Chinese
FOR
DUMMIES®
2ND EDITION

by Dr. Wendy Abraham

WILEY

John Wiley & Sons, Inc.

Chinese For Dummies®, 2nd Edition

Published by
John Wiley & Sons, Inc.
111 River St.
Hoboken, NJ 07030-5774
www.wiley.com

Copyright © 2013 by John Wiley & Sons, Inc., Hoboken, New Jersey

Published by John Wiley & Sons, Inc., Hoboken, New Jersey

Published simultaneously in Canada

For general information on our other products and services, please contact our Customer Care Department within the U.S. at 877-762-2974, outside the U.S. at 317-572-3993, or fax 317-572-4002.

For technical support, please visit www.wiley.com/techsupport.

Wiley publishes in a variety of print and electronic formats and by print-on-demand. Some material included with standard print versions of this book may not be included in e-books or in print-on-demand. If this book refers to media such as a CD or DVD that is not included in the version you purchased, you may download this material at http://booksupport.wiley.com. For more information about Wiley products, visit www.wiley.com.

Library of Congress Control Number: 2012955832

ISBN 978-1-118-43666-0 (pbk); ISBN 978-1-118-43654-7 (ebk); ISBN 978-1-118-43657-8 (ebk); ISBN 978-1-118-43658-5 (ebk)

Manufactured in the United States of America

10 9 8 7 6 5 4 3 2 1

WILEY

About the Author

Dr. Wendy Abraham has taught courses on Chinese language, literature, history, and culture at Hunter College, Georgetown University, NYU, and Stanford University. She spent a year researching Shang Dynasty oracle bones in Taiwan, which sparked her deep interest in the development of China's written language. Wendy has directed Chinese language programs for American students in Beijing and Shanghai, and she has interpreted for high-level arts delegations from China. Her doctoral dissertation was on the Chinese Jews of Kaifeng, a subject about which she has written widely and continues to lecture frequently throughout the United States. Her interest in all things Chinese since the age of three continues unabated.

Dedication

This book is dedicated to Oszkar and Shandy, with love for the Iakab family — then and now.

It is also dedicated to my father, György, my mother, Marilyn, my sister, Susan, and my new brother-in-law, Michael.

Author's Acknowledgments

The first million thanks go to my mother for making this past year (and me) possible. It would never have happened without her and our late night Scrabble games, and I will be forever grateful.

The next million thanks go to my father for filling this past year with amazing new conversations, lots of love, and a letter to his newly found cousins.

Thanks also go to my sister and brother-in-law for their collective sense of humor and for reminding us about all the things in life for which we should be grateful.

To Gerard and Jean Russak for extending the welcome mat, music, and deep friendship to me and the ever-growing brood of cats on the Upper West Side.

To all those who made miracles happen this year: Csongor Nyulas (Hungarian translator par excellence), Bob Edelstein, Anna Mekulinova, Hila Turkienicz, Itzhak Fouxon, Nehama Rosenberg, Malka Spitzberg, Leon Fishbein, my wonderful Elly Ne'eman, and Am Hazikaron. My family will always be grateful for your help in finding Oszkar and Shandy while writing this second edition of *Chinese For Dummies*.

Needless to say, this book would not have been possible without the remarkable folks at Wiley: Stacy Kennedy (the wonderful and efficient Acquisitions Editor), Tim Gallan (the calm and collected Project Editor), Constance Carlisle (who labored tirelessly to get the audio CD just right), and Megan Knoll (whose eye for Chinese typos without even knowing the language was stupefying). Great team, all.

Finally, thank you Cynthia Reidlinger, Ollie, Tommy, and the extended Sargent clan for contributing so much to this book and providing a great dose of inspiration along the way.

Publisher's Acknowledgments

We're proud of this book; please send us your comments at `http://dummies.custhelp.com`. For other comments, please contact our Customer Care Department within the U.S. at 877-762-2974, outside the U.S. at 317-572-3993, or fax 317-572-4002.

Some of the people who helped bring this book to market include the following:

Acquisitions, Editorial, and Vertical Websites

Senior Project Editor: Tim Gallan

Acquisitions Editor: Stacy Kennedy

Copy Editor: Megan Knoll

Assistant Editor: David Lutton

Editorial Program Coordinator: Joe Niesen

Technical Editors: Language Training Centers, Yang Wen

Editorial Manager: Michelle Hacker

Editorial Assistants: Rachelle S. Amick, Alexa Koschier

Vertical Websites: Melanie Orr

Audio Produced by: Her Voice Unlimited, LLC

(hervoice@iquest.net)

Cover Photos: © Idealink Photography / Alamy

Cartoons: Rich Tennant (`www.the5thwave.com`)

Composition Services

Project Coordinator: Sheree Montgomery

Layout and Graphics: Carrie A. Cesavice, Jennifer Creasey, Melanee Habig, Joyce Haughey

Proofreader: Joni Heredia Language Services

Indexer: Potomac Indexing, LLC

Publishing and Editorial for Consumer Dummies

   Kathleen Nebenhaus, Vice President and Executive Publisher

   David Palmer, Associate Publisher

   Kristin Ferguson-Wagstaffe, Product Development Director

Publishing for Technology Dummies

   Andy Cummings, Vice President and Publisher

Composition Services

   Debbie Stailey, Director of Composition Services

Contents at a Glance

Table of Contents

Introduction

Globalization has made familiarity with other people, cultures, and languages not only preferable but also essential in the 21st century. With the help of the Internet, reaching out and touching someone on the other side of the earth has become as easy as clicking a mouse or using a smartphone. And yet nothing quite beats the excitement of a face-to-face encounter with someone who hails from the other side of the globe in his or her own language. Communication in cyberspace doesn't even come close.

Whether you're an inveterate traveler, going overseas for business, about to study overseas, interested in frequenting Chinatown, befriending a Chinese-speaking classmate or coworker, or just plain curious about China, *Chinese For Dummies,* 2nd Edition, can help you get acquainted with enough Chinese to carry on a decent conversation on any number of topics. You won't become fluent instantly, of course, but this book helps you greet a stranger, buy a plane ticket, and order some food. It also gives you some invaluable cultural tips so that you can not only rattle off those newly acquired words and phrases but also back them up with the right behavior at the right time.

I designed this book to help guide you toward the successful use of one of the most difficult languages on earth. Chinese should also just be plain fun to learn.

About This Book

The good news is that you can use *Chinese For Dummies,* 2nd Edition, anytime, anywhere. No mandatory class sessions, no exams, and no homework assignments to dread. Need to get to a new city for a business meeting? Just turn to the chapter on travel to find out how to buy a plane ticket, get through customs, and get to the airport on time. Have to make a sudden trip to the doctor? Turn to the chapter on your health and figure out in advance how to tell your caregivers exactly what ails you.

The beauty of this book is that it can be all things to all people. You don't have to memorize Chapter 5 before moving on to Chapter 6 if what Chapter 6 deals with is what you really need. Each chapter provides you with different bits of information about the Chinese language and highlights different parts of Chinese grammar. Read as much or as little as you want, as quickly or as slowly as you like. Whatever interests you is what you should focus on. And remember: You're discovering a language that simultaneously represents one of the world's oldest civilizations and one of its fastest growing economies in the 21st century.

Conventions Used in This Book

Pay attention to a few conventions that can help you navigate this book's contents:

- ✔ Chinese terms are set in **boldface** to make them stand out.

- ✔ Pronunciations and meanings appear in parentheses immediately after the Chinese terms. The English translations are in *italics*.

- ✔ This book uses the **pīnyīn** 拼音 (pin-yin) (Literally: *spelling the way it sounds*) Romanization system of Chinese words. What does that mean? Well, if you go to China, you see signs in Chinese characters all around, but if you look for something in English, you may be hard pressed to find it. Whatever signs you see in Roman letters will be of **pīnyīn,** the Romanization system developed by the Communists in the 1950s, so seeing **pīnyīn** in this book is good practice for you.

- ✔ In this edition of *Chinese For Dummies,* Chinese characters have been added in many places and appear after the initial transliteration from the **pīnyīn.** Chinese characters are fun to try to decipher. The Chinese have been working at precisely that for thousands of years, especially for the more complicated characters that took as many as 20 separate strokes of the traditional Chinese writing brush to create.

  Lucky for you, many of the more complicated Chinese characters were simplified in the early 20th century to make them easier to read and write, and these are used in mainland China today. (You can read more about Chinese characters in Chapter 2.) The original (or *traditional*) characters are still used in Taiwan. In this book, simplified characters appear first, followed in parentheses by the traditional characters. Characters that were never simplified don't have any separate notation in parentheses.

- ✔ Another thing you should keep in mind as you begin to understand Chinese is that many of the English translations you see in this book aren't exactly literal. Knowing the gist of what you hear or see is more important than knowing what individual words in any given phrase mean. For example, the Chinese phrase meaning *so-so* literally translates as *horse horse tiger tiger* even though you're not actually talking about animals. Whenever I give a literal translation, I preface it with "Literally."

The following elements in this book help reinforce the new terms and phrases you're studying:

- ✔ **Talkin' the Talk dialogues:** Nothing beats seeing and hearing an actual conversation to learn Chinese, so I intersperse dialogues throughout the book under the heading "Talkin' the Talk." They show you the Chinese words, the pronunciations, and the English translations, and I often put cultural do's and don'ts into context, which should come in handy. Many of these dialogues appear in the accompanying audio tracks so you can practice the sentences after you hear how they should sound. With the tonal nature of the Chinese language, this feature is indispensable as you learn Chinese.

- ✔ **Words to Know blackboards:** These boxes come after the Talkin' the Talk dialogues and highlight important words from each dialogue.

- ✔ **Fun & Games activities:** Working through word games can be a fun way to review the words and phrases you encounter in each chapter. This element is a great way to gauge your progress and tease your brain at the same time. Look for these activities at the end of each chapter.

Foolish Assumptions

Some of the foolish assumptions I made about you while writing *Chinese For Dummies,* 2nd Edition, are that

- ✔ You don't know any Chinese, except for maybe a couple of words you picked up from a good kung-fu movie or the word *tofu,* which you picked up while grocery shopping.

- ✔ Your goal in life isn't to become an interpreter of Chinese at the U.N.; you just want to pick up some useful words, phrases, and sentence constructions to make yourself understood in a Chinese-speaking environment.

- ✔ You have no intention of spending hours and hours memorizing Chinese vocabulary and grammar patterns.

- ✔ You basically want to have fun while speaking a little Chinese.

How This Book Is Organized

This book is divided by topic into parts, chapters, and appendixes. Each part focuses on one aspect of the Chinese language, and the chapters cover different useful topics, such as how to dine at a restaurant, how to handle emergencies, or how to plan a vacation. The following sections tell you what types of information you can expect to find in each part.

Part 1: Getting Started

This part familiarizes you with some basics of Chinese: how to pronounce words, how to create the proper pitch (also known as *tone*) for each word, and so on. Because Chinese is a tonal language, if you pronounce a word with an incorrect tone, you may say a whole different word. Sometimes the only way to know whether you've said something you didn't intend is by the look on the listener's face, so you should pay particular attention to the tones as you speak.

Part II: Chinese in Action

In this part, you really begin to use Chinese. Instead of focusing strictly on grammar, this part helps guide you through everyday situations that you encounter while meeting people, eating at restaurants, going shopping, or yakking on the phone.

Part III: Chinese on the Go

This part of the book gives you the tools you need to use Chinese in any number of practical real-world settings. You find out how to change money, how to ask for directions, how to book a room at a hotel, and how to tell a doctor what ails you. Whether your travels take you all the way to Shanghai or just to your cubicle at work is up to you.

Part IV: The Part of Tens

This part begins with some tips on how to learn Chinese quickly, and it offers reminders of what not to do in a Chinese setting.

Part V: Appendixes

This part contains helpful references that you may want to refer to occasionally as you snoop through the rest of the chapters. Appendix A is a handy mini-dictionary of both Chinese to English and English to Chinese. Feel free to check this section when you encounter unfamiliar words on a need-to-know basis. Appendix B contains a useful verb list, which can help in any setting.

Appendix C provides a list of the audio tracks that come with this book. This appendix comes in handy when you're ready to hear a selection of the Talkin' the Talk dialogues from the book. Finally, Appendix D contains the answers to the Fun & Games exercises at the end of each chapter.

Icons Used in This Book

Cute little icons occasionally appear in the left-hand margins, next to sidebars, and with the Talkin' the Talk dialogues throughout this book. These beacons shed light on what kind of information you're looking at and can help you locate certain types of information in a hurry. The six icons used in this book are as follows:

The bull's-eye appears wherever I've highlighted a great idea to help make your study of Chinese easier.

This icon, appropriately showing a string around a finger, should serve as a reminder about particularly important information concerning Chinese.

The bomb in this icon should act as a stop sign in your mind. It warns you about things to avoid saying or doing so that you don't make a fool of yourself overseas or with a new Chinese-speaking acquaintance.

This icon clues you in on fascinating bits of information about China and Chinese culture. Knowledge of a culture goes hand in hand with knowledge of a foreign language, so these icons help light the way as you embark on your journey.

This icon highlights various rules of grammar that may be out of the norm. Even though this book doesn't focus primarily on grammar, your successful execution of the language can only be enhanced by paying attention to little grammatical rules as they pop up.

The audio tracks that come with this book give you the chance to hear native Chinese speakers so you can better understand the way Chinese really sounds. This opportunity proves especially helpful because of all the tones you have to keep in mind. This icon indicates the basic sounds and Talkin' the Talk dialogues you can find in these tracks. *Note:* If you're reading this text in an electronic format, please go to the table of contents for access to the additional content.

Where to Go from Here

Chinese is often considered one of the toughest languages in the world to master. Don't worry. The good news is that you're not trying to master it. All you want to do is be understandable when you open your mouth so that you don't ask for the men's room when you really want the ladies' room. All you have to do now is keep listening to and repeating the words and phrases you find in this book. Turn to whichever chapter piques your curiosity, listen to the accompanying audio tracks at home or in your car, and keep practicing your favorite Chinese phrases when you're with your family and friends in Chinatown.

Part I
Getting Started

The 5th Wave · By Rich Tennant

"You mean, 'wo,' 'ta,' 'baba,' and 'mama' are all words in Mandarin? My gosh, Alice, our baby's been speaking Chinese the last few weeks!"

In this part . . .

Part I warmly welcomes you to the Chinese language. I give you the lowdown on all the essentials of Chinese: how to pronounce Chinese sounds (and tones) like a native, how to read Chinese script, how to string Chinese words together so that they make sense, how to count in Chinese, how to speak Chinese around your home, and how to communicate in Chinese with all the cultural trimmings. **Wǒmen kāishǐ ba!** 我们开始吧! (我們開始吧!) (waw-mun kye-shir bah!) (*Let's begin!*)

Chapter 1

Chinese in a Nutshell

*T*ime to get your feet wet with the basics of Chinese. This chapter gives you guidelines that help you pronounce words in standard Mandarin (the official language of both the People's Republic of China and Taiwan) like a native speaker and helps you get a handle on the four tones that distinguish Mandarin Chinese. After you have the basics down, I show you how to construct basic Chinese phrases.

But before you dive in, here's a bit of advice: Don't be intimidated by all the tones! The best thing you can do when learning a foreign language is to not worry about making mistakes the minute you open your mouth. Practice speaking Chinese first to your dog or cat, and then work your way up to a couple of goldfish or a niece or nephew under the age of ten. When you finally get the nerve to rattle off a few phrases to your local Chinatown grocer, you'll know you've made it. And when you visit China for the first time, you discover how incredibly appreciative the Chinese are of anyone who even remotely attempts to speak their language. All the hours you spent yakking away with the family pet start to pay off, and you'll be rewarded greatly. Still have doubts? You'll be amazed at how much you can say after snooping through *Chinese For Dummies,* 2nd Edition.

Encountering the Chinese culture is just as important as exploring the Chinese language. In fact, you can't quite master the language without absorbing a little of the culture by osmosis. Just making the effort to speak Chinese is an act of positive diplomacy. Don't worry about how you sound when you open your mouth — you're contributing to international friendship no matter what comes out.

Grasping Chinese Dialects

Give yourself a big pat on the back right now. Yup, right now — before you even begin to utter one iota of Chinese. If you don't do it now, you may be too shocked later on when it sinks in that you've taken on a language that has hundreds (yes, hundreds) of dialects — each one mutually incomprehensible to speakers of the other ones. Practically every major town, and certainly every province, in China has its own regional dialect that folks grow up learning. Of the seven major dialects (outlined in Table 1-1), Shanghainese, Taiwanese, and Cantonese are the ones you may have heard of before.

And then you have Mandarin, dialect of the masses. Mandarin Chinese is spoken by more people on earth than any other language today. Pretty much a quarter of humanity uses it, given China's immense population. So just why was this particular dialect chosen to become the official dialect taught in all schools throughout China, regardless of whatever additional dialects people speak at home or in their communities?

With only four tones, **Guānhuà** 官话 (官話) (gwan-hwah) (*Mandarin* [Literally: *the language of the officials*, who were also known as Mandarins]) has served as the hybrid language of China since the 15th century because this dialect was based on the educated speech of the region around Beijing. Instead of referring to it as Guānhuà, mainlanders in China now call it **Pǔtōnghuà** 普通话 (普通話) (poo-toong-hwah) (Literally: *the common language*). People in Taiwan, in Hong Kong, and in overseas Chinese communities call it **Guóyǔ** 国语 (國語) (gwaw-yew) (Literally: *the national language*). You may also hear it referred to as **Zhōngwén** 中文 (joong-one) (*the language of the Chinese people*) and **Hànyǔ** 汉语 (漢語) (hahn-yew) (*the language of the Han people*), because the Chinese have often referred to themselves as descendants of the Han dynasty (206 BCE-220 CE), one of the golden eras of Chinese history. Because Chinese is the language of ethnic Chinese and China's minority groups, the more all-encompassing term **Zhōngwén** is preferred.

Table 1-1	**Major Chinese Dialects**	
Dialect	*Pronunciation*	*Region Where Spoken*
Pǔtōnghuà/Guóyǔ (Mandarin) 普通话 (普通話) ／国语 (國語)	poo-toong-hwah/gwaw-yew	North of the Yangzi River, but is taught in schools everywhere; official language of the People's Republic of China and is spoken all over Taiwan
Wú 吴 (吳)	woo	Shanghai, southeastern Anhui, and much of Zhejiang

Dialect	Pronunciation	Region Where Spoken
Xiāng 湘	shyahng	Hunan
Gàn 赣 (贛)	gahn	Jiangxi, southern Anhui, and southeastern Hubei
Kèjiā (Hakka) 客家	kuh-jyah	Scattered parts of eastern and southwestern Guangxi and in northern Guangdong (Canton)
Yuè (Cantonese) 粤 (粵)	yweh	Southeastern Guangxi, Guangdong (Canton), and Hong Kong
Mín (Taiwanese) 闽 (閩)	meen	Fujian, southern Zhejiang, northeastern Guangdong, Hainan, and Taiwan.

The term **Pǔtōnghuà** is used to refer to Mandarin in the People's Republic of China, and the term **Guóyǔ** is the term used for Mandarin in Taiwan. You can simply say **Hànyǔ** anywhere.

Pīnyīn Spelling: Beijing, Not Peking

To spell the way it sounds . . . that's the literal meaning of **pīnyīn** 拼音. For decades, Chinese had been *transliterated* (written/spelled with the characters of other languages' alphabets) in any number of ways. Finally, in 1979, the People's Republic of China (PRC) officially adopted **pīnyīn** as its official Romanization system. After the adoption, U.S. libraries and government agencies diligently changed all their prior records from other Romanization systems into **pīnyīn**.

You should keep in mind the following quick facts about some of the initial sounds in Mandarin when you see them written in the relatively new **pīnyīn** system:

- **J:** Sounds like the **g** in *gee whiz*. An **i** often follows a **j. Jǐ kuài qián?** 几块钱? (幾塊錢?) (jee kwye chyan?) means *How much money?*

- **Q:** Sounds like the **ch** in *cheek*. In Chinese, you never see it followed by a **u** like it is in English, but an **i** always follows it, possibly before another vowel or a consonant. **Qīngdǎo** 青岛 (青島) (cheeng-daow) beer used to be spelled **ch'ing tao** or **Tsingtao.**

- **X:** Sounds like the **sh** in *she*. It's the third letter that's often followed by an **i**. One famous Chinese leader, **Dèng Xiǎopíng** 邓小平 (鄧小平) (dung shyaow-peeng), boasted this letter in his name.

✔ **Zh:** Unlike **j,** which often precedes a vowel to make it sound like you're opening your mouth, **zh** is followed by vowels that make it sound like your mouth is a bit more closed — like the *ger* sound in the word *German.* Take **Zhōu Enlái** 周恩来 (周恩來) (joe un-lye), the great statesman of 20th-century China, for example. When you say his name, it should sound like Joe Un-lye.

✔ **Z:** Sounds like a **dz.** You see it in the name of the PRC's first leader, **Máo Zédōng** 毛泽东 (毛澤東) (maow dzuh-doong), which used to be spelled **Mao Tse-tung.**

✔ **C:** Pronounced like **ts** in such words as **cài** 菜 (tsye) (*food*) or **cèsuǒ** 厕所 (廁所) (tsuh-swaw) (*bathroom*).

✔ **B, D, and G:** In the past, the sounds made by these three letters were represented by **p, t,** and **k,** respectively. In the past, if the corresponding initial sounds were *aspirated* (had air coming out of the speaker, like in the words *pie, tie,* and *kite*), they would've been written as **p', t',** and **k'.** Today, the letters **p, t,** and **k** represent the aspirated sounds.

Sounding Off: Basic Chinese Sounds

Don't worry about sounding like a native speaker the first time you utter a Chinese syllable — after all, who can? But the longer you procrastinate about becoming familiar with the basic elements of Chinese words, the greater your fear of this unique language may become. After you begin to practice the sounds (and eventually the tones) out loud, you may wonder if you'll ever come close to sounding like Bruce Lee in a kung-fu movie or even like your local Chinatown grocer. Hearing Chinese spoken at a normal speed is definitely intimidating at the beginning, so you should enjoy taking plenty of baby steps and reveling in the praise from waiters who appreciate all your effort the next time you frequent a Chinese restaurant.

The main thing to remember about the Chinese language is that each *morpheme* (the smallest unit of meaning in a language) is represented by one syllable, which in turn consists of an initial sound and a final sound, topped off by a tone. This rule applies to each and every syllable. Without any one of these three components, your words may be incomprehensible to the average Chinese person. For example, the syllable **mā** 妈 (媽) is comprised of the initial **m** and the final **a,** and you pronounce it with what's called a first tone. Together, the parts mean *mother.* If you substitute the first tone for a third tone, which is written as **mǎ,** 马 (馬) you say the word *horse.* So be careful not to call your mother a horse when you practice the initials, finals, and tones. The following sections break up the three parts and give each their due.

Before you can participate in sports or play games, you must become familiar with all the rules. The same goes for practicing a new language. Do your best to understand the basic rules of pronunciation, and keep practicing over and over to begin feeling comfortable speaking the language.

Starting off with initials

In Chinese, initials always consist of consonants. Table 1-2 lists the initials you encounter in the Chinese language.

Listen to these sounds on the accompanying audio tracks as you practice pronouncing initials. (Track 2)

Table 1-2		Chinese Initials
Chinese Letter	*Sound*	*English Example*
b	b	bore
p	p	paw
m	m	more
f	f	four
d	d	done
t	t	ton
n	n	null
l	l	lull
g	g	gull
k	k	come
h	h	hunt
j	g	gee
q	c	cheat
x	s	she
z	d	ds in *suds*
c	t	ts in *huts*
s	s	sun
zh	jir	germ
ch	chir	churn

(continued)

Table 1-2 *(continued)*

Chinese Letter	Sound	English Example
sh	sh	*shirt*
r	ir	*er* in *bigger*
w	w	*won*
y	y	*yup*

The initials **-n** and **-r** in Table 1-2 can also appear as part of finals, so don't be surprised if you see them in Table 1-3, where I list finals.

Ending with finals

Chinese boasts many more consonants than vowels. In fact, the language has only six vowels all together: **a, o, e, i, u,** and **ü.** If you pronounce the vowels in sequence, your mouth starts off very wide and your tongue starts off very low. Eventually, when you get to **ü,** your mouth becomes much more closed and your tongue ends pretty high. You can also combine the vowels in various ways to form compound vowels. Table 1-3 lists the vowels and some possible combinations, which comprise all the finals in Chinese.

Table 1-3   Chinese Finals

Chinese Vowel	Sound	English Example
a	ah	*hot*
ai	i	*eye*
ao	ow	*chow*
an	ahn	*on*
ang	ahng	*thong*
o	aw	*straw*
ong	oong	*too* + ng
ou	oh	*oh*
e	uh	*bush*
ei	ay	*way*
en	un	*fun*

Chinese Vowel	Sound	English Example
eng	ung	tongue
er	ar	are
i	ee	tea
ia	ya	gotcha
iao	yaow	meow
ie	yeh	yet
iu	yo	leo
ian	yan	Cheyenne
iang	yahng	y + angst
in	een	seen
ing	eeng	going
iong	yoong	you + ng
u	oo	too
ua	wa	suave
uo	waw	war
ui	way	way
uai	why	why
uan	wan	want
un	one	one
uang	wahng	wan + ng
ueng	wung	one + ng
ü	yew	ewe
üe	yweh	you + eh
üan	ywan	you + wan
ün	yewn	you + n

Tone marks in **pīnyīn** always appear above the vowel, but if you see a couple of vowels in a row, the tone mark appears above the first vowel in that sequence. One exception is when you see the vowels **iu** and **ui** together. In that case, the tone mark falls on the second vowel.

Sometimes vowels appear without initial consonant accompaniment, but they still mean something. The word **ǎi** 矮, meaning *short* (of stature), is one example.

Perfect pitch: Presenting the four tones

Mee meeeee (cough cough)! Pardon me. I'm getting carried away with warming up before I get into the four tones. Just think of the tones this way: They can be your best friends when it comes to being understood in Chinese, and they're the hip part of this ancient language.

If you combine all the possible initial sounds of Chinese with all the possible permutations of the final sounds, you come up with only about 400 sound combinations — not nearly enough to express all the ideas in your head. If you add the four basic tones of Mandarin to the mix, the number of possible permutations increases fourfold. Tones are also a great way to reduce the number of homophones in Chinese. Even so, any given syllable with a specific tone can often have more than one meaning. Sometimes, the only way to decipher the intended meaning is to see the written word.

Mandarin has only four tones. The best way to imagine what each of the four tones sounds like is to visualize these short descriptions:

- ✔ **First tone:** High level. The first tone is supposed to be as high as your individual pitch range can be without wavering. It appears like this above the letter *a:* **ā.**

- ✔ **Second tone:** Rising. The second tone sounds like you're asking a question. It goes from the middle level of your voice to the top. It doesn't automatically indicate that you're asking a question, however — it just sounds like you are. It appears like this above the letter *a:* **á.**

- ✔ **Third tone:** Falling and then rising. The third tone starts in the middle level of your voice range and then falls deeply before slightly rising at the end. It looks like this above the letter *a:* **ǎ.**

- ✔ **Fourth tone:** Falling. The fourth tone sounds like you're giving someone an order (unlike the more plaintive-sounding second tone). It falls from the high pitch level it starts at. Here's how it looks above the letter *a:* **à.**

I know this tone business (especially the nuances in the following sections) all sounds very complicated, but when you get the hang of tones, pronunciation becomes second nature. Just keep listening to the audio tracks throughout the book. These concepts will sink in quicker than you expect.

One third tone after another

Here's something interesting about tones: When you have to say one third tone followed by another third tone out loud in consecutive fashion, the first one actually becomes a second tone. If you hear someone say **Tā hěn hǎo.** 她很好. (tah hun how.) (*She's very well.*), you may not realize that both **hěn** 很 and **hǎo** 好 individually are third tone syllables. It sounds like **hén** is a second tone and **hǎo** is a full third tone.

Half-third tones

Whenever a third tone is followed by any of the other tones — first, second, fourth, or even a neutral tone — it becomes a half-third tone. You pronounce only the first half of the tone — the falling half — before you pronounce the other syllables with the other tones. In fact, a half-third tone barely falls at all. It sounds more like a level, low tone (kind of the opposite of the high-level first tone). Get it?

Neutral tones

A fifth tone exists that you can't exactly count among the four basic tones because it's actually toneless, or *neutral.* You never see a tone mark over a fifth tone, and you say it only when you attach it to grammatical particles or the second character of repetitive syllables, such as **bàba** 爸爸 (bah-bah) (*father*) or **māma** 妈妈 (媽媽) (mah-mah) (*mother*).

Tonal changes in yī and bù

Just when you think you're getting a handle on all the possible tones and tone changes in Chinese, I have one more aspect to report: The words **yī** 一 (ee) (*one*) and **bù** 不 (boo) (*not* or *no*) are truly unusual in Chinese, in that their tones may change automatically depending on what comes after them. You pronounce **yī** by itself with the first tone. However, when a first, second, or third tone follows it, **yī** instantly turns into a fourth tone, such as in **yìzhāng zhǐ** 一张纸 (一張紙) (ee-jahng jir) (*a piece of paper*). If a fourth tone follows **yī,** however, it automatically becomes a second tone, such as in the word **yíyàng** 一样 (一樣) (ee-yahng) (*the same*).

Adding Idioms and Popular Expressions to Your Repertoire

The Chinese language has thousands of idiomatic expressions known as **chéngyǔ** 成语 (成語) (chung-yew). Most of these **chéngyǔ** originated in anecdotes, fables, fairy tales, or ancient literary works, and some of the expressions are thousands of years old. The vast majority consist of four characters, succinctly expressing morals behind very long, ancient stories. Others are more than four characters. Either way, the Chinese pepper these pithy expressions throughout any given conversation.

Here are a few **chéngyǔ** you frequently hear in Chinese:

- **àn bù jiù bān** 按部就班 (ahn boo jyoe bahn) (*to take one step at a time*)
- **hú shuō bā dào** 胡说八道 (胡說八道) (hoo shwaw bah daow) (*to talk nonsense* [Literally: *to talk nonsense in eight directions*])
- **huǒ shàng jiā yóu** 火上加油 (hwaw shahng jyah yo) (*to add fuel to the fire/to aggravate the problem*)
- **Mò míng qí miào.** 莫名其妙. (maw meeng chee meow.) (Literally: *No one can explain the wonder and mystery of it all.*) This saying describes anything that's tough to figure out, including unusual behavior.
- **quán xīn quán yì** 全心全意 (chwan sheen chwan ee) (*wholeheartedly* [Literally: *entire heart, entire mind*])
- **Rù xiāng suí sú.** 入乡随俗. (入鄉隨俗.) (roo shyahng sway soo.) (*When in Rome, do as the Romans do.*)
- **yì jǔ liǎng dé** 一举两得 (一舉兩得) (ee jyew lyahng duh) (*to kill two birds with one stone*)
- **yì mó yí yàng** 一模一样 (一模一樣) (ee maw ee yahng) (*exactly alike*)
- **yǐ shēn zuò zé** 以身作则 (以身作則) (ee shun dzwaw dzuh) (*to set a good example*)
- **yì zhēn jiàn xiě** 一针见血 (一針見血) (ee jun jyan shyeh) (*to hit the nail on the head*)

Another fact you quickly become aware of when you start speaking with **chéngyǔ** is that the expressions are sometimes full of references to animals. Here are some of those:

- **chē shuǐ mǎ lóng** 车水马龙 (車水馬龍) (chuh shway mah loong) (*heavy traffic* [Literally: *cars flowing like water and horses, creating a solid line looking like a dragon*])
- **dǎ cǎo jīng shé** 打草惊蛇 (打草驚蛇) (dah tsaow jeeng shuh) (*to give a warning* [Literally: *to beat the grass to frighten the snake*])
- **duì niú tán qín** 对牛弹琴 (對牛彈琴) (dway nyo tahn cheen) (*to cast pearls before swine* [Literally: *to play music to a cow*])

✔ **Gǒu zhàng rén shì.** 狗仗人势. (狗仗人勢.) (go jahng run shir.) (*to take advantage of one's connections with powerful people* [Literally: *The dog acts fierce when his master is present.*])

✔ **guà yáng tóu mài gǒu ròu** 挂羊头卖狗肉 (掛羊頭賣狗肉) (gwah yahng toe my go roe) (*to cheat others with false claims* [Literally: *to display a lamb's head but sell dog meat*])

✔ **huà shé tiān zú** 画蛇添足 (畫蛇添足) (hwah shuh tyan dzoo) (*to gild the lily/to do something superfluous* [Literally: *to paint a snake and add legs*])

✔ **hǔ tóu shé wěi** 虎头蛇尾 (虎頭蛇尾) (hoo toe shuh way) (*to start strong but end poorly* [Literally: *with the head of a tiger but the tail of a snake*])

✔ **xuán yá lè mǎ** 悬崖勒马 (懸崖勒馬) (shywan yah luh mah) (*to halt* [Literally: *to rein in the horse before it goes over the edge*])

Fun & Games

Listen to the accompanying audio to see whether you can imitate the following words, which are distinguished only by their tones. (Be on the lookout: Any given sound with the same accompanying tone may have several other meanings, distinguishable only by context or by seeing the appropriate written character.) Good luck! (Track 3)

- ✔ **mā** 妈 (媽) (*mother*)
- ✔ **má** 麻 (*hemp*)
- ✔ **mǎ** 马 (馬) (*horse*)
- ✔ **mà** 骂 (罵) (*to scold*)
- ✔ **fēi** 飞 (飛) (*to fly*)
- ✔ **féi** 肥 (*fat*)
- ✔ **fěi** 匪 (*bandit*)
- ✔ **fèi** 肺 (*lungs*)
- ✔ **qīng** 清 (*clear*)
- ✔ **qíng** 情 (*affection*)
- ✔ **qǐng** 请 (請) (*please*)
- ✔ **qìng** 庆 (慶) (*celebrate*)
- ✔ **zhū** 猪 (豬) (*pig/pearl*)
- ✔ **zhú** 竹 (*bamboo*)
- ✔ **zhǔ** 主 (*master*)
- ✔ **zhù** 住 (*to reside*)

Chapter 2

The Written Word: Checking out Chinese Characters

In This Chapter

▶ Familiarizing yourself with the Six Scripts

▶ Using Chinese radicals as clues to the meaning of a character

▶ Getting a handle on character type, writing, and order

▶ Knowing how to use a Chinese dictionary

Make no bones about it. (Oracle bones, that is.) China has literally hundreds of spoken dialects but only one written language. That's right: When a headline hits the news, people in Shanghai, Chongqing, and Henan are all yakking about it to their neighbors in their own regional dialects, but they're pointing to the exact same characters in the newspaper headlines. The written word is what's kept the Chinese people unified for over 4,000 years.

This chapter gives you the low down on how Chinese **wénzì** 文字 (wuhn-dzuh) (*writing*) actually began, how characters are constructed, and which direction they're going in when you read them. I describe how you may be able to identify the basic meaning of a character by looking at a key portion of it (called the radical) and how characters used by people living in Taiwan are different from characters used by people in mainland China. And because Chinese has no **zìmǔ** 字母 (dzuh-moo) (*alphabet*), I show you all sorts of ways you can look words up in a Chinese dictionary.

Chinese has the multiple distinction of being the mother tongue of the oldest continuous civilization on earth as well as the language spoken by the greatest number of people. It arguably has one the most intricate written languages in existence, with about 50,000 characters in a comprehensive Chinese dictionary. To read a newspaper with relative ease, though, you only need to know about 3,000 to 4,000 characters.

Perusing Pictographs, Ideographs, and the Six Scripts

You already know that Chinese words are written in beautiful, sometimes symbolic configurations called *characters*. But did you know that you can classify the characters in a variety of ways?

During the **Hàn** 汉 (漢) dynasty, a lexicographer named **Xǔ Shèn** 许慎 (許慎) (shyew shuhn) identified six ways in which Chinese characters reflect meanings and sounds. These designations are known as the **liù shū** 六书 (六書) (lyoe shoo) (*the Six Scripts*). Of the six, four were the most common:

- **Xiàngxíng** 象形 (shyahng-sheeng) (*pictographs*): These characters resemble the shape of the objects they represent, such as **shān** 山 (shahn) (*mountain*) or **guī** 龜 (gway) (the traditional character for *turtle*; the simplified character for turtle — 龟 — doesn't really look as much like a turtle). Pictographs show the meaning of the character rather than the sound.

- **Biǎoyì** *or* **zhǐshì** 表意 *or* 指事 (byaow-ee *or* jir-shir) (*ideographs*): These characters represent more abstract concepts. The characters for **shàng** 上 (shahng) (*above*) and **xià** 下 (shyah) (*below*), for example, each have a horizontal line representing the horizon and another stroke leading out above or below the horizon.

- **Huì yì** 会意 (會意) (hway ee) (*compound ideographs*): These characters are combinations of simpler characters that together represent more things. For example, by combining the characters for *sun* (日) and *moon* (月), you get the character 明 **míng** (meeng), meaning *bright.*

- **Xíngshēng** 形声 (形聲) (sheeng-shuhng) (*phonetic compounds*): These characters are formed by two graphic elements — one hinting at the meaning of the word (called the radical; see the following section), and the other providing a clue to the sound. More than 90 percent of all Chinese characters are phonetic compounds.

An example of a phonetic compound is the character **gū** 蛄 (goo). It's a combination of the radical **chóng** 虫 (choong) (*insect*) and the sound element of the character **gū** 古 (goo) (*ancient*). Put them together, and you have the character 蛄, meaning *cricket* (the insect, not the sport). It's pronounced with a first tone **(gū)** rather than a third tone **(gǔ).** So the sound of the word is similar to the term for *ancient,* even though that term has nothing to do with the meaning of the word. The actual meaning is connected to the radical referring to insects. Table 2-1 summarizes the Six Scripts.

Table 2-1		The Six Scripts	
Type of Character	*Chinese Character*	*Romanization and Pronunciation*	*Description*
Pictographs	象形	**xiàngxíng** (shy-ahng-sheeng)	Simplified line drawings of concrete objects
Ideographs	表意 *or* 指事	**biǎoyì** *or* **zhǐshì** (byaow-ee *or* jir-shir)	Graphic representations of abstract ideas
Compound ideographs	会意 (會意)	**huìyì** (hway-ee)	Literally *joined meaning;* combination of two or more characters into a new compound character
Phonetic compounds	形声 (形聲)	**xíngshēng** (sheeng-shuhng)	Literally *form and sound;* combination of a visual meaning element with a phonetic element
Derivative cognates	轉注	**zhuǎn zhù** (jwahn joo)	Literally *reciprocal meaning;* characters given a new written form to better reflect a changed pronunciation over time
Phonetic loan characters	假借	**jiǎjiè** (jyah-jyeh)	Characters used to represent a homophone unrelated in meaning to the new word they represent

The Chinese Radical: A Few Clues to a Character's Meaning

What a radical idea! Two hundred and fourteen radical ideas, in fact.

The Chinese written language contains a total of 214 *radicals* — parts of the character that can help identify what it may signify. For example, if you see two or three dots on the left-hand side of the character, you know the word is something connected to water. Here are some characters with the water radical appearing on the left-hand side:

冰 **bīng** (beeng) (*ice*)

冲 **chōng** (choong) (*to pour boiling water on something/to rinse or flush*)

汗 **hàn** (hahn) (*sweat*)

河 **hé** (huh) (*river*)

湖 **hú** (hoo) (*lake*)

Another example: The radical meaning *wood* — 木 **mù** (moo) — originally represented the shape of a tree with branches and roots). Here are some characters with the wood radical in them (also on the left-hand side):

板 **bǎn** (bahn) (*board/plank*)

林 **lín** (leen) (*forest*)

树 (樹) **shù** (shoo) (*tree*)

Sometimes you find the radical at the top of the character rather than on the left-hand side. The radical meaning *rain* — 雨 **yú** (yew) — is one such character. Look for the rain radical at the top these characters. (Hint: It looks slightly squished compared to the actual character for rain by itself.)

雹 **bǎo** (baow) (*hail*)

雷 **léi** (lay) (*thunder*)

露 **lù** (loo) (*dew*)

One of the most complicated radicals (number 214, to be precise) is the one that means *nose:* 鼻 **bí** (bee). It's so complicated to write, in fact, that only one other character in the whole Chinese language uses it: 鼾 **hān** (hahn) (*to snore*).

Following the Rules of Stroke Order

If you want to study **shū fǎ** 书法 (書法) (shoo-fah) (*calligraphy*) with a traditional Chinese **máo bǐ** 毛笔 (毛筆) (maow-bee) (*writing brush*), or even just learn how to write Chinese characters with a plain old ballpoint pen, you need to know which stroke goes before the next. This progression is known as **bǐ shùn** 笔顺 (筆順) (bee shwun) (*stroke order*).

All those complicated-looking Chinese characters are actually created by several individual strokes of the Chinese writing brush. **Bǐ shùn** follows nine (count 'em) rules, which I lay out in the following sections.

Nowadays you don't have to master the art of Chinese calligraphy to write beautiful characters. All you have to do is press a key on a computer, and the character magically appears.

Rule 1

The first rule of thumb is that you write the character by starting with the topmost stroke.

For example, among the first characters students usually learn is the number *one,* which is written with a single horizontal line: 一. Because this character is pretty easy and has only one stroke, it's written from left to right.

The character for *two* has two strokes: 二. Both strokes are written from left to right; the top stroke is written first, following the top-to-bottom rule. The character for *three* has three strokes (三)and follows the same stroke-making pattern.

In the case of more complicated characters (for example, those with radicals that appear on the left-hand side), the radical on the left is written first, followed by the rest of the character. For example, to write the character meaning *tree* — 树 (樹) **shù** (shoo) — you first write the radical on the left (木) before adding the rest of the character to the right of the radical. To write the character meaning *thunder* — 雷 **léi** (lay) — you have to write the radical that appears on top (雨) first before writing the rest of the character underneath it.

Rules 2 through 9

Don't worry; the remaining rules require a lot less explanation than rule 1 does:

- ✔ **Rule 2:** Write horizontal strokes before vertical strokes. For example, the character meaning *ten* (十) is composed of two strokes, but the first one you write is the one appearing horizontally: 一. The vertical stroke downward is written after that.

- ✔ **Rule 3:** Write strokes that have to pass through the rest of the character last. Vertical strokes that pass through many other strokes are written after the strokes they pass through (like in the second character for the city of **Tiānjīn**: 天津 [tyan-jeen]), and horizontal strokes that pass through all sorts of other strokes are written last (like in the character meaning *boat:* 舟 **zhōu** [joe]).

✔ **Rule 4:** Create diagonal strokes that go from right to left before writing the diagonal strokes that go from left to right. You write the character meaning *culture* — 文 **wén** (wuhn) — with four separate strokes: First comes the dot on top, then the horizontal line underneath it, then the diagonal stroke that goes from right to left, and finally the diagonal stroke that goes from left to right.

✔ **Rule 5:** In characters that are vertically symmetrical, create the center components before those on the left or the right. Then write the portion of the character appearing on the left before the one appearing on the right. An example of such a character is the one meaning *to take charge of:* 承 **chéng** (chuhng).

✔ **Rule 6:** Write the portion of the character that's an outside enclosure before the inside portion, such as in the word for *sun:* 日 **rì** (*ir*). Some characters with such enclosures don't have bottom portions, such as with the character for *moon:* 月 **yuè** (yweh).

✔ **Rule 7:** Make the left vertical stroke of an enclosure first. For example, in the word meaning *mouth* — 口 **kǒu** (ko) — you write the vertical stroke on the left first, followed the horizontal line on top and the vertical stroke on the right (those two are written as one stroke) and finally the horizontal line on the bottom.

✔ **Rule 8:** Bottom enclosing components usually come last, such as with the character meaning *the way:* 道 **(dào)** (daow).

✔ **Rule 9:** Dots come last. For example, in the character meaning *jade* — 玉 **yù** (yew) — the little dot you see between the bottom and middle horizontal lines is written last.

Which Way Did Those Characters Go? Unraveling Character Order

Because each Chinese character can be a word in and of itself or part of a compound word, you can read and understand them in any order — right to left, left to right, or top to bottom. If you see a Chinese movie in Chinatown, you can often choose between two types of subtitles: English, which you read from left to right, on one line and Chinese characters, which you read from right to left, on another (usually; the Chinese line can also go from left to right, so be careful.) You may go cross-eyed for a while trying to follow them both.

Right to left and left to right are common enough, but why top to bottom, you may ask? Because before the invention of paper around the 8th century BCE, Chinese was originally written on pieces of bamboo, which required the vertical writing direction.

You can see the role of bamboo strips in the character for *volume* (as in a volume of a book): 册 (冊) **cè** (tsuh). The simplified character consists of two bamboo strips connected by a piece of string. The traditional character (in parentheses) looks like even more bamboo strips are tied together by the string. I tell you more about simplified and traditional characters in the following section.

See whether you can tell what the following saying means, regardless of which way these characters are going. First, I tell you what the four characters each mean individually; then you can string them together and take a stab at the whole saying.

- ✔ 知 **zhī** (jir) (*to know*)
- ✔ 者 **zhě** (juh) (possessive article, such as *the one who*)
- ✔ 不 **bù** (boo) (negative prefix, such as *no, not, doesn't*)
- ✔ 言 **yán** (yeahn) (classical Chinese for *to speak*)

Okay, here's the saying in three different directions. See whether you can figure it out by the time it's written top to bottom.

Left to right: 知者不言, 言者不知

Right to left: 知不者言, 言不者知

Top to bottom:

知
者
不
言,
言
者
不
知

不知者不罪
　　zhě　zuì

不言不语 — to not to say a word
yán　　yǔ

不言自明 — self-evidence
yán zì míng

Give up? It means *Those who know do not speak, and those who speak do not know*. How's that for wisdom?

The saying "Those who know do not speak, and those who speak do not know." has been attributed to the sage **Lǎo Zǐ** 老子 (laow dzuh) in the 6th century BCE. It comes from the **Dào Dé Jīng** 道德经 (道德經) (daow duh jeeng) (more commonly spelled **Tao Te Ching**), which contains many inspirational sayings; portions of the **Dào Dé Jīng** appear in many Chinese paintings, poems, and works of calligraphy.

Separating Traditional and Simplified Characters

Whether you're planning on visiting Taiwan or doing business in the People's Republic of China, you need to know the difference between **fántǐ zì** 繁体字 (繁體字) (fahn-tee dzuh) (*traditional characters*) and **jiántǐ zì** 简体字 (簡體字) (jyan-tee dzuh) (*simplified characters*).

Fántǐ zì haven't changed much since **kǎi shū** 楷书 (楷書) (kye shoo) (*standard script*) was first created around 200 CE. These traditional characters are still used in Taiwan, Hong Kong, Macao, and many overseas Chinese communities today, where the proud but arduous process of learning complicated characters begins at a very early age and the art of deftly wielding a Chinese writing brush comes with the territory.

Jiántǐ zì are used solely in the People's Republic of China, Singapore, and Malaysia. When the People's Republic of China was established in 1949, the illiteracy rate among the general populace was about 85 percent — in large part because learning to write Chinese was difficult, especially when most of the population consisted of farmers who had to work on the land from dawn to dusk.

The new Communist government decided to simplify the writing process by reducing the number of strokes in many characters. Table 2-2 shows you some examples of the before (traditional characters) and after (simplified characters).

Table 2-2	Traditional and Simplified Chinese Characters		
Traditional Character (# of Strokes)	**Simplified Character (# of Strokes)**	**Romanization and Pronunciation**	**Meaning**
見 (7 strokes)	见 (4 strokes)	**jiàn** (jyan)	*to see*
車 (6 strokes)	车 (4 strokes)	**chē** (chuh)	*vehicle*
聲 (17 strokes)	声 (7 strokes)	**shēng** (shuhng)	*sound*
國 (11 strokes)	国 (8 strokes)	**guó** (gwaw)	*country*
較 (13 strokes)	较 (10 strokes)	**jiào** (jyaow)	*relatively*

Simplification of the Chinese writing system has political overtones, so if you're planning on doing business in Taiwan, for example, make sure your business cards and other company materials are printed with traditional Chinese characters.

Using a Chinese Dictionary . . . without an Alphabet!

Whether you're looking at simplified or traditional characters (see the preceding section), you don't find any letters stringing them together like you see in English. So how in the world do Chinese people consult a Chinese dictionary? (Bet you didn't know I could read your mind.) In several different ways.

- **Count the number of strokes in the overall character.** Because Chinese characters are composed of several strokes of the writing brush, one way to look up a character is by counting the number of strokes and then looking up the character under the portion of the dictionary that notes characters by strokes. But to do so, you have to know which radical to check under first.

- **Determine the radical.** Each radical is itself composed of a certain number of strokes, so you have to first look up the radical by the number of strokes it contains. After you locate that radical, you start looking under the number of strokes left in the character after that radical to locate the character you wanted to look up in the first place.

- **Check under the pronunciation of the character.** You can always just check under the pronunciation of the character (assuming you already know how to pronounce it), but you have to sift through every single *homonym* (characters with the same pronunciation) to locate just the right one. You also have to look under the various tones to see which pronunciation comes with the first, second, third, or fourth tone you want to locate. And because Chinese has so many homonyms, this task isn't as easy as it may sound (no pun intended). (You can read more about tones in Chapter 1).

I bet now you feel really relieved that you're only focusing on spoken Chinese and not the written language.

Fun & Games

Fill in the blanks below to test your knowledge of the Chinese writing system. Refer to Appendix D for the correct answers.

1. The Chinese written language contains _____ radicals.

   a) 862   b) 194   c) 214   d) 2,140

2. The origins of the Chinese writing system can be found on _____.

   a) oracle bones   b) bronze inscriptions   c) chopped liver   d) rice cakes

3. The direction of Chinese writing is _____.

   a) right to left   b) left to right   c) top to bottom   d) all of the above

4. The most complicated radical to write (鼻) means _____.

   a) eye   b) ear   c) nose   d) throat

5. Chinese characters that are simple line drawings representing an object are _____.

   a) ideographs   b) compound ideographs   c) pictographs
   d) phonetic compounds

Chapter 3

Warming Up with the Basics: Chinese Grammar

*M*aybe you're one of those people who cringe at the mere mention of the word *grammar*. Just the thought of all those rules on how to construct sentences can put you into a cold sweat.

Hey, don't sweat it! This chapter can just as easily be called "Chinese without Tears." It gives you some quick and easy shortcuts on how to combine the basic building blocks of Chinese (which, by the way, are the same components that make up English) — nouns to name things; adjectives to qualify the nouns; verbs to show action or passive states of being; and adverbs to describe the verbs, adjectives, or other adverbs. After you know how to combine these parts of any given sentence, you can express your ideas and interests spanning the past, present, and future.

When you speak English, I bet you don't sit and analyze the word order before opening your mouth to say something. Well, the same can hold true when you begin speaking Chinese. You probably didn't even know the word for grammar before someone taught you that it was the framework for analyzing the structure of a language. Instead of overwhelming you, this chapter makes understanding Chinese grammar as easy as punch.

If you're patient with yourself, have fun following the dialogues illustrating basic sentences, and listen to them on the accompanying audio tracks, you'll do just fine.

The Basics of Chinese Nouns, Articles, and Adjectives

Admit it. Most of us took the better part of our first two years of life to master the basics when it came to forming English sentences. With this book, you can whittle this same skill in Chinese down to just a few minutes. Just keep reading this chapter. I promise it'll save you a lot of time in the long run.

The basic word order of Chinese is exactly the same as in English. Hard to imagine? Just think of it this way: When you say *I love spinach,* you're using the subject (I), verb (love), object (spinach) sentence order. It's the same in Chinese. Only in Beijing, the sentence sounds more like **Wǒ xǐhuān bōcài.** 我喜欢菠菜. (我喜歡菠菜.) (waw she-hwahn baw-tsye.).

And if that isn't enough to endear you to Chinese, maybe these tidbits of information will:

✔ You don't need to distinguish between singular and plural nouns.

✔ You don't have to deal with gender-specific nouns.

✔ You can use the same word as both the subject and the object.

✔ You don't need to conjugate verbs.

✔ You don't need to master verb tenses. (Don't you just love it already?)

How could such news not warm the hearts of all those who've had grammar phobia since grade school? I get to the verb-related issues later in the chapter; in this section, I pull you up to speed on nouns and their descriptors.

The way you can tell how one part of a Chinese sentence relates to another is generally by the use of particles and what form the word order takes. (*Particles,* for those of you presently scratching your heads, can be found at the beginning or end of sentences and serve mainly to distinguish different types of emphatic statements but can't be translated in and of themselves.)

Nouns

Common nouns represent tangible things, such as **háizi** 孩子 (hi-dzuh) (*child*) or **yè** 叶(葉) (yeh) (*leaf*). Like all languages, Chinese is just chock-full of nouns:

✔ Proper nouns for such things as names of countries or people, like **Fǎguó** 法国 (法國) (fah-gwaw) (*France*) and **Zhāng Xiānshēng** 张先生 (張先生) (jahng shyan-shung) (*Mr. Zhang*)

✔ Material nouns for such nondiscrete things as **kāfēi** 咖啡 (kah-fay) (*coffee*) or **jīn** 金 (jin) (*gold*)

✔ Abstract nouns for such things as **zhèngzhì** 政治 (juhng-jir) (*politics*) or **wénhuà** 文化 (one-hwah) (*culture*)

Pronouns

Pronouns are easy to make plural in Chinese. Just add the plural suffix **-men** to the three basic pronouns:

✔ **Wǒ** 我 (waw) (*I/me*) becomes **wǒmen** 我们 (我們) (waw-mun) (*we/us*).

✔ **Nǐ** 你 (nee) (*you*) becomes **nǐmen** 你们 (你們) (nee-mun) (*you [plural]*).

✔ **Tā** 他/她/它 (tah) (*he/him, she/her, it*) becomes **tāmen** 他们/她们/它们 (他們/她們/它們) (tah-mun) (*they/them*).

Sometimes you hear the term **zánmen** 咱们 (咱們) (dzah-mun) for *us* rather than the term **wǒmen. Zánmen** is used in very familiar settings when the speaker wants to include the listener in an action, like when you say **Zánmen zǒu ba.** 咱们 走吧. (咱們走吧.) (dzah-mun dzoe bah.) (*Let's go.*).

When you're speaking to an elder or someone you don't know too well and the person is someone to whom you should show respect, you need to use the pronoun **nín** 您 (neen) rather than the more informal **nǐ** 你 (nee). On the other hand, if you're speaking to several people who fit that description, the plural remains **nǐmen** 你们 (你們) (nee-men).

Classifiers

Classifiers are sometimes called *measure words,* even though they don't really measure anything. They actually help classify particular nouns. For example, the classifier **běn** 本 (bun) can refer to books, magazines, dictionaries, and just about anything else that's printed and bound like a book. You may hear **Wǒ yào yìběn shū.** 我要一本书. (我要一本書.) (waw yaow ee-bun shoo.) (*I want a book.*) just as easily as you hear **Wǒ yào kàn yìběn zázhì.** 我要看一本杂志. (我要看一本雜志.) (waw yaow kahn ee-bun dzah-jir.) (*I want to read a magazine.*).

Classifiers are found between a number (or a demonstrative pronoun such as *this* or *that*) and a noun. They're similar to English words such as *herd* (of elephants) or *school* (of fish). Although English doesn't use classifiers too often, in Chinese you find them wherever a number is followed by a noun, or at least an implied noun (such as *I'll have another one,* referring to a cup of coffee).

Because you have so many potential classifiers to choose from in Chinese, here's the general rule of thumb: When in doubt, use **ge** 个 (個) (guh). It's the all-purpose classifier and the one used the most in the Chinese language. You usually can't go wrong by using **ge.** If you're tempted to leave a classifier out altogether because you're not sure which one is the right one, don't give in! You may not be understood at all.

Chinese has lots of different classifiers because they're each used to refer to different types of things. For example, Table 3-1 lists classifiers for natural objects. Here are some other examples:

- ✔ **gēn** 根 (gun): Used for anything that looks like a stick, such as a string or even a blade of grass

- ✔ **zhāng** 张 (張) (jahng): Used for anything with a flat surface, such as a newspaper, table, or bed

- ✔ **kē** 颗 (顆) (kuh): Used for anything round and tiny, such as a pearl

Table 3-1	Typical Classifiers for Natural Objects	
Classifier	*Pronunciation*	*Use*
duǒ 朵	dwaw	flowers
kē 棵	kuh	trees
lì 粒	lee	grain (of rice, sand, and so on)
zhī 只(隻)	jir	animals, insects, birds
zuò 座	dzwaw	hills, mountains

Whenever you have a pair of anything, you can use the classifier **shuāng** 双(雙) (shwahng). That goes for **yì shuāng kuàizi** 一双筷子 (一雙筷子) (ee shwahng kwye-dzuh) (*a pair of chopsticks*) as well as for **yì shuāng shǒu** 一双手 (一雙手) (ee shwahng show) (*a pair of hands*). Sometimes a pair is indicated by the classifier **duì** 对 (對) (dway), as in **yí duì ěrhuán** 一对耳环 (一對耳環) (ee dway are-hwahn) (*a pair of earrings*).

Singular and plural: It's a non-issue

Chinese makes no distinction between singular and plural. If you say the word **shū** 书 (書) (shoo), it can mean *book* just as easily as *books*. The only way you know whether it's singular or plural is if a number followed by a classifier precedes the word **shū**, as in **Wǒ yǒu sān běn shū.** 我有三本书. (我有三本書.) (waw yo sahn bun shoo.) (*I have three books.*).

One way to indicate plurality after personal pronouns **wǒ** 我 (waw) (*I*), **nǐ** 你 (nee) (*you*), and **tā** 他/她/它 (tah) (*he/she/it*) and human nouns such as **háizi** 孩子 (hi-dzuh) (*child*) and **xuéshēng** 学生 (學生) (shweh-shuhng) (*student*) is by adding the suffix **-men** 们 (們) (men). It acts as the equivalent of adding an *s* to nouns in English.

So many Chinese words are pronounced largely the same way (although each with different tones) that the only way to truly know the meaning of the word is by looking at the character. For example, the third person singular is pronounced "tah" regardless of whether it means *he, she,* or *it,* but each one is written with a different Chinese character.

Talkin' the Talk

Susan and Michael are looking at a beautiful field.

Susan: **Zhèr de fēngjǐng zhēn piàoliàng!**
jar duh fung-jeeng juhn pyaow-lyahng.
This scenery is really beautiful!

Michael: **Nǐ kàn! Nà zuò shān yǒu nàmme duō shù, nàmme duō huā.**
nee kahn! nah dzwaw shahn yo nummuh dwaw shoo, nummuh dwaw hwah.
Look! That mountain has so many trees and flowers.

Susan: **Duì le. Nèi kē shù tèbié piàoliàng. Zhè duǒ huā yě hěn yǒu tèsè.**
dway luh. nay kuh shoo tuh-byeh pyaow-lyahng. jay dwaw hwah yeah hun yo tuh-suh.
You're right. That tree is particularly beautiful. And this flower is also really unique.

Michael: **Nà kē shù shàng yě yǒu sān zhī niǎo.**
nah kuh shoo shahng yeah yo sahn jir nyaow.
That tree also has three birds in it.

Words to Know

fēngjǐng 风景 (風景)	fung-jeeng	scenery
piàoliàng 漂亮	pyaow-lyahng	beautiful
shān 山	shahn	mountain(s)
shù 树 (樹)	shoo	tree(s)
huā 花	hwah	flower(s)

If a number and a measure word already appear in front of a pronoun or human noun, such as **sānge háizi** 三个孩子 (三個孩子) (sahn-guh hi-dzuh) (*three children*), don't add the suffix **-men** after **háizi** because plurality is already understood.

Never attach the suffix **-men** to anything not human. People will think you're nuts if you start referring to your two pet cats as **wǒde xiǎo māomen** 我的小猫们 (我的小貓們) (waw-duh shyaow maow-mun). Just say **Wǒde xiǎo māo hěn hǎo, xièxiè.** 我的小猫很好, 谢谢. (我的小貓很好, 謝謝.) (waw-duh shyaow maow hun how, shyeh-shyeh.) (*My cats are fine, thank you.*), and that should do the trick.

Definite versus indefinite articles

If you're looking for those little words in Chinese you can't seem to do without in English, such as *a, an,* and *the* — articles, as grammarians call them — you'll find they simply don't exist in Chinese. The only way you can tell if something is being referred to specifically (hence, considered definite) or just generally (and therefore indefinite) is by the word order. Nouns that refer specifically to something are usually found at the beginning of the sentence, before the verb:

Háizimen xǐhuān tā. 孩子们喜欢她. (孩子們喜歡她.) (hi-dzuh-mun she-hwahn tah.) (*The children like her.*)

Pánzi zài zhuōzishàng. 盘子在桌子上. (盤子在桌子上.) (pahn-dzuh dzye jwaw-dzuh-shahng.) (*There's a plate on the table.*)

Shū zài nàr. 书在那儿. (書在那兒.) (shoo dzye nar.) (*The book[s] are there.*)

Nouns that refer to something more general (and are therefore indefinite) can more often be found at the end of the sentence, after the verb:

Nǎr yǒu huā? 哪儿有花? (哪兒有花?) (nar yo hwah?) (*Where are some flowers?/Where is there a flower?*)

Nàr yǒu huā. 那儿有花. (那兒有花.) (nar yo hwah.) (*There are some flowers over there./There's a flower over there.*)

Zhèige yǒu wèntí. 这个有问题. (這個有問題.) (jay-guh yo one-tee.) (*There's a problem with this./There are some problems with this.*)

These rules have some exceptions: If you find a noun at the beginning of a sentence, it may actually refer to something indefinite if the sentence makes a general comment (instead of telling a whole story), like when you see the verb **shì** 是 (shir) (*to be*) as part of the comment:

Xióngmāo shì dòngwù. 熊猫是动物. (熊貓是動物.) (shyoong-maow shir doong-woo.) (*Pandas are animals.*)

Same thing goes if an adjective comes after the noun, such as

Pútáo hěn tián. 葡萄很甜. (poo-taow hun tyan.) (*Grapes are very sweet.*)

Or if there's an auxiliary verb, such as

> **Xiǎo māo huì zhuā lǎoshǔ.** 小貓会抓老鼠. (小貓會抓老鼠.) (shyaow maow hway jwah laow-shoo.) (*Kittens can catch mice.*)

Or a verb indicating that the action occurs habitually, such as

> **Niú chī cǎo.** 牛吃草. (nyo chir tsaow.) (*Cows eat grass.*)

Nouns that are preceded by a numeral and a classifier, especially when the word **dōu** 都 (doe) (*all*) exists in the same breath, are also considered definite:

> **Sìge xuéshēng dōu hěn cōngmíng.** 四个学生都很聪明. (四個學生都很聰明.) (suh-guh shweh-shung doe hun tsoong-meeng.) (*The four students are all very smart.*)

If the word **yǒu** 有 (yo) (*to exist*) comes before the noun and is then followed by a verb, it can also mean the reference is indefinite:

> **Yǒu shū zài zhuōzishàng.** 有书在桌子上. (有書在桌子上.) (yo shoo dzye jwaw-dzuh-shahng.) (*There are books on top of the table.*)

If you see the word **zhè** 这 (這) (juh) (*this*) or **nà** 那 (nah) (*that*), plus a classifier used when a noun comes after the verb, it indicates a definite reference:

> **Wǒ yào mǎi nà zhāng huà.** 我要买那张画. (我要買那張畫.) (waw yaow my nah jahng hwah.) (*I want to buy that painting.*)

Adjectives

As you learned in grade school (you were paying close attention, weren't you?), adjectives describe nouns. The question is where to put them. The general rule of thumb in Chinese is that if the adjective is pronounced with only one syllable, it appears immediately in front of the noun it qualifies:

> **cháng zhītiáo** 长枝条 (長枝 條) (chahng jir-tyaow) (*long stick*)
>
> **lǜ chá** 绿茶 (綠茶) (lyew chah) (*green tea*)

If the adjective has two syllables, though, the possessive particle **de** 的 (duh) comes between it and whatever it qualifies:

> **cāozá de wǎnhuì** 嘈杂的晚会 (嘈雜的晚會) (tsaow-dzah duh wahn-hway) (*noisy party*)
>
> **gānjìng de yīfu** 干净的衣服 (乾淨的衣服) (gahn-jeeng duh ee-foo) (*clean clothes*)

And if a numeral is followed by a classifier, those should both go in front of the adjective and what it qualifies:

sān běn yǒuyìsī de shū 三本有意思的书 (三本有意思的書) (sahn bun yo-ee-suh duh shoo) (*three interesting books*)

yí jiàn xīn yīfu 一件新衣服 (一件新服裝) (ee jyan shin ee-foo) (*a [piece of] new clothing*)

One unique thing about Chinese is that when an adjective is also the predicate, appearing at the end of a sentence, it follows the subject or the topic without needing the verb **shì**:

Nà jiàn yīfu tài jiù. 那件衣服太旧. (那件衣服太舊.) (nah jyan ee-foo tye jyoe.) (*That piece of clothing [is] too old.*)

Tā de fángzi hěn gānjìng. 他的房子很干净. (他的房子很乾淨.) (tah duh fahng-dzuh hun gahn-jeeng.) (*His house [is] very clean.*)

Getting Into Verbs, Adverbs, Negation, and Possession

Some interesting characteristics of the Chinese language include the fact that there's no such thing as first, second, or third person (for example, *I eat* versus *he eats*); no such thing as active or passive voices (for example, *hear* versus *be heard*); and no such thing as past or present (*I like him* versus *I liked him*). In addition, Chinese language has only two aspects — complete and continuous — whereas English has all sorts of different aspects: indefinite, continuous, perfect, perfect continuous, and so on. (Examples include ways of distinguishing among *I eat, I ate, I will eat, I said I would eat, I am eating,* and so on.) *Aspects* are what characterize the Chinese language in place of tenses. They refer to how a speaker views an event or state of being.

The following sections give you the lowdown on verbs, their friends the adverbs, and ways you can negate statements and express possession.

Verbs

Good news! You never have to worry about conjugating a Chinese verb in your entire life! If you hear someone say **Tāmen chī Yìdàlì fàn.** 他们吃意大利饭. (他們吃意大利飯.) (tah-men chir ee-dah-lee fahn.), it may mean *They eat Italian food.* just as easily as it may mean *They're eating Italian food.* Table 3-2 presents some common verbs; check out Appendix B for a more extensive list.

Table 3-2	Common Chinese Verbs	
Chinese	*Pronunciation*	*English*
chī 吃	chir	*to eat*
kàn 看	kahn	*to see*
mǎi 买 (買)	my	*to buy*
mài 卖 (賣)	my	*to sell*
rènshi 认识 (認識)	run-shir	*to know (a person)*
shì 是	shir	*to be*
yào 要	yaow	*to want/to need*
yǒu 有	yo	*to have*
zhīdào 知道	jir-daow	*to know (a fact)*
zǒu lù 走路	dzoe loo	*to walk*
zuò fàn 做饭 (做飯)	dzwaw fahn	*to cook*

To be or not to be: The verb shì

Does the Chinese verb **shì** 是 (shir) really mean *to be?* Or is it not to be? **Shì** is indeed similar to English in usage because it's often followed by a noun that defines the topic, such as **Tā shì wǒde lǎobǎn.** 他是我的老板. (他是我的老闆.) (tah shir waw-duh laow-bahn.) (*He's my boss.*) or **Nà shì yīge huài huà.** 那是一个坏话. (那是一個壞 話.) (nah shir ee-guh hwye hwah.) (*That's a bad word.*).

Be careful not to put the verb **shì** in front of an adjective unless you really mean to make an emphatic statement. In the course of normal conversation, you may say **Nà zhī bǐ tài guì.** 那支笔太贵. (那支筆太貴.) (nah jir bee tye gway.) (*That pen [is] too expensive.*). You wouldn't say **Nà zhī bǐ shì tài guì.** 那支笔是太贵. (那支筆是太貴.) (nah jir bee shir tye gway.) unless you really want to say *That pen IS too expensive!*, in which case you'd emphasize the word **shì** when saying it.

To negate the verb **shì,** put the negative prefix **bù** 不 (boo) in front of it:

> **Shì bú shì?** 是不是? (shir boo shir?) (*Is it or isn't it?*)

> **Zhè bú shì táng cù yú.** 这不是糖醋鱼. (這不是糖醋魚.) (jay boo shir tahng tsoo yew.) (*This isn't sweet and sour fish.*).

Flip to the later section "Bù and méiyǒu: Total negation" for more on negation prefixes.

Feeling tense? Le, guò, and other aspect markers

Okay, you can relax now. No need to get tense about Chinese, because verbs don't indicate tenses all by themselves. That's the job of *aspect markers,* which are little syllables that indicate whether an action has been completed, is continuing, has just begun, and just about everything in between.

Take the syllable **le** 了 (luh), for example. If you use it as a suffix to a verb, it can indicate that an action has been completed:

> **Nǐ mǎi le hěn duō shū.** 你买了很多书. (你買了很多書.) (nee my luh hun dwaw shoo.) (*You bought many books.*)
>
> **Tā dài le tāde yǔsǎn.** 他带了他的雨伞. (他帶了他的雨傘.) (tah dye luh tah-duh yew-sahn.) (*He brought his umbrella.*)

And if you want to turn the sentence into a question, just add **méiyǒu** 没有 (mayo) at the end. It automatically negates the action completed by **le:**

> **Nǐ mǎi le hěn duō shū méiyǒu?** 你买了很多书没有? (你買了很多書没有?) (nee my luh hun dwaw shoo mayo?) (*Have you bought many books?/Did you buy many books?*)
>
> **Tā dài le tāde yǔsǎn méiyǒu?** 他带了他的雨伞没有? (他帶了他的雨傘没有?) (tah dye luh tah-duh yew-sahn mayo?) (*Did he bring his umbrella?*)

Another aspect marker is **guò** 过 (過) (gwaw). It basically means that something has been done at one point or another even though it's not happening right now:

> **Tā qù guò Měiguó.** 他去过美国. (他去過美國.) (ta chyew gwaw may-gwaw.) (*He has been to America.*)
>
> **Wǒmen chī guò Fǎguó cài.** 我们吃过法国菜. (我們吃過法國菜.) (waw-mun chir gwaw fah-gwaw tsye.) (*We have eaten French food before.*)

If an action is happening just as you speak, you use the aspect marker **zài** 在 (dzye):

> **Nǐ māma zài zuòfàn.** 你妈妈在做饭. (你媽媽在做飯.) (nee mah-mah dzye dzwaw-fahn.) (*Your mother is cooking.*)
>
> **Wǒmen zài chīfàn.** 我们在吃饭. (我們在吃飯.) (waw-mun dzye chir-fahn.) (*We are eating.*)

When using the aspect marker **zài,** you can also add the word **zhèng** 正 (juhng) in front of it to add emphasis. It can be translated as *to be right in the middle of [doing something].*

If something is or was happening continually and resulted from something else you did, just add the syllable **zhe** 着 (juh) to the end of the verb to say things like the following:

Nǐ chuān zhe yí jiàn piàoliàng de chènshān. 你穿着一件漂亮的衬衫. (你穿著一件漂亮的襯衫.) (nee chwan juh ee jyan pyaow-lyahng duh chuhn-shahn.) (*You're wearing a pretty shirt.*)

Tā dài zhe yíge huáng màozi. 他戴着一个黄帽子. (他戴著一個黃帽子.) (tah dye juh ee-guh hwahng maow-dzuh.) (*He's wearing a yellow hat.*)

Another way you can use **zhe** is when you want to indicate two actions occurring at the same time:

Tā zuò zhe chīfàn. 她坐着吃饭. (她坐著吃飯.) (tah dzwaw juh chir-fahn.) (*She is/was sitting there eating.*)

Talkin' the Talk

Carol and Joe have fun people-watching on the streets of Shanghai.

Carol:	**Nǐ kàn! Nàge xiǎo háizi dài zhe yíge hěn qíguài de màozi, shì bú shì?**
	nee kahn! nah-guh shyaow hi-dzuh dye juh ee-guh hun chee-gwye duh maow-dzuh, shir boo shir?
	Look! That little kid is wearing a really strange hat, isn't she?
Joe:	**Duì le. Tā hái yìbiān zǒu, yìbiān chàng gē.**
	dway luh. tah hi ee-byan dzoe, ee-byan chahng guh.
	Yeah. She's also singing while she walks.
Carol:	**Wǒ méiyǒu kàn guò nàmme kě'ài de xiǎo háizi.**
	waw mayo kahn gwaw nummuh kuh-eye duh shyaow hi-dzuh.
	I've never seen such a cute child.
Joe:	**Zài Zhōngguó nǐ yǐjīng kàn le tài duō kě'ài de xiǎo háizi.**
	dzye joong-gwaw nee ee-jeeng kahn luh tye dwaw kuh-eye duh shyaow hi-dzuh.
	You've already seen too many adorable little kids in China.

Words to Know

qíguài 奇怪	chee-gwye	strange
shì bú shì? 是不是	shir boo shir	Isn't that so?
chàng gē 唱歌	chahng-guh	to sing
kě'ài 可爱 (可愛)	kuh-eye	cute; adorable

The special verb: Yǒu (to have)

Do you **yǒu** 有 (yo) a computer? No?! Too bad. Everyone else seems to have one these days. How about a sports car? Do you **yǒu** one of those? If not, welcome to the club. People who have lots of things use the word **yǒu** pretty often, translated as *to have* like in the following examples:

> **Wǒ yǒu sānge fángzi: yíge zài Ōuzhōu, yíge zài Yàzhōu, yíge zài Měiguó.**
> 我有三个房子: 一个在欧洲, 一个在亚洲, 一个在美国. (我有三個房子: 一個在歐洲, 一個在亞洲, 一個在美國.) (waw yo sahn-guh fahng-dzuh: ee-guh dzye oh-joe, ee-guh dzye yah-joe, ee-guh dzye may-gwaw.) (*I have three homes: one in Europe, one in Asia, and one in America.*)

> **Wǒ yǒu yí wàn kuài qián.** 我有一万块钱. (我有一萬塊錢.) (waw yo ee wahn kwye chyan.) (*I have $10,000.*)

Another way **yǒu** can be translated is as *there is* or *there are:*

> **Yǒu hěn duō háizi.** 有很多孩子. (yo hun dwaw hi-dzuh.) (*There are many children.*), as opposed to **Wǒ yǒu hěn duō háizi.** 我有很多孩子. (waw yo hun dwaw hi-dzuh.) (*I have many children.*)

> **Shūzhuōshàng yǒu wǔ zhāng zhǐ.** 书桌上有五张纸. (書桌上有五張紙.) (shoo-jwaw-shahng yo woo jahng jir.) (*There are five pieces of paper on the desk.*)

To negate the verb **yǒu,** you can't use the usual negative prefix **bù.** Instead, you must use another term indicating negation, **méi** 没 (may):

> **Méiyǒu hěn duō háizi.** 没有很多孩子. (mayo hun dwaw hi-dzuh.) (*There aren't many children.*)

> **Shūzhuōshàng méiyǒu wǔ zhāng zhǐ.** 书桌上没有五张纸. (書桌上沒有五張紙.) (shoe-jwaw-shahng mayo woo jahng jir.) (*There aren't five pieces of paper on the desk.*)

You can read more about negation prefixes in "Bù and méiyǒu: Total negation" later in the chapter.

Asking for what you want: The verb yào

After Yao Ming, the 7-foot-6-inch basketball superstar from China, came on the scene, the verb **yào** 要 (yaow) (_to want_) got some great publicity in the United States. The character for his name isn't written quite the same as the verb **yào,** but at least everyone knows how to pronounce it already: yow!

Yào is one of the coolest verbs in Chinese. When you say it, you usually get what you want. In fact, the mere mention of the word **yào** means you want something:

Wǒ yào gēn nǐ yìqǐ qù kàn diànyǐng. 我要跟你一起去看电影. (我要跟你一起去看電影.) (waw yaow gun nee ee-chee chyew kahn dyan-yeeng.) (_I want to go to the movies with you._)

Wǒ yào yì bēi kāfēi. 我要一杯咖啡. (waw yaow ee bay kah-fay.) (_I want a cup of coffee._)

You can also give someone an order with the verb **yào,** but only if it's used with a second-person pronoun:

Nǐ yào xiǎoxīn! 你要小心! (nee yaow shyaow-sheen!) (_You should be careful!_)

Nǐ yào xǐ shǒu. 你要洗手. (nee yaow she show.) (_You need to wash your hands._)

Adverbs

Adverbs serve to modify verbs or adjectives and always appear in front of them in Chinese. The most common adverbs you find in Chinese are **hěn** 很 (hun) (_very_) and **yě** 也 (yeah) (_also_).

If you want to say that something isn't just **hǎo** 好 (how) (_good_) but rather that it's very good, you say it's **hěn hǎo** 很好 (hun how) (_very good_). If your friend wants to put his two cents in and say that something else is also really good, he says **Zhèige yě hěn hǎo.** 这个也很好 (這個也很好) (jay guh yeah hun how.) (_This is also very good._) because **yě** always comes before **hěn** (as well as before the negative prefix **bù;** refer to the following section.)

Bù and méiyǒu: Total negation

Boo! Scare you? Don't worry. I'm just being negative in Chinese. That's right: The word **bù** is pronounced the same way a ghost would say it (boo) and is often spoken with the same intensity.

Bù can negate something you've done in the past or the present (or at least indicate you don't generally do it these days), and it can also help negate something in the future:

> **Diànyǐngyuàn xīngqīliù bù kāimén.** 电影院星期六不开门. (電影院星期六不開門.) (dyan-yeeng-ywan sheeng-chee-lyo boo kye-mun.) (*The movie theatre won't be open on Saturday.*)

> **Tā xiǎo de shíhòu bù xǐhuān chī shūcài.** 他小的时候不喜欢吃蔬菜. (他小的時候不喜歡吃蔬菜.) (tah shyaow duh shir-ho boo she-hwahn chir shoo-tsye.) (*When he was young, he didn't like to eat vegetables.*)

> **Wǒ bú huà huàr.** 我不画画儿. (我不畫畫兒.) (waw boo hwah hwar.) (*I don't paint.*)

> **Wǒ búyào chàng gē.** 我不要唱歌. (waw boo-yaow chahng guh.) (*I don't want to sing.*)

The negative prefix **bù** is usually spoken with a fourth (falling) tone. However, when it precedes a syllable with another fourth tone, **bù** becomes a second (rising) tone instead, as in such words as **búqù** 不去 (boo-chew) (*won't/didn't/doesn't go*) and **búyào** 不要 (boo-yaow) (*don't/didn't/won't want*). For more about tones, head to Chapter 1.

In addition to being part of the question **yǒu méiyǒu** (*do you have/did it*), **méiyǒu** is another negative prefix that also goes before a verb. It refers only to the past, though, and means either something didn't happen, or at least didn't happen on a particular occasion:

> **Wǒ méiyǒu kàn nèi bù diànyǐng.** 我没有看那部电影. (我沒有看那部電影.) (waw mayo kahn nay boo dyan-yeeng.) (*I didn't see that movie.*)

> **Zuótiān méiyǒu xiàyǔ.** 昨天没有下雨. (昨天沒有下雨.) (dzwaw-tyan mayo shyah-yew.) (*It didn't rain yesterday.*)

If the aspect marker **guò** is at the end of the verb **méiyǒu**, it means the action never happened (up until now) in the past. By the way, you'll sometimes find that **méiyǒu** is shortened just to **méi:**

Wǒ méi qù guò Fǎguó. 我没去过法国. (我沒去過法國.) (waw may gwaw fah-gwaw.) (*I've never been to France.*)

Wǒ méi chī guò Yìndù cài. 我没吃过印度菜. (我沒吃過印度菜.) (wo may chir gwaw een-doo tsye.) (*I've never eaten Indian food.*)

Talkin' the Talk

Harvey, Stella, and Laurie discuss where to go for dinner. (Track 4)

Harvey: **Nǐmen jīntiān wǎnshàng yào búyào qù fànguǎn chīfàn?**
你们今天晚上要不要去饭馆吃饭?
nee-mun jin-tyan wahn-shahng yaow boo-yaow chyew fahn-gwahn chir-fahn?
Do you both want to go to a restaurant tonight?

Stella: **Nà tài hǎole. Dāngrán yào.**
那太好了 当然要
nah tye how-luh. dahng-rahn yaow.
That's a great idea. Of course I'd like to go.

Laurie: **Wǒ búyào. Wǒ méiyǒu qián.**
我不要 我没要 钱
waw boo-yaow. waw mayo chyan.
I don't want to. I have no money.

Harvey: **Wǒ yě méiyǒu qián, dànshì méiyǒu guānxi. Wǒ zhīdào yíge hěn hǎo, hěn piányì de Zhōngguó fànguǎn.**
我也没有钱 只是 没有 关系 我知道一个很好
很便宜的 中国饭馆
waw yeah mayo chyan, dahn-shir mayo gwahn-she. waw jir-daow ee-guh hun how, hun pyan-yee duh joong-gwaw fahn-gwan.
I don't have any money either, but it doesn't matter. I know a great but very inexpensive Chinese restaurant.

Laurie: **Hǎo ba. Zánmen zǒu ba.**
好吧 咱们 走吧 走
how bah. dzah-men dzoe bah.
Okay. Let's go.

要 不要 — to do
但是 (dàn shì) — but
没有 关系 (mei) it doesn't matter.
当然 (dāng rán) — off course
且是 (dàn shì) — but, yet still

Words to Know

jīntiān wǎnshàng 今天晚上	jin-tyan wahn-shahng	tonight
tài hǎole 太好了	tye how-luh	that's great
dāngrán 当然 (當然)	dahng-rahn	of course
dànshì 但是	dahn-shir	but/however
zǒu ba 走吧	dzoe bah	let's go

Getting possessive with the particle de

The particle **de** 的 is ubiquitous in Chinese. Wherever you turn, there it is. **Wǒde tiān!** 我的天! (waw-duh tyan) (*My goodness!*) Oops . . . there it is again. It's easy to use. All you have to do is attach it to the end of the pronoun, such as **nǐde chē** 你的车 (你的車) (nee-duh chuh) (*your car*), or other modifier, such as **tā gōngsī de jīnglǐ** 他公司的经理 (他公司的經理) (tah goong-suh duh jeeng-lee) (*his company's manager*), and — voilà — it indicates possession.

The particle **de** acts as the *'s* in English when it's not attached to a pronoun. It also makes the process of modification exactly the opposite of the French possessive **de** or the English *of,* with which you may be tempted to compare it.

Asking Questions

You have a few easy ways to ask questions in Chinese at your disposal. Hopefully you're so curious about the world around you these days that you're itching to ask lots of questions when you know how. I break them down in the following sections.

The question particle ma

By far the easiest way to ask a question is simply to end any given statement with a **ma.** That automatically makes it into a question. For example, **Tā chīfàn.** 他吃饭. (他吃飯.) (tah chir-fahn.) (*He's eating./He eats.*) becomes **Tā chīfàn ma?** 他吃饭吗? (他吃飯嗎?) (tah chir-fahn mah?) (*Is he eating?/Does he eat?*) **Nǐ shuō Zhōngwén.** 你说中文. (你說中文.) (nee shwaw joong-one.) (*You speak Chinese.*) becomes **Nǐ shuō Zhōngwén ma?** 你说中文吗? (你說中文嗎?) (nee shwaw joong-one mah?) (*Do you speak Chinese?*)

Yes/no choice questions using bù between repeating verbs

Another way you can ask a Chinese question is to repeat the verb in its negative form. The English equivalent is to say something like *Do you eat, not eat?* ***Remember:*** This format can be used for only yes-or-no questions, though. Here are some examples:

> **Nǐ shì búshì Zhōngguórén?** 你是不是中国人? (你是不是中國人?) (nee shir boo-shir joong-gwaw-run?) (*Are you Chinese?*)
>
> **Tāmen xǐhuān bùxǐhuān chī Zhōngguó cài?** 他们喜欢不喜欢吃中国菜? (他們喜歡不喜歡吃中國菜?) (tah-men she-hwahn boo-she-hwahn chir joong-gwaw tsye?) (*Do they like to eat Chinese food?*)
>
> **Tā yào búyào háizi?** 他要不要孩子? (tah yaow boo-yaow hi-dzuh?) (*Does he want children?*)

To answer this type of question, all you have to do is omit either the positive verb or the negative prefix and the verb following it:

> **Nǐ hǎo bù hǎo?** 你好不好? (nee how boo how?) (*How are you?* [Literally: *Are you good or not good?*])
>
> **Wǒ hǎo.** 我好. (waw how.) (*I'm okay.*) or **Wǒ bùhǎo.** 我不好. (waw boo-how.) (*I'm not okay.*)

Some Chinese verbs, such as **xǐhuān** 喜欢 (喜歡) (she-hwan) (*to like/to want*), have two syllables. When Chinese people speak quickly, they may leave out the second syllable in a few bisyllabic verbs and even a few auxiliary verbs the first time they come up in the verb-**bù**-verb pattern. So instead of saying **Tā xǐhuān bùxǐhuān hē jiǔ?** 她喜欢不喜欢喝酒? (她喜歡不喜歡喝酒?) (tah she-hwan boo-she-hwan huh jyo?) to mean *Does he or she like to drink wine?*, someone may say **Tā xǐ bùxǐhuān hē jiǔ?** 她喜不喜欢喝酒? (她喜不喜歡喝酒?) (tah she boo-she-hwan huh jyoe?).

Interrogative pronouns

A third way to ask questions in Chinese is to use interrogative pronouns. The following are pronouns that act as questions in Chinese:

- **nǎ** 哪 (nah) + classifier (*which*)
- **nǎr** 哪儿 (哪兒) (nar) (*where*)
- **shéi** 谁 (誰) (shay) (*who/whom*)
- **shéi de** 谁的 (誰的) (shay duh) (*whose*)
- **shénme** 什么 (甚麼) (shummuh) (*what*)
- **shénme dìfāng** 什么地方 (甚麼地方) (shummah dee-fahng) (*where*)

Don't confuse **nǎ** with **nǎr.** That one extra letter makes the difference between saying *which* **(nǎ)** and *where* **(nǎr).**

Figuring out where such interrogative pronouns should go in any given sentence is easy. Just put them wherever the answer would be found. For example

Question: **Nǐ shì shéi?** 你是谁? (你是誰?) (nee shir shay?) (*Who are you?*)

Answer: **Nǐ shì wǒ péngyǒu.** 你是我朋友. (nee shir waw puhng-yo.) (*You're my friend.*)

Question: **Tāde nǚpéngyǒu zài nǎr?** 他的女朋友在哪儿? (他的女朋友在哪兒?) (tah duh nyew-puhng-yo dzye nar?) (*Where is his girlfriend?*)

Answer: **Tāde nǚpéngyǒu zài jiālǐ.** 他的女朋友在家里. (他的女朋友在家裡.) (tah-duh nyew-puhng-yo dzye jyah-lee.) (*His girlfriend is at home.*)

A way to ask *who* or *which person* without sounding rude or too familiar is to use the term **něi wèi** 哪位 (nye way) (Literally: *which person*). For example, **Nǐ yéye shì něi wèi?** 你爷爷是哪位? (你爺爺是哪位?) (nee yeh-yeh shir nay way?) (*Which one is your grandfather?*)

You often find interrogative pronouns at the beginning of sentences if they're followed by the verb **yǒu** 有 (yo) (*to exist*), such as **Shéi yǒu wǒde bǐ?** 谁有我的笔? (誰有我的筆?) (shay yo waw-duh bee?) (*Who has my pen?*)

Fun & Games

Match the Chinese questions with the English translations. (See Appendix D for the correct answer.)

1. **Shì bú shì?** 是不是?

2. **Nǐ shuō Zhōngwén ma?** 你说中文吗? (你說中文嗎?)

3. **Nǐ shì shéi?** 你是谁? (你是誰?)

4. **Nà yǒu shénme guānxi?** 那有什么关系? (那有甚麼關係?)

5. **Nǐ yǒu méiyǒu yíge shǒutíshì?** 你有没有一个手提式? (你有沒有一個手提式?)

a. *Who are you?*

b. *Isn't that so?*

c. *Do you have a laptop?*

d. *Who cares?*

e. *Do you speak Chinese?*

Chapter 4

Getting Started with Basic Expressions: Nǐ Hǎo!

. . . .

In This Chapter

▶ Introducing yourself and others

▶ Greeting and chatting with family, friends, and colleagues

. . . .

Nǐ **hǎo!** 你好! (nee how) (*Hello!/How are you?*) Those are probably the two most important words you need to know to start a conversation with your Chinese neighbors, with your Chinese in-laws coming into town, with a Chinese classmate, or with airport personnel upon your arrival in China. When you say them, you take the first step in making new friends and establishing contact with just about anybody.

In this chapter, I show you how to start your new connection off with just the right words. The only other thing you have to do is smile. That's something all people understand, no matter what country they're from.

Making Introductions

Nothing beats making new friends at a **wǎnhuì** 晚会 (晚會) (wahn-hway) (*party*), a **xīn gōngzuò** 新工作 (sheen goong-dzaw) (*new job*), on the **dìtiě** 地铁 (地鐵) (dee-tyeh) (*subway*), or just **zài lùshàng** 在路上 (dzye loo-shahng) (*on the street*). You may meet someone right after reading this chapter who becomes a good friend for life. This section gives you a head start in making a good first impression. Go ahead and practice these greetings to get ready for anything.

Acquainting yourself

When you make Chinese acquaintances or travel abroad, you soon discover that a little knowledge of even a few key expressions in their native language goes a long way in creating good will between your two cultures. Chinese people in particular are very appreciative of anyone who takes the time to learn their intricate and difficult language, so your efforts will be rewarded many times over.

You have options other than **nǐ hǎo** when you first meet someone, such as **Hěn gāoxìng jiàndào nǐ.** 很高兴见到你 (很高興見到你) (hun gaow-sheeng jyan-daow nee.) (*Glad to meet you.*) or **Wǒ hěn róngxìng.** 我很荣幸 (我很榮幸) (waw hun roong-sheeng.) (*I'm honored to meet you.*). Go ahead and tell the person your **míngzi** 名字 (meeng-dzuh) (*name*) and take the conversation from there.

Don't know what to say after the first **nǐ hǎo?** Here are a few common opening lines to get you started:

- **Nǐ jiào shénme míngzi?** 你叫什么名字? (你叫甚麼名字?) (nee jyaow shummuh meeng-dzuh?) (*What's your name?*)

- **Qǐng ràng wǒ jièshào wǒ zìjǐ.** 请让我介绍我自己. (請讓我介紹我自己.) (cheeng rahng waw jyeh-shaow waw dzuh-jee) (*Please let me introduce myself.*)

- **Wǒ jiào ____. Nǐ ne?** 我叫 ____. 你呢? (waw jyaow ____. nee nuh?) (*My name is ____. What's yours?*)

- **Wǒ shì Měiguórén.** 我是美国人. (我是美國人.) (waw shir may-gwaw-run.) (*I'm an American.*)

Introducing your friends and family

You can help your friends make even more friends if you start introducing them to each other. All you have to do is say **Qǐng ràng wǒ jièshào wǒde péngyǒu, Carl.** 请让我介绍我的朋友, Carl. (請讓我介紹我的朋友, Carl.) (cheeng rahng waw jyeh-shaow waw-duh puhng-yo, Carl.) (*Let me introduce my friend, Carl.*) In addition to introducing your **péngyǒu** 朋友 (puhng-yo) (*friend*), you can introduce these important people:

- **bàba** 爸爸 (bah-bah) (*father*)
- **lǎobǎn** 老板 (老闆) (laow-bahn) (*boss*)

- ✔ **lǎoshī** 老师 (老師) (laow-shir) (*teacher*)

- ✔ **māma** 妈妈 (媽媽) (mah-mah) (*mother*)

- ✔ **nán péngyǒu** 男朋友 (nahn puhng-yo) (*boyfriend*)

- ✔ **nǚ péngyǒu** 女朋友 (nyew pung-yo) (*girlfriend*)

- ✔ **tàitai** 太太 (tye-tye) (*wife*)

- ✔ **tóngshì** 同事 (toong-shir) (*colleague*)

- ✔ **tóngwū** 同屋 (toong-woo) (*roommate*)

- ✔ **tóngxué** 同学 (同學) (toong-shweh) (*classmate*)

- ✔ **wǒde péngyǒu** 我的朋友 (waw-duh puhng-yo) (*my friend*)

- ✔ **zhàngfu** 丈夫 (jahng-foo) (*husband*)

When introducing two people to each other, always introduce the one with the lower social status and/or age to the person with the higher social status. The Chinese consider this progression polite.

Asking people for their names

Many situations call for informal greetings like **Wǒ jiào Sarah. Nǐ ne?** 我叫 Sarah. 你呢? (waw jyaow Sarah. nee nuh?) (*My name is Sarah. And yours?*) or **Nǐ jiào shénme míngzi?** 你叫什么名字? (你叫甚麼名字?) (nee jyaow shum-muh meeng-dzuh?) (*What's your name?*), but you can show a greater level of politeness and respect by asking **Nín guì xìng?** 您贵姓? (您貴姓?) (neeng gway sheeng?) (Literally: *What's your honorable surname?*) But if you're asking this question of someone who's younger than you or lower in social status, you can easily just say **Nǐ jiào shénme míngzi?** 你叫什么名字? (你叫甚麼名字?) (nee jyaow shummah meeng-dzuh?) (*What's your name?*) Even though **míngzi** usually means *given name,* asking this question may elicit an answer of first and last name. Keep practicing these different opening lines to ask who people are, and you're bound to make friends quickly (or you're at least bound to get to know a lot of Chinese names).

If someone asks you **Nín guì xìng?,** don't refer to yourself with the honorific **guì** when you answer. Your new acquaintance would consider you too boastful. Such a response is like saying "My esteemed family name is Smith." The best way to answer is to say **Wǒ xìng Smith.** 我姓 Smith. (waw sheeng Smith.) (*My family name is Smith.*)

If a guy tells you his name in Chinese, you can be sure the first syllable he utters will be his surname, not his given name. So if he says his name is **Lǐ Shìmín,** for example, his family name is **Lǐ** and his given name is **Shìmín.** You should keep referring to him as **Lǐ Shìmín** (rather than just **Shìmín**) until you become really good friends. If you want to address him as **Xiānshēng** 先生 (shyan-shuhng) (*Mr.*), or if you're addressing a female as **Xiǎojiě** 小姐 (shyaow-jyeh) (*Miss*) or **Tàitài** 太太 (tye-tye) (*Mrs.*), you put that title after his or her last name and say **Lǐ Xiānshēng** or **Lǐ Xiǎojiě.** Even though the Chinese language has words for *Mr., Miss,* and *Mrs.,* it has no equivalent term for *Ms.* At least not yet.

Talkin' the Talk

Eva introduces her friends Oscar and David to each other. (Track 5)

Eva: **Oscar, qǐng ràng wǒ jièshào wǒde péngyǒu David.**
Oscar, cheeng rahng waw jyeh-shaow waw-duh puhng-yo David.
Oscar, allow me to introduce my friend David.

Oscar: **Nǐ hǎo. Hěn gāoxìng jiàndào nǐ.**
nee how. hun gaow-sheeng jyan-daow nee.
Hi. Nice to meet you.

David: **Hěn gāoxìng jiàndào nǐ. Wǒ shì Eva de tóngxué.**
hun gaow-sheeng jyan-daow nee. waw shir Eva duh toong-shweh.
Good to meet you. I'm Eva's classmate.

Oscar: **Hěn gāoxìng jiàndào nǐ.**
hun gaow-sheeng jyan-daow nee.
Nice to meet you.

David: **Nǐmen zénme rènshì?**
nee-mun dzummuh run-shir?
How do you happen to know each other?

Eva: **Wǒmen shì tóngshì.**
waw-mun shir toong-shir.
We're co-workers.

Words to Know

péngyǒu 朋友	puhng-yo	friend
Hěn gāoxìng jiàndào nǐ. 很高兴见到你. (很高興見到你.)	hun gaow-sheeng jyan-daow nee.	Nice to meet you.
tóngxué 同学 (同學)	toong-shweh	classmate
tóngshì 同事	toong-shir	colleague

Greeting and Chatting

When you **dǎ zhāohu** 打招呼 (dah jaow-who) (*extend greetings*), you're sure to maintain and possibly even improve your connections with others. This goes for starting the day right with your **àirén** 爱人 (愛人) (eye-run) (*spouse*), showing respect for your **lǎoshī** 老师 (老師) (laow-shir) (*teacher*), keeping on the good side of your **lǎobǎn** 老板 (老闆) (laow-bahn) (*boss*), or paving the way for that deal with your new **shēngyì huǒbàn** 生意伙伴 (生意夥伴) (shuhng-yee hwaw-bahn) (*business partner*).

After the opening greeting, stick around to chat for a bit so you can get to know each other better. You can make new friends and find out more about each other through small conversations. This section gives you the important phrases to know.

Addressing new friends and strangers

In your hometown or home country, you may have plenty of **lǎo péngyǒu** 老朋友 (laow puhng-yo) (*old friends*), but in any other city or country, you need to get off on the right foot by addressing people the way they're used to being addressed. You can get chummier as time goes by, but try to avoid sounding too friendly or presumptuous too soon.

You can always safely greet people in professional settings by announcing their last name followed by their title, such as **Wáng Xiàozhǎng** 王校长 (王校長) (wahng shyaow-jahng) (*President [of an educational institution] Wang*) or **Jīn Zhǔrèn** 金主任 (jeen joo-run) (*Director Jin*). Here are some other examples of occupational titles:

- ✔ **bùzhǎng** 部长 (部長) (boo-jahng) (*department head or minister*)
- ✔ **fùzhǔrèn** 副主任 (foo-joo-run) (*assistant director*)
- ✔ **jiàoshòu** 教授 (jyaow-show) (*professor*)
- ✔ **jīnglǐ** 经理 (經理) (jeeng-lee) (*manager*)
- ✔ **lǎoshī** 老师 (老師) (laow-shir) (*teacher*)

If you don't know someone's title, you can safely address the person by saying his or her family name and then either **Xiānshēng** 先生 (shyan-shuhng) (*Mr.*) or **Xiǎojiě** 小姐 (shyaow-jyeh) (*Miss*).

Chinese folks often instruct their young children to address older people as **shúshu** 叔叔 (shoo-shoo) (*uncle*) or **āyí** 阿姨 (ah-yee) (*aunt*). Getting to know a Chinese family makes you feel like you're actually part of the family in a new country.

Sometimes people add the terms **lǎo** 老 (laow) (*old*) or **xiǎo** 小 (shyaow) (*young*) in front of the last name and omit the first name completely. It indicates a comfortable degree of familiarity and friendliness that can only develop over time. But make sure you know which one to use — **lǎo** is for someone who's older than you, and **xiǎo** is for someone who's younger than you. Also keep in mind that these names can sometimes sound kind of funny to non-Chinese. If someone's surname is pronounced **Yáng** (yahng), which sounds like the word for *goat,* you may end up sounding like you're calling the person an old goat when you become good friends.

Conversing around the clock

You can always say **nǐ hǎo** when you meet someone, but at certain times of the day, you can use specific ways to express your greetings.

When you meet family, friends, co-workers, or fellow students in the morning, you can say **Zǎo.** 早. (dzaow.) (*Good morning.*) or **Zǎo ān.** 早安. (dzaow ahn.) (*Good morning.* [Literally: *early peace*]).

A word about culturally acceptable behavior

The Chinese are very friendly people and sometimes don't hesitate to come up to a foreigner on the street in order to practice their English. Such a situation can be a great chance to practice your Chinese as well. You have all sorts of cultural differences to get used to, however, so don't be surprised if a person you meet for the first time starts asking you about your salary or the cost of that cute sweater you're wearing. Subjects that are taboo as conversation pieces in the United States aren't off limits in China. (Try not to inquire about a person's political views or love life unless you know the person really well, though, or you may hit a brick wall.)

In general, Chinese people are loath to show negative emotions in public. Anger and disappointment or disapproval are major no-nos. Try to do the same when you're in a Chinese setting, because you may run the risk of insulting someone unintentionally. To do so means that you make them lose face — a cardinal sin if you want to get along in China. The last thing you want to do is insult, yell at, or otherwise embarrass anyone publicly, so keep a lid on any negative reactions you may have. You earn respect by controlling your emotions.

You may be surprised that many Chinese have no compunction about performing certain bodily functions in public. The Chinese don't consider it rude, for example, to belch, spit, or even pass gas in front of others. And because there's no such thing as a nonsmoking area, most smokers don't even think to ask whether you mind their lighting up near you. In addition, you may find people pointing or even staring at you — especially in smaller towns and villages, which rarely get foreign visitors. These behaviors are considered perfectly acceptable, so don't let them get your dander up. Just go with the flow and offer a polite smile in return.

The Chinese have a different idea about keeping a certain polite physical distance when speaking to someone. You'll commonly find someone standing or sitting pretty close to you, no matter how much you keep trying to inch away. And if you find two friends of the same sex walking arm in arm or holding hands, don't jump to any conclusions. It just means that they're friends.

Note: Despite the more relaxed view of personal space, however, avoid slaps on the back to Chinese people you don't know well, no matter how excited you are to meet them. And when dealing with members of the opposite sex, any physical contact with folks you don't know too well will be misinterpreted, so try to avoid it.

In the evening or before you go to sleep, you can say **Wǎn ān.** 晚安. (wahn ahn.) (*Good night.*). Just as **zǎo** means early, **wǎn** means late. So if someone says **Nǐ lái de tài wǎn.** 你来得太晚. (你來得太晚.) (nee lye duh tye wahn.) or **Nǐ lái de tài zǎo.** 你来得太早. (你來得太早.) (nee lye duh tye dzaow.), he means *You came too late.* or *You came too early.*

Talkin' the Talk

Julia and Christopher are good friends who meet in front of school one morning. Julia introduces Christopher to a new student named Lǐ.

Julia: **Zǎo. Nǐ zěnme yàng?**
dzaow. nee dzummuh yahng?
Good morning. How's it going?

Christopher: **Hěn hǎo, xièxiè. Nǐ ne?**
hun how, shyeh-shyeh. nee nuh?
Very well, thanks. And you?

Julia: **Wǒ yě hěn hǎo. Zhè wèi shì wǒmen de xīn tóngxué.**
waw yeah hun how. jay way shir waw-mun duh sheen toong-shweh.
I'm good, too. This is our new classmate.

Christopher: **Nǐ hǎo. Qǐng wèn, nǐ xìng shénme?**
nee how. cheeng one, nee sheeng shummuh?
Hi. What's your (sur)name?

Lǐ: **Wǒ xìng Lǐ. Nǐ jiào shénme míngzi?**
waw sheeng Lǐ. nee jyaow shummuh meeng-dzuh?
My last name is Lǐ. What's your (first) name?

Christopher: **Wǒ jiào Christopher. Nǐ xué shénme?**
waw jyaow Christopher. nee shweh shummuh?
My name is Christopher. What do you study?

Lǐ: **Wǒ xué lìshǐ. Nǐ ne?**
waw shweh lee-shir. nee nuh?
I study history. How about you?

Christopher: **Wǒ xué kuàijì.**
waw shweh kwye-jee.
I study accounting.

Words to Know

tóngxué 同学 (同學)	toong-shweh	classmate
míngzi 名字	meeng-dzuh	first name
xìng 姓	sheeng	last name
xué 学 (學)	shweh	to study
lìshǐ 历史 (歷史)	lee-shir	history
kuàijì 会计 (會計)	kwye-jee	accounting

Talking about the weather

Talking about the **tiānqì** 天气 (天氣) (tyan-chee) (*weather*) is always a safe topic in any conversation. In fact, it's kind of the universal ice breaker. If the skies are blue and all seems right with the world, you can start by saying **Jīntiān de tiānqì zhēn hǎo, duì bú duì?** 今天的天气真好,对不对? (今天的天氣真好, 對不對?) (jin-tyan duh tyan-chee juhn how, dway boo dway?) (*The weather today sure is nice, isn't it?*) Here are some adjectives to describe temperature and humidity:

- ✔ **lěng** 冷 (lung) (*cold*)
- ✔ **liángkuài** 凉快 (涼快) (lyahng-kwye) (*cool*)
- ✔ **mēnrè** 闷热 (悶熱) (mun-ruh) (*muggy*)
- ✔ **nuǎnhuó** 暖和 (nwan-hwaw) (*warm*)
- ✔ **rè** 热 (熱) (ruh) (*hot*)

Only use the word **rè** to describe hot weather. For food that's hot temperature-wise, you say **tàng** 烫 (燙) (tahng). And if your food is spicy hot, you have to say it's **là** 辣 (lah) instead.

The **sìjì** (suh-jee) (*four seasons*) — **dōngtiān** 冬天 (doong-tyan) (*winter*), **chūntiān** 春天 (chwun-tyan) (*spring*), **xiàtiān** 夏天 (shyah-tyan) (*summer*), and **qiūtiān** 秋天 (chyo-tyan) (*fall*) — all have their charms. They also all have their distinctive characteristics when it comes to the weather, which you can express with the following words in any conversation:

- **bàofēngxuě** 暴风雪 (暴風雪) (baow-fuhng-shweh) (*blizzard*)

- **dàfēng** 大风 (大風) (dah-fuhng) (*gusty winds*)

- **duōyún** 多云 (多雲) (dwaw-yewn) (*cloudy*)

- **fēng hěn dà** 风很大 (風很大) (fuhng hun dah) (*windy*)

- **léiyǔ** 雷雨 (lay-yew) (*thunderstorm*)

- **qínglǎng** 晴朗 (cheeng-lahng) (*sunny*)

- **qíngtiān** 晴天 (cheeng-tyan) (*clear*)

- **xià máomáoyǔ** 下毛毛雨 (shyah maow-maow-yew) (*drizzle*)

- **xiàwù** 下雾 (下霧) (shyah-woo) (*fog*)

- **xiàxuě** 下雪 (shyah-shweh) (*snow*)

- **xiàyǔ** 下雨 (shyah-yew) (*rainy*)

- **yīntiān** 阴天 (陰天) (yeen-tyan) (*overcast*)

Talkin' the Talk

Gerry and Jean discuss the weather in Harbin, one of the coldest places in northern China.

Jean: **Hā'ěrbīn dōngtiān hěn lěng. Chángcháng xiàxuě.**
hah-are-been doong-tyan hun lung. chahng-chahng shyah shweh.
Harbin is very cold in the winter. It snows often.

Gerry: **Zhēnde ma?**
jun-duh mah?
Really?

Jean: **Zhēnde. Yě yǒu bàofēngxuě. Xiàtiān hái hǎo. Bǐjiào nuǎnhuó.**
jun-duh. yeh yo baow-fuhng-shweh. shyah-tyan hi how. bee-jyaow nwan-hwaw.
Really. There are also blizzards. Summertime is okay, though. It's relatively warm.

Gerry: **Lěng tiān kéyǐ qù huáxuě, hái kéyǐ qù liūbīng.**
           Nèmme Hā'ěrbīn dōngtiān de shíhòu dàgài hěn hǎo
           wán.
           lung tyan kuh yee chyew hwah-shweh, hi kuh yee
           chyew lyo-beeng. nummah hah-are-been doong-tyan
           duh shir-ho dah gye hun how wahn.
           In cold weather, you can go skiing or ice skating. So
           Harbin during the winter is probably a lot of fun.

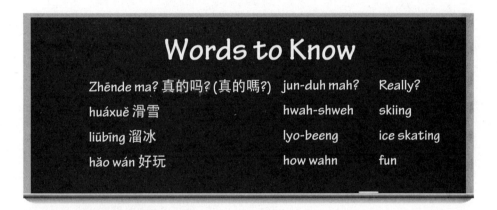

Words to Know

Zhēnde ma? 真的吗? (真的嗎?)	jun-duh mah?	Really?
huáxuě 滑雪	hwah-shweh	skiing
liūbīng 溜冰	lyo-beeng	ice skating
hǎo wán 好玩	how wahn	fun

Finding out where people are from

Wondering where people are from when you first meet them is natural. Maybe they hail from your hometown. Maybe your new friend's mother and your father went to the same high school way back when. Whatever motivates you to pose the question, you ask it by saying **Nǐ shì nǎr de rén?** 你是哪儿的人? (你是哪兒的人?) (nee shir nar duh run?) (*Where are you from?*) To answer this question, you replace the word **nǐ** 你 (nee) (*you*) with **wǒ** 我 (waw) (*I*) and put the name of wherever you're from where the word **nǎr** is.

People in Taiwan say **nálǐ** 哪里 (哪理) (nah-lee) rather than **nǎr** 哪儿 (哪兒) (nar) for the word *where*. **Nǎr** indicates a northern accent and is used primarily by people from mainland China.

Here's a list of countries that may come up in conversation:

- **Fǎguó** 法国 (法國) (fah-gwaw) (*France*)
- **Měiguó** 美国 (美國) (may-gwaw) (*America*)
- **Rìběn** 日本 (ir-bun) (*Japan*)

- **Ruìdiǎn** 瑞典 (rway-dyan) (*Sweden*)

- **Ruìshì** 瑞士 (rway-shir) (*Switzerland*)

- **Yìdàlì** 意大利 (ee-dah-lee) (*Italy*)

- **Yuènán** 越南 (越南) (yweh-nahn) (*Vietnam*)

- **Zhōngguó** 中国 (中國) (joong-gwaw) (*China*)

Talkin' the Talk

Cynthia has just introduced herself to Adrienne at their mutual friend's house. Cynthia asks Adrienne where she is from.

Cynthia:　**Adrienne, nǐ shì nǎr de rén?**
Adrienne, nee shir nar duh run?
Adrienne, where are you from?

Adrienne:　**Wǒ shì Jiāzhōu rén. Nǐ ne?**
waw shir jyah-joe-run. nee nuh?
I'm from California. How about you?

Cynthia:　**Wǒ búshì Měiguórén. Wǒ shì Yīngguó Lúndūn láide.**
waw boo-shir may-gwaw-run. waw shir eeng-gwaw lwun-dun lye duh.
I'm not American. I'm from London, England.

Adrienne:　**Nà tài hǎole.**
nah tye how-luh.
That's great.

Words to Know

Jiāzhōu 加州	jyah-joe	California
Měiguórén 美国人 (美國人)	may-gwaw-run	American
Yīngguó 英国 (英國)	eeng-gwaw	England
Nà tài hǎole. 那太好了.	nah tye how-luh.	That's great.

Taking (that is, rejecting) compliments

Chinese people are always impressed whenever they meet a foreigner who has taken the time to learn their language. So when you speak **Zhōngwén** 中文 (joong-one) (*Chinese*) to a **Zhōngguórén** 中国人 (中國人) (joong-gwaw-run) (*Chinese person*), he may very well say **Nǐde Zhōngwén tài hǎole.** 你 的中文太好了. (nee-duh joong-one tye how-luh.) (*Your Chinese is fantastic.*) Instead of patting yourself on the back, however, you should be slightly self-deprecating in your response. Don't give in to the temptation to accept the compliment easily and say **Xièxiè.** 谢谢 (謝謝). (shyeh-shyeh.) (*Thanks.*), because doing so implies that you agree wholeheartedly with the compli-mentary assessment. Instead, try one of the following replies. Each of them can be roughly translated as *It's nothing.* or the equivalent of *No, no, I don't deserve any praise.*:

✔ **Guò jiǎng guò jiǎng.** 过讲过讲. (過講過講.) (gwaw jyahng gwaw jyahng.)

✔ **Nálǐ nálǐ.** 哪里哪里. (哪裡哪裡.) (nah-lee nah-lee.)

✔ **Nǎr de huà.** 哪儿的话. (哪兒的話.) (nar duh hwah.)

Saying goodbye

When it comes time to say goodbye, you can always say **Zài jiàn.** 再见. (再見.) (dzye jyan.) (*Goodbye.*). If you're just leaving for a little while and plan to be back soon, you can say **Yīhuǐr jiàn.** 一会儿见. (一會兒見.) (ee-hwahr jyan.) (*See you in a bit.*). And if you won't see someone until the next day, you can say **Míngtiān jiàn.** 明天见. (明天見.) (meeng-tyan jyan.) (*See you tomorrow.*). For a quick *See you later.*, you can say **Huítóu jiàn.** 回头见. (回頭見.) (hway-toe jyan.). Here are some other phrases you can use to say goodbye:

✔ **Míngnián jiàn.** 明年见. (明年見.) (meeng-nyan jyan.) (*See you next year.*)

✔ **Xiàge lǐbài jiàn.** 下个礼拜见. (下個禮拜見.) (shyah-guh lee-bye jyan.) (*See you next week.*)

✔ **Xīngqī'èr jiàn.** 星期二见. (星期二見.) (sheeng-chee-are jyan.) (*See you on Tuesday.*)

✔ **Yílù píng'ān.** 一路平安. (ee-loo peeng ahn.) (*Have a good trip.*)

For more days-of-the-week options to use in the next to last item in the list, head to Chapter 5.

Fun & Games

Activity 1: Here's a list of words that got loose. See if you can put them back where they belong in the following text. The answers are in Appendix D.

míngzi 名字, **bàofēngxuě** 暴风雪 (暴風雪), **jiàn** 见 (見), **Déguórén** 德国人 (德國人), **hǎo** 好

Zǎo. Nǐ ____. Wǒde _____ jiào John. Wǒ shì _____. Jīntiān de tiānqì hěn hǎo. Méiyǒu _____. Huítóu _____.

早。你 —— 。 我的 —— 叫 John. 我是 —— 。 今天的天气(氣) 很好。 没有 —— 。 回头(頭) —— 。

Activity 2: Match the situation with the appropriate expression. You can find the answers in Appendix D.

1. You see someone again after a long time.

2. You see your friend in the evening.

3. You see your teacher in the morning.

4. Someone compliments you on your new hairstyle.

5. Someone introduces you to his brother.

6. Your best friend is about to board a plane for France.

A. **Hěn gāoxìng jiàndào nǐ.** 很高兴见到你. (很高興見到你.)

B. **Yílù píng'ān.** 一路平安.

C. **Hǎo jiǔ méi jiàn.** 好久没见. (好久沒見.)

D. **Wǎn ān.** 晚安.

E. **Zǎo.** 早.

F. **Nǎr de huà.** 哪儿的话. (哪兒的話.)

Chapter 5

Getting Your Numbers, Times, and Measurements Straight

∙ ∙

In This Chapter

▶ Counting to 100 and beyond

▶ Knowing times and periods of the day

▶ Discovering calendar words and Chinese holidays

∙ ∙

Know how they figured out that China has more than a billion people? They counted, silly. Okay, they probably conducted an official census, but if you can learn your ABCs in English, you can at least learn to count to a hundred in Chinese. Just multiply that by ten, and you'll get to a billion. The words for Chinese numbers are really quite logical — easier than you think — and they're the cornerstone of this chapter.

After you know how to count, you can also say the days of the week and the months of the year. The chapter also covers cardinal and ordinal numbers, so you can tell which came first (the chicken or the egg). If you've got a train to catch, you can look to this chapter to figure out how to tell time so you won't be late. You can even tell your Chinese date what the date is in Chinese. Finally, I give you the lowdown on key Chinese holidays so you can plan your work and travel schedule accordingly, including showing you how to extend New Year's greetings and providing a whole list of which animals are coming up in the Chinese zodiac. What more could you ask for?

Counting in Chinese

Figuring out things like how to specify the number of pounds of meat you want to buy at the market, how much money you want to change at the airport, or how much that cab ride from your hotel is really going to cost can be quite an ordeal if you don't know the basic words for numbers. The following sections break down the Chinese counting rules and terms.

Numbers from 1 to 10

Learning to count from 1 to 10 in Chinese is as easy as **yī** 一 (ee) (*one*), **èr** 二 (are) (*two*), **sān** 三 (sahn) (*three*). Table 5-1 lists numbers from 1 to 10. People in China use Arabic numerals as well, though, so you can just as easily write *1, 2, 3,* and everyone will know what you mean.

Table 5-1	Numbers from 1 to 10	
Chinese	*Pronunciation*	*English*
líng 零	leeng	*0*
yī 一	ee	*1*
èr 二	are	*2*
sān 三	sahn	*3*
sì 四	suh	*4*
wǔ 五	woo	*5*
liù 六	lyo	*6*
qī 七	chee	*7*
bā 八	bah	*8*
jiǔ 九	jyoe	*9*
shí 十	shir	*10*

If the number *2* comes before a classifier, use the word **liǎng** rather than **èr**. (As I discuss in Chapter 3, *classifiers* are the equivalent of English words such as *herd* [of elephants] or *school* [of fish]. They help classify particular nouns.) So to say that you have *two books,* you say that you have **liǎng běn shū** 两本书 (兩本書) (lyahng bun shoo) rather than **èr běn shū** 二本书 (二本書) (are bun shoo).

Numbers from 11 to 99

After the number *10,* you create numbers by saying the word *10* followed by the single digit that, when added to it, will combine to create numbers 11 through 19. It's really easy. For example, *11* is **shíyī** 十一 (shir-ee) — literally, *10 plus 1.* Same thing goes for 12, and so on through 19. Table 5-2 lists numbers from 11 to 19.

Table 5-2	Numbers from 11 to 19	
Chinese	**Pronunciation**	**English**
shíyī 十一	shir-ee	*11* (Literally: *10 + 1*)
shí'èr 十二	shir-are	*12* (Literally: *10 + 2*)
shísān 十三	shir-sahn	*13*
shísì 十四	shir-suh	*14*
shíwǔ 十五	shir-woo	*15*
shíliù 十六	shir-lyo	*16*
shíqī 十七	shir chee	*17*
shíbā 十八	shir-bah	*18*
shíjiǔ 十九	shir-jyoe	*19*

When you get to 20, you have to literally think *two 10s* — plus whatever single digit you want to add to that for 21 through 29, as shown in Table 5-3.

Table 5-3	Numbers from 20 to 29	
Chinese	**Pronunciation**	**English**
èrshí 二十	are-shir	*20* (Literally: *two 10s*)
èrshíyī 二十一	are-shir-ee	*21* (Literally: *two 10s + 1*)
èrshí'èr 二十二	are-shir-are	*22*
èrshísān 二十三	are-shir-sahn	*23*
èrshísì 二十四	are-shir-suh	*24*
èrshíwǔ 二十五	are-shir-woo	*25*
èrshíliù 二十六	are-shir-lyo	*26*
èrshíqī 二十七	are-shir-chee	*27*
èrshíbā 二十八	are-shir-bah	*28*
èrshíjiǔ 二十九	are-shir-jyoe	*29*

The same basic idea goes for **sānshí** 三十 (sahn-shir) (*30* [Literally: *three 10s*]), **sìshí** 四十 (suh-shir) (*40*), **wǔshí** 五十 (woo-shir) (*50*), **liùshí** 六十 (lyo-shir) (*60*), **qīshí** 七十 (chee-shir) (*70*), **bāshí** 八十 (bah-shir) (*80*), and **jiǔshí** 九十 (jyoe-shir) (*90*). What could be easier?

Numbers from 100 to 9,999

After the number *99,* you can no longer count by tens. Here's how you say 100 and 1,000:

- ✔ *100* is **yìbǎi** 一百 (ee-bye).

- ✔ *1,000* is **yìqiān** 一千 (ee-chyan).

Chinese people count all the way up to **wàn** 万 (萬) (wahn) (*10,000*) and then repeat in those larger amounts up to **yì** 亿 (億) (ee) (*100 million*).

In Chinese, numbers are represented with the higher units of value first. So the number *387* is **sānbǎi bāshí qī** 三百八十七 (sahn-bye bah-shir chee). The number *15,492* is **yíwàn wǔqiān sìbǎi jiǔshí'èr** 一万五千四百九十二 (一萬五千四百九十二 (ee-wahn woo-chyan suh-bye jyoe-shir-are).

The number *1* (**yī** 一) changes its tone from the first (high) to the fourth (falling) tone when followed by a first tone, as in **yìqiān** 一千 (ee-chyan) (*1,000*); by a second (rising) tone, as in **yì nián** 一年 (ee nyan) (*one year*); and by a third (low dipping) tone, as in **yìbǎi** 一百 (ee-bye) (*100*). And it changes to the second tone when followed by a fourth tone, as in **yíwàn** 一万 (一萬) (ee-wahn) (*10,000*). It retains its original first tone mark only when people count numbers: one, two, three, and so on.

Numbers from 10,000 to 100,000 and beyond

Here are the big numbers:

- ✔ *10,000* is **yíwàn** 一万 (一萬) (ee-wahn) (Literally: *one unit of 10,000*).

- ✔ *100,000* is **shí wàn** 十万 (十萬) (shir wahn) (Literally: *ten units of 10,000*).

- ✔ *1 million* is **yìbǎi wàn** 一百万 (一百萬) (ee-bye wahn) (Literally: *100 units of 10,000*).

- ✔ *100 million* is **yí yì** 一亿 (一億) (ee ee).

Numbers play an interesting role in everyday speech in China. Sometimes you'll hear someone say emphatically **Nǐ qiānwàn búyào xìn tāde huà!** 你千万不要信他的话! (你千萬不要信他的話!) (nee chyan-wahn boo-yaow sheen tah-duh hwah!) (*No matter what, you're not to believe what he says!*) **Qiān** means *1,000,* and **wàn** means *10,000,* but when you put those two words together in front of the negative prefix **bù**, you emphasize a point even more. Another phrase that has been heard often in the Chinese past is the partial phrase **wàn suì** 万岁 (萬歲) (wahn sway) (*long live*). After that phrase, the person may add the name of someone in power, so you hear something like **Máo zhǔxí wàn suì!** 毛主席万岁! (毛主席萬歲!) (maow joo-she wahn sway!) (*Long live Chairman Mao!*) If you use this expression these days, you're kind of parodying a phrase taken extremely seriously just a few short decades ago.

How 'bout those halves?

So what happens if you want to add a half to anything? Well, the word for *half* is **bàn** 半 (bahn), and it can either come at the beginning, such as in **bàn bēi kělè** (半杯可乐) (半杯可樂) (bahn bay kuh-luh) (*a half a glass of cola*), or after a number and classifier but before the object to mean *and a half,* such as in **yí ge bàn xīngqī** 一个半星期 (一個半星期) (ee guh bahn sheeng-chee) (*a week and a half*).

Ordinal numbers

If you want to indicate the order of something, add the word **dì** 第 (dee) before the numeral:

Chinese	Pronunciation	English
dì yī 第一	dee ee	*first*
dì èr 第二	dee are	*second*
dì sān 第三	dee sahn	*third*
dì sì 第四	dee suh	*fourth*
dì wǔ 第五	dee woo	*fifth*
dì liù 第六	dee lyo	*sixth*
dì qī 第七	dee chee	*seventh*
dì bā 第八	dee bah	*eighth*
dì jiǔ 第九	dee jyoe	*ninth*
dì shí 第十	dee shir	*tenth*

If a noun follows the ordinal number, a classifier needs to go between them, such as in **dì bā ge xuéshēng** 第八个学生 (第八個學生) (dee bah guh shweh-shuhng) (*the eighth student*) or **dì yī ge háizi** 第一个孩子 (第一個孩子) (dee ee guy hi-dzuh) (*the first child*).

Asking how many or how much

You have two ways to ask how much something is or how many of something there are. The first is the question word **duōshǎo** 多少 (dwaw-shaow), which you use when referring to something for which the answer is probably more than ten. The second is **jǐ** 几(幾) (jee) or **jǐge** 几个 (幾個) (jee-guh), which you use when referring to something for which the answer is probably going to be less than ten:

> **Nàge qìchē duōshǎo qián?** 那个汽车多少钱? (那個汽車多少錢?) (nah-guh chee-chuh dwaw-shaow chyan?) (*How much is that car?*)

> **Nǐ xiǎo nǚ'ér jīnnián jǐ suì?** 你小女儿今年几岁? (你小女兒今年幾歲?) (nee shyaow nyew-are jin-nyan jee sway?) (*How old is your little girl this year?*)

Telling Time

All you have to do to find out the **shíjiān** 时间 (時間) (shir-jyan) (*time*) is take a peek at your **shǒubiǎo** 手表 (show-byaow) (*watch*) or look at the **zhōng** 钟 (鐘) (joong) (*clock*) on the wall. These days, even your computer or cell-phone shows the time. And you can always revert to that beloved **luòdìshì dà bǎizhōng** 落地式大摆钟 (落地式大擺鐘) (lwaw-dee-shir dah bye-joong) (*grandfather clock*) in your parents' living room. You no longer have any excuse to **chídào** 迟到 (遲到) (chir-daow) (*be late*), especially if you own a **nào zhōng** 闹钟 (鬧鐘) (now-joong) (*alarm clock*)!

Asking and stating the time

Want to know what time it is? Just walk up to someone and say **Xiànzài jǐdiǎn zhōng?** 现在几点钟? (現在幾點鐘?) (shyan-dzye jee-dyan joong?). It almost literally translates into *Now how many hours are on the clock?* In fact, you can even leave off the word *clock* and still ask for the time: **Xiànzài jǐdiǎn?** 现在几点? (現在幾點?) (shyan-dzye jee-dyan?). Isn't that easy?

To understand the answers to those questions, though, you need to understand how to tell time in Chinese. You can express time in Chinese by using the words **diǎn** 点 (點) (dyan) (*hour*) and **fēn** 分 (fun) (*minute*). Isn't using **fēn** fun? You can even talk about time in **miǎo** 秒 (meow) (*seconds*) if you like and sound like a cat. Table 5-4 shows you how to pronounce all the hours on the clock.

You can indicate the hour by saying **sān-diǎn** or **sān-diǎn zhōng. Diǎn** 点 (點) (dyan) means *hour,* but it's also a classifier, and **zhōng** 钟 (鐘) (joong) means *clock.* Feel free to use either to say what time it is.

Table 5-4	Telling Time in Chinese	
Chinese	*Pronunciation*	*English*
yī diǎn zhōng 一点钟 (一點鐘)	ee-dyan joong	*1:00*
liǎng diǎn zhōng 两点钟 (兩點鐘)	lyahng-dyan joong	*2:00*
sān diǎn zhōng 三点钟 (三點鐘)	sahn-dyan joong	*3:00*
sì diǎn zhōng 四点钟 (四點鐘)	suh-dyan joong	*4:00*
wǔ diǎn zhōng 五点钟 (五點鐘)	woo-dyan joong	*5:00*
liù diǎn zhōng 六点钟 (六點鐘)	lyo-dyan joong	*6:00*
qī diǎn zhōng 七点钟 (七點鐘)	chee-dyan joong	*7:00*
bā diǎn zhōng 八点钟 (八點鐘)	bah-dyan joong	*8:00*
jiǔ diǎn zhōng 九点钟 (九點鐘)	jyo-dyan joong	*9:00*
shí diǎn zhōng 十点钟 (十點鐘)	shir-dyan joong	*10:00*
shíyī diǎn zhōng 十一 点钟 (十一點鐘)	shir-ee-dyan joong	*11:00*
zhōngwǔ 中午	joong-woo	*noon*
bànyè 半夜	bahn-yeh	*midnight*

When mentioning 12:00, be careful! The way to say *noon* is simply **zhōngwǔ** 中午 (joong-woo), and the way to say *midnight* is **bànyè** 半夜 (bahn-yeh).

Specifying the time of the day

The Chinese are very precise when they tell time. You can't just say **sān diǎn zhōng** 三点钟 (三點鐘) (sahn dyan joong) when you want to say *3:00.* Do you mean to say **qīngzǎo sān diǎn zhōng** 清早三点钟 (清早三點鐘)

(cheeng-dzaow sahn dyan joong) (*3:00 a.m.*) or **xiàwǔ sāndiǎn zhōng** 下午三点钟 (下午三點鐘) (shyah-woo sahn-dyan joong) (*3:00 p.m.*)? Another wrinkle: Noon and midnight aren't the only dividers the Chinese use to split up the day.

Here's a list of the major segments of the day:

 ✔ **qīngzǎo** 清早 (cheeng-dzaow): the period from midnight to 6:00 a.m.

 ✔ **zǎoshàng** 早上 (dzaow-shahng): the period from 6:00 a.m. to noon

 ✔ **xiàwǔ** 下午 (shyah-woo): the period from noon to 6:00 p.m.

 ✔ **wǎnshàng** 晚上 (wahn-shahng): the period from 6:00 p.m. to midnight

The segment of the day that you refer to needs to come before the actual time itself in Chinese. Here are some samples of combining the segment of the day with the time of day:

qīngzǎo yì diǎn yí kè 清早一点一刻 (清早一點一刻) (cheeng-dzaow ee dyan ee kuh) (*1:15 a.m.*)

wǎnshàng qī diǎn zhōng 晚上七点钟 (晚上七點鐘) (wahn-shahng chee dyan joong) (*7:00 p.m.*)

xiàwǔ sān diǎn bàn 下午三点半 (下午三點半) (shyah-woo sahn dyan bahn) (*3:30 p.m.*)

zǎoshàng bā diǎn èrshíwǔ fēn 早上八点二十五分 (dzaow-shahng bah dyan are-shir-woo fun) (*8:25 a.m.*)

If you want to indicate half an hour, just add **bàn** (bahn) (*half*) after the hour:

sān diǎn bàn 三点半 (三點半) (sahn-dyan bahn) (*3:30*)

shíyī diǎn bàn 十一点半 (十一點半) (shir-ee-dyan bahn) (*11:30*)

sì diǎn bàn 四点半 (四點半) (suh-dyan bahn) (*4:30*)

Do you want to indicate a quarter of an hour or three quarters of an hour? Just use the phrases **yí kè** 一刻 (ee kuh) and **sān kè** 三刻 (sahn kuh), respectively, after the hour:

liǎng diǎn yí kè 两点一刻 (兩點一刻) (lyahng-dyan ee kuh) (*2:15*)

qī diǎn sān kè 七点三刻 (七點三刻) (chee-dyan sahn kuh) (*7:45*)

sì diǎn yí kè 四点一刻 (四點一刻) (suh-dyan ee kuh) (*4:15*)

wǔ diǎn sān kè 五点三刻 (五點三刻) (woo-dyan sahn kuh) (*5:45*)

When talking about time, you may prefer to indicate a certain number of minutes before or after a particular hour. To do so, you use either **yǐqián** 以前 (ee-chyan) (*before*) or **yǐhòu** 以后 (以後) (ee-ho) (*after*) along with the time (though you can also use it with days and months, concepts that I cover later in the chapter). Here are a couple of examples:

> **qīngzǎo 4-diǎn bàn yǐhòu** 清早四点半以后 (清早四點半以後) (cheeng-dzaow suh-dyan bahn ee-ho) (*after 4:30 a.m.*)

> **xiàwǔ 3-diǎn zhōng yǐqián** 下午三点钟以前 (下午三點鐘以前) (shyah-woo sahn-dyan joong ee-chyan) (*before 3 p.m.*)

Of course, you have other ways to indicate time in Chinese. On the hour, half hour, and quarter of an hour aren't the only parts of time that exist, after all. For example, instead of saying **qī diǎn wǔshí fēn** 七点五十分 (七點五十分) (chee dyan woo-shir fun) (*7:50*), you can say **bā diǎn chà shí fēn** 八点差十分 (八點差十分) (bah dyan chah shir fun) (*10 minutes to 8* [Literally: *8:00 minus 10 minutes*]). **Chà** 差 (chah) means *to lack*. Unlike **fēn** 分 (fun) (*minute*), **kè** 刻 (kuh) (*quarter of an hour*), and **bàn** 半 (bahn) (*half*), you can use **chà** either before or after **diǎn** 点 (點) (dyan) (*hour*).

Here are some other examples of alternative ways to indicate the time:

> **chà shí fēn wǔ diǎn** 差十分五点 (差十分五點) (chah shir fun woo dyan) (*10 minutes to 5:00*)

> **wǔ diǎn chà shí fēn** 五点差十分 (五點差十分) (woo dyan chah shir fun) (*10 minutes to 5:00*)

> **sì diǎn wǔshí fēn** 四点五十分 (四點五十分) (suh dyan woo-shir fun) (*4:50*)

> **chà yí kè qī diǎn** 差一刻七点 (差一刻七點) (chah ee kuh chee dyan) (*a quarter to 7:00*)

> **qī diǎn chà yí kè** 七点差一刻 (七點差一刻) (chee dyan chah ee kuh) (*a quarter to 7:00*)

> **liù diǎn sān kè** 六点三刻 (六點三刻) (lyo dyan sahn kuh) (*6:45*)

> **liù diǎn sìshíwǔ fēn** 六点四十五分 (六點四時五分) (lyo dyan suh-shir-woo fun) (*6:45*)

Talkin' the Talk

 Xiǎo Huá and Chén Míng discuss their plans to see a movie. (Track 6)

Xiǎo Huá:	**Wǒmen jīntiān wǎnshàng qù kàn diànyǐng hǎo bùhǎo?**
	waw-men jin-tyan wahn-shahng chyew kahn dyan-yeeng how boo-how?
	Let's go see a movie tonight, okay?
Chén Míng:	**Bùxíng. Wǒde fùmǔ jīntiān wǎnshàng yídìng yào wǒ gēn tāmen yìqǐ chī wǎnfàn.**
	boo-sheeng. waw-duh foo-moo jin-tyan wahn-shahng ee-deeng yaow waw gun tah-men ee-chee chir wahn-fahn.
	No can do. My parents are adamant that I have dinner with them tonight.
Xiǎo Huá:	**Nǐmen jǐdiǎn zhōng chīfàn?**
	nee-men jee-dyan joong chir-fahn?
	What time do you eat?
Chén Míng:	**Píngcháng wǒmen liùdiǎn zhōng zuǒyòu chīfàn.**
	peeng-chahng waw-men lyo-dyan joong dzwaw yo chir-fahn.
	We usually eat around 6:00.
Xiǎo Huá:	**Hǎo ba. Nǐ chīfàn yǐhòu wǒmen qù kàn yíbù jiǔdiǎn zhōng yǐqián de piānzi, hǎo bùhǎo?**
	how-bah. nee chir-fahn ee-ho waw-men chyew kahn ee-boo jyo-dyan joong ee-chyan duh pyan-dzuh, how boo-how?
	Okay. How about we see a movie that starts before 9:00 after you're finished eating?
Chén Míng:	**Hěn hǎo. Yìhuǐr jiàn.**
	hun how. ee-hwar jyan.
	Okay. See you later.

Words to Know

diànyǐng 电影 (電影)	dyan-yeeng	movie
fùmǔ 父母	foo-moo	parents
chīfàn 吃饭 (吃飯)	chir-fahn	to eat
Yíhuǐr jiàn. 一会儿见. (一會兒見.)	ee-hwar jyan.	See you later.

Save the Date: Using the Calendar and Stating Dates

So what day is **jīntiān** 今天 (jin-tyan) (*today*)? Could it be **xīngqīliù** 星期六 (sheeng-chee-lyo) (*Saturday*), when you can sleep late and go see a movie in the evening with friends? Or is it **xīngqīyī** 星期一 (sheeng-chee-ee) (*Monday*), when you have to be at work by 9:00 a.m. to prepare for a 10:00 a.m. meeting? Or maybe it's **xīngqīwǔ** 星期五 (sheeng-chee-woo) (*Friday*), and you already have two tickets for the symphony that begins at 8:00 p.m. In the following sections, I give you the words you need to talk about days and months and put them together into specific dates. I also give you the lowdown on some major Chinese holidays.

Dealing with days of the week

You may not be a big fan of going to work Monday to Friday, but when the **zhōumò** 周末 (週末) (joe-maw) (*weekend*) comes, you have two days of freedom and fun. Before you know it, though, Monday comes again. Chinese people recognize seven days in the week just as Americans do, and the Chinese week begins on Monday and ends on **xīngqītiān** 星期天 (sheeng-chee-tyan) (*Sunday*). Table 5-5 spells out the days of the week.

Table 5-5	Days of the Week	
Chinese	*Pronunciation*	*English*
xīngqīyī 星期一	sheeng-chee-ee	*Monday*
xīngqī'èr 星期二	sheeng-chee-are	*Tuesday*
xīngqīsān 星期三	sheeng-chee-sahn	*Wednesday*
xīngqīsì 星期四	sheeng-chee-suh	*Thursday*
xīngqīwǔ 星期五	sheeng-chee-woo	*Friday*
xīngqīliù 星期六	sheeng-chee-lyo	*Saturday*
xīngqītiān 星期天	sheeng-chee-tyan	*Sunday*

If you're talking about **zhèige xīngqī** 这个星期 (這個星期) (jay-guh sheeng-chee) (*this week*) in Chinese, you're talking about any time between this past Monday through this coming Sunday. Anything earlier is considered **shàngge xīngqī** 上个星期 (上個星期) (shahng-guh sheeng-chee) (*last week*). Any day after this coming Sunday is automatically part of **xiàge xīngqī** 下个星期 (下個星期) (shyah-guh sheeng-chee) (*next week*) at the earliest. Here a few more week-related terms:

- ✔ **hòutiān** 后天 (後天) (ho-tyan) (*the day after tomorrow*)

- ✔ **míngtiān** 明天 (meeng-tyan) (*tomorrow*)

- ✔ **qiántiān** 前天 (chyan-tyan) (*the day before yesterday*)

- ✔ **zuótiān** 昨天 (dzwaw-tyan) (*yesterday*)

So **jīntiān xīngqījǐ?** 今天星期几? (今天星期幾?) (jin-tyan sheeng-chee-jee) (*What day is it today?*) Where does today fit in your weekly routine?

- ✔ **Jīntiān xīngqī'èr.** 今天星期二. (jin-tyan sheeng-chee-are.) (*Today is Tuesday.*)

- ✔ **Wǒmen měige xīngqīyī kāihuì.** 我们每个星期一开会. (我們每個星期一開會.) (waw-men may-guh sheeng-chee-ee kye-hway.) (*We have meetings every Monday.*)

- ✔ **Wǒ xīngqīyī dào xīngqīwǔ gōngzuò.** 我星期一到星期五工作. (waw sheeng-chee-ee daow sheeng-chee-woo goong-dzwaw.) (*I work from Monday to Friday.*)

- ✔ **Xiàge xīngqīsān shì wǒde shēngrì.** 下个星期三是我的生日. (下個星期三是我的生日.) (shyah-guh sheeng-chee-sahn shir waw-duh shung-ir.) (*Next Wednesday is my birthday.*)

Naming the months

When you know how to count from 1 to 12 (refer to the earlier section "Counting in Chinese"), naming the months in Chinese is really easy. Just think of the cardinal number for each month and put that in front of the word **yuè** 月 (yweh) (*month*). For example, *January* is **yīyuè** 一月 (ee-yweh), *February* is 二月 **èryuè** (are-yweh) and so on. I list the months of the year in Table 5-6. Which month is your **shēngrì** 生日 (shung-ir) (*birthday*)?

Table 5-6	Months of the Year and Other Pertinent Terms	
Chinese	*Pronunciation*	*English*
yīyuè 一月	ee-yweh	*January*
èryuè 二月	are-yweh	*February*
sānyuè 三月	sahn-yweh	*March*
sìyuè 四月	suh-yweh	*April*
wǔyuè 五月	woo-yweh	*May*
liùyuè 六月	lyo-yweh	*June*
qīyuè 七月	chee-yweh	*July*
bāyuè 八月	bah-yweh	*August*
jiǔyuè 九月	jyo-yweh	*September*
shíyuè 十月	shir-yweh	*October*
shíyīyuè 十一月	shir-ee-yweh	*November*
shí'èryuè 十二月	shir-are-yweh	*December*
shàngge yuè 上个月 (上個月)	shahng-guh-yweh	*last month*
xiàge yuè 下个月 (下個月)	shyah-guh-yweh	*next month*
zhèige yuè 这个月 (這個月)	jay-guh-yweh	*this month*

Shí'èryuè, yīyuè, and **èryuè** together make up one of the **sì jì** 四季 (suh-jee) (*four seasons*); check it out with the others in Table 5-7.

Table 5-7	The Four Seasons	
Chinese	*Pronunciation*	*English*
dōngjì 冬季	doong-jee	*winter*
chūnjì 春季	chwun-jee	*spring*
xiàjì 夏季	shyah-jee	*summer*
qiūjì 秋季	chyo-jee	*fall*

47

Specifying dates

To ask what today's date is, you simply say **Jīntiān jǐyuè jǐhào?** 今天几月 几号? (今天幾月幾號?) (jin-tyan jee-yweh jee-how?) (Literally: *Today is what month and what day?*) To answer that question, remember that the larger unit of the month always comes before the smaller unit of the date in Chinese:

> **sānyuè sì hào** 三月四号 (三月四號) (sahn-yweh suh how) (*March 4*)
>
> **shí'èryuè sānshí hào** 十二月三十号 (十二月三十號) (shir-are-yweh sahn-shir how) (*December 30*)
>
> **yīyuè èr hào** 一月二号 (一月二號) (ee-yweh are how) (*January 2*)

Days don't exist in a vacuum — or even just in a week — and four whole weeks make up one whole month. So if you want to be more specific, you have to say the month before the day, followed by the day of the week:

> **liùyuè yī hào, xīngqīyī** 六月一号星期一 (六月一號星期一) (lyo-yweh ee how, sheeng-chee ee) (*Monday, June 1*)
>
> **sìyuè èr hào, xīngqītiān** 四月二号星期天 (四月二號星期天 (suh-yweh are how, sheeng-chee-tyan) (*Sunday, April 2*)

The same basic idea goes for saying the days of the week. All you have to do is add the number of the day of the week (Monday: Day 1), preceded by the word **lǐbài** 礼拜 (禮拜) (lee-bye) or **xīngqī** 星期 (sheeng-chee), meaning *week*, to say the day you mean. For example, *Monday* is **xīngqī yī** 星期一 (sheeng chee ee) or **lǐbài yī** 礼拜一 (禮拜一), *Tuesday* is **xīngqī èr** 星期二 (sheeng chee are) or **lǐbài èr** 礼拜二 (禮拜二), and so on. The only exception is Sunday, when you have to add the word **tiān** 天 (tyan) (*heaven, day*) in place of a number. **Wǒde tiān!** 我的天! (waw-duh tyan!) (*My heavens!*) Isn't this easy?

You say each month by adding the number of the month in front of the word **yuè,** but if you add the classifier **ge** 个 (個) (guh) between the number and the word **yuè,** you say *one month, two months,* and so on. For example, **bāyuè** 八月 (bah-yweh) means *August* (which is the 8th month), but **bāge yuè** 八个月 (八個月) (bah-guh yweh) means *eight months.*

Talkin' the Talk

Joseph asks Julia about her birthday.

Joseph: **Julia, nǐde shēngrì shì jǐyuè jǐhào?**
           Julia, nee-duh shung-ir shir jee-yweh jee-how?
           Julia, when's your birthday?

Julia: **Wǒde shēngrì shì liùyuè èr hào. Nǐde ne?**
           waw-duh shung-ir shir lyo-yweh are how. nee-duh nuh?
           My birthday is June 2. How about yours?

Joseph: **Wǒde shēngrì shì wǔyuè qī hào.**
           waw-duh shung-ir shir woo-yweh chee how.
           My birthday is May 7.

Julia: **Nèmme, xiàge xīngqīyī jiù shì nǐde shēngrì! Zhù nǐ chàjǐtiān shēngrì kuàilè!**
           nummuh, shyah-guh sheeng-chee-ee jyo shir nee-duh shung-ir! joo nee chah-jee-tyan shung-ir kwye-luh!
           In that case, next Monday is your birthday! Happy almost birthday!

Words to Know

Nǐde ne? 你的呢?	nee-duh nuh?	How about yours?
xiàge xīngqīyī 下个星期一 (下個星期一)	shyah-guh sheeng-chee-ee	next Monday
Zhù nǐ shēngrì kuàilè! 祝你生日快乐! (祝你生日快樂!)	joo nee shung-ir kwye-luh!	Happy birthday!

Celebrating Chinese holidays

When was the last time you saw a **wǔshī** 舞狮 (舞獅) (woo-shir) (*lion dance*) in Chinatown? You can catch this colorful (and noisy) dance and all the other festivities during **nónglì xīn nián** 农历新年 (農曆新年) (noong-lee sheen nyan) (*the Lunar New Year*), also known as **chūnjié** 春節 (chwun-jyeh) (*the Spring Festival*). Just be careful not to get too close to all the **yān huǒ** 烟火 (焰火) (yan hwaw) (*fireworks*).

To extend New Year's greetings, you can say **Xīn nián kuàilè!** 新年快乐! (新年快樂!) (shin nyan kwye-luh!) (*Happy New Year!*) or, better yet, **Gōngxī fācái!** 恭喜发财! (恭喜發財!) (goong-she fah-tsye!) (*Congratulations, and may you prosper!*). In fact, you can start saying this on **chúxī** 除夕 (choo-shee) (*Chinese New Year's Eve*), the night when Chinese families get together to share a big, traditional dinner. The next morning children wish their parents a happy New Year and get **hóng bāo** 红包 (紅包) (hoong baow) (*red envelopes*) with money in them. What a great way to start the year!

Table 5-8 helps you keep track of which animal year we're in according to the **shēngxiào** 生肖 (shung-shyaow) (*Chinese zodiac*), which runs in 12-year cycles.

Table 5-8	Animals of the Chinese Zodiac		
Chinese	*Pronunciation*	*English*	*Year*
shǔ 鼠	shoo	*Rat*	2008
niú 牛	nyo	*Ox*	2009
hǔ 虎	hoo	*Tiger*	2010
tù 兔	too	*Rabbit*	2011
lóng 龙(龍)	loong	*Dragon*	2012
shé 蛇	shuh	*Snake*	2013
mǎ 马 (馬)	ma	*Horse*	2014
yáng 羊	yahng	*Goat*	2015
hóu 猴	ho	*Monkey*	2016
jī 鸡 (雞)	jee	*Rooster*	2017
gǒu 犬 (狗)	go	*Dog*	2018
zhū 猪 (豬)	joo	*Pig*	2019

Here are some other major Chinese holidays:

- **Yuán xiāo jié** 元宵节 (元宵節) (ywan shyaow jyeh) (*Lantern Festival*): Lantern parades and lion dances help celebrate the first full moon, which marks the end of the Chinese New Year, in either January or February.

- **Qīngmíng jié** 清明节 (清明節) (cheeng-meeng jyeh) (Literally: *the Clear and Bright Festival*): This celebration at the beginning of April is actually Tomb Sweeping Day, when families go on spring outings to clean and make offerings at the graves of their ancestors.

- **Duānwǔ jié** 端午节 (端午節) (dwan-woo jyeh) (*Dragon Boat Festival*): To commemorate the ancient poet **Qū Yuán** 屈原 (chew ywan), who drowned himself to protest government corruption, Chinese people eat **zòngzǐ** 粽子 (dzoong-dzuh) (*glutinous rice dumplings wrapped in lotus leaves*), drink yellow rice wine, and hold dragon boat races on the river. This holiday often falls in late May or early June.

- **Zhōngqiū jié** 中秋节 (中秋節) (joong-chyo jyeh) (*Mid-Autumn Festival*): This popular lunar harvest festival celebrates **Cháng'é** 嫦娥 (chahng-uh), the Chinese goddess of the moon (and of immortality). Red bean and lotus seed pastries called *mooncakes* are eaten, romantic matches are made, and all's right with the world. This holiday usually comes in September.

Sizing Up Weights and Measures

The metric system is standard in both mainland China and Taiwan. The basic unit of weight is the **gōngkè** 公克 (goong-kuh) (*gram*), so you usually buy fruits and vegetables in multiples of that measure. The standard liquid measurement is the **shēng** 升 (shung) (*liter*). One liter equals about 1.06 quarts. Table 5-9 gives you a list of weights and measures.

Table 5-9	Weights and Measures	
Chinese	*Pronunciation*	*English*
Volume		
àngsi 盎司	ahng-suh	*ounce*
jiālún 加仑 (加侖)	jyah-lwun	*gallon*
kuātuō 夸脱 (夸脫)	kwah-twaw	*quart*
pǐntuō 品脱 (品脫)	peen-twaw	*pint*
shēng 升	shung	*liter*

(continued)

Table 5-9 *(continued)*

Chinese	Pronunciation	English
Weight/Mass		
bàng 镑 (鎊)	bahng	pound
háokè 毫克	how-kuh	milligram
gōngkè 公克	goong-kuh	gram
jīn; gōngjīn 斤; 公斤	jeen; goong-jeen	kilogram
Distance		
gōnglǐ 公里	goong-lee	kilometer
límǐ 厘米	lee-mee	centimeter
mǎ 码 (碼)	mah	yard
mǐ 米	mee	meter
yīngchǐ 英尺	eeng-chir	foot
yīngcùn 英寸	eeng-tswun	inch
yīnglǐ 英里	eeng-lee	mile

Although the Chinese use the metric system, more often than not you encounter traditional measurement terms that predate the metric system, such as the words **yīngcùn** for *inch* and **yīngchǐ** for *foot*.

Fun & Games

Count to 10 and then to 100 in multiples of 10 by filling in the blanks with the correct numbers. Turn to Appendix D for the answers.

yī 一

èr 二

sān 三

sì 四

_____

liù 六

_____

bā 八

jiǔ 九

_____

èrshí 二十

_____

sìshí 四十

wǔshí 五十

_____

qīshí 七十

bāshí 八十

_____

yìbǎi 一百

Chapter 6

Speaking Chinese at Home

If you're one of those people who believes your **jiā** 家 (jyah) (*home*) is your **chéngbǎo** 城堡 (chuhng-baow) (*castle*), then this chapter's for you. Maybe you just transferred to Beijing for a new job, or are taking a year off to study kung fu in Taipei. Either way, you're going to want to call your new environment home for a while, and what better way to do that than to buy or rent your own place?

Planning on relocating with your spouse and children? Or maybe even your in-laws? All the more reason to make your new digs as comfortable as possible and carry on as if you weren't suddenly half way around the world. This chapter helps you get settled and be so comfortable that you can start asking for the **yǎokòngqì** 遥控器 (遙控器) (yaow-koong-chee) (*remote*) again when you want to change channels.

Hanging Out at Home

Whether you're in the bedroom taking a nap, in the living room watching TV, or in the dining room having dinner, the one thing you want to feel is at home. Want the dog to fetch your slippers? Want the kids to quiet down? Just remember that the character for *family* (家) is the same ideograph used for the word *home:* a pig underneath a roof (as in, domesticated animals). Sometimes the domestication just takes a little longer.

In China, you commonly see **sān dài** 三代 (sahn-dye) (*three generations*) living under one roof. It's the ideal Chinese family, in fact, where grandparents are taken care of in old age and children have lots of love and attention all around. Especially in the countryside, **sān dài** live in the same traditional family compound for generations, sharing a common courtyard with a hall in the center to honor the family's ancestors.

Hunting for an Apartment

Are you one of the thousands of people considering making a long-term move to China for business purposes? Starting to think about purchasing some **fángdìchǎn** 房地产 (房地產) (fahng-dee-chahn) (*real estate*) in the form of a **gōngyùfáng** 公寓房 (goong-yew-fahng) (*condominium*) or a **hézuò gōngyù** 合作公寓 (huh-dzwaw goong-yew) (*co-op*) in Beijing or Shanghai? Just a few decades ago, contemplating such a purchase of **cáichǎn** 财产 (財產) (tsye-chahn) (*property*) was unthinkable. These days, though, with the enormous influx of foreign investment and joint-venture companies, countless foreigners are beginning to take advantage of the many reputable **fángdìchǎn jīngjìrén** 房地产经纪人 (房地產經紀人) (fahng-dee chahn-jeeng jee run) (*realtors*) to help them do just that.

And if you've already purchased some **cáichǎn,** you may want to **chūzū** 出租 (choo-dzoo) (*rent*) or **zhuǎnzū** 转租 (轉租) (jwan-dzoo) (*sublet*) a **kōng gōngyù fángjiān** 空公寓房间 (空公寓房間) (koong goong-yew fahng-jyan) (*vacant apartment*) to a trustworthy **chéngzūrén** 承租人 (chung-dzoo-run) (*tenant*). Here are some terms you may want to know when thinking of buying a place in China:

- **ànjiēfèi** 按揭费 (按揭費) (ahn-jyeh-fay) (*closing costs*)
- **dàilǐ** 代理 (dye-lee) (*agent*)
- **dǐyājīn** 抵押金 (dee-yah-jeen) (*mortgage*)
- **gǔběn** 股本 (goo-bun) (*equity*)
- **hétóng** 合同 (huh-toong) (*contract*)
- **jiànzhù guīzé** 建筑规则 (建築規則) (jyan-joo gway-dzuh) (*building code*)
- **jīngjìrén** 经纪人 (經紀人) (jeeng-jee-run) (*broker*)
- **lìxī** 利息 (lee-she) (*interest*)

- **píngjià** 评价 (評價) (peeng-jya) (*appraisal*)
- **tóubiāo** 投标 (投標) (toe-byaow) (*bid*)
- **tóukuǎn** 头款 (頭款) (toe-kwahn) (*down payment*)
- **xìnyòng bàogào** 信用报告 (信用報告) (sheen-yoong baow-gaow) (*credit report*)

Talkin' the Talk

Serena contacts a realtor about buying a condo in Shanghai. (Track 7)

Serena:	**Nǐ hǎo. Wǒ xiǎng zài Shànghǎi mǎi yíge gōngyùfáng.** nee how. waw shyahng dzye shahng-hi my ee-guh goong-yew-fahng. *Hi. I'm thinking of buying a condo in Shanghai.*
Realtor:	**Méiyǒu wèntí. Wǒ jiù shì yíge fángdìchǎn jīngjìrén. Hěn yuànyì bāngmáng.** mayo one-tee. waw jyo shir ee-guh fahng-dee-chahn jeeng-jee-run. hun ywan-yee bahng-mahng. *No problem. I'm a real estate broker. I'd be more than happy to help you.*
Serena:	**Nà tài hǎole. Zài něige dìqū mǎi fángzi zuì hǎo?** nah tye haow-luh. dzye nay-guh dee-chyew my fahng-dzuh dzway how? *That's great. Which area do you consider to be the best to buy some property?*
Realtor:	**Shànghǎi yǒu hěn duō hěn hǎo de fángdìchǎn. Kěnéng zuì qiǎngshǒu de shì Hóngqiáo hé Jīnqiáo. Hěn duō wàiguó bàngōngshì xiànzài zài Pǔdōng.** shahng-hi yo hun dwaw hun how duh fahng-dee-chahn. kuh-nung dzway chyahng-show duh shir hoong-chyaow huh jeen-chyaow. hun dwaw why-gwaw bahn-goong shir shyan-dzye dzye poo-doong. *Shanghai has many excellent properties. Perhaps the most popular locations are Hongqiao and Jinqiao. Many foreign offices are now in Pudong.*

Words to Know

mǎi yíge gōngyùfáng 买一个 公寓房 (買一個公寓房)	my ee-guh goong-yew-fahng	to buy a condo
fángdìchǎn jīngjìrén 房地产 经纪人 (房地產經紀人)	fahng-dee-chahn jeeng-jee-run	realtor
dìqū 地区 (地區)	dee-chyew	area/location
liúxíng 流行	lyoe-sheeng	popular

Be sure you're using the correct tone when you pronounce the letters **m-a-i** (pronounced my) in Chinese. If you say it with a third (dipping) tone, **mǎi,** it means *to buy.* If you say it with a fourth (falling) tone, however — **mài** — it means *to sell.* If you're not careful, you may end up selling something you had hoped to live in yourself.

The Chinese language is fascinating and incredibly logical. If you put **mǎi** and **mài** together and add the word **zuò** (dzwaw) (*to do*) in front of them, to say **zuò mǎimài** 做买卖 (做買賣) (dzwaw my-my), it means *to do business.* (To buy and to sell . . . get it?)

The growth of Pudong

Pǔdōng 浦东 (浦東) (poo-doong) is the stretch of land east of the Huangpu River in the city of Shanghai. (**Pǔ** is short for the Huangpu River, and **dōng** means *east.*) Just a decade ago, this area was indistinguishable from many other backwater Chinese villages — just farmland and countryside. Today, it's a city within a city, boasting a population of over 5 million on a piece of real estate larger than the entire country of Singapore. Foreign investment in this part of Shanghai is enormous. In addition to its claim to fame as the fastest growing business area in China, it also boasts Asia's largest department store, its highest TV tower, and, needless to say, the Shanghai Stock Exchange.

Decorating Your New Digs

Whether you've bought a condo or a co-op, have rented an apartment, or are spending a semester in a **sùshè** 宿舍 (soo-shuh) (*dormitory*), you probably want to start buying some **jiājù** 家具 (jyah-jyew) (*furniture*) or to otherwise **zhuāngshì** 装饰 (裝飾) (jwahng-shir) (*decorate*) your new digs and put your individual stamp on the place.

Does your new place have a **hòu yuànzi** 后院子 (後院子) (ho ywan-dzuh) (*backyard*) with a pretty **huāyuán** 花园 (花園) (hwah-ywan) (*garden*), perhaps? How about a **yángtái** 阳台 (陽台) (yahng-tye) (*balcony*) or a more romantic little **zǒuláng** 走廊 (dzoe-lahng) (*veranda*)? You can put some really nice **zhíwù** 植物 (jir-woo) (*plants*) out there, or even some **huā** 花 (hwah) (*flowers*), like **júhuā** 菊花 (jyew-hwah) (*chrysanthemums*) or **lánhuā** 兰花 (蘭花) (lahn-hwah) (*orchids*), or even some **méihuā** 梅花 (may-hwah) (*plum blossoms*). Wouldn't that be nice?

Is there a **lóushàng** 楼上 (樓上) (low-shahng) (*upstairs*) as well as a **lóuxià** 楼下 (樓下) (low-shyah) (*downstairs*)? Do you have a grand **ménkǒu** 门口 (門口) (mun-koe) (*entrance*) or at least a **diàntī** 电梯 (電梯) (dyan-tee) (*elevator*) if you're on the top floor? Does the place have lots of floor-to-ceiling **chuānghu** 窗户 (chwahng-hoo) (*windows*) with great views, or do they look straight into an air shaft, forcing you to cover them with **chuānglián** 窗帘 (窗簾) (chwahng-lyan) (*curtains*) the first chance you get? No matter. At least you finally have a place you can call your own.

With all these new things to buy, just try not to run up too much of a **xìnyòng kǎ** 信用卡 (sheen-yoong kah) (*credit card*) bill, or you may regret having made that move from Poughkeepsie to Pudong in the first place.

Wondering what to plant in your new garden? Consider one (or all) of the **suìhǎn sānyǒu** 岁寒三友 (歲寒三友) (sway-hahn sahn-yo) (*the three friends of winter*): plum, pine, and bamboo. When other plants have long withered away, these three still thrive in the winter months. Representing both resilience and the possibility of renewal, they're often depicted in Chinese literature, painting, and garden design.

Appointing Your Rooms, Fēng Shuǐ Style

Literally translated as *wind and water*, the goal of **fēng shuǐ** 风水 (風水) (fuhng shway) is to create harmony between the flow of **qì** 气 (氣) (chee) (*energy*) in the environment and the good fortune of the person who is in it. Buildings, rooms, and even graves are all built with **fēng shuǐ** principles in mind.

Fēng shuǐ is no joke in Asia. Entire buildings depend on the expert placement and location chosen by **fēng shuǐ** geomancers, and an entire industry is booming as a result. (Not the construction industry, silly; the **fēng shuǐ** consultant industry.) Even U.S. realtors are sure to make houses and apartments they show **fēng shuǐ** friendly. Ideally, the building should have some kind of elevated landscape in back of it and a water feature in the front, like a pond, river, or well.

Check out the rooms that you may need a **fēng shuǐ** master to help you organize in Table 6-1.

Table 6-1	Areas of the Home	
Chinese	*Pronunciation*	*English*
chūfáng 厨房 (廚房)	choo-fahng	kitchen
dīnglóu 顶楼 (頂樓)	deeng-low	attic
dìxiàshì 地下室	dee-shyah-shir	basement
fángjiān 房间 (房間)	fahng-jyan	room(s)
fàntīng 饭厅 (飯廳)	fahn-teeng	dining room
kètīng 客厅 (客廳)	kuh-teeng	living room
kōngfáng 空房	koong-fahng	spare room
shūfáng 书房 (書房)	shoo-fahng	study
wòshì 卧室	waw-shir	bedroom
xiūxishì 休息室	shyo-she-shir	den
yùshì 浴室	yew-shir	bathroom

According to **fēng shuǐ** principles, color helps balance the energy of a room. So the color of the décor of each room is pretty important. Bathrooms, for example, should reflect **yīn** qualities of peace and seclusion (for self-explanatory reasons).

The Chinese associate colors with one of each of the **wǔ xíng** 五行 (woo sheeng) (*five elements*): wood, water, fire, earth, and metal. Table 6-2 lists each of these elements.

You can think of the five elements as different phases of nature. For example, wood creates fire; fire creates earth (ashes); elements from the earth create metal; objects made of metal (such as buckets) carry water; and water nourishes wood, bringing the cycle right back to the first element again.

Table 6-2	The Five Elements	
Chinese	*Pronunciation*	*English*
mù 木	moo	*wood*
huǒ 火	hwaw	*fire*
tǔ 土	too	*earth*
jīn 金	gin	*metal*
shuǐ 水	shway	*water*

The bedroom

After you move in and discover how much empty space you really have, you probably want to go out and buy at least the bare bones basics as far as furniture is concerned. How about some of these for the **wòshì** 卧室 (卧室) (waw-shir) (*bedroom*)?

✔ **bèizi** 被子 (bay-dzuh) (*quilt*)

✔ **chuáng** 床 (chwahng) (*bed*)

✔ **chuángdān** 床单 (床單) (chwahng-dahn) (*sheets*)

✔ **chuángdiàn** 床垫 (床墊) (chwahng-dyan) (*mattress*)

✔ **chuángzhào** 床罩 (chwahng-jaow) (*bedspread*)

✔ **tǎnzi** 毯子 (tahn-dzuh) (*blanket*)

✔ **yīguì** 衣柜 (衣櫃) (ee-gway) (*chest of drawers*)

✔ **zhěntóu** 枕头 (枕頭) (juhn-toe) (*pillow*)

The good news, of course, is that after you've purchased all these items, you can actually collapse on your own new bed. The bad news is that now you have no excuse not to **pūchuáng** 铺床 (鋪床) (poo-chwahng) (*make the bed*) every morning.

Here are three quick **fēng shuǐ** tips for the bedroom:

✔ Place the bed as far away from the door as possible for more control over your life.

✔ Don't put your bed against a side wall if you want more flexibility in life.

✔ Put lots of space between the front of your bed and the rest of the room if you want your life to expand.

And if you have kids, you'll probably want to make sure there's a **shūzhuō** 书桌 (書桌) (shoo-jwaw) (*desk*) somewhere in their bedroom so that they can get some studying in after school. (You don't have to be a **fēng shuǐ** expert to know that.)

The bathroom

Okay, I'll cut to the chase. The bathroom is the one room in the house no one can do without. Here are the basics: You need a **cèsuǒ** 厕所 (廁所) (tsuh-swaw) (*toilet*), a **yùgāng** 浴缸 (yew-gahng) (*bathtub*) or **línyùjiān** 淋浴间 (淋浴間) (leen-yew-jyan) (*shower*), and a **shuǐcéng** 水槽 (shway-tsuhng) (*sink*).

One last thing you don't want to realize you've forgotten to stock up on before turning in for the night: **weìshēngzhǐ** 卫生纸 (衛生紙) (way-shung-jir) (*toilet paper*). While you're at it, make sure you have some **féizào** 肥皂 (fay-dzaow) (*soap*) on hand in this room, too. Don't say I didn't warn you.

Here are some **fēng shuǐ** tips for the bathroom:

- ✔ To prevent **qì** from escaping, keep the door closed when the room isn't in use. (Actually, keep the door closed when it's in use, too.)
- ✔ Close the toilet lid after you're done.
- ✔ Make sure there are no leaks.
- ✔ Put a potted plant or ceramic bowl with pebbles on the toilet tank. (Using a non-water color or element helps balance out all the water already in the room.)

The kitchen

Now you're cookin'. The kitchen is a room everyone can wrap their minds (or at least their stomachs) around. Aside from the one piece of furniture every kitchen usually needs — a **chúfáng cānzhuō** 厨房餐桌 (廚房餐桌) (choo-fahng tsahn-jwaw) (*kitchen table*) — and basic food prep appliances like a **kǎo lú** 烤炉 (烤爐) (cow loo) (*oven*) and a **diànbīngxiǎng** 电冰箱 (電冰箱) (dyan-beeng-shyahng) (*refrigerator*), you may need some dishware and smaller appliances. Here are some things you may want to know how to say:

- ✔ **bēizi** 杯子 (bay-dzuh) (*glasses*)
- ✔ **jiǔ bēi** 酒杯 (jyo bay) (*wine glasses*)
- ✔ **kāfēi bēi** 咖啡杯 (kah-fay bay) (*coffee cups*)

The Kitchen God

In Chinese mythology, **Zào Jūn** 灶君 (dzaow jyewn) (*the Kitchen God* [Literally: *the Master of the Stove,* because you hang his image over the stove]) is the most important deity of the entire home. A week before the Lunar New Year, he goes to the Jade Emperor, who rules the heavens, to report on the family's behavior from the prior year. To ensure that he gives a good report to the Jade Emperor, families smear the Kitchen God's mouth with honey to sweeten his tongue. They then burn his image, and his spirit is sent to the heavens with the good report. On New Year's Eve, each family puts up a new Kitchen God, and thus begins another year of watching over the family.

- **wǎndié** 碗碟 (wahn-dyeh) (*dishes*)
- **wēibō lú** 微波炉 (微波爐) (way-baw loo) (*microwave*)
- **yǐnqì** 银器 (銀器) (yin-chee) (*silverware*)

The best way to **fēng shuǐ** your kitchen is simply to keep it simple. Eliminate the clutter to avoid stagnant energy in your life. Old, stale food has old, stale energy, so clean out the fridge regularly. An unused stove implies untapped resources or ignored opportunities, so start using all the burners on the stove, and use the oven once in a while, too. (It can't hurt. Plus, you'll save a ton of money by not eating in restaurants.)

The living room

Now here's one room everyone loves to hang out in and watch some **diànshì** 电视 (電視) (dyan-shir) (*TV*) — the **kètīng** 客厅 (客廳) (kuh-teeng) (*living room*). Want to put your feet up on the **chájī** 茶几 (chah-jee) (*coffee table* [Literally: *tea table*]) while you're watching? Don't even think about it. The **chájī** was meant for **kāfēi** 咖啡 (kah-fay) (*coffee*), not **jiǎo** 脚 (腳) (jyaow) (*feet*). (Don't ask me why it's not called a **kāfēijī** rather than a **chájī** — I don't have a clue.) The reality is that you can put coffee, tea, soda, and (when no one else is looking) even your feet on this table. Just don't say I said so.

You almost always find a **shāfā** 沙发 (沙發) (shah-fah) (*sofa*) in the **kètīng,** and possibly a **yáoyǐ** 摇椅 (搖椅) (yaow-ee) (*rocking chair*), too. In fact, some apartments are so small that the **kètīng** doubles as a **fàntīng** 饭厅 (飯廳) (fahn-teeng) (*dining room*). In those cases, you may not have an actual

fàntīng shèbèi 餐厅设备 (餐廳設備) (fahn-teeng shuh-bay) (*dining room set*) with a big table and chairs, but then again, that's what **chájī** are sometimes for.

Here are some **fēng shuǐ** tips for the living room:

✔ Keep the living room well lit and clutter-free, and make sure the air quality is good.

✔ Avoid an L-shaped furniture arrangement because it creates a lack of balance in the room and in your life.

✔ Don't crowd the living room with too many pieces of furniture, or the **qì** in the room and in your family's life will be blocked.

The basement

Some people find the **dìxiàshì** 地下室 (dee-shyah-shir) (*basement*) pretty scary. In addition to ghosts and spiders, though, it can actually have some really cool things in it. Table 6-3 lists what you may find in a basement.

Table 6-3	Things You Find in a Basement	
Chinese	*Pronunciation*	*English*
cúnchǔ kōngjiān 存储空间 (存儲空間)	tswun-choo koong-jyan	*storage space*
guǐ 鬼	gway	*ghosts*
hǒnggānjī 烘干机 (烘乾機)	hoong-gahn-jee	*dryer*
mùgōng chējiān 木工车间 (木工車間)	moo-goong chuh-jyan	*carpentry workshop*
táiqiú zhuō 台球桌	tye-chyo jwaw	*pool table*
xǐyījī 洗衣机 (洗衣機)	shee-ee-jee	*washing machine*
zhīzhū 蜘蛛	jir-joo	*spiders*

Here are some **fēng shuǐ** tips for the basement:

✔ Improve the air quality in normally stuffy basements with plants that purify the air, such as bamboo palm, English ivy, or rubber plants.

✔ Make sure the basement has enough light and that you augment this light with brightly colored wall hangings.

CULTURAL WISDOM

Bats are good fortune, and other traditions

In Chinese architecture, door gods are placed on doorways to ward off evil and bring good fortune. Because bats actually represent good fortune in China, they can often be found in designs within the home. Another thing you may see in traditional homes is a raised piece of wood that you need to step over to get into each room. These pieces have a serious purpose: to trip the evil spirits, because evil spirits travel only in straight lines. (That's why you see a lot of curved roofs as well.) Similarly, spirit walls are placed in courtyards in front of the doors to the entrance of the house so that evil spirits will have to go around them.

The attic

The **gé lóu** 阁楼 (閣樓) (guh-low) (*attic*) is another part of the house some people try to avoid. Sure, there are bound to be some **zhīzhū wǎng** 蜘蛛网 (蜘蛛網) (jir-joo wahng) (*spider webs*) up there, but you may also find your grandmother's **jiǔ yīfú** 旧衣服 (舊衣服) (jyo ee-foo) (*old clothes*) and, if you're lucky, maybe even some **chuǎnjiā bǎo** 传家宝 (傳家寶) (chwan-jyah baow) (*heirlooms*). Okay, you may also see an occasional **bīngfǔ** 蝙蝠 (beeng-foo) (*bat*), but in China, those are auspicious creatures.

Here are some **fēng shuǐ** tips for the attic:

- ✔ Attics represent the future in **fēng shuǐ,** so definitely keep this area free of clutter and open to all sorts of possibilities.

- ✔ Consider making the attic into a quiet meditation room instead of a willy-nilly storage space.

- ✔ Use the energy of the attic for reflective pursuits. You may want to make it into a research area or library.

Fun & Games

For the following household items, match the English word to the corresponding Chinese word. Check Appendix D for the answers.

yùshì 浴室	*dining room*
wòshì 卧室	*balcony*
fàntīng 饭厅 (飯廳)	*sofa*
tǎnzi 毯子	*desk*
yángtái 阳台 (陽台)	*quilt*
zhěntóu 枕头 (枕頭)	*bedroom*
bèizi 被子	*bathroom*
shūzhuō 书桌 (書桌)	*blanket*
shāfā 沙发 (沙發)	*pillow*

Part II
Chinese in Action

"This is why you shouldn't use the Chinese you picked up in oriental restaurants when making a reservation. We've got a room with a view and a queen size eggroll."

In this part . . .

This part helps you jump right in to everyday activities: shooting the breeze with friends, eating, drinking, shopping 'til you drop, working at the office, and just plain ol' enjoying your spare time. I cover it all so that you can do it in Chinese. Choose your favorite topic and start putting your Chinese into action!

Chapter 7

Getting to Know You: Making Small Talk

In This Chapter

▶ Exchanging friendly banter with someone you just met

▶ Yakking on the job

▶ Sharing information about your home

Small talk can really break the ice when you're interacting with someone you've just met or barely know. It's how you get to know someone, have a brief chat with the man sitting next to you on the plane, or get acquainted with the folks you'll be working with. This chapter helps you master a few key phrases and questions you can use to establish a relationship.

Xiánliáo 闲聊 (閒聊) (shyan-lyaow) means *small talk* in Chinese. **Xiántán** 闲谈 (閒談) (shyan-tahn) is *to chat.* Either term does the trick.

Establishing a Connection

A surefire way of initiating a conversation is to ask someone a question. Here are some basic question words to keep in mind as you approach the moment of acquaintance:

✔ **Duō jiǔ?** 多久? (dwaw jyoe?) (*For how long?*)

✔ **Shéi?** 谁? (誰?) (shay?) (*Who?*)

✔ **Shénme?** 什么? (甚麼?) (shummuh?) (*What?*)

✔ **Shénme shíhòu?** 什么时候? (甚麼時候?) (shummuh shir-ho?) (*When?*)

✔ **Wèishénme?** 为什么? (為甚麼?) (way-shummuh?) (*Why?*)

✔ **Zài nǎr?** 在哪儿? (在哪兒?) (dzye nar?) (*Where?*)

✔ **Zěnme?** 怎么? (怎麼?) (dzummuh?) (*How?*)

Here are a few examples of how to use these question words in simple sentences; sometimes you can also use some of the words on their own, just as in English:

Cèsuǒ zài nǎr? 厕所在哪儿? (廁所在哪兒?) (tsuh-swaw dzye nar?) (*Where's the bathroom?*)

Jǐ diǎn zhōng? 几点钟? (幾點鐘?) (jee dyan joong?) (*What time is it?*)

Nǐ shénme shíhòu chī fàn? 你什么时候吃饭? (你甚麼時候吃飯?) (nee shummuh shir-ho chir fahn?) (*When do you eat?*)

Nǐ wèishénme yào qù Zhōngguó? 你为什么要去中国? (你為甚麼要去中國?) (nee way-shummuh yaow chyew joong-gwaw?) (*Why do you want to go to China?*)

Nǐ yào shénme? 你要什么? (你要甚麼?) (nee yaow shummuh?) (*What would you like?*)

Nǐ zěnme yàng? 你怎么样? (你怎麼樣?) (nee dzummuh yahng?) (*How's it going?*)

Nǐ yǐ jīng zài zhèr duō jiǔ le? 你已经在这儿多久了? (你已經在這兒多久了?) (nee ee-jeeng dzye jar dwaw jyoe luh?) (*How long have you been here already?*)

Tā shì shéi? 他/她是谁? (他/她是誰?) (tah shir shay?) (*Who is he/she?*)

Xiànzài jǐ diǎn zhōng? 现在几点钟? (現在幾點鐘?) (shyan-dzye jee dyan joong?) (*What time is it now?*)

You can also use the following responses to the questions in the preceding list if someone happens to approach you. These statements are the basics of small talk and really come in handy when you're learning a foreign language:

✔ **Duìbùqǐ.** 对不起. (對不起.) (dway-boo-chee.) (*Excuse me.*)

✔ **Hěn bàoqiàn.** 很抱歉. (hun baow-chyan.) (*I'm so sorry.*)

✔ **Wǒ bùdǒng.** 我不懂. (waw boo-doong.) (*I don't understand.*)

✔ **Wǒ búrènshi tā.** 我不认识他/她. (我不認識他/她.) (waw boo-run-shir tah.) (*I don't know him/her.*)

✔ **Wǒ bùzhī dào.** 我不知道. (waw boo-jir daow.) (*I don't know.*)

Talkin' the Talk

几点钟

 Beverly doesn't have a watch and wants to know what time it is.
She asks a man on the street. (Track 8)

Beverly:	**Duìbùqǐ. Qǐngwèn, xiànzài jǐdiǎn zhōng?**
	dway-boo-chee. cheeng-one, shyan-dzye jee-dyan joong?
	Excuse me. May I ask what time it is?

对不起, 请问,
现在几点钟?

Man:	**Xiànzài yī diǎn bàn.**
	shyan-dzye ee dyan bahn.
	It's 1:30.

1点半

Beverly:	**Hǎo. Xièxiè nǐ.**
	how. shyeh-shyeh nee.
	Great. Thank you.

谢谢你

65

Man:	**Bú kèqì.**
	boo kuh-chee.
	You're welcome.

Beverly:	**Máfán nǐ, sì lù chēzhàn zài nǎr?**
	mah-fahn nee, suh loo chuh-jahn dzye nar?
	Sorry to trouble you again, but where's the #4 bus stop?

Man:	**Chēzhàn jiù zài nàr.**
	chuh-jahn jyoe dzye nar.
	The bus stop is just over there.

Beverly:	**Hǎo. Xièxiè.**
	how. shyeh-shyeh.
	Okay. Thanks.

Man:	**Méi wèntí.**
	may one-tee.
	No problem.

没问题

Words to Know

Xiànzài jǐ diǎn zhōng? 现在几点钟? (現在幾點鐘?)	shyan-dzye jee dyan joong?	What time is it?
chēzhàn 车站 (車站)	chuh-jahn	bus stop
Méi wèntí. 没问题. (沒問題.)	may one-tee.	No problem.

Posing simple introductory questions

Flash card conversation

The following is a list of simple questions you can use when you meet people. (To find out how to respond, or to talk about yourself, flip to Chapter 4.)

- **Nǐ huì jiǎng Zhōngwén ma?** 你会讲中文吗? (你會講中文嗎?) (nee hway jiahng joong-one mah?) (*Do you speak Chinese?*)

- **Nǐ jiào shénme míngzi?** 你叫什么名字? (你叫甚麼名字?) (nee jyaow shummuh meeng-dzuh?) (*What's your name?*)

- **Nǐ jiéhūn le méiyǒu?** 你结婚了没有? (你結婚了沒有?) (nee jyeh-hwun luh mayo?) (*Are you married?*)

- **Nǐ niánjì duō dà?** 你年纪多大? (你年紀多大?) (nee nyan-jee dwaw dah?) (*How old are you?*)

- **Nǐ shénme shíhòu zǒu?** 你什么时候走? (你甚麼時候走?) (nee shummuh shir-ho dzoe?) (*When are you leaving?*)

- **Nǐ xǐhuān kàn diànyǐng ma?** 你喜欢看电影吗? (你喜歡看電影嗎?) (nee she-hwahn kahn dyan-yeeng mah?) (*Do you like to see movies?*)

- **Nǐ yǒu háizi ma?** 你有孩子吗? (你有孩子嗎?) (nee yo hi-dzuh mah?) (*Do you have children?*)

- **Nǐ zhù zài nǎr?** 你住在哪儿? (你主在哪兒?) (nee joo dzye nar?) (*Where do you live?*)

- **Nǐ zuò shénme gōngzuò?** 你做什么工作? (你做甚麼工作?) (nee dzwaw shummuh goong-dzwaw?) (*What kind of work do you do?*)

Chatting about family

外三寸

If you want to talk about your family when answering questions or making small talk, you need to know these common words:

- ✓ **àirén** 爱人 (愛人) (eye-run) (*spouse* [used mostly in mainland China])
- ✓ **dìdì** 弟弟 (dee-dee) (*younger brother*)
- ✓ **érzi** 儿子 (兒子) (are-dzuh) (*son*)
- ✓ **fùmǔ** 父母 (foo-moo) (*parents*)
- ✓ **fùqīn** 父亲 (父親) (foo-cheen) (*father*)
- ✓ **gēgē** 哥哥 (guh-guh) (*older brother*)

- ✓ **háizi** 孩子 (hi-dzuh) (*children*)
- ✓ **jiějiě** 姐姐 (jyeh-jyeh) (*older sister*)
- ✓ **jiěmèi** 姐妹 (jyeh-may) (*sisters*)
- ✓ **mèimèi** 妹妹 (may-may) (*younger sister*)
- ✓ **mǔqīn** 母亲 (母親) (moo-cheen) (*mother*)
- ✓ **nǚ'ér** 女儿 (女兒) (nyew-are) (*daughter*)
- ✓ **qīzi** 妻子 (chee-dzuh) (*wife*)
- ✓ **sūnnǚ** 孙女 (swun-nyew) (*granddaughter*)
- ✓ **sūnzi** 孙子 (swun-dzuh) (*grandson*)
- ✓ **tàitài** 太太 (tye-tye) (*wife* [used mostly in Taiwan])
- ✓ **wàigōng** 外公 (wye-goong) (*maternal grandfather*)
- ✓ **wàipó** 外婆 (wye-paw) (*maternal grandmother*)
- ✓ **xiōngdì** 兄弟 (shyoong-dee) (*brothers*)
- ✓ **xiōngdì jiěmèi** 兄弟姐妹 (shyoong-dee jyeh-may) (*siblings*)
- ✓ **zhàngfu** 丈夫 (jahng-foo) (*husband*)
- ✓ **zǔfù** 祖父 (dzoo-foo) (*paternal grandfather*)
- ✓ **zǔmǔ** 祖母 (dzoo-moo) (*paternal grandmother*)

Talkin' the Talk

Deborah meets her daughter's classmate, Samantha, and asks about Samantha's family.

Deborah: **Samantha, nǐ yǒu méiyǒu xiōngdì jiěmèi?**
Samantha, nee yo mayo shyoong-dee jyeh-may?
Samantha, do you have any brothers or sisters?

Samantha: **Wǒ yǒu yíge jiějie.**
waw yo ee-guh jyeh-jyeh.
I have an older sister.

Deborah: **Tā yě huì jiǎng Zhōngwén ma?**
tah yeah hway jyahng joong-one-mah?
Can she also speak Chinese?

Samantha: **Búhuì. Tā zhǐ huì Yīngyǔ.**
boo-hway. tah jir hway eeng-yew.
No. She only speaks English.

Deborah: **Nǐde fùmǔ zhù zài nǎr?**
nee-duh foo-moo joo dzye nar?
Where do your parents live?

Samantha: **Wǒmen dōu zhù zài Běijīng. Wǒ bàba shì wàijiāoguān.**
waw-mun doe joo dzye bay-jeeng. waw bah-bah shir why-jyaow-gwan.
We all live in Beijing. My father is a diplomat.

Deborah: **Nà tài hǎo le.**
nah tye how luh.
That's great.

Words to Know

jiǎng 讲 (講)	jyahng	to talk
Zhōngwén 中文	joong-one	Chinese (language)
Yīngyǔ 英语 (英語)	eeng-yew	English (language)
zhù 住	joo	to live
wàijiāoguān 外交官	why-jyaow-gwahn	diplomat

Making Small Talk on the Job

The kind of job you have can say plenty about you. It can also be a great topic of conversation or spice up an otherwise-dull exchange. To ask someone about his or her **gōngzuò** 工作 (goong-dzwaw) (*work*), you can say **Nǐ zuò shénme gōngzuò?** 你做什么工作? (你做甚麼工作?) (nee dzwaw shummuh goong-dzwaw?) (*What kind of work do you do?*) You may even try to guess and say, for example, **Nǐ shì lǎoshī ma?** 你是老师吗? (你是老師嗎?) (nee shir laow-shir mah?) (*Are you a teacher?*)

The following are some occupations you or the person you're talking with may hold:

- ✔ **biānjí** 编辑 (編輯) (byan-jee) (*editor*)
- ✔ **cáiféng** 裁缝 (裁縫) (tsye-fung) (*tailor*)
- ✔ **chéngwùyuán** 乘务员 (乘務員) (chuhng-woo-ywan) (*flight attendant*)
- ✔ **chūnàyuán** 出纳员 (出納員) (choo-nah-ywan) (*bank teller*)
- ✔ **diàngōng** 电工 (電工) (dyan-goong) (*electrician*)
- ✔ **fēixíngyuán** 飞行员 (飛行員) (fay-sheeng-ywan) (*pilot*)
- ✔ **hǎiguān guānyuán** 海关官员 (海關官員) (hi-gwan gwan-ywan) (*customs agent*)
- ✔ **hùshì** 护士 (護士) (who-shir) (*nurse*)

- **jiàoshòu** 教授 (jyaow-show) (*professor*)
- **jiēxiànyuán** 接线员 (接線員) (jyeh-shyan-ywan) (*telephone operator*)
- **kèfáng fúwùyuán** 客房服务员 (客房服務員) (kuh-fahng foo-woo-ywan) (*housekeeper*)
- **kuàijì** 会计 (會計) (kwye-jee) (*accountant*)
- **lǎoshī** 老师 (老師) (laow-shir) (*teacher*)
- **lièchēyuán** 列车员 (列車員) (lyeh-chuh-ywan) (*train conductor*)
- **lùshī** 律师 (律師) (lyew-shir) (*lawyer*)
- **qiántái fúwùyuán** 前台服务员 (前台服務員) (chyan-tye foo-woo-ywan) (*receptionist*)
- **shuǐnuǎngōng** 水暖工 (shway-nwan-goong) (*plumber*)
- **yǎnyuán** 演员 (演員) (yan-ywan) (*actor*)
- **yī shēng** 医生 (醫生) (ee-shung) (*doctor*)
- **yóudìyuán** 邮递员 (郵遞員) (yo-dee-ywan) (*mail carrier*)
- **zhǔguǎn** 主管 (joo-gwan) (*CEO*)

The following are some useful job terms and job-related expressions:

- **bàn rì gōngzuò** 半日工作 (bahn ir goong-dzwaw) (*part-time work*)
- **gùyuán** 雇员 (僱員) (goo-ywan) (*employee*)
- **gùzhǔ** 雇主 (goo-joo) (*employer*)
- **jīnglǐ** 经理 (經理) (jeeng-lee) (*manager*)
- **miànshì** 面试 (面試) (myan-shir) (*interview*)
- **quán rì gōngzuò** 全日工作 (chwan ir goong-dzwaw) (*full-time work*)
- **shī yè** 失业 (失業) (shir-yeh) (*unemployed*)

In China, your **dānwèi** 单位 (單位) (dahn-way) (*work unit*) is an important part of your life. (This term refers to your place of work, which can be anywhere in the country. Your **dānwèi** is the group that's responsible for both taking care of you and being responsible for any missteps you happen to make.) In fact, when people ask you to identify yourself over the phone, they often say **Nǐ nǎr?** 你哪儿? (你哪兒?) (nee nar?) (Literally: *Where are you from?*) to find out what **dānwèi** you belong to. Under Chairman Mao Zedong (the leader of the Chinese Communist Party, who founded the People's Republic of China in 1949), people were assigned jobs right out of high school and didn't even think of marrying until they knew the location of their assignment. A man could've been given a job in the northern hinterlands of China, and his fiancée could've been sent south — only to see each other once a year during the Chinese New Year. The **dānwèi** continues to provide housing for its employees and also enforces government policies, such as the one-child-per-family policy. As recently as 2003, you needed the unit's permission to get married, have a child, or receive any government benefits.

Talkin' the Talk

 Yáng and Xiǎo Liú discuss their respective professions, which are quite different from each other. Xiǎo Liú is a nurse in a city located in Henan Province, not far from the famed Shaolin Temple. (Track 9)

Xiǎo Liú: **Yáng, nǐ zuò shénme gōngzuò?**
yahng, nee dzwaw shummuh goong-dzwaw?
Yang, what kind of work do you do?

Yáng: **Wǒ shì yǎnyuán.**
waw shir yan-ywan.
I'm an actor.

Xiǎo Liú: **Nà hěn yǒuyìsi.**
nah hun yo-ee-suh.
That's very interesting.

Yáng: **Nǐ ne?**
nee nuh?
How about you?

Xiǎo Liú: **Wǒ shì hùshì. Wǒ zài Kāifēng dìyī yī yuàn gōngzuò.**
waw shir hoo-shir. waw dzye kye-fung dee-ee ee ywan goong-dzwaw.
I'm a nurse. I work at Kaifeng's No. 1 Hospital.

Yáng: **Nán bùnán?**
nahn boo-nahn?
Is it difficult?

Xiǎo Liú: **Bùnán. Wǒ hěn xǐhuān wǒde zhíyè.**
boo-nahn. waw hun she-hwahn waw-duh jir-yeh.
It's not difficult. I really like my profession.

Words to Know

gōngzuò 工作	goong-dzwaw	to work
hùshī 护士 (護士)	hoo-shir	nurse
yī yuàn 医院 (醫院)	ee ywan	hospital
nán 难 (難)	nahn	difficult
xǐhuān 喜欢 (喜歡)	she-hwahn	to like; to enjoy
zhī yè 职业 (職業)	jir yeh	profession

Talking About Where You Live

After folks get to know each other through small talk, they may exchange addresses and phone numbers to keep in touch. That introductory question covered earlier in this chapter, **Nǐ zhù zài nǎr?** 你住在哪儿? (你主在哪兒?) (nee joo dzye nar?) (*Where do you live?*), may pop up. You may also want to ask a few of these questions:

- ✔ **Nǐde diànhuà hàomǎ duōshǎo?** 你的电话号码多少? (你的電話號碼多少?) (nee-duh dyan-hwah how-mah dwaw-shaow?) (*What's your phone number?*)

- ✔ **Nǐde dìzhǐ shì shénme?** 你的地址是什么? (你的地址是甚麼?) (nee-duh dee-jir shir shummuh?) (*What's your address?*)

- ✔ **Nǐ shénme shíhòu zài jiā?** 你什么时侯在家? (你甚麼時候在家?) (nee shummuh shir-ho dzye jyah?) (*When will you be at home?/When are you home?*)

You may also talk about your home from time to time. These words and phrases can come in handy:

- ✔ **Wǒ zhù de shì gōngyù.** 我住的是公寓. (waw joo duh shir goong-yew.) (*I live in an apartment.*)

- ✔ **Wǒmen zhù de shì fángzi.** 我们住的是房子. (我們住的是房子) (waw-mun joo duh shir fahng-dzuh.) (*We live in a house.*)

✔ **Wǒ zhù zài chénglǐ.** 我住在城里. (我住在城裡.) (waw joo dzye chuhng-lee.) (*I live in the city.*)

✔ **Wǒ zhù zài jiāowài.** 我住在郊外. (waw joo dzye jyaow-why.) (*I live in the suburbs.*)

✔ **Wǒ zhù zài nóngcūn.** 我住在农村. (我住在農村.) (waw joo dzye noong-tswun.) (*I live in the countryside.*)

In addition to your **diànhuà hàomǎ** 电话号码 (電話號碼) (dyan-hwah how-mah) (*phone number*) and your **dìzhǐ** 地址 (dee-jir) (*address*), most people also want to know your **diànzǐ yóuxiāng dìzhǐ** 电子邮箱地址 (電子郵箱地址) (dyan-dzuh yo-shyahng dee-jir) (*e-mail address*). And if you find yourself in a more formal situation, giving someone your **míngpiàn** 名片 (meeng-pyan) (*business card*) may be appropriate. (To find out how to pronounce numbers, refer to Chapter 5.)

Fun & Games

Match these people with the words that identify their professions. Check out Appendix D for the answers.

yīshēng 医生 (醫生)   *accountant*

lǎoshī 老师 (老師)   *doctor*

fēixíngyuán 飞行员 (飛行員)   *pilot*

kuàijì 会计 (會計)   *teacher*

Chapter 8

Dining Out and Shopping for Food

. . . .

In This Chapter

▶ Eating, Chinese style

▶ Ordering and conversing in restaurants

▶ Drinking up tea knowledge

▶ Shopping for groceries

. . . .

*Y*ou may think you already know what Chinese food is all about, but if you suddenly find yourself a guest in a Chinese friend's home or the guest of honor at a banquet for your company's new branch in Shanghai, you may want to keep reading. This chapter not only helps you communicate when you're hungry or thirsty, go grocery shopping, and order food in a restaurant but also gives you some useful tips on how to be both a wonderful guest and a gracious host when you have only one shot at making a good impression.

Feeling hungry yet? Allow me to whet your appetite by inviting you to take a closer look at world-renowned Chinese cuisine. No doubt you're already familiar with a great many Chinese dishes, from chow mein and chop suey to sweet and sour pork to that delicious favorite of all Chinese fare, **dim sum.**

Exploring Chinese food and Chinese eating etiquette is a great way to discover Chinese culture. You can also use what you discover in this chapter to impress your date by ordering in Chinese the next time you eat out.

All About Meals

If you feel hungry when beginning this section, you should stop to **chī** 吃 (chir) (*eat*) **fàn** 饭 (飯) (fahn) (*food*). In fact, **fàn** always comes up when you talk about meals in China. Different meals throughout the day, for example, are called

- ✔ **zǎofàn** 早饭 (早飯) (dzaow-fahn) (*breakfast*)
- ✔ **wǔfàn** 午饭 (午飯) (woo-fahn) (*lunch*)
- ✔ **wǎnfàn** 晚饭 (晚飯) (wahn-fahn) (*dinner*)

For centuries, Chinese people greeted each other not by saying **Nǐ hǎo ma?** 你好吗? (你好嗎?) (nee how ma?) (*How are you?*) but rather by saying **Nǐ chīfàn le méiyǒu?** 你吃饭了没有? (你 吃飯了沒有?) (nee chir-fahn luh mayo?) (Literally: "*Have you eaten?*")

In China, **fàn** actually means some kind of grain or starch-based staple. You can have **mǐfàn** 米饭 (米飯) (mee-fahn) (*rice*), which can be **chǎo fàn** 炒饭 (炒饭) (chaow fahn) (*fried white rice*) or **bái mǐfàn** 白米饭 (白米飯) (bye mee-fahn) (*boiled white rice*); **miàntiáo** 面条 (面條) (myan-tyaow) (*noodles*); **mántóu** 馒头 (饅頭) (mahn-toe) (*steamed bread*); **bāozi** 包子 (baow-dzuh) (*steamed buns*); or **jiǎozi** 饺子 (餃子) (jyaow-dzuh) (*dumplings*). As you can see, you have many types of **fàn** to choose from.

Satisfying your hunger

If you're hungry, you can say **Wǒ hěn è.** 我很饿. (我很餓.) (waw hun uh.) (*I'm very hungry.*) and wait for a friend to invite you for a bite to eat. If you're thirsty, just say **Wǒde kǒu hěn kě.** 我的口很渴. (waw-duh ko hun kuh.) (Literally: *My mouth is very dry.*) to hear offers for all sorts of drinks. You may not get a chance to even utter these words, however, because Chinese rules of hospitality dictate offering food and drink to guests right off the bat.

You have a few subtle ways to get across the idea that you're hungry without appearing too forward. You can say any of the following:

- ✔ **Nǐ è bú è?** 你饿不饿? (你餓不餓?) (nee uh boo uh?) (*Are you hungry?*)
- ✔ **Nǐ è ma?** 你饿吗? (你餓嗎?) (nee uh mah?) (*Are you hungry?*)
- ✔ **Nǐ hái méi chī wǎnfàn ba.** 你还没吃晚饭吧. (你還沒吃晚飯吧.) (nee hi may chir wahn-fahn bah.) (*I bet you haven't had dinner yet.*)

By checking to see whether the other person is hungry first, you display the prized Chinese sensibility of consideration for others, and you give yourself a chance to gracefully get out of announcing that you, in fact, are really the one who's dying for some Chinese food. If you want, you can always come right out and say that you're the one who's hungry by substituting **wǒ** 我 (waw) (*I*) for **nǐ** 你 (nee) (*you*).

If you hear the sound **ba** 吧 (bah) at the end of a sentence, you can probably interpret it as *I bet,* as in **Nǐ hái méi chī wǎnfàn ba.** in the previous bulleted list, or as *let's,* as in **Wǒmen qù chīfàn ba.** 我们去吃饭吧. (我們去吃飯吧.) (waw-men chyew chir-fahn bah.) (*Let's go have dinner.*). One little utterance serves to soften the sound of making a request (or a command).

You can say something like **Nǐ xiān hē jiǔ.** 你先喝酒. (nee shyan huh jyoe.) (*Drink wine first.*), but you sound nicer and friendlier if you say **Nǐ xiān hē jiǔ ba.** 你先喝酒吧. (nee shyan huh jyoe bah.) (*Better drink some wine first./Why not have some wine first?*)

When an acquaintance invites you over for dinner, he may ask **Nǐ yào chī fàn háishì yào chī miàn?** 你要吃饭还是要吃面? (你要吃飯還是要吃麵?) (nee yaow chir fahn hi-shir yaow chir myan) (*Do you want to eat rice or noodles?*) Naturally, your host doesn't just serve you a bowl of rice or noodles; he wants to know what basic staple to prepare before he adds the actual **cài** 菜 (tsye) (*the various dishes that go with the rice or noodles*).

The many varieties of **cài** have made China the envy of the culinary world. Centuries of subsistence-level existence have taught the Chinese not to waste one morsel of an animal, mineral, or vegetable when they can use the morsel as food. Chronic shortages of food at various points in Chinese history have lent credence to the saying "Necessity is the mother of invention." The Chinese say it another way, however: They eat "anything with legs that's not a table and anything with wings that's not an airplane." Either way, you get the idea.

Do you prefer meat háishì fish?

When you can choose between more than one item on a Chinese menu, you can use the alternative question structure for interrogative expressions by placing the word **háishì** 还是 (還是) (hi-shir) (*or*) between the two choices.

If you use the term *or* in affirmative sentences, however — such as when you say she's arriving either today or tomorrow — you should use the word **huò** 或 (hwaw) or **huò zhe** 或者 (hwaw juh) instead.

Sitting down to eat and practicing proper table manners

After you've chosen what staple you want and it actually sits staring you in the face on the table, you probably want to know what utensils to use in order to eat the meal. Don't be shy about asking for a good old fork and knife, even if you're in a Chinese restaurant. The idea that Chinese people all eat with chopsticks is a myth anyway. Table 8-1 presents a handy list of utensils you need to know how to say at one point or another.

Table 8-1	Utensils	
Chinese	*Pronunciation*	*English*
bēizi 杯子	bay-dzuh	*cup*
cānjīnzhǐ 餐巾纸 (餐巾紙)	tsahn-jeen-jir	*napkin*
chāzi 叉子	chah-dzuh	*fork*
dāozi 刀子	daow-dzuh	*knife*
pánzi 盘子 (盤子)	pahn-dzuh	*plate*
tiáogēng 调羹 (調羹)	tyaow-gung	*spoon*
wǎn 碗	wahn	*bowl*
yì shuāng kuàizi 一双筷子 (一雙筷子)	ee shwahng kwye-dzuh	*a pair of chopsticks*

When you receive an invitation to someone's home, always remember to bring a small gift and to toast others before you take a drink yourself during the meal. The Chinese have no problem slurping their soup or belching during or after a meal, by the way, so don't be surprised if you witness both at a perfectly formal gathering. And to remain polite and in good graces, you should always make an attempt to serve someone else before yourself when dining with others; otherwise, you run the risk of appearing rude and self-centered. (Check out Chapter 21 for a list of other etiquette considerations.)

Don't hesitate to use some of these phrases at the table:

✔ **Duō chī yìdiǎr ba!** 多吃一点儿吧! (多吃一點兒吧!) (dwaw chir ee-dyar bah!) (*Have some more!*)

✔ **Gānbēi!** 干杯! (幹杯!) (gahn-bay!) (*Bottoms up!*)

✔ **Màn chī** *or* **màn màn chī!** 慢吃 *or* 慢慢吃! (mahn chir! *or* mahn mahn chir!) (*Bon appetite!*) This phrase literally means *Eat slowly.*, but it's loosely translated as *Take your time and enjoy your food.*

✔ **Wǒ chībǎo le.** 我吃饱了. (我吃飽了.) (waw chir-baow luh.) (*I'm full.*)

✔ **Zìjǐ lái.** 自己来. (自己來.) (dzuh-jee lye.) (*I'll help myself.*)

Whenever a dining partner begins to serve you food, as is the custom, you must always feign protest with a few mentions of **Zìjǐ lái.** so you don't appear to assume that someone *should* be serving you. In the end, you should permit the person to follow proper etiquette by serving you portions from each dish if you're the guest.

And whatever you do, don't use a **yáqiān** 牙签 (牙籤) (yah-chyan) (*toothpick*) without covering your mouth. One of the ultimate dining faux pas is to make your teeth visible during toothpick use.

Getting to Know Chinese Cuisines

You may have already discovered that different regions of China specialize in different types of cuisine. Each province has its own specialties, cooking style, and favorite ingredients. Some corner the market on spicy food, and others showcase rather bland food. But no matter where you go, you're sure to discover a new taste bud or two along the way.

Northern Chinese food, found in places such as Beijing, is famous for all sorts of meat dishes. You find plenty of beef, lamb, and duck (remember Peking Duck?). Garlic and scallions garnish the meat for good measure; otherwise, though, Northern cooking is bland because of the lack of excessive condiments. So don't expect anything overtly salty, sweet, or spicy.

Shanghai dining, as well as that of the neighboring Jiangsu and Zhejiang provinces, represents Eastern cuisine. Because these places are close to the sea and boast many lakes, you can find an infinite variety of seafood in this part of China. Fresh vegetables, different kinds of bamboo, and plenty of soy sauce and sugar are also hallmarks of this region's cuisine.

Food from Sichuan and Hunan provinces is considered Western Chinese cuisine. Western Chinese food is common in Chinese restaurants in the United States. Because this part of China is hot and humid, hot peppers and salt are commonly found here. (The food isn't the only thing considered fiery in these parts; some famous revolutionaries, such as Mao Zedong, have hailed from this region of China.)

Southern Chinese cuisine comes from Guangdong (formerly known as Canton) province, as well as from Fujian and Taiwan. Like Shanghai cuisine, it offers plentiful amounts of seafood, fresh fruits, and vegetables. One of the most famous types of food from Guangdong that you've no doubt heard of is **dim sum** (deem sum), which in standard Mandarin is pronounced **diǎn xīn** 点心 (點心) (dyan sheen). You can read more about this fare in the later section "Dipping into some dim sum."

Dining Out

Breaking bread with friends at home is great, but sometimes you want the Chinese dining experience out on the town. Taking on a menu in a foreign language can be daunting (and even that won't help you find the restroom), so the following sections take you through all sorts of restaurant basics, from sorting through the food options (including checking out **dim sum**) to ordering, paying the bill, and yes, locating the facilities.

You ask for something politely by saying **Qǐng nǐ gěi wǒ . . . ?** 请你给我 . . . ? (請你給我 . . . ?) (cheeng nee gay waw . . . ?) (*Would you mind please getting me a . . . ?*). You can also say **Máfan nǐ gěi wǒ . . .** 麻烦你给我 . . . (麻煩你給我 . . .) (mah-fahn nee gay waw . . .) (*May I trouble you to please get me a . . . ?*).

Flip to Table 8-1 earlier in the chapter for a list of common utensils. Here are a couple of additional items you commonly encounter or need to ask for when dining out:

- **yíge rè máojīn** 一个热毛巾 (一個熱毛巾) (ee-guh ruh maow-jeen) (*a hot towel*)

- **yíge shī máojīn** 一个湿毛巾 (一個濕毛巾) (ee-guh shir maow-jeen) (*a wet towel*)

When in doubt, use the measure word **ge** 个 (個) (guh) in front of the noun you want to modify by a numeral or a specifier, such as **zhè** 这 (這) (jay) (*this*) or **nà** 那 (nah) (*that*). The word for *a* always begins with **yī** 一 (ee), meaning the number *1* in Chinese. In between **yī** and the noun is the measure word. For chopsticks, it's **shuāng** 双 (雙) (shwahng), meaning *pair;* for napkin, it's **zhāng** 张 (張) (jahng), used for anything with a flat surface (such as paper, a map, or even a bed); and a toothpick's measuring word is **gēn** 根 (gun), referring to anything resembling a stick, such as rope, a thread, or a blade of grass. Chinese has many different measure words, but **ge** (guh) is by far the most common.

Talkin' the Talk

Audrey and William meet after work in New York and decide where to eat.

William:	**Audrey, nǐ hǎo!** Audrey, nee how! *Audrey, hi!*

Audrey:	**Nǐ hǎo. Hǎo jiǔ méi jiàn.** nee how. how jyoe may jyan. *Hi there. Long time no see.*

William:	**Nǐ è bú è?** nee uh boo uh? *Are you hungry?*

Audrey:	**Wǒ hěn è. Nǐ ne?** waw hun uh. nee nuh? *Yes, very hungry. How about you?*

William:	**Wǒ yě hěn è.** waw yeah hun uh. *I'm also pretty hungry.*

Audrey:	**Wǒmen qù Zhōngguóchéng chī Zhōngguó cài, hǎo bù hǎo?** waw-men chyew joong-gwaw-chuhng chir joong-gwaw tsye, how boo how? *Let's go to Chinatown and have Chinese food, okay?*

William:	**Hǎo. Nǐ zhīdào Zhōngguóchéng nǎ jiā cānguǎn hǎo ma?** how. nee jir-daow joong-waw-chuhng nah jya tsahn-gwahn how ma? *Okay. Do you know which restaurant in Chinatown is good?*

Audrey:	**Běijīng kǎo yā diàn hǎoxiàng bú cuò.** bay-jeeng cow ya dyan how-shyang boo tswaw. *The Peking Duck place seems very good.*

William:	**Hǎo jíle. Wǒmen zǒu ba.** how jee-luh. waw-men dzoe bah. *Great. Let's go.*

Words to Know

Nǐ è bú è? 你饿不饿? (你餓不餓?)	nee uh boo uh?	Are you hungry?
Zhōngguó cài 中国菜 (中國菜)	joong-gwaw tsye	Chinese food
cānguǎn 餐馆 (餐館)	tsahng-gwahn	restaurant

Nǐ hǎo 你好 (nee how), which appears in the nearby Talkin' the Talk dialogue, can be translated as *Hi., Hello.,* or *How are you?*.

Understanding what's on the menu

Are you a vegetarian? If so, you want to order **sùcài** 素菜 (sue-tsye) (*vegetable dishes*). If you're a dyed-in-the-wool carnivore, however, you should definitely keep your eye on the kind of **hūncài** 荤菜 (葷菜) (hwun-tsye) (*meat or fish dishes*) listed on the **càidān** 菜单 (菜單) (tsye-dahn) (*menu*). Unlike the rice or noodles you may order, which come in individual bowls for everyone at the table, the **cài** 菜 (tsye) (*dishes*) you order arrive on large plates, which you're expected to share with others.

You should become familiar with the basic types of food on the menu in case you have only Chinese characters and **pīnyīn** Romanization to go on. Having this knowledge allows you to immediately know which section to focus on (or, likewise, to avoid).

Take meat, for example. In English, the words for *pork, beef,* and *mutton* have no hints of the words for the animals themselves, such as **zhū** 猪 (豬) (joo) (*pig*), **niú** 牛 (nyoe) (*cow*), or **yáng** 羊 (yahng) (*lamb*). Chinese is much simpler. Just combine the word for the animal and the word **ròu** 肉 (row), meaning *meat,* such as **zhū ròu** 猪肉 (豬肉) (joo row) (*pork*), **niú ròu** 牛肉 (nyoe row) (*beef*), or **yáng ròu** 羊肉 (yahng row) (*mutton*). Voilà! You have the dish.

Table 8-2 shows the typical elements of a Chinese menu.

Table 8-2	Typical Sections of a Chinese Menu	
Chinese	**Pronunciation**	**English**
diǎnxīn 点心 (點心)	dyan-sheen	dessert
hǎixiān 海鲜 (海鮮)	hi-shyan	seafood dishes
jī lèi 鸡类 (雞類)	jee lay	poultry dishes
kāiwèicài 开胃菜 (開胃菜)	kye-way-tsye	appetizer
ròu lèi 肉类 (肉類)	row lay	meat dishes
sùcài 素菜	soo-tsye	vegetarian dishes
tāng 汤 (湯)	tahng	soup
yǐnliào 饮料 (飲料)	een-lyaow	drinks

Talkin' the Talk

Ernest, Otto, and Cecilia meet at a restaurant in Shanghai after work, and a host greets them on the way in. (Track 10)

Host: **Jǐ wèi?**
jee way?
How many are in your party?

Otto: **Sān wèi.**
sahn way.
There are three of us.

The host shows them to their table. The three must now decide what to order for their meals.

Host: **Qǐng zuò zhèr. Zhè shì càidān.**
cheeng dzwaw jar. jay shir tsye-dahn.
Please sit here. Here's the menu.

Otto: **Nǐ yào chī fàn háishì yào chī miàn?**
nee yaow chir fahn hi-shir yaow chir myan?
Do you want to eat rice or noodles?

Ernest: **Liǎngge dōu kěyǐ.**
lyahng-guh doe kuh-yee.
Either one is fine.

Cecilia: **Wǒ hěn xǐhuān yāoguǒ jīdīng. Nǐmen ne?**
waw hun she-hwan yaow-gwaw jee-deeng. nee-men nuh?
I love diced chicken with cashew nuts. How about you guys?

Ernest: **Duìbùqǐ, wǒ chī sù. Wǒmen néng bù néng diǎn yìdiǎr dòufu?**
dway-boo-chee, waw chir soo. waw-mun nung boo nung dyan ee-dyar doe-foo?
Sorry, I'm a vegetarian. Can we order some tofu?

Cecilia: **Dāngrán kěyǐ.**
dahng-rahn kuh-yee.
Of course we can.

Otto: **Bù guǎn zěnme yàng, wǒmen lái sān píng píjiǔ, hǎo bù hǎo?**
boo gwahn dzummuh yahng, waw-mun lye san peeng pee-jyoe, how boo how?
No matter what, let's get three bottles of beer, okay?

Ernest: **Hěn hǎo!**
hun how!
Very good!

Words to Know

Jǐ wèi? 几位? (幾位?)	jee way?	How many are in your party?
bù guǎn zěnme yàng 不管怎么样 (不管怎麼樣)	boo gwahn dzum-mah yahng	no matter what
píjiǔ 啤酒	pee-jyoe	beer

Vegetarian's delight

If you're a vegetarian, you may feel lost when looking at a menu filled with mostly pork (the staple meat of China), beef, and fish dishes. Not to worry. As long as you memorize a couple of the terms shown in Table 8-3, you won't go hungry.

Table 8-3	Vegetables Commonly Found in Chinese Dishes	
Chinese	*Pronunciation*	*English*
bōcài 菠菜	baw-tsye	*spinach*
dòufu 豆腐	doe-foo	*bean curd*
fānqié 番茄	fahn-chyeh	*tomato*
gāilán 芥兰 (芥蘭)	gye-lahn	*Chinese broccoli*
mógū 蘑菇	maw-goo	*mushroom*
qiézi 茄子	chyeh-dzuh	*eggplant*
qīngjiāo 青椒	cheeng-jyaow	*green pepper*
sìjídòu 四季豆	suh-jee-doe	*string bean*
tǔdòu 土豆	too-doe	*potato*
xīlánhuā 西兰花 (西蘭花)	she-lahn-hwah	*broccoli*
yáng báicài 洋白菜	yahng bye-tsye	*cabbage*
yùmǐ 玉米	yew-me	*corn*
zhúsǔn 竹笋 (竹筍)	joo-swoon	*bamboo shoot*

When you have a good understanding of the vegetables that go into Chinese dishes, you, oh proud vegetarian, can start to order specialized vegetarian dishes at all your favorite restaurants. Table 8-4 shows some vegetarian dishes good for a night on the town.

Table 8-4	Vegetarian Dishes	
Chinese	*Pronunciation*	*English*
dànhuā tāng 蛋花汤 (蛋花湯)	dahn-hwah tahng	*egg drop soup*
gānbiān sìjìdòu 干煸四季豆 (乾煸四季豆)	gahn-byan suh-jee-doe	*sautéed string beans*

(continued)

Table 8-4 *(continued)*

Chinese	Pronunciation	English
hóngshāo dòufu 红烧豆腐 (紅燒豆腐)	hoong-shaow doe-foo	*braised bean curd in soy sauce*
suān là tāng 酸辣汤 (酸辣湯)	swan lah tahng	*hot-and-sour soup*
yúxiāng qiézi 鱼香茄子 (魚香茄子)	yew-shyang chyeh-dzuh	*spicy eggplant with garlic*

You may be tempted to **chī** 吃 (chir) (*eat*) your soup in a Chinese restaurant, but you should actually **hē** 喝 (huh) (*drink*) it instead. If it tastes really good, you can say the soup is **hěn hǎohē** 很好喝 (hun how-huh) (*very tasty*), just like anything else you may have ordered to drink.

Some favorite Chinese dishes

You may be familiar with many of the following dishes if you've ever been in a Chinese restaurant:

- **Běijīng kǎo yā** 北京烤鸭 (北京烤鴨) (bay-jeeng cow yah) (*Peking roast duck*)

- **chūnjuǎn** 春卷 (春捲) (chwun-jwan) (*spring roll*)

- **dòufu gān** 豆腐干 (豆腐乾) (doe-foo gahn) (*dried beancurd*)

- **gàilán niúròu** 芥兰牛肉 (芥蘭牛肉) (guy-lahn nyoe-row) (*beef with broccoli*)

- **gōngbǎo jīdīng** 宫保鸡丁 (宮保雞丁) (goong-baow jee-deeng) (*diced chicken with hot peppers*)

- **háoyóu niúròu** 蚝油牛肉 (蠔油牛肉) (how-yo nyoe-row) (*beef with oyster sauce*)

- **húntūn tāng** 馄饨汤 (餛飩湯) (hwun-dwun tahng) (*wonton soup*)

- **shuàn yángròu** 涮羊肉 (shwahn yahng-row) (*Mongolian hot pot*)

- **tángcù yú** 糖醋鱼 (糖醋魚) (tahng-tsoo yew) (*sweet-and-sour fish*)

- **yān huángguā** 腌黄瓜 (醃黃瓜) (yan hwahng-gwah) (*pickled cucumber*)

CULTURAL WISDOM

Chowing down on the Chinese New Year

On the eve of the Chinese lunar New Year, known as **chú xī** 除夕 (choo she), the Chinese eat a big **niányèfàn** 年夜饭 (年夜飯) (nyan-yeh-fahn) (*New Year's Eve dinner*). The dinner almost always includes a whole cooked **yú** 鱼 (魚) (yew) (*fish*), because the word for fish rhymes with the word for *abundance* **(yù),** even though the written characters for the words look quite different. In some of the poorer parts of northern China, people often eat **jiǎozi** 饺子 (餃子) (jyaow-dzuh) (*dumplings*) rather than fish because their shape resembles traditional **yuánbāo** 元宝 (元寶) (ywan-baow) (*gold*

ingots) used in pre-modern times by people of means. These people hope that the prosperity and abundance of such wealthy families will also come into their lives through the eating of the **jiǎozi.** Southerners often eat **fā cài** 发菜 (fah tsye) (*a kind of stringy black vegetable*), which rhymes with **fā cái** 发财 (發財) (fah tsye), although you pronounce the words in different tones. **Fā cái** means to get wealthy and prosper; in fact, the most common greeting on New Year's day is **Gōngxǐ fā cái!** 恭喜发财! (恭喜發財!) (goong-she fah tsye) (*Congratulations, and may you prosper!*)

Sauces and seasonings

The Chinese use all kinds of seasonings and sauces to make their dishes so tasty. Check out *Chinese Cooking For Dummies* by Martin Yan (Wiley) for much more info. Here are just a few of the basics:

- ✔ **cù** 醋 (tsoo) (*vinegar*)
- ✔ **jiǎng** 姜 (jyahng) (*ginger*)
- ✔ **jiàngyóu** 酱油 (醬油) (jyahng-yo) (*soy sauce*)
- ✔ **làyóu** 辣油 (lah-yo) (*hot sauce*)
- ✔ **máyóu** 麻油 (mah-yo) (*sesame oil*)
- ✔ **yán** 盐 (鹽) (yan) (*salt*)

Even though Chinese food is so varied and great you could have it three meals a day forever, once in a while you might really find yourself hankering for a good old American hamburger or a stack of French fries. In fact, you may be surprised to find places like McDonald's and Kentucky Fried Chicken in Asia when you least expect to. Table 8-5 lists some items you can order when you're in need of some old fashioned comfort food, and Table 8-6 lists common beverages.

Table 8-5	Western Food	
Chinese	*Pronunciation*	*English*
bǐsā bǐng 比萨饼 (比薩餅)	bee-sah beeng	*pizza*
hànbǎobāo 汉堡包 (漢堡包)	hahn-baow-baow	*hamburger*
káo tǔdòu 烤土豆	cow too-doe	*baked potato*
règǒu 热狗 (熱狗)	ruh-go	*hot dog*
sānmíngzhì 三明治	sahn-meeng-jir	*sandwich*
shālā jiàng 沙拉酱 (沙拉醬)	shah-lah jyahng	*salad dressing*
shālā zìzhùguì 沙拉自助柜 (沙拉自助櫃)	shah-lah dzuh-joo-gway	*salad bar*
tǔdòuní 土豆泥	too-doe-nee	*mashed potatoes*
yáng pái 羊排	yahng pye	*lamb chops*
yìdàlì shì miàntiáo 意大利式面条 (意大利式麵條)	ee-dah-lee shir myan-tyaow	*spaghetti*
zhà jī 炸鸡 (炸雞)	jah jee	*fried chicken*
zhà shǔtiáo 炸薯条 (炸薯條)	jah shoo-tyaow	*French fries*
zhà yángcōng quān 炸洋葱圈 (炸洋蔥圈)	jah yahng-tsoong chwan	*onion rings*
zhū pái 猪排 (豬排)	joo pye	*pork chops*

Table 8-6	Beverages	
Chinese	*Pronunciation*	*English*
chá 茶	chah	*tea*
gān hóng pútáojiǔ 干红葡萄酒 (干紅葡萄酒)	gahn hoong poo-taow-jyoe	*dry red wine*
guǒzhī 果汁	gwaw-jir	*fruit juice*
kāfēi 咖啡	kah-fay	*coffee*
kělè 可乐 (可樂)	kuh-luh	*soda*
kuāngquánshuǐ 矿泉水 (礦泉水)	kwahng-chwan-shway	*mineral water*
níngmén qìshuǐ 柠檬汽水 (檸檬汽水)	neeng-muhng chee-shway	*lemonade*
niúnǎi 牛奶	nyoe-nye	*milk*
píjiǔ 啤酒	pee-jyoe	*beer*

Placing an order and chatting with the wait staff

I bet you're used to everyone ordering one dish for themselves, right? Well, in China, diners almost always share dishes by putting them on common platters smack in the middle of the table where everyone can pick and choose. You get used to ordering with the whole group in mind, not just yourself — just one more example of how the collective is always considered before the individual in Chinese culture.

Chinese table etiquette dictates that everyone decides together what to order. The two main categories you must decide on are the **cài** 菜 (tsye) (*food dishes*) and the **tāng** 汤 (湯) (tahng) (*soup*). Feel free to be the first one to ask **Wǒmen yīnggāi jiào jǐge cài jǐge tāng?** 我们应该叫几个菜几个汤? (我們 應該叫幾個菜幾個湯?) (waw-men eeng-gye jyaow jee-guh tsye jee-guh tahng?) (*How many dishes and how many soups should we order?*) Ideally, one of each of the five major tastes should appear in the dishes you choose for your meal to be a "true" Chinese meal: **suān** 酸 (swan) (*sour*), **tián** 甜 (tyan) (*sweet*), **kǔ** 苦 (koo) (*bitter*), **là** 辣 (lah) (*spicy*), and **xián** 咸 (shyan) (*salty*).

I know it can be hard to choose what to eat from all the fantastic choices staring back at you from most any Chinese menu; after all, the Chinese perfected the art of cooking long before the French and Italians appeared on the scene. But when you finally hit on something you like, you have to figure out how to tell the waiter what you want to **chī** 吃 (chir) (*eat*), whether you like spicy food, if you want to avoid **wèijīng** 味精 (way-jeeng) (*MSG*), what kind of beer you want to **hē** 喝 (huh) (*drink*), and that you want to know what kind of **náshǒu cài** 拿手菜 (nah-show tsye) (*house specialty*) the restaurant has going today.

Here are some questions your waiter or waitress is likely to ask you:

- ✔ **Nǐmen yào hē diǎr shénme?** 你们要喝点儿什么? (你們要喝點兒甚麼?) (nee-men yaow huh dyar shummuh?) (*What would you like to drink?*)

- ✔ **Nǐmen yào shénme cài?** 你们要什么菜? (你們要甚麼菜?) (nee-men yaow shummuh tsye?) (*What would you like to order?* [Literally: *What kind of food would you like?*])

- ✔ **Yào jǐ píng píjiǔ?** 要几瓶啤酒? (要幾瓶啤酒?) (yaow jee peeng pee-jyoe?) (*How many bottles of beer do you want?*)

When addressing waiters or waitresses, you can call them by the same name: **fúwùyuán** 服务员 (服務員) (foo-woo-ywan) (*service personnel*). In fact, *he, she,* and *it* all share the same Chinese word, too: **tā** 他/她/它 (tah). Isn't that easy to remember? Here are some questions, requests, and statements that may come in handy:

- **Dà shīfu náshǒu cài shì shénme?** 大师傅拿手菜是什么? (大師傅拿手菜是甚麼?) (dah shir-foo nah-show tsye shir shummuh?) (*What's the chef's specialty?*)

- **Nǐ gěi wǒmen jièshào cài, hǎo ma?** 你给我们介绍菜, 好吗? (你給我們介紹菜, 好嗎?) (nee gay waw-men jyeh-shaow tsye how ma?) (*Can you recommend some dishes?*)

- **Nǐmen yǒu kuàngquán shuǐ ma?** 你们有矿泉水吗? (你們有礦泉水嗎?) (nee-men yo kwahng-chwan shway mah?) (*Do you have any mineral water?*)

- **Qǐng bǎ yǐnliào sòng lái.** 请把饮料送来. (請把飲料送來.) (cheeng bah yin-lyaow soong lye.) (*Please bring our drinks.*)

- **Qǐng bié fàng wèijīng, wǒ guòmǐn.** 请别放味精, 我过敏. (請別放味精, 我過敏.) (cheeng byeh fahng way-jeeng, waw gwaw-meen.) (*Please don't use any MSG, I'm allergic.*)

- **Qǐng cā zhuōzi.** 请擦桌子. (請擦桌子.) (cheeng tsah jwaw-dzuh.) (*Please wipe off the table.*)

- **Qǐng gěi wǒ càidān.** 请给我菜单. (請給我菜單.) (cheeng gay waw tsye-dahn.) (*Please give me the menu.*)

- **Wǒ bù chī zhūròu.** 我不吃猪肉. (我不吃豬肉.) (waw boo chir joo-row.) (*I don't eat pork.*)

- **Wǒ bù néng chī yǒu táng de cài.** 我不能吃有糖的菜. (waw boo nuhng chir yo tahng duh tsye.) (*I can't eat anything made with sugar.*)

- **Wǒ bú yào là de cài.** 我不要辣的菜. (waw boo yaow lah duh tsye.) (*I don't want anything spicy.*)

- **Wǒ bú yuànyì chī hǎishēn.** 我不愿意吃海参. (我不願意吃海參.) (waw boo ywan-yee chir hi-shun) (*I don't want to try sea slugs.*)

- **Wǒ méi diǎn zhèige.** 我没点这个. (我没点這個.) (waw may dyan jay-guh.) (*I didn't order this.*)

- **Wǒmen yào yíge suān là tāng.** 我们要一个酸辣汤. (我們要一個酸辣湯.) (waw-men yaow ee-guh swan lah tahng.) (*We'd like a hot-and-sour soup.*)

- **Yú xīnxiān ma?** 鱼新鲜吗? (魚新鮮嗎?) (yew shin-shyan mah?) (*Is the fish fresh?*)

Regular nouns in Chinese make no distinction between singular and plural. Whether you want to talk about one **píngguǒ** 苹果 (蘋果) (peeng-gwaw) (*apple*), two **júzi** 桔子 (jyew-dzuh) (*oranges*), or both **píngguó hé júzi** 苹果和桔子 (peeng gwaw huh jyew dzuh) (*apples and oranges*), the fruits always sound the same in Chinese. On the other hand, if you want to refer to human beings, you can always add the suffix **men** 们 (們) (mun). The word for *I* or *me* is **wǒ** 我 (waw), but *we* becomes **wǒmen** 我们 (我們) (waw-mun). The same goes for **nǐ** 你 (nee) (*you*) and **tā** 他/她/它 (tah) (*he/she/it*). *Both of you* or *all of you* becomes **nǐmen** 你们 (你們) (nee-mun) and *both of them* or *all of them* becomes **tāmen** 他们 他們) / 她们 (她們) / 它们 (它們) (tah-mun). If you want to refer to a specific number of apples, however, you don't use **men** as a suffix. You can either say **píngguǒ** for *apple* (or *apples*) or **liǎngge píngguǒ** 两个苹果 (兩個蘋果) (lyahng-guh peeng-gwaw), meaning *two apples*. How do you like them apples?

Dipping into some dim sum

Dim sum is probably the most popular food of Chinese folks in the United States and of people in Guangdong Province and all over Hong Kong, where you can find it served for breakfast, lunch, and sometimes dinner. Vendors even sell dim sum snacks in subway stations.

The dish's main claim to fame is that it takes the shape of mini portions, and it's often served with tea to help cut through the oil and grease afterwards. You have to signal the waiters when you want a dish of whatever is on the dim sum cart they push in the restaurant, however, or they just pass on by. Dim sum restaurants are typically crowded and noisy, which only adds to the fun.

Part of the allure of dim sum is that you get to sample a whole range of different tastes while you catch up with old friends. Dim sum meals can last for hours, which is why most Chinese people choose the weekends to have dim sum. No problem lingering on a Saturday or Sunday.

Because dim sum portions are so small, your waiter often tallys the total by the number of plates left on your table. You can tell the waiter you want a specific kind of dim sum by saying **Qǐng lái yì dié** _____. 请来一碟 _____. (請來一碟 _____.) (cheeng lye ee dyeh _____.) (*Please give me a plate of _____.*). Fill in the blank with one of the tasty choices I list in Table 8-7.

Table 8-7	Common Dim Sum Dishes	
Chinese	*Pronunciation*	*English*
chūnjuǎn 春卷 (春捲)	chwun-jwan	*spring rolls*
dàntǎ 蛋挞 (蛋撻)	dahn-tah	*egg tarts*
dòushā bāo 豆沙包	doe-shah baow	*sweet bean buns*

(continued)

Table 8-7 (continued)

Chinese	Pronunciation	English
guō tiē 锅贴 (鍋貼)	gwaw tyeh	fried pork dumplings
luóbō gāo 萝卜糕 (蘿蔔糕)	law-baw gaow	turnip cake
niàng qīngjiāo 酿青椒 (釀青椒)	nyahng cheeng-jyaow	stuffed peppers
niúròu wán 牛肉丸	nyoe-row wahn	beef balls
xiā jiǎo 虾饺 (蝦餃)	shyah jyaow	shrimp dumplings
xiǎolóng bāo 小笼包 (小籠包)	shyaow-loong baow	steamed pork buns
xiā wán 虾丸 (蝦丸)	shyah wahn	shrimp balls
yùjiǎo 芋饺 (芋餃)	yew-jyaow	deep fried taro root

Have you ever used the particle **guò** 过 (過) (gwaw)? If you want to ask whether someone has ever done something, use this word directly after the verb to get your point across:

> **Nǐ qù guò Měiguó méiyǒu?** 你去过美国没有? (你去過美國沒有?) (nee chew gwaw may-gwaw mayo?) (*Have you ever been to America?*)

> **Nǐ chī guò Yìdàlì fàn ma?** 你吃过意大利饭吗? (你吃過意大利飯嗎?) (nee chir gwaw ee-dah-lee fahn ma?) (*Have you ever eaten Italian food?*)

Finding the restrooms

After you have a bite to eat, you may be in need of a restroom. The need may be dire if you're smack in the middle of a 12-course banquet in Beijing and already have a couple of glasses of **máotái** 茅台 (maow-tye), the stiffest of all Chinese drinks, under your belt.

Now all you have to do is garner the energy to ask *Where's the restroom?*: **Cèsuǒ zài nǎr?** 厕所在哪儿? (廁所在哪兒?) (tsuh-swaw dzye nar?) if you're in mainland China or **Cèsuǒ zài nǎlǐ?** 厕所在哪里? (廁所在哪理?) (tsuh-swaw dzye nah-lee?) if you're in Taiwan. You can also ask **Nǎlǐ kěyǐ xǐ shǒu?** 哪里可以洗手? (哪裡可以洗手?) (nah-lee kuh-yee she show?) (*Where can I wash my hands?*)

If you're in mainland China, don't forget to take some toilet paper with you before you leave the hotel, because many public restrooms don't supply it there. In most cases, the pictures on the bathroom doors are self-explanatory, but you may also see 男, the **pīnyīn** for **nán** (nahn) (*male*) and 女, the **pīnyīn**

for **nǚ** (nyew) (*female*) before the word **cèsuǒ.** Those are the words you want to pay attention to above all else.

You can also find the word **cèsuǒ** in the term for graffiti: **cèsuǒ wénxué** 厕所 文学 (廁所文學) (tsuh-swaw one-shweh) (Literally: *bathroom literature*). How apropos.

Finishing your meal and paying the bill

After you're through sampling all possible permutations of Chinese cuisine (or French or Italian, for that matter), you won't be able to just slink away unnoticed out the front door and into the sunset. Time to pay the bill, my friend. Hopefully it was worth the expense. Here are some phrases you should know when the time comes:

- ✔ **Bāokuò fúwùfèi.** 包括服务费. (包括服務費.) (baow-kwaw foo-woo-fay.) (*The tip is included.*)

- ✔ **fēnkāi suàn** 分开算 (分開算) (fun-kye swahn) (*to go Dutch*)

- ✔ **jiézhàng** 结账 (結賬) (jyeh-jahng) (*to pay the bill*)

- ✔ **Qǐng jiézhàng.** 请结账. (請結賬.) (cheeng jyeh-jahng.) (*The check, please.*)

- ✔ **Qǐng kāi shōujù.** 请开收据. (請開收據.) (cheeng kye show-jyew.) (*Please give me the receipt.*)

- ✔ **Wǒ kěyǐ yòng xìnyòng kǎ ma?** 我可以用信用卡吗? (我可以用信用卡嗎?) (waw kuh-yee yoong sheen-yoong kah mah?) (*May I use a credit card?*)

- ✔ **Wǒ qǐng kè.** 我请客. (我請客.) (waw cheeng kuh.) (*It's on me.*)

- ✔ **Zhàngdān yǒu cuò.** 账单有错. (賬單有錯.) (jahng-dahn yo tswaw.) (*The bill is incorrect.*)

All the Tea in China

You encounter about as many different kinds of tea as you do Chinese dialects. Hundreds, in fact. To make ordering or buying this beverage easier, however, you really need to know only the most common kinds of tea:

- ✔ **Lǜ chá** 绿茶 (綠茶) (lyew chah) (*Green tea*): Green tea is the oldest of all the teas in China, with many unfermented subvarieties. The most famous kind of Green tea is called **lóngjǐng chá** 龙井茶 (龍井茶) (loong-jeeng chah), meaning *Dragon Well tea.* You can find it near the famous West Lake region in Hangzhou, but people in the south generally prefer this kind of tea.

✔ **Hóng chá** 红茶 (紅茶) (hoong chah) (*Black tea*): Even though **hóng** means *red* in Chinese, you translate this phrase as *Black tea* instead. Unlike Green tea, Black teas are fermented; they're enjoyed primarily by people in Fujian province.

✔ **Wūlóng chá** 乌龙茶 (烏龍茶) (oo-loong chah) (*Black Dragon tea*): This kind of tea is semi-fermented. It's a favorite in Guangdong and Fujian provinces in the South, and in Taiwan.

✔ **Mòlì huā chá** 茉莉花茶 (茉莉花茶) (maw-lee hwah chah) (*Jasmine*): This kind of tea is made up of a combination of Black, Green, and Wūlóng teas in addition to some fragrant flowers such as jasmine or magnolia thrown in for good measure. Most northerners are partial to Jasmine tea, probably because the north is cold and this type of tea raises the body's temperature.

Tea is always offered to guests the minute they enter a Chinese home. The hosts aren't just being polite; the offering of tea shows respect to the guest and presents a way to share something that all parties can enjoy together. It may be considered rude not to at least take a sip. Chinese custom says that a host only fills the teacup to 70 percent of its capacity. The other 30 percent is supposed to contain friendship and affection. Isn't that a nice concept?

You often use the adjective **hǎo** 好 (how) (*good*) with a verb to create an adjective that means *good to.* Here are a few examples:

hǎochī 好吃 (how-chir) (*tasty* [Literally: *good to eat*])

hǎohē 好喝 (how-huh) (*tasty* [Literally: *good to drink*])

hǎokàn 好看 (how-kahn) (*pretty, interesting* [Literally: *good to look at or watch*]) This designation can apply to people or even movies.

hǎowán 好玩 (how-wahn) (*fun, interesting* [Literally: *good to play*])

The Chinese night market

Night markets are great places to stroll, shop, eat, and otherwise hang out with family and friends. Vendors hawk their wares from clothes to **xiǎo chī** 小吃 (shyaow chir) (*snacks* [Literally: *small eats*]) of every kind in noisy, crowded stalls in what can only be described as a carnival-like atmosphere. The most famous night market in Taiwan is in the **Shìlín** 士林 (shir-leen) district of Taipei, which closes well after midnight. In mainland China, don't miss the **Kāifēng yèshì** 开封夜市 (開封夜市) (kye-fuhng yeh-shir) (*Kaifeng night market*), in northern China's Henan province. At night, Kaifeng's streets turn into veritable restaurants, with the specialty being northern-style dumplings.

Taking Your Chinese to Go

Restaurants are great, but once in a while you may want to mingle with the masses as people go about buying food for a home-cooked family dinner. Outdoor food markets abound in China and are great places to see how the locals shop and what they buy. And what better way to try out your Chinese? You can always point to what you want and discover the correct term for it from the vendor.

In addition to clothes, books, and kitchen utensils, outdoor markets may offer all sorts of food items:

✔ **Ròu** 肉 (row) (*meat*): **niú ròu** 牛肉 (nyoe row) (*beef*), **yáng ròu** 羊肉 (yahng row) (*lamb*), or **jī ròu** 鸡肉 (雞肉) (jee row) (*chicken*)

✔ **Shuǐguǒ** 水果 (shway-gwaw) (*fruit*): **píngguǒ** 苹果 (蘋果) (peeng-gwaw) (*apples*) or **júzi** 桔子 (jyew-dzuh) (*oranges*)

✔ **Yú** 鱼 (魚) (yew) (*fish*): **xiā** 虾 (蝦) (shyah) (*shrimp*), **pángxiè** 螃蟹 (pahng-shyeh) (*crab*), **lóngxiā** 龙虾 (龍蝦) (loong-shyah) (*lobster*), or **yóuyú** 鱿鱼 (魷魚) (yo-yew) (*squid*)

Chinese people generally don't eat any raw food. The idea of a raw salad bar is truly foreign to them. In fact, **shēngcài** 生菜 (shung-tsye) (*lettuce*) literally translates as raw food, and the Chinese generally consider it fit only for farm animals.

Making comparisons

When you want to compare people or objects, you generally put the word **bǐ** 比 (*bee*) (*compared to*) between two nouns, followed by an adjective: A **bǐ** B (adjective). This construction means *A is more _____ than B*.

Here are a few examples:

Píngguǒ bǐ júzi hǎochī. 苹果比桔子好吃。(蘋果比橘子好吃。) (peeng-gwaw bee jyew-dzuh how-chir.) (*Apples are tastier than oranges.*)

Tā bǐ nǐ niánqīng. 她比你年轻 (年輕)。(tah bee nee nyan-cheeng.) (*She's younger than you.*)

Zhèige fànguǎr bǐ nèige fànguǎr guì. 这个饭馆比那个饭馆贵。(這個飯館比那個飯館貴。) (jay-guh fahn-gwar bee nay-guh fahng-gwar gway.) (*This restaurant is more expensive than that one.*)

How much is that thousand-year-old egg?

When you're ready to buy some foodstuffs, here are two simple ways to ask how much the products cost:

- **Duōshǎo qián?** 多少钱? (多少錢?) (dwaw-shaow chyan?) (*How much money is it?*)

- **Jǐkuài qián?** 几块钱? (幾塊錢?) (jee-kwye chyan?) (Literally: *How many dollars does it cost?*)

The only difference between the two questions is the implied amount of the cost. If you use the question word **duōshǎo** 多少 (dwaw-shaow), you want to inquire about something that's most likely more than $10. If you use **jǐ** 几 (幾) (jee) in front of **kuài** 块 (塊) (kwye) (*dollars*), you assume the product costs less than $10. (You can also use **jǐ** in front of **suì** 岁 (歲) (sway) (*years*) when you want to know how old a child under 10 is.)

Talkin' the Talk

 At the local open-air market in Kaifeng, Margaret and Emmanuel eye some vegetables and discuss the price with the older man selling them in his stall. (Track 11)

Margaret:	**Shīfu, qǐng wèn, nǐ yǒu méiyǒu bōcài?** shir-foo, cheeng one, nee yo mayo baw-tsye? *Sir, may I ask, do you have any spinach?*
Shīfu:	**Dāngrán. Yào jǐjīn?** dahng-rahn. yaow jee-jeen? *Of course. How many kilograms would you like?*
Emmanuel:	**Wǒmen mǎi sānjīn, hǎo bùhǎo?** waw-men my sahn-jeen, how boo-how? *Let's get three kilograms, okay?*
Margaret:	**Hǎo. Sānjīn ba.** how. sahn-jeen bah. *Okay. It'll be three kilograms then.*

师傅，你有没有
波菜？

学然 要几斤？

我们买三斤，好不好？

好 三斤吧

Shīfu: **Méi wèntí. Yìjīn sān kuài qián. Nèmme, yígòng jiǔ kuài.**
may one-tee. ee-jeen sahn kwye chyan. nummuh, ee-goong jyoe kwye.
No problem. It's $3 a kilogram. So that will be $9 all together.

Emmanuel: **Děng yíxià. Bōcài bǐ gàilán guì duōle. Wǒmen mǎi gàilán ba.**
dung ee-shyah. baw-tsye bee guy-lahn gway dwaw-luh. waw-mun my guy-lahn bah.
Wait a minute. Spinach is more expensive than Chinese broccoli. Let's buy Chinese broccoli then.

Shīfu: **Hǎo. Gàilán liǎngkuài yìjīn. Hái yào sānjīn ma?**
how. guy-lahn lyahng-kwye ee-jeen. hi yaow sahn-jeen mah?
Okay. Chinese broccoli is $2 a kilogram. Do you still want three kilograms?

Margaret: **Shì de.**
shir duh.
Yes.

Shīfu: **Nà, sānjīn yígòng liù kuài.**
nah, sahn-jeen ee-goong lyo kwye.
In that case, three kilograms will be $6.

Emmanuel: **Hǎo. Zhè shì liù kuài.**
how. juh shir lyoe kwye.
Okay. Here's $6.

Shīfu: **Xièxiè.**
shyeh-shyeh.
Thank you.

Emmanuel: **Xièxiè. Zàijiàn.**
shyeh-shyeh. dzye-jyan.
Thanks. Goodbye.

Shīfu: **Zàijiàn.**
dzye-jyan.
Goodbye.

Words to Know

shīfu 师傅 (師傅)	shir-foo	sir
Hǎo. 好.	how.	Okay.
Děng yíxià. 等一下.	dung ee-shyah.	Wait a minute.

Shīfu 师傅 (師傅) (shir-foo) is a term used to indicate someone providing a service; it shows more respect due to age than the term **fúwùyuán** 服务员 (服務員) (foo-woo-ywan), which indicates any kind of attendant, does.

Fun & Games

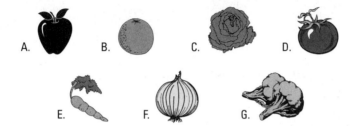

Identify these fruits and vegetables and write their Chinese names below. Check out Appendix D for the answers.

A. _____

B. _____

C. _____

D. _____

E. _____

F. _____

G. _____

Chapter 9

Shopping Made Easy

. . . .

In This Chapter

▶ Checking out the stores

▶ Looking for clothes and other items

▶ Bargaining for a better price

. . . .

Ever dreamed of shopping till you dropped in a foreign country where the rate of exchange is really great? Or in faraway lands where lively outdoor night markets abound? This chapter helps you navigate both small shops and fancy department stores; get a handle on prices, colors, and merchandise; and in general negotiate the best deal wherever possible.

To **mǎi dōngxi** 买东西(買東西) (my doong-she) (*buy things*) is one of the most enjoyable pastimes for people the world over. Whether you're just going **guàngshāngdiàn** 逛商店 (gwahng-shahng-dyan) (*window shopping*) or actually about to **mǎi dōngxi** doesn't matter. You can still enjoy looking at all the **shāngpǐn** 商品 (shahng-peen) (*merchandise*), fantasizing about buying that **zuànshí jièzhǐ** 钻石戒指 (鑽石戒指) (dzwan-shir jye-jir) (*diamond ring*), and haggling over the **jiàgé** 价格 (價格) (jyah-guh) (*price*).

Going to Stores

You can find all sorts of stores to meet your shopping needs throughout China. Table 9-1 presents some common store options.

Table 9-1	Kinds of Stores	
Chinese	*Pronunciation*	*English*
bǎihuò shāngdiàn 百货商店 (百貨商店)	bye-hwaw shahng-dyan	*department store*
cài shìchǎng 菜市场 (菜市場)	tsye shir-chahng	*food market*
chàngpiàn diàn 唱片店	chahng-pyan-dyan	*record store*
chāojí shìchǎng 超级市场 (超級市場)	chow-jee shir-chahng	*supermarket*
fúzhuāng diàn 服装店 (服裝店)	foo-jwahng dyan	*clothing store*
lǐpǐn diàn 礼品店 (禮品店)	lee-peen dyan	*gift shop*
shūdiàn 书店 (書店)	shoo-dyan	*bookstore*
wánjù diàn 玩具店	wahn-jyew dyan	*toy store*
wǔjīn diàn 五金店	woo-jeen dyan	*hardware store*
xiédiàn 鞋店	shyeh-dyan	*shoe store*
yàofáng 药房 (藥房)	yaow-fahng	*drugstore*
zhūbǎo diàn 珠宝店	joo-baow dyan	*jewelry store*

Here are some things you can find in various stores:

- **Zài yíge shūdiàn nǐ kéyǐ mǎi shū, zázhì hé bàozhǐ.** 在一个书店你可以买书, 杂志和报纸. (在一個書店你可以買書, 雜誌和報紙.) (dzye ee-guh shoo-dyan nee kuh-yee my shoo, dzah-jir huh baow-jir.) (*In a bookstore, you can buy books, magazines, and newspapers.*)

- **Zài yíge wǔjīn diàn nǐ kéyǐ mǎi zhuǎnjiē qì, chātóu hé yānwù bàojǐng qì.** 在一个五金店你可以买转接器, 插头和烟雾报警器. (在一個五金店你可以買轉接器, 插頭和煙霧報警器.) (dzye ee-guh woo-jeen dyan nee kuh-yee my jwan-jyeh chee, chah-toe huh yan-woo baow-jeeng chee.) (*In a hardware store, you can buy adaptors, plugs, and smoke detectors.*)

- **Zài yíge zhūbǎo diàn nǐ kéyǐ mǎi shǒuzhuó, ěrhuán, xiàngliàn, xiōngzhēn hé jièzhi.** 在一个珠宝店你可以买手镯, 耳环, 项链, 胸针和戒指. (在一個珠寶店你可以買手鐲, 耳環, 項鍊, 胸針和戒指.) (dzye ee-guh joo-baow dyan nee kuh-yee my show-jwaw, are-hwahn, shyahng-lyan, shyoong-juhn huh jyeh-jir.) (*In a jewelry store, you can buy bracelets, earrings, necklaces, pins, and rings.*)

When you finally make up your mind about what to shop for, you may want to call ahead to check out the store's hours. Here are some questions that can help:

✔ **Nǐmen wǔdiǎn zhōng yǐhòu hái kāi ma?** 你们五点钟以后还开吗? (你們五點鐘以後還開嗎?) (nee-men woo-dyan joong ee-hoe hi kye mah?) (_Are you open after 5:00 p.m.?_)

✔ **Nǐmen xīngqītiān kāi bùkāi?** 你们星期天开不开? (你們星期天開不開?) (nee-mun sheeng-chee-tyan kye boo-kye?) (_Are you open on Sundays?_)

✔ **Nǐn jǐdiǎn zhōng kāi/guān mén?** 您几点钟开/关门? (您幾點鐘開/關門?) (neen jee-dyan joong kye/gwahn mun?) (_What time do you open/close?_)

Most stores in China are open quite early, around 8:00 a.m., and don't close until 8:00 p.m. or even later. If you want a less harried shopping experience, avoid shopping on the weekends, when seemingly a quarter of humanity is out doing the same thing.

Talkin' the Talk

Helaine and Jeffrey discuss going shopping for the day. Here's how they start out.

Helaine:	**Wǒ jīntiān xiǎng qù mǎi dōngxi.** 我今天想去買東西。 waw jin-tyan shyahng chyew my doong-she. _I want to go shopping today._
Jeffrey:	**Nǐ qù nǎr mǎi dōngxi?** 你哪儿買東西? 去 在 nee chyew nar my doong-she? _Where will you go to shop?_
Helaine:	**Wǒ yào qù bǎihuò shāngdiàn mǎi yīfu.** 我要去百貨商店買衣服。 waw yaow chyew bye-hwaw shahng-dyan my ee-foo. _I want to go to the department store to buy some clothes._
Jeffrey:	**Tīngshuō zài zhèige chénglǐ dōngxi dōu hěn guì.** 听說在这个城里 teeng-shwaw dzye jay-guh chuhng-lee doong-she doe hun gway. _I've heard that everything's very expensive in this city._

Helaine: **Nà bùyídìng. Kàn shì shénme diàn. Yǒude hěn guì, yǒude yìdiǎn dōu búguì.**
nah boo-ee-deeng. kahn shir shummuh dyan. yo-duh hun gway, yo-duh ee-dyan doe boo-gway.
Not necessarily. It depends on the store. Some are really expensive, and some aren't expensive at all.

Jeffrey: **Hǎo ba. Wǒmen zǒu ba. Wǒmen qù mǎi yīfu.**
how bah. waw-mun dzoe bah. waw-mun chyew my ee-foo.
Great. Let's go. Let's buy some clothes.

Words to Know

bǎihuò shāngdiàn 百货商店 (百貨商店)	bye hwaw shahng dyan	department store
tīngshuō 听说 (聽說)	teeng-shwaw	I've heard that . . .
bùyídìng 不一定	boo-ee-deeng	not necessarily
Wǒmen zǒu ba. 我们走吧。(我們走吧。)	waw-mun dzoe bah.	Let's go.

Whenever you see the words **yìdiǎn dōu bú** 一点都不 (一點都不) (ee-dyan doe boo) before an adjective, it means *not at all (adjective).* This construction is a great way to emphasize something. You can say something like **Wǒ yìdiǎn dōu búlèi.** 我一点都不累. (我一點都不累.) (waw ee-dyan doe boo-lay.) (*I'm not tired in the least.*) or **Tā yìdiǎn dōu búpiàoliàng.** 她一点都不漂亮. (她一點都不漂亮.) (tah ee-dyan doe boo-pyaow-lyahng.) (*She's not at all pretty.*) to get your point across.

Getting What You Want at a Department Store

If you don't have a clue how to begin shopping in China, much less what you want to buy, you may want to start off at one of the many luxury department stores that have sprouted up throughout China in the last decade. Here, you can get almost any name-brand thing you're looking for, from **zhūbǎo** 珠宝 (joo-baow) (*jewelry*) and **huāpíng** 花瓶 (hwah-peeng) (*vases*) to **yīfu** 衣服 (ee-foo) (*clothing*) and **yuèqì** 乐器 (樂器) (yweh-chee) (*musical instruments*).

Department stores aren't the only places you can shop, but they're certainly the easiest because everything is right there within walking distance and you can browse without fighting off vendors trying to push their wares.

Even though traditional alley markets and shop fronts still exist in China, Western-style shopping malls are quickly putting their imprint on places like Beijing and Shanghai. You can still get the best prices, though, at the many open-air markets and street vendors, which sell traditional arts and crafts and other specialties. Beijing's number one shopping area isn't far from **Tiān'ānmén Square** 天安门 (天安門) (tyan-ahn-mun square) on **Wángfǔjǐng** 王府井 (wahng-foo-jeeng) and **Dōngdān** 东单 (東單) (doong-dahn) Streets. Or on **Jiànguóménwài Dàjiē** 建国门外大街 (建國門外大街) (jyan-gwaw mun-why dah-jyeh) Street.

Just browsing

You may want to call ahead of time to see when the biggest department store in town opens before you decide to stroll on over. It's a nice day outside, you're in a mellow mood, all's right with the world, and all you want to do is just window shop — inside the store. You start out on the **dì yī céng** 第一层 (第一層) (dee ee tsuhng) (*first floor*), take the **zìdòng lóutī** 自动楼梯 (自動樓梯) (dzuh-doong low-tee) (*escalator*) all the way up to the **dì sān céng** 第三层 (第三層) (dee sahn tsuhng) (*third floor*), and enjoy checking out tons of **shāngpǐn** 商品 (shahng-peen) (*merchandise*) quietly by yourself, when all of a sudden a **shòuhuòyuán** 售货员 (售貨員) (show-hwaw-ywan) (*salesperson*) sneaks up behind you and says **Nǐ xiǎng mǎi shénme?** 你想买什么? (你想買甚麼?) (nee shyahng my shummuh?) (*What would you like to buy?*)

At this point, you really just want to be left alone, so you say **Wǒ zhǐ shì kànkàn. Xièxiè.** 我只是看看. 谢谢. (我只是看看. 謝謝.) (waw jir shir kahn-kahn. shyeh-shyeh) (*I'm just looking. Thanks.*)

Asking for help

But what if you really do want help? First, you'd better look around for that salesperson you just told to go away. You may not find too many others nearby when you finally need them. If your luck holds, though, here are some questions you may want to ask:

✔ **Nǎr yǒu wàitào?** 哪儿有外套? (哪兒有外套?) (nar yo why-taow?) (*Where are the jackets?*)

✔ **Néng bùnéng bāngmáng?** 能不能帮忙? (能不能幫忙?) (nung boo-nung bahng-mahng?) (*Can you help me?*)

✔ **Nǐ yǒu méiyǒu Yīngwén de shū?** 你有没有英文的书? (你有沒有英文的書?) (nee yo mayo eeng-one duh shoo?) (*Do you have any books in English?*)

✔ **Nǐmen mài búmài guāngpán?** 你们卖不卖光盘? (你們賣不賣光盤?) (nee-mun my boo-my gwahng-pahn?) (*Do you sell CDs?*)

✔ **Qǐng nǐ gěi wǒ kànkàn nǐde xīzhuāng.** 请你给我看看你的西装. (請你給我看看你的西裝.) (cheeng nee gay waw kahn-kahn nee-duh she-jwahng.) (*Please show me your [Western] suits.*)

✔ **Wǒ zhǎo yì běn yǒu guān Zhōngguó lìshǐ de shū.** 我找一本有关中国历史的书. (我找一本有關中國歷史的書.) (waw jaow ee bun yo gwan joong-gwaw lee-shir duh shoo.) (*I'm looking for a book about Chinese history.*)

Talkin' the Talk

Tania and Klara are in a clothing store. They try to get a **fúwùyuán** (foo-woo-ywan) (*attendant*) to help them locate dresses in their sizes. (Track 12)

Tania: **Xiǎojiě! Nǐ néng bāng wǒmen ma?**
shyaow-jyeh! nee nung bahng waw-men mah?
Miss! Can you help us?

Fúwùyuán: **Kéyǐ. Qǐng děng yíxià.**
kuh-yee. cheeng dung ee-shyah.
Yes. Just a moment.

After the store attendant puts some boxes away, she returns to help Tania and Klara.

Fúwùyuán: **Hǎo. Nǐmen yào mǎi shénme?**
how. nee-men yow my shummuh?
Okay. What did you want to buy?

Tania: **Nǎr yǒu qúnzi?**
nar yo chwun-dzuh?
Where are the skirts?

Fúwùyuán: **Qúnzi jiù zài nàr.**
chwun-dzuh jyo dzye nar.
The skirts are just over there.

Words to Know

xiǎojiě 小姐	shyaow-jyeh	Miss
Qǐng děng yíxià. 请等一下. (請等一下.)	cheeng dung ee-shyah.	Just a moment.
Qúnzi jiù zài nàr. 裙子就在那儿. (裙子就在那兒.)	chwun-dzuh jyo dzye nar.	The skirts are just over there.

Shopping for Clothes

Going shopping for clothes is an art — one requiring lots of patience and fortitude, not to mention lots of new vocabulary if you're going to do it in Chinese. You need to know how to ask for your own size, how to see whether something is available in a different color or fabric, and in general how to compare apples and oranges (or at least skirts and shirts).

What's your size?

If you ask for clothing in the **dàxiǎo** 大小 (dah-shyaow) (*size*) you're used to quoting in the United States when you're in Taiwan or mainland China, you're in for a surprise. The numbers you generally throw out when talking to sales-people in the United States are vastly different from the ones you have to get used to using when dealing with Chinese sizes.

Here are some useful phrases you may want to know:

- **Dàxiǎo búduì.** 大小不对. (大小不對.) (dah-shyaow boo-dway.) (*It's the wrong size.*)

- **Hěn héshēn.** 很合身. (hun huh-shun.) (*It fits really well.*)

- **Nín chuān duō dà hào?** 您穿多大号? (您穿多大號?) (neen chwan dwaw dah how?) (*What size are you?*)

- **Zài Měiguó wǒde chǐcùn shì wǔ hào.** 在美国我的尺寸是五号. (在美國我的尺寸是五號.) (dzye may-gwaw waw-duh chir-tswun shir woo how.) (*In America, I wear a size 5.*)

Instead of using the word **dàxiǎo**, you can say things like the following:

- **Nín chuān jǐ hào de chènshān?** 您穿几号的衬衫? (您穿記號的襯衫?) (neen chwahn jee how duh chun-shahn?) (*What size shirt do you wear?*)

- **Wǒ chuān sānshíqī hào.** 我穿三十七号. (我穿三十七號.) (waw chwahn sahn-shir-chee how.) (*I wear a size 37.*)

- **Wǒ chuān xiǎohào.** 我穿小号. (我穿小號.) (waw chwahn shyaow-how.) (*I wear a size small.*)

Of course, you can always guess your approximate size just by indicating you want to see something in one of the following categories:

- **xiǎo** 小 (shyaow) (*small*)

- **zhōng** 中 (joong) (*medium*)

- **dà** 大 (dah) (*large*)

Talkin' the Talk

Kathryn approaches a salesperson at a department store in Beijing. She's unsure of what size to ask for because the measurement systems are different in China than they are in the United States.

Kathryn:	**Xiǎojiě!** shyaow-jyeh! *Miss!*
Fúwùyuán:	**Nǐ hǎo. Xiǎng mǎi shénme?** nee how. shyahng my shummuh? *Hello. What would you like to buy?*
Kathryn:	**Wǒ xiǎng mǎi yíjiàn jiákè.** waw shyahng my ee-jyan jyah-kuh. *I'm looking for a jacket.*
Fúwùyuán:	**Hǎo ba. Nǐ chuān jǐ hào?** how bah. nee chwahn jee how? *Very well. What size are you?*
Kathryn:	**Wǒ bùzhīdào. Měiguó de hàomǎ hé Zhōngguó de hàomǎ hěn bùyíyàng.** waw boo-jir-daow. may-gwaw duh how-ma huh joong-gwaw duh how-ma hun boo-ee-yahng. *I don't know. American sizes are quite different from Chinese sizes.*

Fúwùyuán: **Wǒ gūjì nǐ chuān xiǎohào.**
waw goo-jee nee chwahn shyaow-how.
I would estimate you wear a size small.

Kathryn: **Hǎo ba. Nà, máfán nǐ gěi wǒ kànkàn xiǎohào de jiákè. Xièxiè.**
how bah. nah, mah-fahn nee gay waw kahn-kahn shyaow-how duh jyah-kuh. shyeh-shyeh.
That sounds about right. Would you mind showing me the small-size jackets, then? Thank you.

Words to Know

Nǐ chuān jǐ hào? 你穿几号? (你穿幾號?)	nee chwahn jee how?	What size are you?
wǒ bùzhīdào 我不知道	waw boo-jir-daow	I don't know
xiǎohào 小号 (小號)	shyaow-how	small

Comparing quality: Good, better, best

When you want to let loose with a superlative in order to say something is absolutely the best — or, for that matter, the worst —always keep this one little word in mind: **zuì** 最 (dzway), which means *the most* (it's the equivalent of the suffix -*est*).

Zuì is a word just waiting for something to follow it; otherwise it doesn't have much meaning. Here are some superlatives you may need to use from time to time:

- **zuì hǎo** 最好 (dzway how) (*best*)
- **zuì lèi** 最累 (dzway lay) (*the most tired*)
- **zuì màn** 最慢 (dzway mahn) (*the slowest*)
- **zuì máng** 最忙 (dzway mahng) (*the busiest*)

✔ **zuì qíguài** 最奇怪 (dzway chee-gwye) (*the strangest*)

✔ **zuì yǒumíng** 最有名 (dzway yo-meeng) (*the most famous*)

✔ **zuì yǒuqián** 最有钱 (最有錢) (dzway yo-chyan) (*the richest*)

If you just want to say that something is better than something else, or more something (not necessarily the best), you use the word **gèng** 更 (guhng) before an adjective. You can consider these the equivalent of the suffix *-er*. Another word that has the meaning of *more* or *-er* is **yìdiǎn** 一点 (一點) (ee-dyan). Although the term **gèng** comes before an adjective, the term **yìdiǎn** must appear after the adjective. Instead of saying **gèng kuài** 更快 (gung kwye) (*faster*), for example, you'd say **kuài yìdiǎn** 快一点 (快一點) (kwye ee-dyan) to mean *faster*.

Here are some examples:

> **gèng cōngmíng** 更聪明 (更聰明) (guhng tsoong-meeng) (*smarter*)
>
> **gèng hǎo** 更好 (guhng how) (*better*)
>
> **gèng guì** 更贵 (更貴) (guhng gway) (*more expensive*)
>
> **gèng piányì** 更便宜 (gung pyan-yee) (*cheaper*)
>
> **piányī yìdiǎn** 便宜一点 (便宜一點) (pyan-yee ee-dyan) (*cheaper*)
>
> **gèng kuài** 更快 (guhng kwye) (*faster*)
>
> **gèng màn** 更慢 (guhng mahn) (*slower*)
>
> **duǎn yìdiǎn** 短一点 (短一點) (dwahn ee-dyan) (*shorter*)
>
> **cháng yìdiǎn** 长一点 (長一點) (chahng ee-dyan) (*longer*)
>
> **xiǎo yìdiǎn** 小一点 (小一點) (shyaow ee-dyan) (*smaller*)
>
> **dà yìdiǎn** 大一点 (大一點) (dah ee-dyan) (*larger*)

Comparing two items

The simplest way to compare two items is by using the *coverb* (the part of speech akin to a preposition) **bǐ** 比 (bee) (*compared with*) between the two things you're comparing, followed by an adjective. If you say **A bǐ B hǎo** A 比 B 好 (A bee B how) you're saying *A is better than B*.

Here are some ways to make comparisons with **bǐ**:

> **Hóngde bǐ huángde hǎo.** 红的比黄的好. (紅的比黄的好.) (hoong-duh bee hwahng-duh how.) (*The red one is better than the yellow one.*)

Tā bǐ wǒ lǎo. 她比我老. (tah bee waw laow.) (*She's older than me.*)

Zhèige wūzi bǐ nèige dà. 这个屋子比那个大. (這個屋子比那個大.) (jay-guh woo-dzuh bee nay-guh dah.) (*This room is bigger than that one.*)

One way to convey similarity between two things is to use the coverbs **gēn** 跟 (gun) or **hé** 和 (huh) between the two things being compared, followed by the word **yíyàng** 一样 (一樣) (ee-yahng) (*the same*) and then the adjective. So if you say **A gēn B yíyàng dà** A 跟 B 一样大 (A 跟 B 一樣大) (A gun B ee-yahng dah), you're saying that A and B are equally large or are as big as each other. You can also just say **A gēn B yíyàng.,** meaning *A and B are the same.* Here are some other things you can say with this sentence pattern:

✔ **Gēge hé dìdi yíyàng gāo.** 哥哥和弟弟一样高. (哥哥和弟弟一樣高.) (guh-guh huh dee-dee ee-yahng gaow.) (*My older brother is as tall as my younger brother.*)

✔ **Māo gēn gǒu yíyàng tiáopí.** 猫跟狗一样调皮. (貓跟狗一樣調皮.) (maow gun go ee-yahng tyaow-pee.) (*Cats are just as naughty as dogs.*)

✔ **Wǒ gēn nǐ yíyàng dà.** 我跟你一样大. (我跟你一樣大.) (waw gun nee ee-yahng dah.) (*You and I are the same age.*)

So what if you want to make a negative comparison, such as *I'm not as tall as him?* For that, you have to use the following sentence pattern: **A méiyǒu B nèmme (adjective).** A 没有B 那么 (那麼) (adjective). (A mayo B nuh muh [adjective].) (*A isn't as [adjective] as B.*). You can see this pattern in action in the following sentences:

Shāyú méiyǒu jīnyú nèmme kě'ài. 鲨鱼没有金鱼那么可爱. (鯊魚沒有金魚那麼可愛.) (shah-yew mayo jeen-yew nummuh kuh-eye.) (*Sharks aren't as cute as goldfish.*)

Yīngwén méiyǒu Zhōngwén nèmme nán. 英文没有中文那么难. (英文沒有中文那麼難.) (eeng-one mayo joong-one nummuh nahn.) (*English isn't as difficult as Chinese.*)

Māo de wěiba méiyǒu tùzi de wěiba nèmme cū. 猫的尾巴没有兔子的尾巴那么粗. (猫的尾巴沒有兔子的尾巴那麼粗.) (maow duh way-bah mayo too-dzuh duh way-bah nummuh tsoo.) (*Cats' tails aren't as thick as the tails of rabbits.*)

Talkin' the Talk

Olivia and Lěiléi go shopping and check out some traditional Chinese women's dresses known as **qípáo** (chee-paow). Those are the ankle-length dresses with high necks and a high slit up the side of one leg.

Olivia: **Zhèi jiàn qípáo zěnmeyàng?**
jay jyan chee-paow dzummuh-yahng?
What do you think of this traditional Chinese dress?

Lěiléi: **Wǒ juéde hěn hǎo.**
waw jweh-duh hun how.
I think it looks great.

Olivia: **Zhēnde ma?**
jun-duh mah?
Really?

Lěiléi: **Zhēnde. Kěshì jīnsède méiyǒu hóngde nèmme piàoliàng.**
jun-duh. kuh-shir jeen-suh-duh mayo hoong-duh nummuh pyaow-lyahng.
Reallly. But the gold one isn't as pretty as the red one.

Olivia: **Jīnsède hé hóngde yíyàng guì ma?**
jeen-suh-duh huh hoong-duh ee-yahng gway mah?
Are the gold one and the red one the same price?

Lěiléi: **Méiyǒu. Jīnsède bǐ hóngde piányi.**
mayo. jeen-suh-duh bee hoong duh pyan-yee.
No. The gold one is less expensive than the red one.

Olivia: **Nà, wǒ jiù mǎi jīnsède.**
nah, waw jyoe my jeen-suh-duh.
In that case, I'll buy the gold one.

You can use two classifiers when it comes to clothing: **jiàn** and **tiáo.** *Classifiers* are the words used between a number or the words *this* or *that* and the clothing you're talking about. You use **jiàn** when you're talking about clothing worn on the upper part of the body and **tiáo** for clothes worn on the lower part. So you say **yíjiàn chènshān** 一件衬衫 (一件襯衫) (ee-jyan chun-shahn) (*one shirt*) or **sāntiáo kùzi** 三条裤子 (三條褲子) (sahn-tyaow koo-dzuh) (*three pairs of pants*).

What are you wearing? Chuān versus dài

Dài 戴 (dye) and **chuān** 穿 (chwan) both mean *to wear,* but they're used for different types of things you put on your body. In English, you can say you're wearing everything from hats to socks to skirts to even a necklace. In Chinese, though, you can only **dài** things like **màozi** 帽子 (maow-dzuh) (*hats*), **yǎnjìng** 眼镜 (镜) (yan-jeeng) (*glasses*), and **xiézi** 鞋子 (shyeh-dzuh) (*shoes*) — in other words, articles more akin to accessories than to actual clothing. However, you **chuān** things like **qúnzi** 裙子 (chewn-dzuh) (*skirts*) and **dàyī** 大衣 (dah-ee) (*coats*).

Here are some things you can **chuān:**

- **bèixīn** 背心 (bay-sheen) (*vest*)
- **chángkù** 长裤 (長褲) (chahng-koo) (*pants*)
- **chángxiù** 长袖 (長袖) (chahng-shyow) (*long-sleeved shirt*)
- **chènshān** 衬衫 (襯衫) (chun-shahn) (*blouse*)
- **dàyī** 大衣 (dah-ee) (*coat*)
- **duǎnkù** 短裤 (短褲) (dwan-koo) (*shorts*)
- **duǎnxiù** 短袖 (dwahn-shyow) (*short-sleeved shirt*)
- **gāogēnxiě** 高跟鞋 (gaow-gun-shyeh) (*high heels*)
- **jiákè** 夹克 (夾克) (jyah-kuh) (*jacket*)
- **kùzi** 裤子 (褲子) (koo-dzuh) (*pants*)
- **nèiyī** 内衣 (nay-ee) (*underwear*)
- **niúzǎikù** 牛仔裤 (牛仔褲) (nyo-dzye-koo) (*blue jeans*)
- **qúnzi** 裙子 (chewn-dzuh) (*skirt*)
- **tuōxié** 拖鞋 (twaw-shyeh) (*slippers*)
- **wàzi** 袜子 (襪子) (wah-dzuh) (*socks*)
- **yǔyī** 雨衣 (yew-ee) (*raincoat*)

Here are some things you can **dài** but not **chuān:**

- **lǐngdài** 领带 (領帶) (leen-dye) (*necktie*)
- **shǒubiǎo** 手表 (show-byaow) (*wristwatch*)
- **shǒutào** 手套 (show-taow) (*gloves*)
- **zhūbǎo** 珠宝 (joo-baow) (*jewelry*)

Asking about the color and material

When you go shopping for clothes, you have a chance to compare all the different **yánsè** 颜色 (顏色) (yan-suh) (*colors*) they come in and choose the one that looks the best on you. Do you generally prefer **dānsè** 单色 (單色) (dahn-suh) (*solid colors*) or **huā** 花 (hwah) (*patterned*) shirts? What about a **shēn yìdiǎn** 深一点 (深一點) (shun ee-dyan) (*darker*) or **dàn yìdiǎn** 淡一点 (淡一點) (dahn ee-dyan) (*lighter*) shade? Whatever your clothing preferences are, after you know how to express your heart's desire with the correct word, you can be sure to ask for what you like.

The following is a list of handy words to use the next time you go shopping either for clothes or for material to create your own. **Shénme yánsè** 什么颜色? (甚麼顏色?) (shummuh yan-suh) (*what color*) is your favorite from the following list? Don't be shy to speak up about your preferences. If someone wants you to wear pink with purple polka dots to a wedding, you can always politely just say, **Yánsè búduì.** 颜色不对. (顏色 不對.) (yan-suh boo-dway.) (*The color is wrong.*) and leave it at that.

- **bái** 白 (bye) (*white*)
- **fēnhóng** 粉红 (粉紅) (fun-hoong) (*pink*)
- **hēi** 黑 (hey) (*black*)
- **hóng** 红 (紅) (hoong) (*red*)
- **huáng** 黄 (hwahng) (*yellow*)
- **júhóng** 橘红 (橘紅) (jyew-hoong) (*orange*)
- **lán** 蓝 (藍) (lahn) (*blue*)
- **zǐ** 紫 (dzuh) (*purple*)

Liàozi 料子 (lyaow-dzuh) (*fabric*) is another important consideration when you're picking out clothes. Check out these terms for common clothing materials:

- **duànzi** 缎子 (緞子) (dwahn-dzuh) (*satin*)
- **kāiīmǐ** 开司米 (開司米) (kye-uh-mee) (*cashmere*)
- **sīchóu** 丝绸 (絲綢) (suh-cho) (*silk*)
- **yángmáo** 羊毛 (yahng-maow) (*wool*)

Talkin' the Talk

Lauren goes shopping for sweaters with her husband Evan and asks him to weigh in on which color looks best on her.

Lauren: **Zhèi jiàn máoyī nǐ juéde zěnmeyàng?**
jay jyan maow-ee nee jweh-duh dzummuh-yahng?
What do you think of this sweater?

Evan: **Nèi jiàn máoyī tài xiǎo. Yánsè yě búpiàoliàng.**
nay jyan maow-ee tye shyaow. yan-suh yeh
boo-pyaow-lyahng.
That sweater is too small. The color doesn't look good either.

Lauren: **Nǐ xǐhuān shénme yánsè?**
nee she-hwahn shummuh yan-suh?
What color do you like?

Evan: **Wǒ xǐhuān hóngde. Búyào nèige hēide.**
waw she-hwahn hoong-duh. boo-yaow nay-guh
hey-duh.
I like the red one. You shouldn't get the black one.

Lauren: **Hǎole. Nà, wǒ jiù mǎi hóngde ba.**
how-luh. Nah, waw jyo my hoong-duh bah.
Okay. In that case, I'll buy the red one.

When the possessive particle **de** is attached to an adjective and there's no noun following it, it can be translated as *the one that is (adjective)*, as in **hóngde** 红的 (紅的) (hoong-duh) (*the red one*), **dà de** 大的 (dah-duh) (*the big one*), **tián de** 甜的 (tyan-duh) (*the sweet one*), and so on.

Shopping for Other Items

Of course, clothes aren't the only things in the world to shop for (although I know some would beg to differ with me). How about some antiques or high-tech toys? The possibilities are endless in this consumer-oriented world.

Hunting for antiques

One of the best places in the world to go searching for **gǔdǒng** 古董 (goo-doong) (*antiques*) is — you guessed it — China. **Gǔdǒng diàn** 古董店 (goo-doong dyan) (*antique shops*) abound in major cities near large stores and in small alleyways. You can buy everything from 200-year-old **diāokè pǐn** 雕刻品 (dyaow-kuh peen) (*carved objects*) to 100-year-old **bí yān hú** 鼻烟壶 (鼻煙壺) (bee yan who) (*snuff bottles*). You can find all sorts of rare things.

After you find the perfect antique item, though, you need to deal with all the possible export restrictions, like for porcelain that is older than 200 years or some types of rare wood products. You have to have a red wax seal put on the item in order to legally take it out of China. The cultural artifacts bureau of the city in which you buy the item must apply the seal.

Slightly southwest of **Tiān'ānmén Square** in **Beijing** lies **Liúlìchǎng** 琉璃厂 (琉璃廠) (lyoe-lee-chahng), an area considered the best in the city for antiques and other traditional arts and crafts. In **Shanghai**, the **Dōngtái** 东台 (東台) (doong-tye) antiques market is the one to look for, not far from **Huáihǎi Lù** 淮海路 (hwye-hi loo). You can even find a Ghost Market in the Old Town Bazaar where folks go for weekend antique shopping. The Ghost Market is so named because of the ungodly hour the vendors begin setting up shop — a time before sunrise when only ghosts can check out what's on sale. Even though you're dealing with antiques, you're still allowed to haggle over the price, so don't be shy trying to get the best deal possible.

Here are some words and phrases that come in handy when you're hunting for antiques:

✔ **dēnglóng** 灯笼 (燈籠) (dung-loong) (*lantern*)

✔ **fóxiàng** 佛像 (faw-shyahng) (*Buddhas*)

✔ **gǔdǒng jiājù** 古董家具 (goo-doong jyah-jyew) (*antique furniture*)

✔ **guìzi** 柜子 (櫃子) (gway-dzuh) (*chest*)

✔ **jìbài yòng de zhuōzi** 祭拜用的桌子 (jee-bye yoong duh jwaw-dzuh) (*altar table*)

✔ **jǐngtàilán** 景泰蓝 (景泰藍) (jeeng-tye-lahn) (*cloisonné*)

✔ **píngfēng** 屏风 (屏風) (peeng-fung) (*screen*)

✔ **shénxiàng** 神像 (shun-shyahng) (*idol*)

✔ **shūfǎ** 书法 (書法) (shoo-fah) (*calligraphy*)

✔ **xiōngzhēn** 胸针 (胸針) (shyoong-juhn) (*brooch*)

✔ **xiùhuā zhìpǐn** 绣花制品 (繡花製品) (shyow-hwah jir-peen) (*embroidery*)

✔ **yù** 玉 (yew) (*jade*)

These sentences can help you find precisely what you're looking for and avoid surprises when you try to take your treasures home:

✔ **Kéyǐ bùkéyǐ jiā zhúnxǔ chūguó de huǒqī yìn?** 可以不可以加准许出国的货器印? (可以不可以加准許出國的貨器印?) (kuh-yee boo-kuh-yee jyah jwun-shyew choo-gwaw duh hwaw-chee yeen?) (*Can you put the export seal on it?*)

✔ **Něige cháodài de?** 哪个朝代的? (哪個朝代的?) (nay-guh chaow-dye duh?) (*Which dynasty is it from?*)

✔ **Néng dài chūguó ma?** 能带出国吗? (能帶出國嗎?) (nung dye choo-gwaw mah?) (*Can it be taken out of China?*)

✔ **Nǐde gǔdǒng dìtǎn zài nǎr?** 你的古董地毯在哪儿? (你的古董地毯在哪兒?) (nee-duh goo-doong dee-tahn dzye nar?) (*Where are your antique carpets?*)

✔ **Zhèige duōshǎo nián?** 这个多少年? (這個多少年?) (jay-guh dwaw-shaow nyan?) (*How old is this?*)

✔ **Zhèi shì něige cháodài de?** 这是哪个朝代的? (這是哪個朝代的?) (jay shir nay-guh chaow-dye duh?) (*Which dynasty is this from?*)

Buying high-tech and electronic things

New electronic gadgets appear on the market every two minutes these days, or so it seems. Just when you think you've gotten the latest model of something, another one comes out with great fanfare. Following is a list of the most commonly used (and most commonly bought) items you may need — even while reading *Chinese For Dummies*. Now you know how to ask for what you want when you walk in that store.

✔ **chuánzhēn jī** 传真机 (傳真機) (chwahn-juhn jee) (*fax machine*)

✔ **dǎyìnjī** 打印机 (打印機) (dah-yeen-jee) (*printer*)

✔ **diànnǎo shèbèi** 电脑设备 (電腦設備) (dyan-now shuh-bay) (*computer equipment*)

✔ **diànshì jī** 电视机 (電視機) (dyan-shir jee) (*TV*)

✔ **gèrén diànnǎo** 个人电脑 (個人電腦) (guh-run dyan-now) (*PC*)

✔ **guāngpán** 光盘 (光盤) (gwahng-pahn) (*CD*)

✔ **shǔbiāo** 鼠标 (鼠標) (shoo-byaow) (*mouse*)

- **jiànpán** 键盘 (鍵盤) (jyan-pahn) (*keyboard*)
- **jìsuàn qī** 计算器 (計算器) (jee-swan chee) (*calculator*)
- **kǎlā'ōukè jī** 卡拉欧克机 (卡拉歐克機) (kah-lah-o-kuh jee) (*karaoke machine*)
- **MP3 bōfàngqì** MP3 播放器 (MP3 baw-fahng-chee) (*MP3 player*)
- **ruǎnjiàn** 软件 (軟件) (rwahn-jyan) (*software*)
- **sǎomiáoyí** 扫描仪 (掃描儀) (saow-myaow-ee) (*scanner*)
- **shèxiàng jī** 摄像机 (攝像機) (shuh-shyahng jee) (*camcorder*)
- **shǒutíshì** 手提式 (show-tee-shir) (*laptop*)
- **xiǎnshìqì** 显示器 (顯示器) (shyan-shir-chee) (*monitor*)
- **xiǎo píngbǎn diànnǎo** 小平板电脑 (小平板電腦) (shyaow peeng-bahn dyan-naow) (*small tablet PC*)
- **yìngjiàn** 硬件 (eeng-jyan) (*computer hardware*)
- **zǔhé yīnxiǎng** 组合音响 (組合音響) (dzoo-huh yeen-shyahng) (*stereo system*)

Getting a Good Price and Paying

Folks the world over want to get good deals on their purchases. At least they should. This section helps you discover the joys (and pitfalls) of haggling in Chinese.

Negotiating prices at the night market

One of the fun things to do in Taiwan and mainland China is to visit one of the lively night markets that abound. There, you can find anything from clothing and jewelry to antiques and food. Because the Chinese love to shop and **tǎojià huánjià** 讨价还价 (討價還價) (taow-jyah hwahn-jyah) (*haggle*), you have plenty of company on your sojourns.

You should always assume that prices are negotiable in an open air market. You can always ask one of the following and see what happens:

- **Néng bùnéng piányì yìdiǎr?** 能不能便宜一点儿? (能不能便宜一點兒?) (nung boo-nung pyan-yee ee-dyar?) (*Can you sell it more cheaply?*)
- **Néng bùnéng shǎo yìdiǎr?** 能不能少一点儿? (能不能少一點兒?) (nung boo-nung shaow ee-dyar?) (*Can you lower the price?*)

Or you can always play hardball and say something like **Zěnme zhèmma guì ah?** 怎么这么贵啊? (怎麼這麼貴啊?) (dzuh-muh juh-muh gway ah?) (*Why is this so expensive?*) in an exasperated voice, start walking away, and see what happens. (Bet they come back with a lower price.)

These haggling-related phrases are also worth knowing:

- **Dǎ zhé, hǎo búhǎo?** 打折, 好不好? (dah juh, how boo-how?) (*How about giving me a discount?*)

- **Kéyǐ jiǎng jià ma?** 可以讲价吗? (可以講價嗎?) (kuh-yee jyahng jyah mah?) (*Can we negotiate the price?*)

- **Nǐmen yào bú yào Měiyuán?** 你们要不要美元? (你們要不要美元?) (nee-men yaow boo yaow may-ywan?) (*Do you want U.S. dollars?*)

- **Zhèige duōshǎo qián?** 这个多少钱 (這個多少錢?) (jay-guh dwaw-shaow chyan?) (*How much is this?*)

If you see something called a **Yǒuyí Shāngdiàn** 友谊商店 (友誼商店) (yo-ee shahng-dyan) (*Friendship Store*), be aware that it's one of the ubiquitous state-run stores in China, so prices are generally fixed. However, bargaining is the norm everywhere else. Beware of goods with no prices marked on them! If you ask about them, you'll probably be quoted a price far different than that charged to the locals. Often, you can get 5 to 10 percent taken off any price quoted verbally, so try to practice bargaining before you set foot in a street market.

Paying for your purchase (or demanding a refund)

When you finish checking out all the merchandise, haggling (or not) over the price, and deciding on just what to buy, you probably start reaching for your **qiánbāo** 钱包 (錢包) (chyan-baow) (*wallet*) to see whether you should take out your **xìnyòng kǎ** 信用卡 (sheen-yoong kah) (*credit card*) or some **xiànqián** 现钱 (現錢) (shyan-chyan) (*cash*) or, if you got a really good deal, just some **língqián** 零钱 (零錢) (leeng-chyan) (*small change*). When you **fùqián** 付钱 (付錢) (foo-chyan) (*pay*), you may also want to get a **shōujù** 收据 (收據) (show-jyew) (*receipt*).

If you end up being **bùyúkuài** 不愉快 (boo-yew-kwye) (*unhappy*) about your purchase, one of these phrases may come in handy when you try to **tuì huí** 退回 (tway hway) (*return*) your merchandise:

- **Duì wǒ bù héshēn.** 对我不合身. (對我不合身.) (dway waw boo huh-shun) (*It doesn't fit me.*)

- **Qǐng nǐ bāo qǐlái.** 请你包起来. (請你包起來.) (cheeng nee baow chee-lye.) (*Please wrap these/this.*)

✔ **Qǐng nǐ bǎ qián jìrù wǒde xìnyòng kǎ.** 请你把钱计入我的信用卡. (請你把錢計入我的信用卡.) (cheeng nee bah chyan jee-roo waw-duh sheen-yoong kah.) (*Please refund my credit card.*)

✔ **Wǒ néng bùnéng jiàn zǒngjīnglǐ?** 我能不能见总经理? (我能不能見總經理?) (waw nung boo-nung jyan dzoong-jeeng-lee?) (*May I see the manager?*)

✔ **Wǒ yào tuìkuǎn.** 我要求退款. (waw yaow tway-kwahn.) (*I want a refund.*)

✔ **Wǒ yào tuì huò.** 我要退货. (我要退貨.) (waw yaow tway hwaw.) (*I would like to return this.*)

Here's how you ask for change:

Nǐ yǒu méiyǒu yí kuài qián de língqián? 你有没有一块钱的零钱? (你有没有一塊錢的零錢?) (nee yo mayo ee kwye chyan duh leeng-chyan?) (*Do you have change for a dollar?*)

Fun & Games

A.　　　　B.　　　　C.

D.　　　　E.

Take a look at the illustrations. In what type of store would you find these items? The answers are in Appendix D.

  A. **Zhūbǎo diàn** 珠宝店 (珠寶店) _____

  B. **Cài shìchǎng** 菜市场 (菜市場) _____

  C. **Huādiàn** 花店 _____

  D. **Yàofáng** 药房 (藥方)_____

  E. **Wánjù diàn** 玩具店_____

Chapter 10

Exploring the Town

- -

In This Chapter

▶ Dropping in on a show

▶ Checking out museums and historical sites

▶ Taking in a movie or concert

▶ Hanging out in bars and clubs

- -

Don't even think of staying around your hotel or house on a beautiful sunny day — especially if you're about to explore a new **chéngshì** 城市 (chuhng-shir) (*city*) in China. You have so much to see and do. You may want to check out a performance of Peking Opera or head over to the nearest museum to take in an art exhibit. Or perhaps a movie or concert and a night-cap are more your style. However you want to spend your time in town, this chapter gives you the vocab you need.

Attending a Performance

Plan on taking in a few **yǎnchū** 演出 (yan-choo) (*shows*) in the near future? You have so much to choose from nowadays. You can check out some **gējù** 歌剧 (歌劇) (guh-jyew) (*operas*), or, if you prefer, a **bāléiwú** 芭蕾舞 (bah-lay-woo) (*ballet*) or a **yīnyuèhuì** (yin-yweh-hway) (*music concert*).

Shanghai in particular is pretty famous for its **zájì tuán** 杂技团 (雜技團) (dzah-jee twahn) (*acrobatics troupes*).

The following sections help you talk about all sorts of performances, from naming your favorite kind of music to getting your tickets and chatting about others' experiences.

Exploring different types of music

You often hear that the language of music crosses international boundaries. If you're feeling a bit exhausted after practicing Chinese, you can head to a musical event in the evening where you can relax. Let the music transport you to another mental space.

Here are some terms to help you talk about music and performances:

- **dàiwèiyuán** 带位员 (帶位員) (dye-way-ywan) (*usher*)
- **gē chàng huì** 歌唱会 (歌唱會) (guh chahng hway) (*choral recital*)
- **gǔdiǎn yīnyuè** 古典音乐 (古典音樂) (goo-dyan een-yweh) (*classical music*)
- **jiāoxiǎng yuè** 交响乐 (交響樂) (jyaow-shyahng yweh) (*symphonic music*)
- **jiémùdān** 节目单 (節目單) (jyeh-moo-dahn) (*program*)
- **jùchǎng** 剧场 (劇場) (jyew-chahng) (*theatre*)
- **juéshì yīnyuè** 爵士音乐 (爵士音樂) (jyweh-shir een-yweh) (*jazz music*)
- **lǐtáng** 礼堂 (禮堂) (lee-tahng) (*auditorium*)
- **míngē** 民歌 (meen-guh) (*folk song*)
- **mùjiān xiūxi** 幕间休息 (幕間休息) (moo-jyan shyo-she) (*intermission*)
- **qì yuè** 器乐 (器樂) (chee yweh) (*instrumental music*)
- **shìnèi yuè** 室内乐 (室內樂) (shir-nay yweh) (*chamber music*)
- **yáogǔn yuè** 摇滚乐 (搖滾樂) (yaow-gun yweh) (*rock 'n' roll*)
- **Zhōngguó gǔdiǎn yīnyuè** 中国古典音乐 (中國古典音樂) (joong-gwaw goo-dyan yeen-yweh) (*classical Chinese music*)

At the end of a concert in China, you don't hear anyone yelling "Encore!" What you do hear is **Zài lái yíge, zài lái yíge!** 再来一个! (再來一個!) (dzye lye ee-guh, dzye lye ee-guh!) (*Bring on one more!*)

Talkin' the Talk

Lydia and Nelson discuss what kind of concert to attend this weekend.

Nelson: **Wǒmen zhèige zhōumò qù yīnyuè tīng tīng Zhōngguó gǔdiǎn yīnyuè ba.**
waw-men jay-guh joe-maw chyew een-yweh teeng teeng joong-gwaw goo-dyan een-yweh bah.
Let's go to the concert hall to hear a classical Chinese music concert this weekend.

Lydia: **Wǒ bùxǐhuān Zhōngguó gǔdiǎn yīnyuè. Wǒ gèng xǐhuān juéshì yīnyuè.**
waw boo-she-hwahn joong-gwaw goo-dyan yeen-yweh. waw gung she-hwahn jyweh-shir een-yweh.
I don't like classical Chinese music. I prefer jazz.

Nelson: **Juéshì yīnyuè tài qíguài. Yáogǔn yuè yě bùxǐhuān.**
jyweh-shir een-yweh tye chee-gwye. yaow-gwun yweh yeh boo-she-hwahn.
Jazz is too strange. I also don't like rock 'n' roll.

Lydia: **Nǐ dàgài zhǐ xǐhuān jiāoxiǎng yuè nèi lèi de yīnyuè ba.**
nee dah-gye jir she-hwahn jyaow-shyahng yweh nay lay duh een-yweh bah.
You probably only like symphonic music and that sort of thing.

Nelson: **Duì le.**
dway luh.
Yup.

Words to Know

yīnyuè tīng 音乐厅 (音樂廳)	yin-yweh teeng	concert hall
Zhōngguó gǔdiǎnyīnyuè 中国古典音乐 (中國古典音樂)	joong-gwaw goo-dyan-yeen-yweh	classical Chinese music
juéshì yīnyuè 爵士音乐 (爵士音樂)	jyweh-shir een-yweh	jazz music
qíguài 奇怪	chee-gwye	strange
yáogǔn yuè 摇滚乐 (搖滾樂)	yaow-gwun yweh	rock 'n' roll
jiāoxiǎng yuè 交响乐 (交響樂)	jyaow-shyahng yweh	symphonic music
Duì le. 对了. (對了.)	dway luh.	Yup.

Buying a ticket

Before you can attend any performances, however, you have to buy a **piào** 票 (pyaow) (*ticket*) or two. The following phrases should help you get what you want, or at least understand what you're being told:

- **Duìbùqǐ, jīntiān wǎnshàng de piào dōu màiwán le.** 对不起, 今天晚上的票都卖完了. (對不起, 今天晚上的票都賣完了.) (dway-boo-chee, jin-tyan wahn-shahng duh pyaow doe my-wahn luh.) (*I'm sorry, tickets for tonight are all sold out.*)

- **Shénme shíhòu kāiyǎn?** 什么时侯开演? (甚麼時候開演?) (shummuh shir-ho kye-yan?) (*What time does the show begin?*)

- **Shénme shíhòu yǎn wán?** 什么时侯演完? (甚麼時候演完?) (shummuh shir-ho yan wahn?) (*What time does the show end?*)

- **Wǒ yào mǎi yì zhāng dàrén piào, liǎng zhāng értóng piào.** 我要买一张大人票, 两张儿童票. (我要買一張大人票, 兩張兒童票.) (waw yaow my ee jahng dah-run pyaow, lyahng jahng are-toong pyaow) (*I'd like to buy one adult ticket and two kid's tickets.*)

- **Yǒu méiyǒu jīntiān wǎnshàng yǎnchū de piào?** 有没有今天晚上演出的票? (yo mayo jin-tyan wahn-shahng yan-choo duh pyaow?) (*Are there any tickets to tonight's performance?*)

- **Zài nǎr kéyǐ mǎidào piào?** 在哪儿可以买到票? (在哪兒可以買到票?) (dzye nar kuh-yee my-daow pyaow?) (*Where can I buy tickets?*)

Asking whether someone has done something

If you're thinking of going out on the town with a new date, and you want to ask them whether they have ever done something so you can plan something special, just add the particle **-guò** 过 (過) (gwaw) to the verb and use the question word **ma** 吗 (嗎) (mah) or **méiyǒu** 没有 (mayo) at the end. Here are some examples:

Nǐ kànguò Jīngjù ma? 你看过京剧吗? (你看過京劇嗎?) (nee kahn-gwaw jeeng-jyew mah?) (*Have you ever seen Peking Opera?*)

Nǐ chīguò xiā méiyǒu? 你吃过虾没有? (你吃過蝦沒有?) (nee chir-gwaw shyah mayo?) (*Have you ever eaten shrimp?*)

Nǐ qùguò Měiguó ma? 你去过美国吗? (你去過美國嗎?) (nee chyew-gwaw may-gwaw mah?) (*Have you ever been to America?*)

Take a peek at Peking Opera

Have you ever been to **Jīngjù** (jeeng-jyew) (_Peking Opera_)? This Chinese opera is one of the most beloved art forms in China, with a history of over 200 years. The opera is a great spectacle of music, song, and acrobatics, telling and retelling great works of Chinese history and literature. Performances abound, especially during the traditional festivals when everyone is off work.

Even though its title is Peking (Beijing) Opera, it actually originated in the Anhui and Hubei provinces. Originally staged for the royal family, it came to Beijing in 1790 and later became familiar to the general public. Thousands of local branches of Chinese Opera exist (including Peking), each with a unique dialect. Opera is the one art form in a country of over 1 billion people that appeals to every level of society.

To answer any of these questions, you can repeat the verb plus **guò** if the answer is yes, or simply say **méiyǒu,** meaning _No, I haven't._ You can also say **méiyǒu** [verb] **guò** if you want.

If you happen to do something **chángcháng** 常常 (chahng-chahng) (_often_) or just **yǒude shíhòu** 有的时侯 (yo-duh shir-ho) (_sometimes_), don't be shy about saying so. You can use these adverbs in both the questions and the answers.

Exploring Museums and Galleries

Theatre shows and live musical performances aren't the only forms of entertainment you can see to get your fill of **wénhuà** 文化 (one-hwah) (_culture_). One of the nicest, calmest activities to do at your own pace is to visit a **bówùguǎn** 博物馆 (博物館) (baw-woo-gwahn) (_museum_) or **huàláng** 画廊 (畫廊) (hwah-lahng) (_gallery_).

You can check out anything from **gǔdàide yìshù pǐn** 古代的艺术品 (古代的藝術品) (goo-dye-duh ee-shoo peen) (_ancient artifacts_) to **shānshuǐ huà** 山水画 (山水畫) (shahn-shway hwah) (_landscape painting_) to **xiàndài yìshù** 现代艺术 (現代藝術) (shyan-dye ee-shoo) (_modern art_). Sometimes the best reason to go to a **bówùguǎn** is to buy some **lǐwù** 礼物 (禮物) (lee-woo) (_gifts_) and some cool **zhāotiē** 招贴 (招貼) (jaow-tyeh) (_posters_) for yourself.

Here are some questions you may want to ask in a museum or gallery:

  ✔ **Bówùguǎn jǐdiǎn zhōng kāimén?** 博物馆几点钟开门? (博物館幾點鐘開門?) (baw-woo-gwahn jee-dyan joong kye-mun?) (_What time does the museum open?_)

✔ **Lǐpǐn shāngdiàn shénme shíhòu guānmén?** 礼品商店什么时侯关门? (禮品商店甚麼時候關門?) (lee-peeng shahng-dyan shummuh shir-ho gwahn-mun?) (*What time does the gift shop close?*)

✔ **Nǐmen mài búmài zhāotiē?** 你们卖不卖招贴? (你們賣不賣招貼?) (nee-mun my boo-my jaow-tyeh?) (*Do you sell posters?*)

Talkin' the Talk

George arrives at the local art museum pretty late in the day, so he approaches the clerk to ask some questions. (Track 13)

George:	**Qǐngwèn, nǐmen jǐdiǎn zhōng guānmén?**
	cheeng-one, nee-mun jee-dyan joong gwahn-mun?
	Excuse me, what time do you close?
Clerk:	**Zhèige bówùguǎn wǎnshàng liù diǎn zhōng guānmén.**
	jay-guh baw-woo-gwahn wahn-shahng lyo dyan joong gwahn-mun.
	This museum closes at 6:00 p.m.
George:	**Xiànzài yǐjīng wǔdiǎn duō le. Wǒ néng bùnéng miǎnfèi jìnqù?**
	shyan-dzye ee-jeeng woo-dyan dwaw luh. waw nung boo-nung myan-fay jeen-chyew?
	It's now already after 5:00. May I enter for free?
Clerk:	**Bùxíng. Hái yào fùqián. Shí kuài yì zhāng.**
	boo-sheeng. hi yaow foo-chyan. shir kwye ee jahng.
	No. You still have to pay. It's $10 a ticket.
George:	**Nà, wǒ míngtiān zài lái, duō huā yìdiǎr shíjiān zài zhèr. Xièxiè.**
	nah, waw meeng-tyan dzye lye, dwaw hwah ee-dyar shir-jyan dzye jar. shyeh-shyeh.
	In that case, I'll come back tomorrow to spend a little more time here. Thanks.

Words to Know

Qǐngwèn 请问 (請問)	cheeng-one	May I ask . . . ?
bówùguǎn 博物馆 (博物館)	baw-woo-gwahn	museum
miǎnfèi 免费 (免費)	myan-fay	free of charge

Visiting Historical Sites

Make sure to take at least one well-coordinated trip to a historical site if you visit China, even if you have only a week for business. Take the **Cháng Chéng** 长城 (長城) (chahng chung) (*Great Wall*), for example. Just north of Beijing, the wall is one of the greatest man-made objects on earth.

And while you're on your way to the Great Wall, you may want to stop off at the **Míng shísān líng** 明十三陵 (meeng shir-sahn leeng) (*Ming Tombs*), which contain the mausoleums of 13 **Ming** dynasty (1368–1644) emperors guarded by stone animals and warrior statues.

By far the easiest way to see the major historical sites in China is to join a tour. Here are some phrases that may come in handy:

- **Bàn tiān duōshǎo qián?** 半天多少钱? (半天多少錢?) (bahn tyan dwaw-shaow chyan?) (*How much for half a day?*)

- **Lǚxíngshè zài nǎr?** 旅行社在哪儿? (旅行社在哪兒?) (lyew-sheeng-shuh dzye nar?) (*Where's the travel agency?*)

- **Nǐ yǒu méiyǒu lǚyóu shǒucè?** 你有没有旅游手册? (你有沒有旅遊手冊?) (nee yo mayo lyew-yo show-tsuh?) (*Do you have a guidebook?*)

- **Yǒu méiyǒu shuō Yīngwén de dǎoyóu?** 有没有说英文的导游? (有沒有說英文的導遊?) (yo mayo shwaw eeng-one duh daow-yo?) (*Are there any English-speaking guides?*)

Some of China's most-visited historical sites include the Great Wall, the Forbidden City in Beijing, and the terra-cotta warriors of Xi'an, where an army of over 6,000 carved warriors and horses stands guard over the tomb of China's first Emperor, **Qín Shǐhuáng** (chin shir-hwahng), who dates back to the third century BCE.

Talkin' the Talk

Sammy hires a taxi and takes his two children to the Jade Buddha Temple in Shanghai, where he tries to get entrance tickets from the clerk. He's eager to show his children the temple's **Song** dynasty (960–1279) architecture.

Sammy: **Qǐngwèn, zài nǎr kéyǐ mǎi piào?**
cheeng-one, dzye nar kuh-yee my pyaow?
Excuse me, where can I buy tickets for admission?

Clerk: **Jiù zài zhèr.**
jyo dzye jar.
You can buy them here.

Sammy: **Hǎojíle. Piàojià duōshǎo?**
how-jee-luh. pyaow-jyah dwaw-shaow?
Great. How much is the ticket price?

Clerk: **Yìzhāng shí kuài.**
ee-jahng shir kwye.
Tickets are $10 each.

Sammy: **Xiǎo háizi miǎnfèi ma?**
shyaow hi-dzuh myan-fay mah?
Do children get in free?

Clerk: **Bù miǎnfèi, kěshì xiǎo háizi bànpiào.**
boo myan-fay, kuh-shir shyaow hi-dzuh bahn-pyaow.
No, but they're half price.

Sammy: **Wǒmen kě bù kěyǐ zhàoxiàng?**
waw-mun kuh boo kuh-yee jaow-shyahng?
May we take pictures?

Clerk: **Dāngrán kěyǐ. Méiyǒu wèntí.**
dahng-rahn kuh-yee. mayo one-tee.
Of course you can. No problem.

Words to Know

Piàojià duōshǎo? 票价多少 (票價多少?)	pyaow-jyah dwaw-shaow?	How much is the ticket price?
zhàoxiàng 照相	jaow-shyahng	to take a photo
dāngrán 当然 (當然)	dahng-rahn	of course
Méiyǒu wèntí. 没有问题. (沒有問題.)	mayo one-tee.	No problem.

Going to the Movies

After a full day of sightseeing, you may want to relax, kick back, and take in a **diànyǐng** 电影 (電影) (dyan-yeeng) (*movie*). At the movies you can sit and watch what's on the **yínmù** 银幕 (銀幕) (yeen-moo) (*screen*) without walking or talking. But what to do when the lights dim and you suddenly realize the film is completely in **Zhōngwén** 中文 (joong-one) (*Chinese*), without any **Yīngwén zìmù** 英文字母 (eeng-one dzuh-moo) (*English subtitles*) whatsoever? You read this book, of course!

What kind of movie do you want to see? Table 10-1 gives you a few genres to choose from:

Table 10-1	Movie Genres	
Chinese	*Pronunciation*	*English*
àiqíng piān 爱情片 (愛情片)	eye-cheeng pyan	*romance*
dònghuà piān 动画片 (動畫片)	doong-hwah pyan	*cartoon*
dòngzuò piān 动作片 (動作片)	doong-dzwaw pyan	*action*
gùshi piān 故事片	goo-shir pyan	*drama*
jìlù piān 纪录片 (紀錄片)	jee-loo pyan	*documentary*
kǒngbù piān 恐怖片	koong-boo pyan	*horror*
wàiguópiān 外国片 (外國片)	wye-gwaw-pyan	*foreign film*
wǔxiá piān 武侠片 (武俠片)	woo-shyah pyan	*kung-fu*
xǐjù piān 喜剧片 (喜劇片)	she-jyew pyan	*comedy*

Talkin' the Talk

Wendy and Elly decide to go to the movies tonight.

Wendy: **Wǒmen jīntiān wǎnshàng qù kàn yíbù diànyǐng ba.**
waw-men jin-tyan wahn-shahng chyew kahn ee-boo dyan-yeeng bah.
Let's go see a movie tonight.

Elly: **Jīntiān yǎn shénme?**
jin-tyan yan shummuh?
What's playing today?

Wendy: **Yíge Zhāng Yìmóu dǎoyǎn de piānzi. Wǒ wàngle nèige míngzi.**
ee-guh jahng ee-moe daow-yan duh pyan-dzuh. waw wahng-luh nay-guh meeng-dzuh.
A film directed by Zhang Yimou. I forget the name.

Elly:. **Shì shuō Yīngwén de ma?**
shir shwaw eeng-one duh mah?
Is it in English?

Wendy: **Búshì, kěshì yǒu Yīngwén zìmù.**
boo-shir, kuh-shir yo eeng-one dzuh-moo.
No, but there are English subtitles.

Words to Know

Jīntiān yǎn shénme? 今天演什么? (今天演甚麼?)	jin-tyan yan shummuh?	What's playing today?
dǎoyǎn 导演 (導演)	daow-yan	director
Yīngwén zìmù 英文字幕	eeng-one dzuh-moo	English subtitles

Hopping Around Bars and Clubs

Are you a night owl who, after a full day of sightseeing and even an evening concert, still has the energy to go barhopping and carousing around fun clubs? If so, you need to know some common barspeak, especially when you're on vacation in a toddlin' town like Shanghai — or Chicago, for that matter. After all, not everyone you meet or go out with may be fluent in English. The following phrases may come in handy when you're out exploring the local pubs and dance halls:

- **Nǐ xiǎng gēn wǒ tiàowǔ ma?** 你想跟我跳舞吗? (你想根我跳舞嗎?) (nee shyahng gun waw tyaow-woo mah?) (*Would you like to dance?*)

- **Qǐng lái yìpíng píjiǔ.** 请来一瓶啤酒. (請來一瓶啤酒.) (cheeng lye ee-peeng pee-jyoe.) (*Please bring me a bottle of beer.*)

- **Wǒmen dào nǎr qù tiàowǔ?** 我们到哪儿去跳舞? (我們到哪兒去跳舞?) (waw-men daow nar chyew tyaow-woo?) (*Where can we go to dance?*)

- **Wǒ néng bùnéng qǐng nǐ hē jiǔ?** 我能不能请你喝酒? (我能不能請你喝酒?) (waw nung boo-nung cheeng nee huh jyoe?) (*May I get you a drink?*)

- **Yǒu méiyǒu rùchǎng fèi?** 有没有入场费? (有沒有入場費?) (yo mayo roo-chahng fay?) (*Is there a cover charge?*)

When you go to a bar with friends, you may ask for some **bīngzhèn de píjiǔ** 冰镇的啤酒 (冰鎮的啤酒) (beeng-juhn duh pee-jyoe) (*cold beer*) or maybe some **hóng** 红 (紅) (hoong) (*red*) or **bái** 白 (bye) (*white*) **pútáo jiǔ** 葡萄酒 (poo-taow jyoe) (*wine*). And don't forget to ask for some **huāshēngmǐ** 花生米 (hwah-shung-mee) (*peanuts*) or **tǔdòupiàn** 土豆片 (too-doe-pyan) (*potato chips*) so you don't get too sloshed with all that **píjiǔ.**

Fun & Games

Match the English term on the left with the corresponding Chinese term on the right. You can find the answers in Appendix D.

1. *movie theatre*

2. *concert hall*

3. *museum*

4. *art*

5. *concert*

6. *Peking opera*

a. **yīnyuè huì** 音乐会 (音樂會)

b. **Jīngjù** 京剧 (京劇)

c. **yìshù** 艺术 (藝術)

d. **bówùguǎn** 博物馆 (博物館)

e. **yīnyuè tīng** 音乐厅 (音樂廳)

f. **diànyǐng yuàn** 电影院 (電影院)

Chapter 11

Taking Care of Telecommunications

In This Chapter

▶ Picking up the phone

▶ Understanding cellphone lingo

▶ Dealing with answering machines and voicemail

▶ Navigating the Internet and checking e-mail

Although e-mail may be the preferred method of communication these days, you can't duplicate hearing your loved one's **shēngyīn** 声音 (聲音) (shung-yeen) (*voice*) on the other end of the line or reaching just the right person you need to begin discussing a merger over the computer. All the more reason to know how to use the telephone in addition to surfing the Net.

The art of making a phone call in another language, and even in another country, is just that — an art. To master it, you have to feel comfortable with such basics as using the telephone in the first place. What do you actually say when someone picks up on the other end? This chapter helps you navigate the communication terrain, whether you're in Idaho or China.

Getting Familiar with Telephone Terms

Before even going near a **diànhuà** 电话 (電話) (dyan-hwah) (*telephone*), you may want to become familiar with some common Chinese words and phrases connected to using one. In fact, you see so many different kinds of phones nowadays that you shouldn't have a problem finding out which one best suits your needs:

✔ **gōngyòng diànhuà** 公用电话 (公用電話) (goong-yoong dyan-hwah) (*public telephone*)

✔ **shŏujī** 手机 (手機) (show-jee) (*cellphone*)

✔ **wúxiàn diànhuà** 无线电话 (無線電話) (woo-shyan dyan-hwah) (*cordless phone*)

Be sure to check out a few things beforehand, like what **dìqū hàomă** 地区号码 (地區號碼) (dee-chyew how-mah) (*area code*) and **diànhuà hàomă** 电话号码 (電話號碼) (dyan-hwah how-mah) (*telephone number*) to **bō** 拨 (撥) (baw) (*dial*). Sometimes you need the help of a **jiēxiànyuán** 接线员 (接線員) (jyeh-shyan-ywan) (*operator*) for some of the following kinds of calls, but others you can take care of on your own:

✔ **běnshì diànhuà** 本市电话 (本市電話) (bun-shir dyan-hwah) (*local call*)

✔ **chángtú diànhuà** 长途电话 (長途電話) (chahng-too dyan-hwah) (*long-distance call*)

✔ **duìfāng fùfèi diànhuà** 对方付费电话 (對方付費電話) (dway-fahng foo-fay dyan-hwah) (*collect call*)

✔ **guójì diànhuà** 国际电话 (國際電話) (gwaw-jee dyan-hwah) (*international phone calls*)

Here are some other communication tools you may want to use:

✔ **chá diànhuà hàomăbù** 查电话号码簿 (查電話號碼簿) (chah dyan-hwah how-mah-boo) (*look a number up in a phone book*)

✔ **dă diànhuà** 打电话 (打電話) (dah dyan-hwah) (*to make a phone call*)

✔ **diànhuà hàomă** 电话号码 (電話號碼) (dyan-hwah how-mah) (*telephone number*)

✔ **diànhuàkă** 电话卡 (電話卡) (dyan-hwah-kah) (*phone card*)

If you're like me, you need to ask plenty of basic questions before you figure out what you're doing with a telephone overseas. Here are a few questions that may come in handy:

✔ **Běnshì diànhuà shōufèi duōshăo qián?** 本市电话收费多少钱? (本市電話收费多少錢?) (bun-shir dyan-hwah show-fay dwaw-shaow chyan?) (*How much is a local phone call?*)

✔ **Zài năr kéyĭ dă diànhuà?** 在哪儿可以打电话? (在哪兒可以打電話?) (dzye nar kuh-yee dah dyan-hwah?) (*Where can I make a call?*)

✔ **Zěnme dă diànhuà?** 怎么打电话? (怎麼打電話?) (dzummuh dah dyan-hwah?) (*How can I place a phone call?*)

Going Mobile with a Cellphone

The majority of folks in the world don't have telephones in their homes. Can you imagine? That goes for mainland China as well, where almost a quarter of humanity resides. You can find phones everywhere in Taiwan, however, as well as in Singapore and Hong Kong. In big cities across the globe, you're apt to see a million people (sometimes literally millions in places like Shanghai) on the street with their **shǒujī** 手机 (手機) (show-jee) (*cellphone*) in tow . . . or, rather, in hand, right next to their **zuǐbā** 嘴巴 (dzway-bah) (*mouth*), yakking away. It's the preferred mode of communication these days, so most people you meet have a **shǒujī hàomǎ** 手机号码 (手機號碼) (show-jee howmah) (*cellphone number*).

Although the more well-known cellphone brands have tried to make their marks on the vast Chinese market of cellphone users, home-grown brands such as TCL and Ningbo Bird corner the market on their home turf nowadays.

Cellphones have become so wildly popular that even as recently as 1998, more than 10,000 phones were confiscated in northern China after officials discovered that members of high government used them as bribes or gifts for friends and family. The phones even became the subject of a government anti-corruption campaign.

Making a Phone Call

Wéi? 喂 (餵) (way?) (*Hello?*). You hear this word spoken in the second (or rising) tone a lot on the other end of the line when you make a phone call. It's kind of like testing the waters to see if someone is there. You can reply with the same word in the fourth (or falling) tone so you sound like you're making a statement, or you can just get right to asking whether the person you want to speak with is in at the moment. (For more about the four tones, refer to Chapter 1.)

A phrase you may hear on the other end of the line in mainland China is **Nǐ nǎr?** 你哪儿? (你哪兒?) (nee nar?) (Literally: *Where are you?*). It asks what **dānwèi** 单位 (單位) (dahn-way) (*work unit*) you're attached to. After these first little questions, you may finally be ready to ask for the person you intended to call in the first place.

For decades after the Communist rule took over mainland China in 1949, all Chinese people were assigned a **dānwèi,** which pretty much regulated every aspect of their lives — from where they lived to when they married and even when they had children. Even though that particular system has largely fallen by the wayside, asking about a person's **dānwèi** is still pretty common when answering the phone.

Here are some things you can do before, during, or after your call:

- **náqǐ diànhuà** 拿起电话 (拿起電話) (nah-chee dyan-hwah) (*pick up the phone*)

- **dǎ diànhuà** 打电话 (打電話) (dah dyan-hwah) (*make a phone call*)

- **shōudào diànhuà** 收到电话 (收到電話) (show-daow dyan-hwah) (*receive a phone call*)

- **jiē diànhuà** 接电话 (接電話) (jyeh dyan-hwah) (*answer a phone call*)

- **huí diànhuà** 回电话 (回電話) (hway dyan-hwah) (*return a phone call*)

- **liú yíge huà** 留一个话 (留一個話) (lyo ee-guh hwah) (*leave a message*)

- **guà diànhuà** 挂电话 (掛電話) (gwah dyan-hwah) (*hang up*)

Calling your friends

Feel like getting in touch with a friend or co-worker to **liáotiān** 聊天 (lyaow-tyan) (*chat*) after class or work? Want to confer with your classmate about tomorrow's exam? Maybe you two are planning a party over the weekend and you need to confer about the details. To get the party started, you have to pick up that phone and start talking.

Talkin' the Talk

Mary calls to see whether her friend Luò Chéng is at home and speaks with his father. (Track 14)

Mr. Luò: **Wéi?** 喂
          way?
          Hello?

Mary: **Qǐngwèn, Luò Chéng zài ma?** 在吗
          cheeng-one, law chung dzye mah?
          May I please speak to Luo Cheng?

Mr. Luò: **Qǐngwèn, nín shì nǎ yí wèi?** 您是哪一喂
          cheeng-one, neen shir nah ee way?
          May I ask who's calling?

Mary: 我是他的同窗 Mary

Wǒ shì tāde tóngxué Mary.
waw shir tah-duh toong-shweh Mary.
I'm his classmate Mary.

Mr. Luò: 好

Hǎo. Shāoděng. Wǒ qù jiào tā.
how. shaow-dung. waw chyew jyao tah.
Okay. Just a moment. I'll go get him.

Words to Know

Wéi? 喂?	way?	Hello?
Qǐngwèn, nín shì nǎ yí wèi? 请问, 您是哪一位? (請問, 您是哪一位?)	cheeng-one, neen shir nah ee way?	May I ask who's calling?
tóngxué 同学 (同學)	toong-shweh	classmate
Shāoděng. 稍等.	shaow-dung.	Just a moment.

Ringing hotels and places of business

Calling places of business may be a bit different from the more informal call to a friend or co-worker. When you call a **lǚguǎn** 旅馆 (旅館) (lyew-gwahn) (*hotel*), **shāngdiàn** 商店 (shahng-dyan) (*store*), or a particular **gōngsī** 公司 (goong-suh) (*company*), you may be asked what **fēnjī hàomǎ** 分机号码 (分機號碼) (fun-jee how-mah) (*extension*) you want. If you don't know, you can ask for the same: **Qǐngwèn, fēnjī hàomǎ shì duōshǎo?** 请问, 分机号码是多少? (請問, 分機號碼是多少?) (cheeng-one, fun-jee how-mah shir dwaw-shaow?) (*May I ask what the extension number is?*).

After you figure out the extension, the operator will hopefully say **Wǒ xiànzài jiù gěi nǐ jiē hào.** 我现在就给你接号. (我現在就給你接號.) (waw shyan-dzye jyo gay nee jyeh how.) (*I'll transfer you now.*).

Even after all your work thus far, you may find that you **jiē bù tōng** 接不通 (jyeh boo toong) (*can't connect*) or that **méiyǒu rén jiē** 没有人接 (mayo run jyeh) (*no one answers*). Maybe the **diànhuàxiàn duànle** 电话线断了 (電話線 斷了) (dyan-hwah-shyan dwahn-luh) (*the line has been disconnected*). That's really **máfan** 麻烦 (麻煩) (mah-fahn) (*annoying*), isn't it? Here are some other **máfan** problems you may encounter while trying to make a phone call:

- **děnghòu** 等候 (dung-ho) (*be on hold*)
- **diànhuà huàile** 电话坏了 (電話壞了) (dyan-hwah hwye-luh) (*the phone is broken*)
- **méiyǒu bōhàoyīn** 没有拨号音 (沒有撥號音) (mayo baw-how-yeen) (*no dial tone*)
- **nǐ bōcuò hàomǎ le** 你拨错号码了 (你駁錯號碼了) (nee baw-tswaw how-mah luh) (*you dialed the wrong number*)
- **záyīn** 杂音 (雜音) (dzah-yeen) (*static*)
- **zhànxiàn** 占线 (佔線) (jahn-shyan) (*the line is busy*)

If you finally do get through to an employee's office only to discover the person isn't there, you can always leave a **yǒu shēng yóujiàn** 有声邮件 (有聲 郵件) (yo shung yo-jyan) (*voicemail*). Flip to the later section "Sorry, I'm Not Home Right Now . . ." for the ins and outs of leaving and receiving messages.

Phoning a client

If you want to reach your **kèhù** 客户 (kuh-hoo) (*client*) or your **shēng yì huǒ bàn** 生意伙伴 (生意夥伴) (shuhng yee hwaw ban) (*business partner*) in today's business world, you just have to pick up that phone. Personally connecting with a phone call is a good way to maintain good business relationships. It's the next best thing to being there.

Sometimes you need a little help from the **mìshū** 秘书 (秘書) (mee-shoo) (*secretary*) to connect to the person you want to reach.

Talkin' the Talk

Jacob enlists the help of Liú Xiǎojiě (Miss Liu), his trusty secretary in Taipei, to help him make a call.

Jacob: **Liú Xiǎojiě, zěnme jiē wàixiàn?**
lyo shyaow-jyeh, dzummuh jyeh why-shyan?
Miss Liu, how can I get an outside line?

Liú Xiǎojiě: **Méi wèntí. Wǒ bāng nǐ dǎ zhèige hàomǎ.**
may one-tee. waw bahng nee dah jay-guh how-mah.
Don't worry. I'll help you dial the number.

Jacob: **Xièxiè.**
shyeh-shyeh.
Thanks.

Miss Liu gets through and speaks to Mr. Wang's secretary.

Liú Xiǎojiě: **Wéi? Zhè shì Wáng Xiānshēng de bàngōngshì ma?**
way? jay shir wahng shyan-shung duh bahn-goong-shir ma?
Hello? Do I have the office of Mr. Wang?

Secretary: **Duì le. Jiù shì.**
dway luh. jyo shir.
Yes it is.

Liú Xiǎojiě: **Kéyǐ gěi wǒ jiē tā ma?**
kuh-yee gay waw jyeh tah mah?
Can you connect me with him please?

Secretary: **Duìbùqǐ, tā xiànzài kāihuì. Nǐ yào liúyán ma?**
dway-boo-chee, tah shyan-dzye kye-hway. nee yaow lyo-yan mah?
I'm sorry, he's in a meeting at the moment. Would you like to leave a message?

Liú Xiǎojiě: **Máfan nǐ gàosù tā ABC gōngsī de jīnglǐ Jacob Smith gěi ta dǎ diànhuà le?**
mah-fahn nee gaow-soo tah ABC goong-suh duh jeeng-lee Jacob Smith gay tah dah dyan-hwah lah?
May I trouble you to tell him that Jacob Smith, the Manager of ABC Company, called him?

Words to Know

wàixiàn 外线 (外線)	why-shyan	outside line
Nǐ yào liúyán ma? 你要留言吗? (你要留言嗎?)	nee yaow lyo-yan mah?	Would you like to leave a message?
jīnglǐ 经理 (經理)	jeeng-lee	manager

Sorry, I'm Not Home Right Now . . .

Because people lead such busy lives, you often can't get a hold of them directly when you try to **gěi tāmen dǎ diànhuà** 给他们打电话 (給他們打電話) (gay tah-mun dah dyan-hwah) (*give them a call*). You have no choice but to **liúhuà** 留话 (留話) (lyo-hwah) (*leave a message*) on the **lùyīn diànhuà** 录音电话 (錄音電話) (loo-yeen dyan-hwah) (*answering machine*). You can always try to leave a **xìnxī** 信息 (sheen-she) (*message*) with a real person, too. In the following sections, I give you the lowdown on leaving and listening to messages.

Listening to messages that people leave you

If you return home from a long, hard day at work to discover that many callers have **liúle huà** 留了话 (留了話) (lyo-luh hwah) (*left messages*) for you, you may be tempted to **tīng** 听 (聽) (teeng) (*listen to*) them right away rather than **bùlǐ** 不理 (boo-lee) (*ignore*) them. Relax. Take a hot bath. Have a glass of wine while you cook dinner. After a break, you'll be ready to tackle all the messages on that ol' answering machine.

Here's what a typical message sounds like:

> **Wéi? Bob, zhè shì Judy. Zhèige zhōumò wǒmen yìqǐ qù nèige wǎnhuì, hǎo bùhǎo? Yīnggāi hěn bàng. Yǒu kōng gěi wǒ dǎ diànhuà. Wǒde shǒujī hàomǎ shì 212-939-9991. Xièxiè.**

> way? Bob, jay shir Judy. jay-guh joe-maw waw-men ee-chee chyew nay-guh wahn-hway, how boo-how? eeng-guy hun bahng. yo koong gay waw dah dyan-hwah. waw-duh show-jee how-mah shir are ee are, jyo sahn jyo, jyo jyo jyo ee. shyeh-shyeh.

> *Hello? Bob, this is Judy. Want to go to that party together this weekend? It should be awesome. When you get a chance, give me a call. My cell number is 212-939-9991. Thanks.*

Recording and understanding greeting messages

Here are some common greetings you may hear if you reach an answering machine:

✔ **"Zhè shì Barry Katz."**: 这是 Barry Katz. (這是 Barry Katz.) (*You've reached Barry Katz.*)

✔ **Wǒ xiànzài búzài.** 我现在不在. (我現在不在.) (waw shyan-dzye boo-dzye.) (*I'm not in at the moment./I'm away from my desk.*)

✔ **Sān yuè sì hào zhīqián wǒ zài dùjià.** 三月四号之前我在度假. (三月四號之前我在度假.) (sahn yweh suh how jir-chyan waw dzye doo-jyah.) (*I'm on vacation until March 4th.*)

✔ **Nín rúguǒ xiǎng gēn wǒde zhùshǒu tōnghuà, qǐng bō fēnjī 108.** 您如果想跟我的助手通话, 请拨分机一零八. (您如果想跟我的助手通話, 請撥分機一零八.) (neen roo-gwaw shyahng gun waw-duh joo-show toong-hwah, cheeng baw fun-jee yaow leeng bah.) (*If you'd like to speak with my assistant, please dial extension 108.*)

✔ **Qǐng liú xià nínde míngzi, diànhuà hàomǎ hé jiǎnduǎn de liúyán. Wǒ huì gěi nín huí diànhuà.** 请留下您的名字, 电话号码和简短的留言. 我会给你回电话. (請留下您的名字, 電話號碼和簡短的留言. 我會給你回電話.) (cheeng lyo shyah neen-duh meeng-dzuh, dyan-hwah how-mah huh jyan-dwahn duh lyo-yan. waw hway gay neen hway dyan-hwah.) (*Please leave your name, number, and a brief message. I'll get back to you.*)

Answering machines are still something of an oddity in China, so many Chinese don't know quite what to do when they hear your recorded greeting message on the other end of the line. Be clear in your message that the caller should leave a name and phone number after the **hū** (who) (*beep*).

Sometimes you have to press the **jǐnghàojiàn** 井号键 (井號鍵) (jeen-how-jyan) (*pound key*) before leaving a message. In that case, you have to recognize the **jǐngzìhào** 井字号 (井字號) (jeeng-dzuh-how) (*pound sign*): #. When dealing with voicemail, you may have to deal with the following kinds of instructions on a recorded message:

✔ **Nín rúguǒ shǐyòng ànjiàn shì diànhuàjī, qǐng àn 3.** 您如果使用按键式电话机, 请按三. (您如果使用按鍵式電話機, 請按三.) (neen roo-gwaw shir-yoong ahn-jyan shir dyan-hwah jee, cheeng ahn sahn.) (*If you have a touch-tone phone, please press 3 now.*)

✔ **Yào huí dào zhǔ mùlù qǐng àn jǐngzìhào.** 要回到主目录请按井字号. (要回到主目錄請按井字號.) (yaow hway daow joo moo-loo cheeng ahn jeeng-dzuh-how.) (*If you want to return to the main menu, please press pound now.*)

Leaving messages

When you leave a message on an answering machine, be sure to give clear instructions about what you want the person to do:

- ✔ **Bié wàngle huí wǒde diànhuà.** 别忘了回我的电话. (別忘了回我的電話.) (byeh wahng-luh hway waw-duh dyan-hwah.) (*Don't forget to return my call.*)

- ✔ **Nǐ huí jiā zhīhòu qǐng gěi wǒ dǎ diànhuà.** 你回家之后请给我打电话. (你回家之後請給我打電話.) (nee hway jyah jir-ho cheeng gay waw dah dyan-hwah.) (*After you get home, please give me a call.*)

- ✔ **Wǒ zài gěi nǐ dǎ diànhuà.** 我再给你打电话. (我再給你打電話.) (waw dzye gay nee dah dyan-hwah.) (*I'll call you again.*)

If a live person answers and you have to leave a message, be sure to be polite. Here are some good phrases to keep in mind:

- ✔ **Máfan nǐ qǐng tā huí wǒde diànhuà?** 麻烦你请他回我的电话? (麻煩你請他回我的電話?) (mah-fahn nee cheeng tah hway waw-duh dyan-hwah?) (*May I trouble you to please have him return my call?*)

- ✔ **Qǐng gàosù tā wǒ gěi tā dǎ diànhuà le.** 请告诉她我给她打电话了. (請告訴她我給她打電話了.) (cheeng gaow-soo tah waw gay tah dah dyan-hwah luh.) (*Please tell her I called.*)

- ✔ **Qǐng gàosù tā wǒ huì wǎn yìdiǎr lái.** 请告诉他我会晚一点儿来. (請告訴他我會晚一點兒來.) (cheeng gaow-soo tah waw hway wahn ee-dyar lye.) (*Please let him know I'll be a little late.*)

- ✔ **Qǐng gěi wǒ zhuǎn tāde liúyánjī?** 请给我转他的留言机? (請給我轉他的留言機?) (cheeng gay waw jwan tah-duh lyo-yan-jee?) (*Could you please transfer me to his voicemail?*)

Talkin' the Talk

Ruben calls Betty and discovers she's not home. He has to leave a message with Betty's mother.

Betty's mom: **Wéi?**
way?
Hello?

Ruben: **Qǐngwèn, Betty zài ma?**
cheeng-one, Betty dzye mah?
Hello, is Betty there?

Betty's mom:	**Tā búzài. Tā qù yóujú le. Qǐngwèn, nín shì nǎ yí wèi?** tah boo-dzye. tah chyew yo-jyew luh. cheeng-one, neen shir nah ee way? *She's not home. She went to the post office. May I ask who this is?*
Ruben:	**Wǒ shì Ruben, tāde tóngbān tóngxué. Máfan nǐ qǐng gàosù tā wǒ gěi tā dǎ diànhuà le.** waw shir Ruben, tah-duh toong-bahn toong-shweh. mah-fahn nee cheeng gaow-soo tah waw gay tah dah dyan-hwah luh. *I'm Ruben, her classmate. May I trouble you to please tell her I called?*
Betty's mom:	**Yídìng huì.** ee-deeng hway. *Certainly.*

Words to Know

yóujú 邮局 (郵局)	yo-jyew	post office
Máfan nǐ? 麻烦你? (麻煩你?)	mah-fahn nee?	May I trouble you?
tóngxué 同学 (同學)	toong-shweh	classmate
Yídìng huì 一定会. (一定會.)	ee-deeng hway.	Certainly.

Using the Internet

These days you can reach your business partner in Beijing in a matter of seconds through **diànzǐ kōngjiān** 电子空间 (電子空間) (dyan-dzuh koong-jyan) (*cyberspace*). With **shǒutí shì** 手提式 (show-tee shir) (*portable*) computers and multiple **jiǎnsuǒ yǐnqíng** 检索引擎 (檢索引擎) (jyan-swaw yeen-cheeng) (*search engines*), you can find just about anything you're looking for. Not sure what you're doing with computers? Forget your **mìmǎ** 密码 (密碼) (mee-mah) (*password*)? **Jìshù fúwù** 技术服务 (技術服務) (jee-shoo foo-woo) (*technical support*) is only a phone call away. Here are some things you can do nowadays with computers and through the Internet:

- ✔ **ānzhuāng tiáozhì jiětiáoqì** 安装调制解调器 (安裝調製解調器) (ahn-jwahng tyaow-jir jyeh-tyaow-chee) (*install a modem*)
- ✔ **chóngxīn kāijī** 重新开机 (重新開機) (choong-sheen kye-jee) (*reboot*)
- ✔ **dǎkāi diànnǎo** 打开电脑 (打開電腦) (dah-kye dyan-now) (*turn on the computer*)
- ✔ **guāndiào diànnǎo** 关掉电话 (關掉電腦) (gwahn-dyaow dyan-now) (*turn off the computer*)
- ✔ **jìn rù** 进入 (進入) (gin roo) (*log on*)
- ✔ **jiànlì yíge zhànghù** 建立一个账户 (建立一個賬戶) (jyan-lee ee-guh jahng-hoo) (*set up an account*)
- ✔ **jiǎnsuǒ guójì yīntè wǎng** 检索因特网 (檢索因特網) (jyan-swaw gwaw-jee een tuh wahng) (*search the Internet*)
- ✔ **liúlǎn** 浏览 (瀏覽) (lyo-lahn) (*browse*)
- ✔ **shàngwǎng** 上网 (上網) (shahng-wahng) (*go online*)
- ✔ **tuì chū** 退出 (tway choo) (*log off*)
- ✔ **xiàzài wénjiàn** 下载文件 (下載文件) (shyah-dzye one-jyan) (*download a file*)
- ✔ **xuǎnzé yìjiā wǎngshàng fúwù tígōng shāng** 选择一家网上服务提供商 (選擇一家網上服務提供商) (shwan-dzuh ee-jya wahng-shahng foo-woo tee-goong shahng) (*choose an Internet service provider*)

By the beginning of the 21st century, China was home to more than 10 million PCs and 26 million Internet users even though the Chinese government strictly controls the web's use.

Talkin' the Talk

Eugene and Sarah discuss the wonders of the Internet.

Eugene: **Yīntèwǎng dàodǐ shì shénme dōngxi?**
een-tuh-wahng daow-dee shir shummuh doong-she?
Just what exactly is the Internet?

Sarah: **Yīntèwǎng shì yìzhǒng diànnǎo de guójì hùlián wǎng. Tā tígòng xìnxī fúwù.**
een-tuh-wahng shir ee-joong dyan-now duh gwaw-jee hoo-lyan wahng. tah tee-goong sheen-she foo-woo.
The Internet is a kind of interconnected international network. It provides information.

Eugene: **Tīngshuō wànwéiwǎng shénme dōu yǒu.**
teeng-shwaw wahn-way-wahng shummuh doe yo.
I've heard that the World Wide Web has everything.

Sarah: **Duì le. Nǐ yī shàngwǎng jiù kěyǐ liúlǎn hěn duō bùtóng de wǎngzhàn.**
dway luh. nee ee shahng-wahng jyo kuh-yee lyo-lahn hun dwaw boo-toong duh wahng-jahng.
That's correct. The minute you go online, you can browse all sorts of different websites.

Words to Know

dàodǐ 到底	daow-dee	Literally: in the end; after all
yīntèwǎng 因特网 (因特網)	een-tuh-wahng	the Internet
guójì 国际 (國際)	gwaw-jee	international
wànwéiwǎng 万维网 (萬維網)	wahn-way-wahng	World Wide Web
wǎngzhàn 网站 (網站)	wahng-jahn	website

142

Checking Your E-Mail

Your **diànzǐ yóuxiāng dìzhǐ** 电子邮箱地址 (電子郵箱地址) (dyan-dzuh yo-shyahng dee-jir) (*e-mail address*) is as important as your **míngzi** 名字 (meeng-dzuh) (*name*) and your **diànhuà hàomǎ** 电话号码 (電話號碼) (dyan-hwah how-mah) (*phone number*) when it comes to keeping in touch.

E-mail is almost indispensable if you want to do business. Just check your **shōuxìnxiāng** 收信箱 (show-sheen-shyahng) (*inbox*) and you'll probably have received a few more **diànzǐ yóujiàn** 电子邮件 (電子郵件) (dyan-dzuh yo-jyan) (*e-mails*) while reading this section alone.

Individuals in China are charged by the minute if they use their own home computers, so folks may not be that keen on checking their e-mail too frequently. If something's really important, you may want to resort to a phone call so you know they'll pick up on the other end of the line.

Here are some things you can do with e-mail when you have your own account:

- ✔ **bǎ wénjiàn fùjiā zài diànzǐ yóujiàn** 把文件附加在电子邮件 (把文件附加在電子郵件) (bah one-jyan foo-jyah dzye dyan-dzuh yo-jyan) (*attach a file to an e-mail*)

- ✔ **fā diànzǐ yóujiàn** 发电子邮件 (發電子郵件) (fah dyan-dzuh yo-jyan) (*send an e-mail*)

- ✔ **sòng wénjiàn** 送文件 (soong one-jyan) (*send a file*)

- ✔ **zhuǎnfā xìnxī** 转发信息 (轉發信息) (jwan-fah sheen-she) (*forward a message*)

Talkin' the Talk

Gary and Laurie discuss how to e-mail each other.

Laurie: **Zěnme fā yíge diànzǐ yóujiàn ne?**
dzummuh fah ee-guh dyan-dzuh yo-jyan nuh?
So how do you send an e-mail?

Gary: **Shǒuxiān nǐ děi dǎkāi "xīn yóujiàn."**
show-shyan nee day dah-kye sheen yo-jyan.
First you have to open up to "new mail."

Laurie: **Ránhòu ne?**
rahn-ho nuh?
And then?

Gary: **Ránhòu tiánhǎo shōujiànrén de diànzǐ yóuxiāng dìzhǐ hé yóujiàn de tímù. Xiěhǎo xìn, jiù kěyǐ fā le.**
rahn-ho tyan-how show-jyan-run duh dyan-dzuh yo-shyahng dee-jir huh yo-jyan duh tee-moo. shyeh-how sheen, jyo kuh-yee fah luh.
After that, you have to fill in the recipient's e-mail address and type in the subject. After you're finished writing the message, you can finally send it.

Words to Know

xīn yóujiàn 新邮件 (新郵件)	sheen yo-jyan	new mail
Ránhòu ne? 然后呢? (然後呢?)	rahn-ho nuh?	And then?
shōujiànrén 收件人	show- jyan-run	recipient
tímù 题目 (題目)	tee-moo	subject

Fun & Games

Match each of the Chinese phrases to the correct English phrase. Turn to Appendix D for the answers.

Just a moment.

Is she at home?

Hello?

Sorry, you dialed the wrong number.

Please leave a message.

Wéi? 喂?

Duìbùqǐ, nǐ bōcuò hàomǎle. 对不起, 你拨错号码了. (對不起, 你撥錯號碼了.)

Shāoděng. 稍等.

Qǐng nǐ liú yíge huà. 请你留一个话. (請你留一個話.)

Tā zài ma? 她在吗? (她在嗎?)

Chapter 12

Chinese at School and at Work

- -

In This Chapter

▶ Navigating the world of school

▶ Keeping your office supplied

▶ Having business meetings

▶ Making presentations

- -

Time to get down to **shēng yì** 生意 (shuhng yee) (*business*). Your **shēng yi,** that is. Want to know how to manage that job in Jiangsu or how to deal with the head honcho? This chapter helps you do business in Chinese — everything from making a business appointment to conducting a meeting.

Because China has the fastest growing economy in the world, it's no wonder you gravitated to this chapter. Think of it. China is the fastest-growing source of international profits for U.S. companies, with over a billion potential customers. The United States is China's second largest trading partner (after Japan) and has hundreds of satellite offices everywhere from Shanghai to Shenzhen. With hundreds of billions (that's right, billions) of dollars in exports throughout the world, China is most decidedly making its mark.

Before you get that job in Wuhan, though, you need to get a good education. This chapter helps you navigate the academic side of things, from kindergarten through college and beyond.

Going to School

You may get out of it for the first 5 or 6 years of life, but eventually we all have to **shàng xué** 上学 (上學) (shahng-shweh) (*go to school*) for about 12 years or so. The following sections break down everything you need to know about school-related terms.

Schools and supplies

Table 12-1 lists all the different kinds of **xué xiào** 学校 (學校) (shweh shyaow) (*school*) you or your children may be ready to attend.

Table 12-1	Schools	
Chinese	**Pronunciation**	**English**
ìrjiān zhàogù zhōngxīn 日间照顾中心 (日间照顧中心)	ir-jyan djaow-goo joong-sheen	*day-care center*
yōu'ér yuán 幼儿园 (幼兒園)	yo-are ywan	*kindergarten*
xiǎo xué 小学 (小學)	shyaow shweh	*elementary school*
zhōng xué 中学 (中學)	joong shweh	*middle school*
gāozhōng xué 高中学 (高中學)	gaow-joong shweh	*high school*
zhuānyè xuéxiào 专业学校 (專業學校)	jwan-yeh shweh-shyaow	*vocational school*
dà xué 大学 (大學)	dah shweh	*college*
wǎng shàng kèchéng 网上课程 (網上課程)	wahng shahng kuh-chuhng	*online courses*
yánjiū yuàn 研究院	yan-jyo ywan	*graduate school*
yī xuéyuàn 医学院 (醫學院)	ee shweh-ywan	*medical school*
fǎ xuéyuàn 法学院 (法學院)	fah shweh-ywan	*law school*
shāng xuéyuàn 商学院 (商學院)	shahng shweh-ywan	*business school*

Say you've applied for **dà xué** and gotten into the one that was (lucky you) your **shǒu xuǎn** 首选 (首選) (show shwan) (*first choice*). By the end of the first day of class, you need to buy **kèběn** 课本 (課本) (kuh-bun) (*textbooks*) and **yòngpǐn** 用品 (yoong-peen) (*supplies*). Here are some supplies you may need, depending on the **kè** 课 (課) (kuh) (*classes*) you register for:

- **bǐjìběn** 笔记本 (筆記本) (bee-jee-bun) (*notebook*)
- **bǐjìběn diànnǎo** 笔记本电脑 (筆記本電腦) (bee-jee-bun dyan-naow) (*laptop*)
- **gāngbǐ** 钢笔 (鋼筆) (gahng-bee) (*ballpoint pens*)
- **jìsuàn qì** 计算器 (計算器) (jee-swan chee) (*calcuator*)
- **mùtàn làbǐ** 木炭蜡笔 (木炭蠟筆) (moo-tahn lah-bee) (*charcoal crayons*)

✔ **qiānbǐ** 铅笔 (鉛筆) (chyan-bee) (*pencils*)

✔ **sùmiáo diàn** 素描垫 (素描墊) (soo-myaow dyan) (*sketch pad*)

✔ **táishì diànnǎo** 台式电脑 (台式電腦 (tye-shir dyan-naow) (*desktop computer*)

The Children's Palace in Shanghai is one of the most prestigious after-school arts programs for gifted children in all of China. Built in 1918 as a private villa by the Iraqi Jewish Kadoorie family, who came to Shanghai in the late 1800s, the palace's ornate features; large fireplaces; huge, winding staircase; and marble hallways lent themselves to its original name: Marble Hall. Tourists often come here to see the children perform as one of the highlights of a trip to Shanghai.

Teachers and subjects

Remember your favorite **xiǎo xué lǎoshī** 小学老师 (小學老師) (shyaow shweh laow-shir) (*elementary school teacher*)? Remember how great it felt to learn how to **yuè dú** 阅读 (閱讀) (yweh doo) (*read*)? Well, soon enough **yuè dú** turns into **xuéxí** 学习 (學習) (shweh-shee) (*studying*) and maybe even some serious academic or scientific **yánjiū** 研究 (yan-jyo) (*research*), and you really have to hunker down. Table 12-2 lists all sorts of subjects you may study with a **lǎoshī** 老师 (老師) (laow-shir) (*teacher*) or **jiào shòu** 教授 (jyaow show) (*professor*).

Table 12-2	Academic Subjects	
Chinese	*Pronunciation*	*English*
dàishù xué 代数学 (代數學)	dye-shoo shweh	*algebra*
Fǎyǔ 法语 (法語)	fah-yew	*French*
guójì guānxì 国际关系 (國際關係)	gwaw-jee gwan-shee	*international relations*
huàxué 化学 (化學)	hwah-shweh	*chemistry*
jǐhéxué 几何学 (幾何學)	jee-huh shweh	*geometry*
jīngjìxué 经济学 (經濟學)	jeeng-jee-shweh	*economics*
lìshǐ 历史 (歷史)	lee-shir	*history*
shēngwùxué 生物学 (生物學)	shung-woo-shweh	*biology*
shùxué 数学 (數學)	shoo-shweh	*mathematics*

(continued)

Table 12-2 *(continued)*

Chinese	*Pronunciation*	*English*
wénxué 文学 (文學)	wuhn-shweh	*literature*
wúdǎo 舞蹈	woo-daow	*dance*
wùlǐ 物理	woo-lee	*physics*
Xībānyáyǔ 西班牙语 (西班牙語)	shee-bahn-yah-yew	*Spanish*
xìjù 戏剧 (戲劇)	shee-jyew	*drama*
Yìdàlìyǔ 意大利語 (意大利語)	ee-dah-lee-yew	*Italian*
Yīngyǔ 英语 (英語)	eeng-yew	*English*
yìshù 艺术 (藝術)	ee-shoo	*art*
zhèngzhìxué 政治学 (政治學)	juhng-jir-shweh	*political science*
zhéxué 哲学 (哲學)	juh-shweh	*philosophy*

Here are some class-related phrases:

- **Nǐ xué shénme?** 你学什么? (你學甚麼?) (nee shweh shummah?) (*What are you studying?*)
- **shàng kè** 上课 (上課) (shahng kuh) (*to go to class*)
- **xué** 学 (學) (shweh) (*to study*)

Exams and semesters

After you get into the swing of the **xuéqí** 学期 (學期) (shweh-chee) (*semester*), you begin to realize your time isn't your own. You have classes to attend, **kè wài huódòng** 课外活动 (課外活動) (kuh wye hwaw-doong) (*extracurricular activities*) to participate in, and a whole bunch of **kǎoshì** 考试 (考試) (*exams*) to take. These words and phrases come in handy during the school year:

- **qīmò kǎo** 期末考 (chee-maw kaow) (*final exam*)
- **qīzhōng kǎo** 期中考 (chee-joong kaow) (*midterm*)
- **suí tǎng cèyàn** 随堂测验 (隨堂測驗) (sway tahng tsuh-yan) (*pop quiz*)
- **wénzhāng** 文章 (wuhn-jahng) (*essay*)
- **Wǒ děi xiě yìpiān wénzhān.** 我得写一篇文章. (我得寫一篇文章.) (waw day shyeh ee-pyan wuhn-jahng.) (*I have to write an essay.*)
- **zuì hòu qīxiàn** 最后期限 (最後期限) (dzway hoe chee-shyan) (*deadline*)

After you've studied hard and taken that **kǎoshì,** you may want to ask your **tóngxué** 同学 (同學) (toong-shweh) (*classmate*) one of these questions:

- **Nǐ déle jǐfēn?** 你得了几分? (你得了幾分?) (nee duh-luh jee-fun?) (*What [grade] did you get?*)

- **Nǐ kǎobù jígē ma?** 你考不及格吗? (你考不及格嗎?) (nee kaow-boo jee-guh mah?) (*Did you fail?*)

- **Nǐ kǎode jígē ma?** 你考得及格吗? (你考得及格嗎) (nee kaow-duh jee-guh mah?) (*Did you pass?*)

Degrees and diplomas

When you're finally done with all the **xuéxí** 学习 (學習) (shweh-shee) (*studying*) and you're ready to **bìyè** 毕业 (畢業) (bee-yeh) (*graduate*), it's a great day. All that hard work has paid off and you're ready to get your **gāozhōng bìyè wénpǐn** 高中毕业文凭 (高中畢業文憑) (gaow-joong bee-yeh wuhn-peen) (*high school diploma*) or a **dàxué xuéwèi** 大学学位 (大學學位) (dah-shweh shweh-way) (*college degree*), you can rest assured that everyone's very proud of you. Here are some of the degrees you may be getting:

- **xuéshì xuéwèi** 学士学位 (學士學位) (shweh-shir shweh-way) (*bachelor's degree*)

- **suòshì xuéwèi** 硕士学位 (碩士學位) (swaw-shir shweh-way) (*master's degree*)

- **bóshì xuéwèi** 博士学位 (博士學位) (baw-shir shweh-way) (*doctorate*)

- **fǎxué bóshì** 法学博士 (法學博士) (fah-shweh baw-shir) (*Juris Doctor*)

- **yīxué bóshì** 医学博士 (醫學博士) (ee-shweh baw-shir) (*medical doctor*)

Settling into Your Office Digs

Whether you're a **mìshū** 秘书 (秘書) (mee-shoo) (*secretary*) or the **zhǔxí** 主席 (joo-she) (*chairman*) of the board, the atmosphere and physical environment of your **bàngōngshì** 办公室 (辦公室) (bahn-goong-shir) (*office*) is pretty important. It can even help get you through an otherwise tough day. May as well make it as comfortable as possible. Why not put a photo of the family dog on your **bàngōngzhuō** 办公桌 (辦公桌) (bahn-goong-jwaw) (*desk*) for starters? That should put a smile on your face as you start the day.

You don't even have to get up out of your **yǐzi** 椅子 (ee-dzuh) (*chair*) to notice all the techie stuff around you. These days, just about any office you work in or visit has the following basic things:

- **chuánzhēn** 传真 (傳真) (chwan-jun) (*fax*)
- **dǎyìnjī** 打印机 (打印機) (dah-een-jee) (*printer*)
- **diànhuà** 电话 (電話) (dyan-hwah) (*telephone*)
- **diànnǎo** 电脑 (電腦) (dyan-now) (*computer*)
- **fùyìnjī** 复印机 (復印機) (foo-een-jee) (*copier*)

Of course, the first thing you may look around for when you get to work in the morning is the **kāfēijī** 咖啡机 (咖啡機) (kah-fay-jee) (*coffee machine*). In fact, the one part of the day you may look forward to the most is the **xiūxi** 休息 (shyo-she) (*coffee break*).

As you look around your **xiǎogéjiān** 小隔间 (小隔間) (shyaow-guh-jyan) (*cubicle*), I bet you can find all these things:

- **bǐjìběn** 笔记本 (筆記本) (bee-jee-bun) (*notebook*)
- **dàng'àn** 档案 (檔案) (dahng-ahn) (*file*)
- **dìngshūjī** 钉书机 (訂書機) (deeng-shoo-jee) (*stapler*)
- **gāngbǐ** 钢笔 (鋼筆) (gahng-bee) (*pen*)
- **huíwénzhēn** 回纹针 (回紋針) (hway-one-jun) (*paper clip*)
- **jiāo dài** 胶带 (膠帶) (jyaow dye) (*transparent tape*)
- **qiānbǐ** 铅笔 (鉛筆) (chyan-bee) (*pencil*)
- **xiàngpíjīn** 橡皮筋 (shyahng-pee-jeen) (*rubber band*)

If you can't find some indispensable item just when you need it, you can always ask someone in the next **xiǎogéjiān** 小隔间 (小隔間) (shyaow-guh-jyan) (*cubicle*). The simplest way to ask is by using the phrase **Nǐ yǒu méiyǒu _____?** 你有没有 _____? (nee yo mayo _____?) (*Do you have any _____?*) Use that phrase as often as you like. Just make sure you can reciprocate whenever your **tóngshì** 同事 (toong-shir) (*co-worker*) needs something as well.

> **Nǐ yǒu méiyǒu dìngshūjī?** 你有没有钉书机? (你有没有訂書機?) (nee yo mayo deeng-shoo-jee?) (*Do you have a stapler?*)

> **Nǐ yǒu méiyǒu gāngbǐ?** 你有没有钢笔? (你有没有鋼筆?) (nee yo mayo gahng-bee?) (*Do you have a pen?*)

Talkin' the Talk

Ollie and Tommy are co-workers in Xi'an. Ollie is about to go into a meeting but can't find his notebook. He quickly checks with his good friend Tommy in the next cubicle.

Ollie: **Tommy! Wǒ jíde yào mìng! Kuài yào kāihuì le, kěshì zhǎobúdào wǒde bǐjìběn.**
Tommy! waw jee-duh yaow meeng! kwye yaow kye-hway luh, kuh-shir jaow-boo-daow waw-duh bee-jee-bun.
Tommy! I'm in such a hurry! We're about to have a meeting, and I can't find my notebook.

Tommy: **Wǒ yǒu bǐjìběn. Jiè gěi nǐ.**
waw yo bee-jee-bun. jyeh gay nee.
I have a notebook. I'll loan it to you.

Ollie: **Tài hǎo le! Xièxiè.**
tye how luh! shyeh-shyeh.
That's great. Thanks.

Words to Know

jiè 借	jyeh	to borrow/to loan
jíde yào mìng 急得要命	jee-duh yaow meeng	in an extreme hurry
bǐjìběn 笔记本 (筆記本)	bee-jee-bun	notebook

Whenever you add **-de yào mìng** 得要命 (duh yaow meeng) right after a verb, you add a touch of drama and emphasize whatever the verb is. For example, if you say you're **lèi** 累 (lay), that means you're tired. But if you say you're **lèi de yào mìng** 累得要命 (lay duh yaow meeng), that means you're absolutely exhausted. If you're not just **máng** 忙 (mahng) (*busy*) but rather **máng de yào mìng** 忙得要命 (mahng duh yaow meeng), you're extremely busy, running around like a chicken without a head. Here are some useful phrases to compare:

Wǒ lěng. 我冷. (waw lung.) (*I'm cold.*)

Wǒ lěng de yào mìng. 我冷得要命. (waw lung duh yaow meeng.) (*I'm freezing.*)

Jīntiān hěn rè. 今天很热. (今天很熱.) (jeen-tyan hun ruh.) (*It's very hot today.*)

Jīntiān rè de yào mìng. 今天热得要命. (今天熱得要命.) (jeen-tyan ruh duh yaow meeng.) (*It's a real scorcher today.*)

If you're going to emphasize a verb by adding **-de yào mìng** after it, you can't also use **hěn** 很 (hun) (*very*) in the same breath. It makes your statement redundant.

Conducting a Meeting

Congratulations! You've finally set up shop in your new office in Beijing or welcomed your business partners from Taiwan and are all set to have your first business meeting. But just what is the purpose of your **huìyì** 会议(會議) (hway-ee) (*meeting*)? Is it to **yǎnshì** 演示 (yan-shir) (*give a presentation*) about a new **chǎnpǐn** 产品 (產品) (chahn-peen) (*product*)? Is it to **tánpàn** 谈判 (談判) (tahn-pahn) (*negotiate*) a **hétóng** 合同 (huh-toong) (*contract*)? How about **shòuxùn** 受训 (受訓) (show-shwun) (*training*) — either you or your Chinese colleagues? Do you have a specific **yìchéng** (议程) 議程 (ee-chung) (*agenda*) in mind already? I hope so. You definitely don't want to look unprepared.

Scheduling and planning a meeting

You may be one of those people who needs to **ānpái huìyì yìchéng** 安排会议议程 (安排會議議程) (ahn-pye hway-ee ee-chung) (*schedule a meeting*) just to prepare for another meeting. Here are some things you may want to do at such a preliminary meeting:

✔ **jiějué wèntí** 解决问题 (解决問題) (jyeh-jweh one-tee) (*solve problems*)

✔ **tǎolùn wèntí** 讨论问题 (討論問題) (taow-lwun one-tee) (*discuss problems*)

✔ **tuánduì jiànshè** 团队建设 (團隊建設) (twan-dway jyan-shuh) (*team building*)

✔ **zhìdìng huìyì yìchéng** 制定会议议程 (制定會議議程) (jir-deeng hway-ee ee-chung) (*set an agenda*)

What is your role at these meetings? Are you the one to **zhǔchí huìyì** 主持会议 (主持會議) (joo-chir hway-ee) (*lead the meeting*) or just to **cānjiā huìyì** 参加会议 (参加會議) (tsahn-jya hway-ee) (*participate in the meeting*)? Are you the **xiétiáorén** 协调人 (協調人) (shyeh-tyaow-run) (*facilitator*) of the meeting, trying to elicit as much **fǎnkuì** 反馈 (反饋) (fahn-kway) (*feedback*) as possible? Or do you always have the unenviable task of contacting everyone to **qǔxiāo huìyì** 取消会议 (取消會議) (chyew-shyaow hway-ee) (*cancel the meeting*)?

Suppose you're the one who's leading the meeting and you want to make sure everyone has a say in matters. Here are some phrases you can use to try to include everyone in the process:

✔ **Jack, nǐ hái yǒu shénme xūyào bǔchōng ma?** Jack, 你还有什么需要补充吗? (Jack, 你還有什麼需要補充嗎?) (Jack, nee hi yo shummuh shyewyaow boo-choong mah?) (*Jack, do you have anything else to add?*)

✔ **Shéi hái yǒu shénme yìjiàn huòzhě wèntí?** 谁还有什么意见或者问题? (誰還有甚麼意見或者問題?) (shay hi yo shummuh ee-jyan hwaw-juh onetee?) (*Who still has any comments or questions?*)

✔ **Wǒmen xūyào duì zhèige xiàngmù biǎojué ma?** 我们需要对这个项目表决吗? (我們需要對這個項目表決嗎?) (waw-men shyew-yaow dway jay-guh shyahng-moo byaow-jweh mah?) (*Do we need to vote on this item?*)

Making the initial greeting

Suppose you've already had some contacts with your business counterparts on the phone or via e-mail but have never actually met them until now. A mere "nice to meet you" may not suffice, especially if you want to emphasize how very glad you are to finally be speaking face to face. Here are a couple of phrases you can use:

✔ **Hěn gāoxìng jiàn dào nín běnrén.** 很高兴见到您本人. (很高興見到您本人.) (hun gaow-sheeng jyan daow neen bun-run.) (*I'm glad to meet you in person.*)

✔ **Zǒngsuàn jiàn dào nín le, shízài ràng wǒ hěn gāoxìng.** 总算见到您了, 实在让我很高兴. (總算見到您了, 實在讓我很高興.) (dzoong-swan jyan daow neen luh, shir-dzye rahng waw hun gaow-sheeng.) (*It's a pleasure to finally meet you.*)

Always greet the person who holds the highest rank first before saying hello to others. Hierarchy is important to the Chinese, so try to always be conscious of this convention, or you may unintentionally cause someone to lose face by not acknowledging his or her importance in the overall scheme of things. This consideration goes for your side of the equation as well. The leader of your team should enter the room first and then wait to be seated by the host of the meeting.

The people you meet with may have one of the following titles:

- **chǎngzhǎng** 厂长 (廠長) (chahng-jahng) (*factory director*)
- **dǒngshì** 董事 (doong-shir) (*director of the board*)
- **fù zǒngcái** 副总裁 (副总裁) (foo dzoong-tsye) (*vice president*)
- **jīnglǐ** 经理 (經理) (jeeng-lee) (*manager*)
- **shǒuxí kuàijì** 首席会计 (首席會計) (show-she kwye-jee) (*chief financial officer*)
- **zhǔrèn** 主任 (joo-run) (*director of a department*)
- **zhǔxí** 主席 (joo-she) (*chairman*)
- **zǒngcái** 总裁 (總裁) (dzoong-tsye) (*president*)
- **zǔzhǎng** 组长 (組長) (dzoo-jahng) (*team leader*)

In Chinese, last names always come first. When addressing someone with a title, always say the last name first, followed by the title. So if you know someone's name is **Lǐ Pēijié** (lee pay-jyeh) (**Lǐ** being the surname), and he's the director of the company, you address him as **Lǐ Zhǔrèn** (lee joo-run) (*Director Li*).

Try to get a list of the names of your Chinese counterparts in advance so you can practice pronouncing them correctly. That's sure to win a few brownie points right there.

Be sure you have business cards ready (preferably in Chinese as well as English) to give out when you go to China. You should always hand and receive each business card with two hands. Feel free to place the cards you receive in the same order as those seated (for example, from left to right as people seat themselves across from you) so you'll remember who is who.

If you're the guest of honor at a dinner banquet, you're seated facing the entrance to the room. Don't worry if you get confused figuring out where to sit when facing a round table. Your host will make sure to show you to your seat. (Refer to Chapter 8 for eating etiquette tips.)

Starting the meeting

Here are some things to say when you're ready to get the business meeting started:

- **Huānyíng nín dào wǒmen de bàngōngshì.** 欢迎您到我们的办公室。(歡迎您到我們的辦公室。) (hwahn-eeng neen daow waw-mun duh bahn-goong-shir.) (*Welcome to our office.*)

✔ **Wǒ xiǎng jièshào yíxià huìyì de cānjiāzhě.** 我想介绍一下会议的参加者. (我想介绍一下會議的參加者.) (waw shyahng jyeh-shaow ee-shyah hway-ee duh tsahn-jya-juh.) (*I'd like to introduce the conference participants.*)

✔ **Zài kāihuì yǐqián, ràng wǒmen zuò yíge zìwǒ jièshào.** 在开会以前, 让我们做一个自我介绍. (在開會以前, 讓我們做一個自我介紹.) (dzye kye-hway ee-chyan, rahng waw-men dzwaw yee-guh dzuh-waw jyeh-shaow.) (*Before the meeting begins, let's introduce ourselves.*)

✔ **Zánmen kāishǐ ba.** 咱们开始吧. (咱們開始吧.) (dzah-mun kye-shir bah.) (*Let's begin.*)

✔ **Zǎoshàng hǎo.** 早上好. (dzaow-shahng how.) (*Good morning.*)

Making a presentation

When you want to give a presentation during the meeting, here are some words that you may want to use:

✔ **bǎnzi** 板子 (bahn-dzuh) (*board*)

✔ **biǎogé** 表格 (byaow-guh) (*charts*)

✔ **cǎibǐ** 彩笔 (彩筆) (tsye-bee) (*marker*)

✔ **caí liào** 材料 (tsye-lyaow) (*handouts*)

✔ **chātú** 插图 (插圖) (chah-too) (*illustrations*)

✔ **fěnbǐ** 粉笔 (粉筆) (fun-bee) (*chalk*)

✔ **huàbǎn** 画板 (畫板) (hwah-bahn) (*easel*)

✔ **túbiāo** 图表 (圖表) (too-byaow) (*diagrams*)

Planning to go high-tech instead? In that case, you may want one of these:

✔ **huàndēngjī** 幻灯机 (幻燈機) (hwahn-dung-jee) (*slide projector*)

✔ **píngmù** 屏幕 (peeng-moo) (*screen*)

✔ **PowerPoint yǎnshì** PowerPoint 演示 (PowerPoint yan-shir) (*PowerPoint presentation*)

✔ **tòu yǐng piàn** 透影片 (toe yeeng pyan) (*transparency*)

If you plan on videotaping your presentation, you need a **lùxiàngjī** 录像机 (錄像機) (loo-shyahng-jee) (*video recorder*), and if the room is pretty big, you may also want to use a **màikèfēng** 麦克风 (麥克風) (my-kuh-fung) (*microphone*).

Ending the meeting

Here are some phrases that may come in handy at the conclusion of the meeting:

- **Gǎnxiè dàjiā jīntiān chūxí huìyì.** 感谢大家今天出席会议. (感謝大家今天 出席會議.) (gahn-shyeh dah-jyah jeen-tyan choo-she hway-ee.) (*Thank you, everyone, for participating in today's meeting.*)

- **Wǒmen xūyào zài kāihuì tǎolùn zhè jiàn shìqíng ma?** 我们需要再开会 讨论这件事情吗? (我們需要再開會討論這件事情嗎?) (waw-men shyew-yaow dzye kye-hway taow-lwun jay jyan shir-cheeng mah?) (*Do we need another meeting to continue the discussion?*)

- **Zài líkāi zhīqián, wǒmen bǎ xià cì huìyì de rìqī dìng xiàlái ba.** 在离开 之前, 我们把下次会议的日期定下来吧. (在離開之前, 我們把下次會議 的日 期定下來吧.) (dzye lee-kye jir-chyan, waw-mun bah shyah tsuh hway-ee duh er-chee deeng shyah-lye bah.) (*Before we leave, let's confirm a date for the next meeting.*)

Talkin' the Talk

Cynthia and Pete have introduced themselves to their Chinese counterparts at the ABC Company in Shenzhen. They plan to give a presentation on their new software product a little later on. (Track 15)

Cynthia: **Dàjiā hǎo. Zhè cì huìyì de mùdì shì gěi nǐmen jièshào ABC gōngsī de xīn chǎnpǐn, yīzhǒng bào biǎo de ruǎnjiàn.**
dah-jyah how. jay tsuh hway-ee duh moo-dee shir gay nee-men jyeh-shaow ABC goong-suh duh sheen chahn-peen, ee-joong baow byaow duh rwahn-jyan.
Hello everyone. The purpose of this meeting is to introduce you all to ABC Company's new product, a type of spreadsheet software.

Pete: **Měi gè rén dōu yǒu huìyì yìchéng ma?**
may guh run doe yo hway-ee ee-chung mah?
Does everyone have a copy of the agenda?

Cynthia: **Xièxiè, Pete. Duì le. Dàjiā dōu yǐjīng nádào zīliào le ma?**
shyeh-shyeh, Pete. dway luh. dah-jyah doe ee-jeeng nah-daow dzuh-lyaow luh mah?
Thank you, Pete. Yes, has everyone already received the materials?

Words to Know

huìyì 会议 (會議)	hway-ee	meeting/conference
mùdì 目的	moo-dee	purpose
zīliào 资料 (資料)	dzuh-lyaow	material
bào biǎo 报表 (報表)	baow byaow	spreadsheet
ruǎnjiàn 软件 (軟件)	rwahn-jyan	software
huìyì yìchéng 会议议程 (會議議程)	hway-ee ee-chung	conference agenda

Discussing Business and Industry

Because China has opened up to the world so quickly since the death of Mao Zedong in 1976 (the United States established diplomatic relations with the People's Republic in 1979), U.S. businesses in many areas have set up shop in many parts of the country. Whether your company has an office in mainland China, Taiwan, Singapore, or Hong Kong, you're sure to find one or more of the industries listed in Table 12-3 represented in those places.

Table 12-3	Industries	
Chinese	**Pronunciation**	**English**
bǎoxiǎn 保险 (保險)	baow-shyan	insurance
cǎikuǎng yú shíyóu 采矿与石油 (採礦與石油)	tsye-kwahng yew shir-yo	mining and petroleum
chūbǎn 出版	choo-bahn	publishing
diànnǎo 电脑 (電腦)	dyan-now	computers
fángdìchǎn 房地产 (房地產)	fahng-dee-chahn	real estate

(continued)

Table 12-3 *(continued)*

Chinese	Pronunciation	English
gōngchéng 工程	goong-chung	engineering
gōngguān 公关 (公關)	goong-gwan	public relations
guǎnggào 广告 (廣告)	gwahng-gaow	advertising
guǎnlǐ zīxún 管理咨询 (管理咨詢)	gwahn-lee dzuh-shwun	management consulting
jiànzào 建造 (建造)	jyan-dzaow	construction
qìchē 汽车 (汽車)	chee-chuh	automotive
shízhuāng 时装 (時裝)	shir-jwahng	fashion
xīnwén 新闻 (新聞)	sheen-one	journalism
yínháng yǔ cáiwù 银行 与财务 (銀行與財物)	yeen-hahng yew tsye-woo	banking and finance
yúlè 娱乐 (娛樂)	yew-luh	entertainment
yùn shū 运输 (運輸)	yewn shoo	shipping
zhìyào 制药 (製藥)	jir-yaow	pharmaceuticals

Regardless of what industry you're in, here are some things you can do to help you decide how to advertise your company and its products or services or to determine how it's going:

- **diàntái yú diànshì guǎnggào** 电台与电视广告 (電台與電視廣告) (dyan-tie yew dyan-shir gwahng-gaow) (*radio and television ads*)

- **dīngdāng** 叮当 (叮噹) (deeng-dahng) (*jingle*)

- **guǎnggào xuānchuán** 广告宣传 (廣告宣傳) (gwahng-gaow shwan-chwan) (*ad campaign*)

- **pǐnpái tuīguǎng** 品牌推广 (品牌推广) (peen-pye tway-gwahng) (*brand-name promotion*)

- **shìchǎng yánjiū** 市场研究 (市場研究) (shir-chahng yan-jyo) (*market research*)

- **xiāofèizhě yánjiū** 消费者研究 (消費者研究) (shyaow-fay-juh yan-jyo) (*consumer research*)

- **xìnxī guǎnggào** 信息广告 (信息廣告) (sheen-she gwahng-gaow) (*infomercial*)

- **zhíxiāo yùndòng** 直销运动 (直銷運動) (jir-shyaow yoon-doong) (*direct marketing campaign*)

And here are some things you should have on hand in meetings or at that **màoyì zhǎnxiāohuì** 贸易展销会 (貿易展銷會) (maow-ee jahn-shyaow-hway) (*trade show*):

▶ **chǎnpǐn mùlù** 产品目录 (產品目錄) (chahn-peen moo-loo) (*catalogue*)

▶ **túbiāo** 图标 (圖標) (too-byaow) (*logo*)

▶ **xiǎocèzǐ** 小册子 (小冊子) (shyaow-tsuh-dzuh) (*brochure*)

Of course, if your product is so good it virtually sells itself, your greatest source of business is undoubtedly going to come from good ol' **kǒuchuán guǎnggào** 口传广告 (口傳廣告) (ko-chwan gwahng-gaow) (*word-of-mouth advertising*).

Talkin' the Talk

William and Douglas, two salesmen, visit Guangdong to see whether the Flying Peacock Company wants to buy their product. They're in a meeting with the Flying Peacock Company president, where they've already gone through the preliminary introductions and small talk.

William: **Zhè shì yǒu guān wǒmen chǎnpǐn de xiǎocèzǐ.**
jay shir yo gwan waw-mun chahn-peen duh shyaow-tsuh-dzuh.
Here's a brochure on our product.

Douglas: **Wǒmen de chǎnpǐn shì yóu wǒmen zìjǐ de zhuānjiā shèjì de érqiě zhèngmíng shì mǎn chénggōng de.**
waw-men duh chahn-peen shir yo waw-men dzuh-jee duh jwan-jyah shuh-jee duh are-chyeh jung-meeng shir mahn chung-goong duh.
Our product was designed by our own experts and has proven to be quite successful.

William: **Duì le, kěshì wǒmen yě kéyǐ gēnjù nǐde guīgé lái shèjì chǎnpǐn.**
dway luh, kuh-shir waw-men yeah kuh-yee gun-jyew nee-duh gway-guh lye shuh-jee chahn-peen.
That's correct, but we can also tailor the product to meet your specifications.

Douglas: **Wǒmen de jiàgé yě hěn yǒu jìngzhēnglì.**
waw-mun duh jyah-guh yeah hun yo jeeng-juhng-lee.
Our prices are also quite competitive.

Words to Know

chǎnpǐn 产品 (產品)	chahn-peen	product
mǎn chénggōng de 满成功的 (滿 成功的)	mahn chung-goong duh	very successful
gēnjù nǐde guīgé 根据你的规格 (根據你的規格)	gun-jyew nee-duh gway-guh	according to your specifications
jiàgé 价格 (價格)	jyah-guh	price
hěn yǒu jìngzhēnglì 很有竞争力 (很有競爭力)	hun yo jeeng-juhng-lee	very competitive

Fun & Games

Match each of the Chinese phrases to the correct English phrase. Turn to Appendix D for the answers.

1. *I'm freezing.*

2. *Let's begin.*

3. *Do you have a pen?*

4. *Who still has any questions?*

5. *I'm cold.*

a. **Wǒ lěng.** 我冷.

b. **Nǐ yǒu méiyǒu bǐ?** 你有没有笔?
   (你有沒有筆?)

c. **Wǒ lěng de yào mìng.** 我冷得要命.

d. **Shéi hái yǒu shénme yìjiàn huòzhě wèntí?** 谁还有什么意见或者问题?
   (誰還有甚麼意見或者問題?)

e. **Zánmen kāishǐ ba.** 咱们开始吧.
   (咱們開始吧.)

Chapter 13

Recreation and Outdoor Activities

In This Chapter

▶ Talking about your hobbies

▶ Appreciating Mother Nature

▶ Pretending to be Picasso

▶ Creating your own tunes

▶ Exercising as an athlete

After a hard day at work, most people are ready to kick back and relax. But where to begin? Do you feel so consumed by your **gōngzuò** 工作 (goong-dzwaw) (*work*) that you can't seem to switch gears? Get a life! Better yet, get a **yèyú àihào** 业余爱好 (業餘愛好) (yeh-yew eye-how) (*hobby*). Play some **yīnyuè** 音乐 (音樂) (yeen-yweh) (*music*) on your **xiǎotíqín** 小提琴 (shyaow-tee-cheen) (*violin*). Paint a **huà** 画 (畫) (hwah) (*picture*). Kick a **zúqiú** 足球 (dzoo-chyo) (*football*) around. Do whatever it takes to make you relax and have some fun. Your outside interests make you more interesting to be around, and you make new friends at the same time — especially if you join a **duì** 队 (隊) (dway) (*team*).

And if you're into **lánqiú** 篮球 (籃球) (lahn-chyo) (*basketball*), just utter the name **Yao Ming** 姚明 (yaow meeng); you'll instantly discover hordes of potential language exchange partners from among the many fans of this 7-foot-6-inch Shanghai native who made it big as a Houston Rockets superstar.

Naming Your Hobbies

Are you someone who likes to collect stamps, play chess, or watch birds in the park? Whatever you enjoy doing, your hobbies are always a good conversation piece. Having at least one **yèyú àihào** 业余爱好 (業餘愛好) (yeh-yew eye-how) (*hobby*) is always a good thing. How about getting involved in some of the following?

✔ **guān niǎo** (gwan-nyaow) 观鸟 (觀鳥) (*birdwatching*)

✔ **jí yóu** 集邮 (集郵) (jee-yo) (*stamp collecting*)

✔ **diàoyú** 钓鱼 (釣魚) (dyaow-yew) (*fishing*)

✔ **kàn shū** 看书 (看書) (kahn shoo) (*reading*)

✔ **pēngtiáo** 烹调 (烹調) (pung-tyaow) (*cooking*)

✔ **yuányì** 园艺 (園藝) (ywan-ee) (*gardening*)

A common verb associated with many hobbies is **dǎ** 打 (dah) (*to do or play with* [Literally: *to strike, hit, or beat*]). You can use it to talk about partaking in hobbies such as **tàijíquán** 太极拳 (太極拳) (tye-jee-chwan) (*a slow form of martial arts commonly referred to just as Tai Ji*) and playing **pú kè** 扑克 (撲克)(poo kuh) (*cards*), **májiàng** 麻将 (麻將) (mah-jyahng) (*mah-jong*), and **guójì xiàngqí** 国际象棋 (國際象棋) (gwaw-jee shyahng-chee) (*chess*). Here are some quick questions with the verb **dǎ** that can help get a conversation started:

✔ **Nǐ huì búhuì dǎ tàijíquán?** 你会不会打太极拳? (你會不會打太極拳?) (nee hway boo-hway dah tye-jee-chwahn?) (*Do you know how to do Tai Ji?*)

✔ **Nǐ dǎ májiàng ma?** 你打麻将吗? (你打麻將嗎?) (nee dah mah-jyahng mah?) (*Do you play mah-jong?*)

Both **tàijíquán** and **májiàng** are quintessential Chinese pastimes. In addition to **tàijíquán,** everyone is familiar with other forms of **wǔshù** 武术 (武術) (woo-shoo) (*martial arts*), including **kung fu** 功夫 — a martial art practiced since the **Tang** 唐 (tahng) dynasty back in the 8th century. In fact, you can still see **kung fu** masters practicing at the Shaolin Temple in Zhengzhou, Henan Province — one great reason for making a trip off the beaten path if you ever visit China.

Tàijíquán is considered an internal martial art and is the most widely practiced form of martial arts throughout the world. The term **tàijí** (*the Great Ultimate*) refers to the interplay between opposing yet complementary forces in the universe — yin and yang — as the basis of creation. **Quán** means *fist,* emphasizing that this art is a kind of unarmed combat. Very early every morning in China, tons of people flock to local parks to practice this slow-motion form of exercise together.

Talkin' the Talk

Donald and Helga discuss their knowledge of **taijiquan** with each other.

Donald: **Nǐ huì búhuì dǎ tàijíquán?**
nee hway boo-hway dah tye-jee-chwan?
Do you know how to do Tai Ji?

Helga: **Búhuì. Kěshì wǒ zhīdào tàijíquán shì yì zhǒng hěn liúxíng de jiànshēn yùndòng.**
boo-hway. kuh-shir waw jir-daow tye-jee-chwan shir ee joong hun lyo-sheeng duh jyan-shun yoon-doong.
No, but I know that Tai Ji is a very popular kind of exercise.

Donald: **Duìle. Měitiān zǎoshàng hěn zǎo hěn duō rén yìqǐ dǎ tàijíquán.**
dway-luh. may-tyan dzaow-shahng hun dzaow hun dwaw run ee-chee dah tye-jee-chwan.
That's right. Very early every morning, lots of people practice Tai Ji together.

Helga: **Tàijíquán de dòngzuò kànqǐlái hěn màn.**
tye-jee-chwan duh doong-dzwaw kahn-chee-lye hun mahn.
Tai Ji movements look very slow.

Donald: **Yòu shuō duìle! Shēntǐ zǒngshì yào wěndìng. Dòngzuò zǒngshì yào xiétiáo.**
yo shwaw dway-luh! shun-tee dzoong-shir yaow one-deeng. doong-dzwaw dzoong-shir yaow shyeh-tyaow.
Right again! The body should always be stable, and the movements should always be well coordinated.

Words to Know

měitiān zǎoshàng hěn zǎo 每天早上很早	may-tyan dzaow-shahng hun dzaow	very early every morning
liúxíng 流行	lyo-sheeng	popular
yùndòng 运动 (運動)	yoon-doong	exercise
dòngzuò 动作 (動作)	doong-dzwaw	movement

Exploring Nature

If you're working overseas in China and want to get really far from the madding crowds, or even just far enough away from your **bàngōngshì** 办公室 (辦公室) (bahn-goong-shir) (*office*) to feel refreshed, try going to one of China's many sacred mountains or a beautiful beach to take in the **shānshuǐ** 山水 (shahn-shway) (*landscape*). You may want to **qù lùyíng** 去露营 (去露營) (chyew lyew-eeng) (*go camping*) or set up camp on the beach and have a **yěcān** 野餐 (yeh-tsahn) (*picnic*) before you **pá shān** 爬山 (pah shahn) (*climb a mountain*).

Traveling through the Chinese countryside is a great way to escape city life. Check out these sights along the way:

- ✔ **bǎotǎ** 宝塔 (寶塔) (baow-tah) (*pagoda*)
- ✔ **dàomiào** 道庙 (道廟) (daow-meow) (*Daoist temple*)
- ✔ **dàotián** 稻田 (daow-tyan) (*rice paddies*)
- ✔ **fómiào** 佛庙 (佛廟) (faw-meow) (*Buddhist temple*)
- ✔ **kǒngmiào** 孔庙 (孔廟) (koong-meow) (*Confucian temple*)
- ✔ **miào** 庙 (廟) (meow) (*temple*)
- ✔ **nóngmín** 农民 (農民) (noong-meen) (*farmers*)

If you're ever exploring **dàzìrán** 大自然 (dah-dzuh-rahn) (*nature*) with a friend who speaks Chinese, a few of these words may come in handy:

- ✔ **àn** 岸 (ahn) (*shore*)
- ✔ **chítáng** 池塘 (chir-tahng) (*pond*)
- ✔ **hǎi** 海 (hi) (*ocean*)
- ✔ **hǎitān** 海滩 (海灘) (hi-tahn) (*beach*)
- ✔ **hé** 河 (huh) (*river*)
- ✔ **hú** 湖 (hoo) (*lake*)
- ✔ **niǎo** 鸟 (鳥) (nyaow) (*birds*)
- ✔ **shāmò** 沙漠 (shah-maw) (*desert*)
- ✔ **shān** 山 (shahn) (*mountains*)
- ✔ **shāndòng** 山洞 (shahn-doong) (*cave*)
- ✔ **shù** 树 (樹) (shoo) (*trees*)
- ✔ **xiǎo shān** 小山 (shyaow-shahn) (*hills*)
- ✔ **yún** 云 (雲) (yewn) (*clouds*)

China's sacred mountains

Both Buddhists and Daoists have traditionally built monasteries high on quiet mountaintops or deep inside lush forests to meditate. Some of China's **shān** 山 (shahn) (*mountains*) — five Daoist and four Buddhist — are still considered sacred today, and they all remain sites of pilgrimage. **Huáng Shān** 黄山 (hwahng shahn) (*Yellow Mountain*) is perhaps China's most famous sacred mountain; it's distinguished by rare pine trees, unusual rock formations, and hot springs and surrounded by lakes and waterfalls.

Talkin' the Talk

Herman and Serena discover the beauty of the seaside resort of **Běidàihé** (bay-dye-huh) in northern China. (Track 16)

Herman: **Nǐ kàn! Zhèr de fēngjǐng duōme piàoliàng!**
nee kahn! jar duh fung-jeeng dwaw-muh pyaow-lyahng!
Look! The scenery here is gorgeous! (Literally: How gorgeous the scenery here is!)

Serena: **Nǐ shuō duìle. Zhēn piàoliàng.**
nee shwaw dway-luh. jun pyaow-lyahng.
You're right. It's truly beautiful.

Herman: **Shénme dōu yǒu: shān, shēn lán de hǎi, qīng lán de tiān.**
shummuh doe yo: shahn, shun lahn duh hi, cheeng lahn duh tyan.
It has everything: mountains, deep blue ocean, and clear sky.

Serena: **Nǐ shuō duìle. Xiàng tiāntáng yíyàng.**
nee shwaw dway-luh. shyahng tyan-tahng ee-yahng.
You're right. It's like paradise.

Words to Know

fēngjǐng 风景 (風景)	fung-jeeng	scenery
piàoliàng 漂亮	pyaow-lyahng	beautiful
shēn lán 深蓝 (深藍)	shun lahn	deep blue
qīng lán 清蓝 (清藍)	cheeng lahn	clear blue
tiāntáng 天堂	tyan-tahng	paradise

To indicate a similarity between two ideas or objects, as in the last line of the Talkin' the Talk involving Serena and Herman, use the phrase **xiàng . . . yíyàng** 像 . . . 一样。(像 . . . 一樣。) (shyahng . . . ee yahng.). Here are some examples:

xiàng nǐ dìdì yíyàng 像你弟弟一样 (像你弟弟一樣) (shyahng nee dee-dee ee-yahng) (*like your younger brother*)

xiàng qīngwā yíyàng 像青蛙一样 (像青蛙一樣) (shyahng cheeng-wah ee-yahng) (*like a frog*)

xiàng fēngzi yíyàng 像疯子一样 (像瘋子一樣) (shyahng fung-dzuh ee-yahng) (*like a crazy person*)

The Shanghai Children's Palace

If you ever visit Shanghai, make time for a visit to the **Shàoniángōng** 少年宫 (shaow-nyan-goong) (*the Children's Palace*), where gifted children take part in an assortment of extracurricular activities in areas such as music, art, dance, and science. Founded in 1953 by Song Qingling (whose husband, Dr. Sun Yat-sen, established the Republic of China, or Taiwan) the Children's Palace is in a grand old building originally known as Marble Hall. It was built by the Baghdadi Jewish tycoon Elly Kadoorie in 1924 and still boasts grand marble hallways, winding staircases, ornate fireplaces, chandeliers, and French windows.

Today you can find such activities as hot-air ballooning and gliding in Anyang. Kind of amazing when you discover Anyang was the capital of China's very first dynasty, almost two millennia before the Common Era. You can even hook up with a hot-air balloon tour of the Great Wall and the Silk Road. These pursuits certainly present a good way to cover such great distances without requiring you to have been a Hun on horseback. Speaking of which, if camel treks are your thing, Chinese travel agencies can now even arrange for you to ride with the Mongols, those horsemen who've perfected the art of riding over the centuries.

Tapping into Your Artistic Side

You may pride yourself on having been the biggest jock, but I bet you still get teary-eyed when you see a beautiful painting or listen to Beethoven. It's okay, just admit it. You're a regular Renaissance man and you can't help it. No more apologies.

Okay, now you're ready to tap into your more sensitive, artistic side in Chinese. Don't be afraid of expressing your **gǎnqíng** 感情 (gahn-cheeng) (*emotions*). The Chinese will appreciate your sensitivity to a **shānshuǐ huà** 山水画 (山水畫) (shahn-shway hwah) (*landscape painting*) from the **Sòng** 宋 (soong) dynasty (960–1279) or to the beauty of a **cíqì** 瓷器 (tsuh-chee) (*porcelain*) from the **Míng** 明 (meeng) dynasty (1368–1644).

I bet you have tons of **chuàngzàoxìng** 创造性 (創造性) (chwahng-dzaow-sheeng) (*creativity*). If so, try your hand at one of these fine arts:

- **diāokè** 雕刻 (雕刻) (dyaow-kuh) (*sculpting*)
- **huà** 画 (畫) (hwah) (*painting*)
- **shūfǎ** 书法 (書法) (shoo-fah) (*calligraphy*)
- **shuǐcǎi huà** 水彩画 (水彩畫) (shway-tsye hwah) (*watercolor*)
- **sùmiáo huà** 素描画 (素描畫) (soo-meow hwah) (*drawing*)
- **táoqì** 陶器 (taow-chee) (*pottery*)

Striking Up the Band

Do you play a **yuè qì** 乐器 (樂器) (yweh chee) (*musical instrument*)? It's never too late to learn, you know. Like kids all over the world, lots of Chinese children take **xiǎo tíqín** 小提琴 (shyaow tee-cheen) (*violin*) and **gāngqín** 钢琴 (鋼琴) (gahng-cheen) (*piano*) classes — often under duress. They appreciate the forced lessons when they get older, though, and have their own kids.

You don't have to become a professional **yīnyuèjiā** 音乐家 (音樂家) (een-yweh-jyah) (*musician*) to enjoy playing an instrument. How about trying your hand (or mouth) at one of these?

- **chángdí** 长笛 (長笛) (chahng-dee) (*flute*)
- **chánghào** 长号 (長號) (chahng-how) (*trombone*)
- **dà hào** 大号 (大號) (dah how) (*tuba*)
- **dà tíqín** 大提琴 (dah tee-cheen) (*cello*)
- **dānhuángguǎn** 单簧管 (單簧管) (dahn-hwahng-gwan) (*clarinet*)
- **gāngqín** 钢琴 (鋼琴) (gahng-cheen) (*piano*)
- **gǔ** 鼓 (goo) (*drums*)
- **lǎbā** 喇叭 (lah-bah) (*trumpet*)
- **liùxiánqín** 六弦琴 (lyo-shyan-cheen) (*guitar*)
- **nán dīyīn** 男低音 (nahn dee-een) (*double bass*)
- **sākèsīguǎn** 萨克斯管 (薩克斯管) (sah-kuh-suh-gwahn) (*saxophone*)
- **shuānghuángguǎn** 双簧管 (雙簧管) (shwahng-hwahng-gwan) (*oboe*)
- **shùqín** 竖琴 (豎琴) (shoo-cheen) (*harp*)
- **xiǎo tíqín** 小提琴 (shyaow tee-cheen) (*violin*)
- **zhōng tíqín** 中提琴 (joong tee-cheen) (*viola*)

The Chinese language has a few different verbs that you can use to indicate the practice of various instruments. People who play stringed instruments should use the verb **lā** 拉 (lah) (*to draw* [as in draw a bow]) before the name of the instrument. For example, you can say that you **lā zhōng tíqín** 拉中提琴 (lah joong tee-cheen) (*play the viola*), but you can only **tán** (tahn) (*play*) a piano. For wind instruments, you have to **chuī** 吹 (chway) (*blow*) them.

Traditional Chinese Instruments

If you've heard any traditional Chinese music at a concert or on a recording, you've probably heard one of these Chinese **yuè qì** 乐器 (樂器) (yweh chee) (*musical instruments*) at one point or another:

- **pípā** 琵琶 (pee-pah): A plucked string instrument with a fretted fingerboard that sits on your lap

- **gǔzhēng** 古筝 (古箏) (goo-juhng): A long, plucked string instrument that rests on a large stand in front of you

- **èrhú** 二胡 (are-hoo): A two-stringed bowed instrument

Playing on a Team

No matter where you go in the world, you'll find a national pastime. In America, it's baseball. In most of Europe, it's soccer. And in China, it's ping pong, although since Yao Ming came on the scene, basketball has gotten some attention as well. Here are the Chinese terms for these and many other popular sports:

- **bàngqiú** 棒球 (bahng-chyo) (*baseball*)
- **bīngqiú** 冰球 (beeng-chyo) (*hockey*)
- **lánqiú** 篮球 (籃球) (lahn-chyo) (*basketball*)
- **lěiqiú** 垒球 (壘球) (lay-chyo) (*softball*)
- **páiqiú** 排球 (pye-chyo) (*volleyball*)
- **pīngpāngqiú** 乒乓球 (peeng-pahng-chyo) (*ping pong*)
- **shǒuqiú** 手球 (show-chyo) (*handball*)
- **tǐcāo** 体操 (體操) (tee-tsaow) (*gymnastics*)
- **wǎngqiú** 网球 (網球) (wahng-chyo) (*tennis*)
- **yīngshì zúqiú** 英式足球 (eeng-shir dzoo-chyo) (*soccer* [Literally: *English-style football*])
- **yóuyǒng** 游泳 (yo-yoong) (*swimming*)
- **yǔmáoqiú** 羽毛球 (yew-maow-chyo) (*badminton*)
- **zúqiú** 足球 (dzoo-chyo) (*football*)

Some sports, such as gymnastics and swimming, actually involve multiple events. Here are the common components of these two sports:

- **ān mǎ** 鞍马 (鞍馬) (ahn mah) (*pommell horse*)
- **dān gàng** 单杠 (單槓) (dahn gahng) (*high bar*)
- **gāo dī gàng** 高低杠 (高低槓) (gaow dee gahng) (*uneven bars*)
- **shuāng gàng** 双杠 (雙槓) (shwahng gahng) (*parallel bars*)
- **zìyóu tǐcāo** 自由体操 (自由體操) (dzuh-yo tee-tsaow) (*floor exercise*)
- **cè yǒng** 侧泳 (側泳) (tsuh yoong) (*sidestroke*)
- **dié yǒng** 蝶泳 (dyeh yoong) (*butterfly stroke*)
- **wā yǒng** 蛙泳 (wah yoong) (*frog-style or breast stroke*)
- **yǎng yǒng** 仰泳 (yahng yoong) (*backstroke*)
- **zìyóu yǒng** 自由泳 (dzuh-yo yoong) (*freestyle*)

And if you're a **tiàoshuǐ yùndòngyuán** 跳水运动员 (跳水運動員) (tyaow-shway yewn-doong-ywan) (*diver*), you'd better not **pà gāo** 怕高 (pah gaow) (*be scared of heights*).

You can use the verb **dǎ** to talk about playing sports as well as pursuing other hobbies (check out the earlier section "Naming Your Hobbies"). But you can also **wán** 玩 (wahn) (*play*) ball games as well.

Remember: Some games require the use of **pīngpāngqiú pāi** 乒乓球拍 (peeng-pahng-chyo pye) (*ping-pong paddles*), **wǎngqiú pāi** 网球拍 (網球拍) (wahng-chyo pye) (*tennis rackets*), or **qiú** 球 (chyo) (*balls*). All games, however, require a sense of **gōngpíng jìngzhēng** 公平竞争 (公平競爭) (goong-peeng jeeng-jung) (*fair play*).

Soccer season in Beijing is from May to October, but in southern China it goes year-round. As in Europe, soccer is the spectator sport of preference throughout the country. And just as in Europe, passionate fans sometimes boil over into brawling hordes. If you ever find yourself in Shanghai, check out the game at the Hong Kou Stadium. In Beijing, try the Workers' Stadium near the City Hotel.

Here are some useful phrases to know, whether you're an amateur or a professional athlete. At one time or another, you've certainly heard (or said) them all.

- ✔ **Nǐ shūle.** 你输了. (你輸了.) (nee shoo-luh.) (*You lost.*)

- ✔ **Wǒ dǎ de bútài hǎo.** 我打得不太好. (waw dah duh boo-tye how.) (*I don't play very well.*)

- ✔ **Wǒ yíngle.** 我赢了. (我贏了.) (waw yeeng-luh.) (*I won.*)

- ✔ **Wǒ zhēn xūyào liànxí.** 我真需要练习. (我真需要練習.) (waw jun shyew-yaow lyan-she.) (*I really need to practice.*)

If you prefer to spectate from the stands (or from your couch), here's a list of terms and phrases you need to know if you want to follow the action:

- ✔ **Bǐfēn duōshǎo?** 比分多少? (bee-fun dwaw-shaow?) (*What's the score?*)

- ✔ **chuī shàozi** 吹哨子 (chway shaow-dzuh) (*to blow a whistle*)

- ✔ **dǎngzhù qiú** 挡住球 (擋住球) (dahng-joo chyo) (*to block the ball*)

- ✔ **dé yì fēn** 得一分 (duh ee fun) (*to score a point*)

- ✔ **fā qiú** 发球 (發球) (fah chyo) (*to serve the ball*)

- ✔ **Něixiē duì cānjiā bǐsài?** 哪些队参加比赛? (哪些隊參加比賽?) (nay-shyeh dway tsahn-jya bee-sye?) (*Which teams are playing?*)

✔ **tījìn yì qiú** 踢进一球 (踢進一球) (tee-jeen ee chyo) (*to make a goal*)

✔ **Wǒ xiǎng qù kàn qiúsài.** 我想去看球赛 (我想去看球賽) (waw shyahng chyew kahn chyo-sye.) (*I want to see a ballgame.*)

Talkin' the Talk

Ernest and Cecilia go to a basketball game together. (Track 17)

Ernest: **Bǐsài shénme shíhòu kāishǐ?**
bee-sye shummuh shir-ho kye-shir?
When does the game begin?

Cecilia: **Kuài yào kāishǐ le.**
kwye yaow kye-shir luh.
It's going to start soon.

A few minutes later, the game finally begins.

Ernest: **Wà! Tā méi tóuzhòng!!**
wah! tah may toe-joong!
Wow! He missed the shot!

Cecilia: **Méi guānxi. Lìngwài nèige duìyuán gāng gāng kòulán défēn.**
may gwahn-she. leeng-why nay-guh dway-ywan gahng gahng ko-lahn duh-fun.
It doesn't matter. That other player just scored with a slam dunk.

Words to Know

kāishǐ 开始 (開始)	kye-shir	to begin
défēn 得分	duh-fun	to score a point
kòulán 扣篮 (扣籃)	ko-lahn	slam dunk

Fun & Games

A.   B.   C.

D.   E.

What are the people in the pictures doing? Use the correct verb in your response. (See Appendix D for the answers.)

A. _____

B. _____

C. _____

D. _____

E. _____

Part III
Chinese on the Go

The 5th Wave   By Rich Tennant

"I'll be screaming in Chinese throughout the ride.
It helps me affect the proper inflections."

In this part . . .

Ah, to travel the world! These chapters help you with every aspect of your travel, from getting a visa and making hotel reservations to deciphering foreign currency, asking for directions, and getting to your destination. I even include a chapter on handling emergencies, although I hope you never have to use it. **Yí lù píng'ān!** 路平安! (ee loo peeng-ahn!) (*Bon voyage!*)

Chapter 14

Planning a Trip

. . . .

In This Chapter

▶ Checking your calendar for open dates

▶ Planning around Chinese holidays

▶ Choosing a travel destination

▶ Filling your luggage

▶ Dealing with travel agents

. . . .

Careful planning is the key to a successful vacation or business trip. You have to keep in mind not only where you want to go but also the best time to travel. This chapter tells you how to prepare for a trip abroad and how to choose the exact day, date, and year you want to travel. When it comes to making sure your **hùzhào** 护照 (護照) (hoo-jaow) (*passport*) is still valid and your **qiānzhèng** 签证 (簽證) (chyan-juhng) (*visa*) is in order, however, you're on your own. **Yí lù píng ān!** 一路平安! (ee loo peeng ahn!) (*Have a good trip!*)

Talking about When You Want to Travel

The time of year you choose to travel can make all the difference in the world for a great (or lousy) vacation. A trip to Beijing during March, just when the dust storms are blowing in from the Gobi Desert, for example, is quite different from a trip during May or October, when pollution is at a minimum and sunny skies are at a maximum. Of course, May and October are peak seasons to travel to China for exactly these reasons, which means hotel prices are also at their peak. Paris in the spring is just as great (and just as expensive) for the same reason. Can't do much to help you there. For more on all things related to dates and seasons, head to Chapter 5.

Want to find out when friends plan to leave on their vacation? Just ask them one of these basic questions:

> ✔ **Nǐ jǐ yuè jǐ hào zǒu?** 你几月几号走? (你幾月幾號走?) (nee jee yweh jee how dzoe?) (*When are you leaving?* [Literally: *What month and day are you leaving?*])

> ✔ **Nǐ jǐ yuè jǐ hào qù Zhōngguó?** 你几月几号去中国? (你幾月幾號去中國?) (nee jee yweh jee how chyew joong-gwaw?) (*When will you be going to China?* [Literally: *What month and day will you be going to China?*])

If you have to answer the preceding questions, just fill in the month and the number of the day you plan on leaving and put those words in place of **yuè** and **hào.** Here are some examples:

> **Wǒ wǔ yuè sānshí hào zǒu.** 我五月三十号走. (我五月三十號走.) (waw woo yweh sahn shir how dzoe) (*I'm leaving on May 30.*)

> **Wǒ sān yuè yī hào qù Zhōngguó.** 我三月一号去中国. (我三月一號去中國.) (waw sahn yweh ee how chyew joong-gwaw) (*I'm going to China on March 1.*)

Bet you can't wait to start making those travel plans now!

Celebrating the Chinese Holidays

If you travel to China during 2013, you arrive during **shé nián** 蛇年 (shuh nyan) (*Year of the Snake*). Want to travel in later years instead?

> ✔ 2014: **mǎ nián** 马年 (馬年) (ma nyan) (*Year of the Horse*)

> ✔ 2015: **yáng nián** 羊年 (yahng nyan) (*Year of the Sheep*)

After the sheep, the following animals come calling: **hóu** 猴 (ho) (*monkey*), 鸡 (雞) (jee) (*rooster*), **gǒu** 狗 (狗) (go) (*dog*), **zhū** 猪 (豬) (joo) (*pig*), **shǔ** 鼠 (shoo) (*rat*), **niú** 牛 (nyo) (*ox*), **hǔ** 虎 (hoo) (*tiger*), **tù** 兔 (too) (*rabbit*), and finally the **lóng** 龙 (龍) (loong) (*dragon*) before the snake comes around again. It's the rat, though (not the snake), who starts the whole new 12-year cycle.

You may want to time your trip to mainland China, Taiwan, or Hong Kong to coincide with certain holidays — or, just as important, to avoid certain days and weeks.

First, you celebrate **xīnnián** 新年 (shin-nyan) (*New Year's Day*), also known as **yuándàn** 元旦 (ywan-dahn), on January 1. That's separate from a three-day celebration coinciding with the lunar New Year known as **chūn jié** 春节 (春節) (chwun jyeh) (*Spring Festival; Chinese New Year*). Every year, the dates for

chūn jié change because — you guessed it — it follows the **yīnlì** 阴历 (陰曆) (yeen-lee) (*lunar calendar*) rather than the **yánglì** 阳历 (陽曆) (yahng-lee) (*solar calendar*). **Chūn jié** always occurs sometime in January or February.

In mainland China, **Láodòng jié** 劳动节 (勞動節) (laow-doong jyeh) (*Labor Day*) is celebrated on May 1, and **Guó qìng jié** 国庆节 (國慶節) (gwaw cheeng jyeh) (*National Day*) is celebrated on October 1 in commemoration of the day Mao Zedong and the Chinese Communist Party declared the founding of **Zhōnghuá rénmín gònghé guó** 中华人民共和国 (中華人民共和國) (joong-hwah run-meen goong-huh gwaw) (*the People's Republic of China*) in 1949. In Taiwan, **Guó qìng jié** is celebrated on October 10 to commemorate the day in 1911 when China's long dynastic history ended and a new era of **Zhōnghuá mín guó** 中华民国 (中華民國) (joong-hwah meen gwaw) (*the Republic of China* [another name for Taiwan]) began, under the leadership of Dr. Sun Yat-sen. National Day in Taiwan is often referred to as **shuāng shí jié** 双十节 (雙十節) (shwahng shir jyeh) (Literally: *double 10 day*), because it occurs on the 10th day of the 10th month.

In Taiwan, you often see years written out that seem to be 11 years short of what you think is correct. That's because the founding of the Republic of China in 1911 is considered the base line for all future years. So 1921 is listed as **mín guó shí nián** 民国十年 (民國十年) (meen gwaw shir nyan); **mín guó** is the abbreviation for **Zhōnghuá mín guó**, and **shí nián,** meaning *10 years,* refers to 10 years following the founding of the Republic of China.

In addition to the major public holidays worthy of closing down businesses, you may want to experience some of the other fun and interesting Chinese holidays first-hand. Refer to Chapter 5 for more on Chinese holidays.

All sorts of folk festivals take place in villages throughout mainland China and Taiwan when you least expect them, so if you suddenly find yourself surrounded by a throng of jovial, clapping and singing people, just follow the crowd and see where the action takes you. You won't be disappointed. Even funeral processions can be the most fascinating and musical of events, with mourners dressed in white sackcloth playing all manner of wind and percussion instruments.

Where To? Deciding on a Destination

Nǐ xiǎng dào nǎr qù? 你想到哪儿去? (你想到哪兒去?) (nee shyahng daow nar chyew?) (*Where do you want to go?*) Planning a trip to **Yàzhōu** 亚洲 (亞洲) (yah-joe) (*Asia*), **Fēizhōu** 非洲 (fay-joe) (*Africa*), **Ōuzhōu** 欧洲 (歐洲) (oh-joe) (*Europe*), or **Měizhōu** 美洲 (may-joe) (*the Americas*)? Will your voyage be **zài guó nèi** 在国内 (在國內) (dzye gwaw nay) (*within the country/domestic*) or **zài guó wài** 在国外 (在國外) (dzye gwaw why) (*outside the country*)? Table 14-1 shows some countries you may choose to visit.

Table 14-1	Places to Visit Around the Globe	
Chinese	*Pronunciation*	*English*
Àiěrlán 爱尔兰 (愛爾蘭)	eye-are-lahn	*Ireland*
Déguó 德国 (德國)	duh-gwaw	*Germany*
Éguó 俄国 (俄國)	uh-gwaw	*Russia*
Fǎguó 法国 (法國)	fah-gwaw	*France*
Jiānádà 加拿大	jyah-nah-dah	*Canada*
Mòxīgē 墨西哥	maw-she-guh	*Mexico*
Nánfēi 南非	nahn-fay	*South Africa*
Rìběn 日本	ir-bun	*Japan*
Ruìdiǎn 瑞典	rway-dyan	*Sweden*
Ruìshì 瑞士	rway-shir	*Switzerland*
Táiwān 台湾 (台灣)	tye-wahn	*Taiwan*
Tǎnsāngníyà 坦桑尼亚 (坦桑尼亞)	tahn-sahng-nee-yah	*Tanzania*
Xiānggǎng 香港	shyahng-gahng	*Hong Kong*
Xiōngyálì 匈牙利	shyoong-yah-lee	*Hungary*
Yǐsèliè 以色列	ee-suh-lyeh	*Israel*
Yuènán 越南	yweh-nahn	*Vietnam*
Zāyīěr 扎伊尔 (扎伊爾)	zah-ee-are	*Zaire*
Zhōngguó dàlù 中国大陆 (中國大陸)	joong-gwaw dah-loo	*Mainland China*

Depending on the type of activities you enjoy doing when you **fàng jià** 放假 (fahng jyah) (*take a vacation*), you may want to consider traveling to a place that has plenty of the following features (or at least one special one to make it well worth the trip) so that you can **yóulǎn** 游览 (遊覽) (yo-lahn) (*sightsee*):

✔ **fó miào** 佛庙 (佛廟) (faw myaow) (*Buddhist temple*)

✔ **gǔdǒngdiàn** 古董店 (goo-doong-dyan) (*antique shop*)

✔ **hǎitān** 海滩 (海灘) (hi-tahn) (*beach*)

✔ **měishùguǎn** 美术馆 (美術館) (may-shoo-gwahn) (*art gallery*)

✔ **mótiāndàlóu** 摩天大楼 (摩天大樓) (maw-tyan-dah-lo) (*skyscraper*)

✔ **shāmò** 沙漠 (shah-maw) (*desert*)

✔ **shān** 山 (shahn) (*mountain*)

- ✔ **tǎ** 塔 (tah) (*pagoda*)

- ✔ **xióngmāo** 熊猫 (熊貓) (shyoong-maow) (*pandas*)

- ✔ **xìyuàn** 剧院 (劇院) (she-ywan) (*theatre*)

- ✔ **yóuliè** 游猎 (遊獵) (yo-lyeh) (*safari*)

- ✔ **zhíwùyuán** 植物园 (植物園) (jir-woo-ywan) (*botanical gardens*)

Unless you're the type who thrives on danger and excitement (or works for a relief agency), try to avoid places where the following natural phenomena occur:

- ✔ **dìzhèn** 地震 (dee-juhn) (*earthquake*)

- ✔ **hànzāi** 旱灾 (旱災) (hahn-dzye) (*drought*)

- ✔ **huǒzāi** 火灾 (火災) (hwaw-dzye) (*fire*)

- ✔ **shuǐzāi** 水灾 (水災) (shway-dzye) (*flood*)

- ✔ **táifēng** 台风 (颱風) (tye-fung) (*typhoon*)

- ✔ **yǔjì** 雨季 (yew-jee) (*rainy season*)

Planning to travel **cóng Xiōngyálì** 从 (從)匈牙利 (tsoong shyoong-yah-lee) (*from Hungary*) **dào Xiānggǎng** 到香港 (daow shyahng-gahng) (*to Hong Kong*) anytime soon? How about **cóng Rìběn** 从日本 (從日本) (tsoong ir-bun) (*from Japan*) **dào Mòxīgē** 到墨西哥 (daow maw-she-guh) (*to Mexico*) instead? Wherever you travel, you always go **cóng** (tsoong) (*from*) one place **dào** (daow) (*to*) another. Here are some good phrases to know when you tell people about your upcoming travel plans, using the **cóng . . . dào** pattern:

> **Cóng Nánfēi dào Zāyīěr duō cháng shíjiān?** 从南非到扎伊尔多长时间? (從南非到扎伊爾多長時間?) (tsoong nahn-fay daow zah-ee-are dwaw chahng shir-jyan?) (*How long does it take to get from South Africa to Zaire?*)

> **Nǐmen shénme shíhòu cóng Zhōngguó dào zhèr lái?** 你们什么时侯从中国到这儿来? (你們甚麼時候從中國到這兒來?) (nee-mun shummuh shir-ho tsoong joong-gwaw daow jar lye?) (*When are you all coming here from China?*)

> **Tā míngtiān cóng Yǐsèliè dào Ruìdiǎn qù.** 她明天从以色列到瑞典去. (她明天從以色列到瑞典去.) (tah meeng-tyan tsoong ee-suh-lyeh daow rway-dyan chyew.) (*She's going from Israel to Sweden tomorrow.*)

> **Wǒ cóng Niǔyuē dào Jiāzhōu qù.** 我从纽约到加州去. (我從紐約到加州去.) (waw tsoong nyo-yweh daow jyah-joe chyew.) (*I'm going from New York to California.*)

Talkin' the Talk

Páng Lǎoshī (pahng laow-shir) (*Professor Pang*) asks his American student, Wendy, where she plans to go during the upcoming winter vacation. She has already been in Tianjin studying Chinese for four months. (Track 18)

Páng Lǎoshī: **Wendy, nǐ hán jià de shíhòu xiǎng qù nǎr?**
Wendy, nee hahn jyah duh shir-ho shyahng chyew nar?
Wendy, where do you plan on going during the winter vacation?

Wendy: **Yīnwèi wǒ yǐjīng zài Tiānjīn sì ge yuè le, suǒyǐ wǒ xiǎng zhōngyú qù Fēizhōu kànkàn.**
een-way waw ee-jeeng dzye tyan-jeen suh guh yweh luh, swaw-yee waw shyahng joong-yew chyew fay-joe kahn-kahn.
Because I've already been in Tianjin for four months, I'd like to finally go to Africa to have a look.

Páng Lǎoshī: **Fēizhōu! Nèmme yuán. Wèishénme yào qù nàr?**
fay-joe! nummuh ywan. way-shummuh yaow chyew nar?
Africa! So far away. Why do you want to go there?

Wendy: **Yīnwèi dōngtiān de shíhòu Tiānjīn tài lěng. Érqiě zài Fēizhōu kěyǐ cānjiā yóuliè!**
een-way doong-tyan duh shir-ho tyan-jeen tye lung. are-chyeh dzye fay-joe kuh-yee tsahn-jyah yo-lyeh!
Because winters in Tianjin are too cold. What's more, in Africa I can take part in a safari!

Páng Lǎoshī: **Cóng Yàzhōu dào Fēizhōu zuò fēijī jǐge xiǎoshí?**
tsoong yah-joe daow fay-joe dzwaw fay-jee jee-guh shyaow-shir?
How many hours is it from Asia to Africa by plane?

Wendy: **Cóng Tiānjīn dào Tǎnsāngníyà yào chàbùduō shísān ge xiǎoshí.**
tsoong tyan-jeen daow tahn-sahng-nee-yah yaow chah-boo-dwaw shir-sahn guh shyaow-shir.
From Tianjin to Tanzania, it takes about 13 hours.

Páng Lǎoshī: **Qǐng dài huí lái hěn duō xiàngpiàn gěi wǒ kànkàn.**
cheeng dye hway lye hun dwaw shyahng-pyan gay waw kahn-kahn.
Please bring back lots of pictures to show me.

Wendy: **Yídìng huì.**
ee-deeng hway.
I certainly will.

Words to Know

hán jià 寒假	hahn jyah	winter vacation
zhōngyú 终于 (終於)	joong-yew	finally
ěrqiě 而且	are-chyeh	what's more

Passports and Visas: Don't Leave Home without 'Em

Surprise! Actually, the fact that you need a valid **hùzhào** 护照 (護照) (hoo-jaow) (*passport*) and a **qiānzhèng** 签证 (簽證) (chyan-juhng) (*visa*) if you want to enter mainland China or Taiwan should come as no surprise. And if you plan on visiting a couple of different countries in the region for any length of time, you may need a couple of different **qiānzhèng** to go with each destination. Check to see what regulations apply before you board your **fēijī** 飞机 (飛機) (fay-jee) (*airplane*), or you may have the shortest vacation experience of your life.

In the course of securing a visa or two, you'll probably have to locate, navigate, deal with, or ask for the following:

- ✔ **B xíng gānyán yìmiáo** B型肝炎疫苗 (pronunciation) (*Hepatitis B shot*)
- ✔ **dāncí rùjìng qiānzhèng** 单次入境签证 (單次入境簽證) (dahn-tsuh roo-jeeng chyan-juhng) (*single-entry visa*)

- ✔ **dàshǐguǎn** 大使馆 (大使館) (dah-shir-gwan) (*embassy*)

- ✔ **duōcí rùjìng qiānzhèng** 多次入境签证 (多次入境簽證) (dwaw-tsuh roo-jeeng chyan-juhng) (*multiple-entry visa*)

- ✔ **guānliáo zhǔyì** 官僚主义 (官僚主義) (gwan-lyaow joo-ee) (*bureaucracy*)

- ✔ **jiànkāng zhèngshū** 健康证书 (健康證書) (jyan-kahng juhng-shoo) (*health certificate*)

- ✔ **línshìguǎn** 领事馆 (領事館) (leen-shir-gwan) (*consulate*)

- ✔ **páiduì** 排队 (排隊) (pye-dway) (*to stand in line*)

- ✔ **qiānzhèng chù** 签证处 (簽證處) (chyan-juhng choo) (*visa section*)

Packing for Your Trip

Are you the type who likes to **zhuāngrù** 装入 (jwahng-roo) (*pack*) everything under the sun in three different pieces of oversized **xíngli** 行李 (sheeng-lee) (*luggage*) before a trip? Or are you more the **bèibāo** 背包 (bay-baow) (*backpack*) type, content to take only the bare essentials? Either way, you have to prepare your bags in advance if you want to qualify them as **shǒutí xíngli** 手提行李 (show-tee sheeng-lee) (*carry-on luggage*) or **tuōyùn xíngli** 托运行李 (托運行李) (twaw-yewn sheeng-lee) (*checked luggage*).

What kind of clothes to pack depends on where you're going; Chapter 9 gives you the lowdown on various items of clothing. No matter where you plan to go, you should pack some of these items:

- ✔ **chúchòu jì** 除臭剂 (除臭劑) (choo-cho jee) (*deodorant*)

- ✔ **féizào** 肥皂 (fay-dzaow) (*soap*)

- ✔ **guālián dāo** 刮脸刀 (刮臉刀) (gwah-lyan daow) (*razor*)

- ✔ **huàzhuāng pǐn** 化妆品 (hwah-jwahng peen) (*makeup*)

- ✔ **nào zhōng** 闹钟 (鬧鐘) (naow joong) (*alarm clock*)

- ✔ **shuāzi** 刷子 (shwah-dzuh) (*brush*)

- ✔ **shùkǒu shuǐ** 漱口水 (shoo-ko shway) (*mouthwash*)

- ✔ **tàiyáng yǎnjìng** 太阳眼镜 (太陽眼鏡) (tye-yahng yan-jeeng) (*sunglasses*)

- ✔ **wèi shēng jīn** 卫生巾 (衛生巾) (way shung geen) (*sanitary napkins*)

- **yágāo** 牙膏 (yah-gaow) (*toothpaste*)

- **yáshuā** 牙刷 (yah-shwah) (*toothbrush*)

- **yuèjīng yòng miánsāi** 月经用棉塞 (月經用棉塞) (yweh-jeeng yoong myan-sye) (*tampons*)

- **yùndǒu** 熨斗 (yewn-doe) (*iron*)

- **yǔsǎn** 雨伞 (雨傘) (yew-sahn) (*umbrella*)

- **zhàoxiàng jī** 照相机 (照相機) (jaow-shyahng jee) (*camera*)

- **zhuǎnjiē qì** 转接器 (轉接器) (jwahn-jyeh chee) (*adaptor*)

The sentence structure for the verb **zhuāng** 装 (裝) (jwahng) (*to pack*) is **bǎ A zhuāngrù B** 把 A 装入 B (bah A jwahng-roo B)**,** which translates into *pack A into B,* even though the word for *pack* comes between what you're packing *(A)* and what you pack it into *(B).*

Enlisting the Help of a Travel Agency

Think you can handle traipsing around the world without an advance plan or hotel reservations? Think again. China, for example, is one country you should travel to as part of a **guānguāng tuán** 观光团 (觀光團) (gwahn-gwahng twahn) (*tour group*). If you don't like the idea of group travel, you should at least make advance reservations for hotels and domestic travel and even for your own private **dǎoyóu** 导游 (導遊) (daow-yo) (*tour guide*) through a **lǚxíngshè** 旅行社 (lyew-sheeng-shuh) (*travel agency*). Remember, you generally hear no **Yīngyǔ** 英语 (英語) (eeng-yew) (*English*) spoken anywhere in China, so having someone who knows the ropes help you iron out the details ahead of time (including arranging an English-speaking tour guide) can help avoid headaches when you're there.

Talkin' the Talk

Daisy and Michael discuss their travel plans with a local travel agent, Miss Lǐ, in Hong Kong. (Track 19)

Miss Lǐ: **Nǐmen hǎo. Wǒ néng bāng shénme máng?**
nee-men how. waw nung bahng shummuh mahng?
Hello. How may I be of help?

Daisy: **Wǒmen hěn xiǎng qù Zhōngguó dàlù. Néng bùnéng yùdìng yíge lǚguǎn?**
waw-men hun shyahng chyew joong-gwaw dah loo. nung boo-nung yew-deeng ee-guh lyew-gwahn?
We're very interested in traveling to mainland China. Would you be able to reserve hotels for us in advance?

Miss Lǐ: **Méiyǒu wèntǐ. Nǐmen shénme shíhòu yào zǒu?**
mayo one-tee. nee-mun shummuh shir-ho yaow dzoe?
No problem. When would you like to go?

Michael: **Tīngshuō wǔ yuè fèn de tiānqì zuì hǎo.**
teeng-shwaw woo yweh fun duh tyan-chee dzway how.
I've heard the weather in May is the best.

Miss Lǐ: **Duì le. Wǒ yě jiànyì nǐmen gēn yíge guānguāng tuán yíkuàr qù.**
dway luh. waw yeah jyan-ee nee-mun gun ee-guh gwahn-gwahng twan ee-kwar chyew.
That's correct. I also suggest you go with a tour group.

Daisy: **Wèishénme?**
way-shummuh?
Why?

Miss Lǐ: **Guānguāng tuán yǒu shuō Yīngyǔ de dǎoyóu hé yóulǎnchē. Nà zuì fāngbiàn.**
gwahn-gwahng twahn yo shwaw eeng-yew duh daow-yo huh yo-lahn-chuh. nah dzway fahng-byan.
Tour groups have an English-speaking tour guide and a sightseeing bus. That's the most convenient way to go.

Michael: **Hǎo. Juédìng le.**
how. jweh-deeng luh.
Okay. It's decided.

Words to Know

yùdìng 预定 (預定)	yew-deeng	to make a reservation
jiànyì 建议 (建議)	jyan-ee	to suggest
guānguāng tuán 光光团 (光光團)	gwahn-gwahng twahn	tour group
dǎoyóu 导游 (導遊)	daow-yo	tour guide
yóulǎnchē 游览车 (遊覽車)	yo-lahn-chuh	sightseeing bus
fāngbiàn 方便	fahng-byan	convenient
juédìng le 决定了 (決定了)	jweh-deeng luh	it's decided

Fun & Games

Fill in the missing words with one of the three possible answers. See Appendix D for the answers.

1. **Wǒmen jīnnián qù** _____. 我们今年去_____. (我們今年去
   _____.) (*This year we're going to Ireland.*)

   a. **Àiěrlán** 爱尔兰 (愛爾蘭)

   b. **Éguó** 俄国 (俄國)

   c. **Nánfēi** 南非

2. **Tāmen** _____ **zǒu.** 他们_____走. (他們_____走.) (*They're
   leaving on June 8.*)

   a. **sì yuè wǔ hào** 四月五号 (四月五號)

   b. **wǔ yuè jiǔ hào** 五月九号 (五月九號)

   c. **liù yuè bā hào** 六月八号 (六月八號)

3. **Wǒmen yídìng yào kàn** _____. 我们一定要看 _____.
   (我們一定要看_____.) (*We definitely want to see Buddhist temples.*)

   a. **xióngmāo** 熊猫 (熊貓)

   b. **fó miào** 佛庙 (佛廟)

   c. **yóuliè** 游猎 (遊獵)

4. **Bié wàngle zhuāngrù** _____. 别忘了装入 _____. (别忘了装入
   _____.) (*Don't forget to pack a toothbrush.*)

   a. **yáshuā** 牙刷

   b. **yágāo** 牙膏

   c. **huàzhuāng pǐn** 化妆品 (化妝品)

5. **Méiyǒu wèntí.** _____. 没有问题 _____. (沒有問題
   _____.) (*No problem. Just kidding.*)

   a. **Juédìng le.** 决定了. (決定了.)

   b. **Kāi wǎn xiào.** 开玩笑. (開玩笑.)

   c. **Jiù wǎn le.** 就完了.

Chapter 15

Making Cents of Money

In This Chapter

▶ Understanding Chinese currencies

▶ Knowing how (and where) to change money

▶ Cashing checks and charging to plastic

▶ Exchanging money at banks and ATMs

▶ Leaving proper tips

*Q*ián 钱 (錢) (chyan) (*money*) makes the world go around. People make their money in all sorts of ways. Most ways are legitimate. (If you've attained yours through nefarious means, I'm not sure I want to know, so don't tell me!) You may be one of those lucky people who win the lottery or receive a large inheritance you use to traipse to the other side of the world. Or perhaps you have a modest amount saved up from working hard and paying your bills on time, and you hope to make it go a long way. However you get your money, you find out how to change it (and then save it or spend it) with the help of this chapter.

Of course, family and friends are priceless, but you can't very well support yourself or help those you love, much less donate to a charity of your choice, unless you have something to give. And that's what life is really all about. (Unless, of course, your main goal in life is to buy a sports car, acquire rare works of art, and live in the south of France . . . in which case you need a lot of **qián.** All the more reason to read this chapter.)

In this chapter, I share with you important words and phrases for acquiring and spending money — things you can easily do nowadays all over the world. I give you some banking terms to help you deal with everything from live tellers to inanimate ATMs. I even give you tips on tipping.

Staying Current with Chinese Currency

Depending on where in Asia (or any place where Chinese is spoken) you live, work, or visit, you have to get used to dealing with different types of **huòbì** 货币 (貨幣) (hwaw-bee) (*currency*), each with its own **duìhuànlǜ** 兑换率 (兌換率) (dway-hwahn-lyew) (*rate of exchange*). See Table 15-1 for the Chinese versions of international currency and the following sections for the main forms of Chinese **huòbì**. I delve into currency exchange in the later section "Making and Exchanging Money."

Table 15-1	International Currencies	
Chinese	*Pronunciation*	*English*
Gǎngbì 港币 (港幣)	gahng-bee	*Hong Kong dollar*
Měiyuán 美元	may-ywan	*U.S. dollar*
Ōu yuán 欧元 (歐元)	oh ywan	*Euro*
Rénmínbì 人民币 (人民幣)	run-meen-bee	*(mainland) Chinese dollar*
Rì yuán 日元	ir ywan	*Japanese dollar*
Xīn bì 新币 (新幣)	shin bee	*Singapore dollar*
Xīn táibì 新台币 (新臺幣)	shin tye-bee	*Taiwan dollar*

Rénmínbì (RMB) in the PRC

In the People's Republic of China (PRC), the equivalent of the U.S. dollar is the **yuán** 元 (ywan), also known as **rénmínbì** 人民币 (人民幣) (run-meen-bee) (*[mainland] Chinese dollars* [Literally: *the people's money*]) or RMB. More than 1 billion people around the globe currently use this currency. As of July 2012, 1 U.S. dollar is equivalent to about 6.38 (mainland) Chinese dollars. Here's how you say that in Chinese:

> **Yì měiyuán huàn liù diǎn sān bā yuán rénmínbì.** 一美元换六点三八元人民币. (一美元換六點三八元人民幣.) (ee may-ywan hwahn lyo dyan sahn ba ywan run-meen-bee.) (*One U.S. dollar is 6.38 (mainland) Chinese dollars.*)

The Chinese **yuán,** which is a paper bill, comes in denominations of 1, 2, 5, 10, 20, 50, and 100 in rénmínbì. One **yuán** is the equivalent of 10 **máo** 毛 (maow), which may also be referred to as **jiǎo** 角 (jyaow) — the equivalent of 10 cents. Each **máo** is the equivalent of 100 **fēn** 分 (fun), which compare to American pennies. Paper bills, in addition to the **yuán,** also come in denominations of 2 and 5 **jiǎo.** Coins come in denominations of 1, 2, and 5 **fēn;** 1, 2, and 5 **jiǎo;** and 1, 2, and 5 **yuán.**

In addition to saying you have **yì yuán,** you can say you have **yí kuài qián** 一块钱 (一塊錢) (ee kwye chyan), which means the exact same thing — one Chinese dollar. The difference between **yuán** and **kuài,** and between **jiǎo** and **máo,** is that **yuán** and **jiǎo** are formal, written ways of saying those denominations and **kuài** and **máo** are the more colloquial forms.

Want to know how much money I have right now in my pocket, Nosy? Why not just ask me?

> ✔ **Nǐ yǒu jǐ kuài qián?** 你有几块钱? (你有幾塊錢?) (nee yo jee kwye chyan?) (*How much money do you have?*)
>
> Use this phrase if you assume the amount is less than $10.
>
> ✔ **Nǐ yǒu duōshǎo qián?** 你有多少钱? (你有多少錢?) (nee yo dwaw-shaow chyan?) (*How much money do you have?*)
>
> Use this phrase if you assume the amount is greater than $10.

Xīn Táibì in the ROC

In Taiwan, also known as the Republic of China or ROC, 1 U.S. dollar equals about 30 **xīn Táibì** 新台币 (新臺幣) (shin tye-bee) (*New Taiwan dollars*). Here's how you say that in Chinese:

> **Yì měiyuán huàn sānshí yuán xīn Táibì.** 一美元 换三十元新台币. (一美元 換三十元新臺幣.) (ee may-ywan hwahn sahn-shir ywan shin tye-bee.) (*One U.S. dollar is 30 New Taiwan dollars.*)

You see bills in denominations of 50, 100, 500, and 1,000 and coins in denominations of 1, 5, 10, and 50 cents. Taiwanese coins are particularly beautiful — they have all sorts of flowers etched into them — so you may want to save a few to bring back to show friends (or just to have). Just make sure you keep enough **língqián** 零钱 (零錢) (leeng-chyan) (*small change*) on hand for all the great items you can buy cheaply at the wonderful night markets.

Hong Kong dollars

Hong Kong, the longtime financial dynamo of Asia, uses the Hong Kong dollar, or the **Găngbì** 港币 (港幣) (gahng-bee). Currently, 1 U.S. dollar is equivalent to 7.75 Hong Kong dollars. Here's how you say that in Chinese:

> **Yì měiyuán huàn qī diǎn qī wǔ yuán Găngbì.** 一美元换七点七五元港币. (一美元換七點七五元港幣.) (ee may-ywan hwahn chee dyan chee woo ywan gahng-bee.) (*One U.S. dollar is 7.75 Hong Kong dollars.*)

Singapore dollars

Singapore is a Mandarin-speaking country in Asia. Its dollars are called **Xīn bì** 新币 (新幣) (shin-bee) and come in denominations of 2, 5, 10, 50, and 100. You can find coins in denominations of 1 cent, 5 cents, 10 cents, 20 cents, 50 cents, and 1 dollar.

In Singapore, if you want to say $1.25, you don't use the number **wǔ** 五 (woo) (*five*) to refer to the final 5 cents in the amount. You use the term **bàn** 半 (bahn), which means *half*: **yí kuài liǎng máo bàn** 一块两毛半 (一塊兩毛半) (ee kwye lyahng maow bahn) rather than **yí kuài liǎng máo wǔ** 一块两毛五 (一塊兩毛五) (ee kwye lyahng maow woo). You can definitely use the number **wǔ** in Taiwan, Hong Kong, or mainland China, however.

Exchanging Money

You can always **huàn qián** 换钱 (換錢) (hwahn chyan) (*exchange money*) the minute you arrive at the airport at the many **duìhuànchù** 兑换处 (兌換處) (dway-hwahn-choo) (*exchange bureaus*), or you can wait until you get to a major bank or check in at your hotel.

The following phrases come in handy when you're ready to **huàn qián**:

- **Jīntiān de duìhuàn lǜ shì shénme?** 今天的兑换率是什么? (今天的兌換率是甚麼?) (jin-tyan duh dway-hwahn lyew shir shummuh?) (*What's today's exchange rate?*)

- **Nǐmen shōu duōshǎo qián shǒuxùfèi?** 你们收多少钱手续费? (你們收多少錢手續費?) (nee-men show dwaw-shaow chyan show-shyew-fay?) (*How much commission do you charge?*)

- Qǐng nǐ gěi wǒ sì zhāng wǔshí yuán de. 请你给我四张五十元的. (請妳
  我四张五十元的.) (cheeng nee gay waw suh jahng woo-shir ywan duh.)
  (*Please give me four 50-yuan bills.*)

- Qǐngwèn, yínháng zài nǎr? 请问, 银行在哪儿? (請問, 銀行在哪兒?)
  (cheeng-one, eeng-hahng dzye nar?) (*Excuse me, where is the bank?*)

- Qǐngwèn, zài nǎr kěyǐ huàn qián? 请问, 在哪儿可以换钱? (請問在哪兒
  可以換錢?) (cheeng-one, dzye nar kuh-yee hwahn chyan?) (*Excuse me,
  where can I change money?*)

- Wǒ yào huàn yì bǎi měiyuán. 我要换一百美元. (我要换一百美元.) (waw
  yaow hwahn ee bye may-ywan.) (*I'd like to change $100.*)

No matter where you get money or how much money you plan to convert into
local currency, you may have to show your **hùzhào** 护照 (護照) (hoo-jaow)
(*passport*), so always have that ready to whip out.

Talkin' the Talk

Jasmine arrives at the airport in Beijing and needs to change some
money. She asks a **xínglǐyuán** (sheeng-lee-ywan) (*porter*) where she
can find a place to exchange money. (Track 20)

Jasmine: **Qǐngwèn, zài nǎr kěyǐ huàn qián?**
              cheeng-one, dzye nar kuh-yee hwahn chyan?
              Excuse me, where can I change money?

Xínglǐyuán: **Duìhuànchù jiù zài nàr.**
              dway-hwahn-choo jyoe dzye nar.
              The exchange bureau is just over there.

Jasmine: **Xièxiè.**
              shyeh-shyeh.
              Thank you.

Jasmine goes to the money exchange counter to change some U.S.
dollars into Chinese **yuán** with the help of the **chūnàyuán** (choo-
nah-ywan) (*cashier*).

Jasmine: **Nǐ hǎo. Wǒ yào huàn yì bǎi měiyuán de rénmínbì.**
              nee how. waw yaow hwahn ee bye may-ywan duh
              run-meen-bee.
              *Hello. I'd like to change USD $100 into (mainland)
              Chinese dollars.*

Chūnàyuán: **Méiyǒu wèntí.**
mayo one-tee.
No problem.

Jasmine: **Jīntiān de duìhuàn lǜ shì duōshǎo?**
jin-tyan duh dway-hwahn lyew shir dwaw-shaow?
What's today's exchange rate?

Chūnàyuán: **Yì měiyuán huàn liù diǎn sān bā yuán rénmínbì.**
ee may-ywan hwahn lyo dyan sahn ba ywan
run-meen-bee.
One U.S. dollar is 6.38 (mainland) Chinese dollars.

Jasmine: **Hǎo. Qǐng gěi wǒ liǎng zhāng wǔshí yuán de.**
how. cheeng gay waw lyahng jahng woo-shir ywan
duh.
Great. Please give me two 50-yuán bills.

Chūnàyuán: **Méiyǒu wèntí. Qǐng gěi wǒ kànkàn nǐde hùzhào.**
mayo one-tee. cheeng gay waw kahn-kahn nee-duh
hoo-jaow.
No problem. Please show me your passport.

Words to Know

duìhuànchù 兑换处 (對換處)	dway-hwahn-choo	exchange counter
Měiyuán 美元	may-ywan	U.S. dollars
rénmínbì 人民币 (人民幣)	run-meen-bee	(mainland) Chinese dollar
duìhuàn lǜ 兑换率 (兌換率)	dway-hwahn lyew	exchange rate
Qǐng gěi wǒ kànkàn nǐde hùzhào. 请给我看看你的护照。(請給我看看你的護照。)	cheeng gay waw kahn-kahn nee-duh hoo-jaow.	Please show me your passport.

Spending Money

I don't think I'll have trouble selling you on (no pun intended) the thought of spending money. Whenever you see something you want, whether in a store, on the street, or at night market, you may as well give in to temptation and buy it, as long as you have enough **qián.** It's as easy as that. Have money, will travel. Or, rather, have money, will spend.

When you're ready to buy something, you can do it with cash, check, or credit card. And when traveling overseas, you often use traveler's checks.

If you end up buying so many items that you can barely hold them all with both hands, here's one adverb you should remember. It comes in handy when you start adding up the cost of everything before you fork over all your money: I'm speaking of **yígòng** 一共 (ee-goong) (*altogether*), as in "How much are these 20 toys and 80 sweaters altogether?"

You may overhear the following conversation in a store:

> **Zhèige hé nèige yígòng duōshǎo qián?** 这个和那个一共多少钱? (這個和那個一共多少錢?) (jay-guh huh nay-guh ee-goong dwaw-shaow chyan?) (*How much are this and that altogether?*)

> **Zhèige sān kuài liǎng máo wǔ, nèige yí kuài liǎng máo, suǒyǐ yígòng sì kuài sì máo wǔ.** 这个三块两毛五, 那个一块两毛, 所以一共四块四毛五. (這個三塊兩毛五, 那個一塊兩毛, 所以一共四塊四毛五.) (jay-guh sahn kwye lyahng maow woo, nay-guh ee kwye lyahng maow, swaw-yee ee-goong suh kwye suh maow woo.) (*This is $3.25, and that is $1.20, so altogether that will be $4.45.*)

Before you decide to **mǎi dōngxi** 买东西 (買東西) (my doong-she) (*buy things*), be sure you have enough money **yígòng** to buy everything you want so you don't feel disappointed after spending many hours in your favorite store.

The term **dōngxi** 买东西 (買東西) (doong-she) (*things*) is literally a combination of **dōng** 东 (東) (*east*) and **xī** 西 (西) (*west*). The Chinese language often combines two such opposite words to come up with various concepts. **Dōngxi** always refers to physical objects.

Overseas, many places accept American Express. Closer to America, businesses may only accept MasterCard or Visa. In some out-of-the-way parts of China, you can't use plastic at all, so have plenty of cash or traveler's checks on hand, just in case.

Using cash

I don't care what anybody tries to tell you, **xiànjīn** 现金 (現金) (shyan-jin) (*cash*) in local currency is always useful, no matter where you are and what time of day it is. Sometimes you can buy things and go places with **xiànjīn** that you can't swing with a credit card. For example, if your kid hears the ice cream truck coming down the street, you can't just whip out your **xìnyòngkǎ** to buy him an ice cream cone when the truck stops in front of your house. You can't even try to convince the ice cream guy to take a **zhīpiào** 支票(紙票) (jir-pyaow) (*check*). For times like these, my friend, you need cold, hard **xiànjīn.** You can use it to buy everything from ice cream on the street to a movie ticket at the theater. Just make sure you put your money in a sturdy **qiánbāo** 钱包 (錢包) (chyan-baow) (*wallet*) and keep it in your front pocket so a thief can't easily steal it.

When you talk about how much something costs, you put the numerical value before the word for bill or coin. For example, you can call a dollar **yí kuài** 一块 (一塊) (ee kwye) (*one dollar*) or **sān kuài** 三块 (三塊) (sahn kwye) (*three dollars*). You translate 10 cents, literally, as one 10-cent coin — **yì máo** 一毛 (ee maow) — or 30 cents, literally, as three 10-cent coins — **sān máo** 三毛 (sahn maow).

Here's how you speak of increasing amounts of money. You mention the larger units before the smaller units, just like in English:

    sān kuài 三块 (三塊) (sahn kwye) (*$3.00*)

    sān kuài yì máo 三块一毛 (三塊一毛) (sahn kwye ee maow) (*$3.10*)

    sān kuài yì máo wǔ 三块一毛五 (三塊一毛五) (sahn kwye ee maow woo) (*$3.15*)

As useful and convenient as **xiànjīn** is, you really have to pay with **zhīpiào** for some things. Take your rent and electricity bills, for example. Can't use cash for these expenses, that's for sure. And when you travel overseas, everyone knows the safest way to carry money is in the form of **lǚxíng zhīpiào** 旅行支票 (lyew-sheeng jir-pyaow) (*traveler's checks*) so you can replace them if they get lost or stolen.

The basic elements of all Chinese currency are the **yuán** (colloquially referred to as a **kuài**), which you can think of as a dollar, the **jiāo** (colloquially referred to as the **máo**), which is the equivalent of a dime, and the **fēn** 分, which is equivalent to the penny. You can read more about the various types of Chinese currency earlier in the chapter.

Talkin' the Talk

Heather goes shopping in Taipei and finds something she likes. She asks the clerk how much it is.

Heather: **Qǐngwèn, zhè jiàn yīfu duōshǎo qián?**
cheeng-one, jay jyan ee-foo dwaw-shaow chyan?
Excuse me, how much is this piece of clothing?

Clerk: **Èrshíwǔ kuài.**
are-shir-woo kwye.
It's $25.

Heather: **Nǐmen shōu bù shōu zhīpiào?**
nee-men show boo show jir-pyaow?
Do you take checks?

Clerk: **Lǚxíng zhīpiào kěyǐ. Xìnyòng kǎ yě kěyǐ.**
lyew-sheeng jir-pyaow kuh-yee. sheen-yoong kah yeah kuh-yee.
Traveler's checks are okay. Credit cards are also okay.

Words to Know

duōshǎo 多少	dwaw-shaow	how much
Nǐmen shōu bù shōu zhīpiào? 你们收不收支票? (你們收不收支票?)	nee-men show boo show jir-pyaow?	Do you take checks?
lǚxíng zhīpiào 旅行支票	lyew-sheeng jir-pyaow	traveler's checks

Paying with plastic

The **xìnyòng kǎ** 信用卡 (sheen-yoong kah) (*credit card*) may be the greatest invention of the 20th century — for credit card companies, that is. Everyone else is often stuck paying all kinds of potentially exorbitant **lìlǜ** 利率 (lee-lyew) (*interest rates*) if they're not careful. Still, credit cards do make paying for things much more convenient, don't you agree?

To find out whether a store accepts credit cards, all you have to say is

> **Nǐmen shōu bù shōu xìnyòng kǎ?** 你们收不收信用卡? (你們收不收信用卡?)
> (nee-men show boo show sheen-yoong kah?) (*Do you accept credit cards?*)

Whether the **jiàgé** 价格 (價格) (jyah-guh) (*price*) of the items you want to buy is **guì** 贵 (貴) (gway) (*expensive*) or **piányì** 便宜 (pyan-yee) (*cheap*), the **xìnyòng kǎ** comes in handy.

Read on for a list of credit-card-related terms:

- ✔ **shēzhàng de zuì gāo é** 赊帐的最高额 (赊帳的最高額) (shuh-jahng duh dzway gaow uh) (*credit line*)
- ✔ **shōu** 收 (show) (*accept*)
- ✔ **xìnyòng** 信用 (sheen-yoong) (*credit*)
- ✔ **xìnyòng xiàn'é** 信用限额 (信用限額) (sheen-yoong shyan-uh) (*credit limit*)

Doing Your Banking

If you plan on staying in Asia for an extended time or you want to continue doing business with a Chinese company, you may want to open a **huóqī zhànghù** 活期账户 (活期賬戶) (hwaw-chee jahng-hoo) (*checking account*) where you can both **cún qián** 存钱 (存錢) (tswun chyan) (*deposit money*) and **qǔ qián** 取钱 (取錢) (chyew chyan) (*withdraw money*). If you stay long enough, you should open a **dìngqī cúnkuǎn hùtóu** 定期存款户头 (定期存款戶頭) (deeng-chee tswun-kwan hoo-toe) (*savings account*) so you can start earning some **lìxí** 利息 (lee-she) (*interest*). Sure beats stuffing large bills under your mattress for years.

How about trying to make your money work for you by investing in one of the following?

- ✔ **chǔxù cúnkuǎn** 储蓄存款 (儲蓄存款) (choo-shyew tswun-kwan) (*certificate of deposit/CD*)
- ✔ **guókù quàn** 国库券 (國庫券) (gwaw-koo chwan) (*treasury bond*)
- ✔ **gǔpiào** 股票 (goo-pyaow) (*stock*)
- ✔ **hùzhù jījīn** 互助基金 (hoo-joo jee-jeen) (*mutual fund*)
- ✔ **tàotóu jījīn** 套头基金 (套頭基金) (taow-toe jee-jeen) (*hedge fund*)
- ✔ **zhàiquàn** 债券 (債券) (jye-chwan) (*bond*)

Larger bank branches in the PRC are generally open seven days a week from 9:00 a.m. to 5:00 p.m., but some close between 12:00 p.m. and 2:00 p.m. In Taiwan, banks close at 3:30 p.m., and in Hong Kong they're usually open from 9:00 a.m. to 4:30 p.m. during the week and from 9:00 a.m. to 12:00 p.m. on Saturdays.

Making withdrawals and deposits

Whether you need to **cún qián** 存钱 (存錢) (tswun chyan) (*deposit money*) or **qǔ qián** 取钱 (取錢) (chyew chyan) (*withdraw money*), you need to make sure you have enough **qián** in the first place to do so. One way to ensure you don't overextend is to make sure you know what your **jiéyú** 结余 (結餘) (jyeh-yew) (*account balance*) is at any given moment. Sometimes you can check your available balance if you go online to see which checks may have already cleared. If someone gives you an **yínháng běnpiào** 银行本票 (銀行本票) (een-hahng bun-pyaow) (*cashier's check*), however, it cashes immediately. Lucky you!

If you plan to cash some checks along with your deposits, here are a couple of useful phrases to know:

- ✔ **Wǒ yào duìxiàn zhèi zhāng zhīpiào.** 我要兑现这张支票. (我要兑現這張 支票. (waw yaow dway-shyan jay jahng jir-pyow.) (*I'd like to cash this check.*)

- ✔ **Bèimiàn qiān zì xiě zài nǎr?** 背面签字写在哪儿? (背面簽字寫在哪兒?) (bay-myan chyan dzuh shyeh dzye nar?) (*Where shall I endorse it?*)

Talkin' the Talk

Freddie decides to open a savings account in Hong Kong. He enters a bank and approaches the teller. (Track 21)

Freddie: **Nín hǎo. Wǒ xiǎng kāi yíge dìngqī cúnkuǎn hùtóu.**
neen how. waw shyahng kye ee-guh deeng-chee tswun-kwan hoo-toe.
Hello. I'd like to open a savings account.

Teller: **Méiyǒu wèntí. Nín yào xiān cún duōshǎo qián?**
mayo one-tee. neen yaow shyan tswun dwaw-shaow chyan?
No problem. How much would you like to deposit initially?

Freddie:	**Wǒ yào cún yìbǎi kuài qián.**
	waw yaow tswun ee-bye kwye chyan.
	I'd like to deposit $100.

Teller:	**Hǎo. Qǐng tián zhèige biǎo. Wǒ yě xūyào kànkàn nínde hùzhào.**
	how. cheeng tyan jay-guh byaow. waw yeah shyew-yaow kahn-kahn neen-duh hoo-jaow.
	Fine. Please fill out this form. I will also need to see your passport.

Words to Know

Wǒ xiǎng kāi yíge dìngqī cúnkuǎn hùtóu. 我想开一个定期存款户头。(我想开一個定期存款戶頭。)	waw shyahng kye ee-guh deeng-chee tswun-kwan hoo-toe.	I'd like to open a savings account.
cún qián 存钱 (存錢)	tswun chyan	to deposit money
Qǐng tián zhèige biǎo. 请填这个表。(請填這個表。)	cheeng tyan jay-guh byaow.	Please fill out this form.
hùzhào 护照 (護照)	hoo-jaow	passport

Accessing an ATM

One of the most convenient ways to access some quick cash is to go to the nearest **zìdòng tíkuǎnjī** 自动提款机 (自動提款機) (dzuh-doong tee-kwan-jee) (*ATM*). ATMs are truly ubiquitous these days. Wherever you turn, there they are, on every other street corner. Sometimes I wonder how we ever survived without them. (Same goes for the personal computer . . . but I digress.)

In order to use a **zìdòng tíkuǎnjī,** you need a **zìdòng tíkuǎn kǎ** 自动提款卡 (自動提款卡) (dzuh-doong tee-kwan kah) (*ATM card*) to find out your account balance or to deposit or withdraw money. And you definitely need to know your **mìmǎ** 密码 (密碼) (mee-mah) (*PIN*); otherwise, the **zìdòng tíkuǎnjī** is useless. Just remember: Make sure you don't let anyone else know your **mìmǎ.** It's a **mìmì** 秘密 (mee-mee) (*secret*).

Tips on Tipping

Usually in the United States, a 15-percent tip is customary at restaurants, and you often give a 10-percent tip to taxi drivers. Giving **xiǎo fèi** 小费 (小費) (shyaow-fay) (*tips*) is expected pretty much everywhere from here to Timbuktu. In some instances, you should even give **xiǎo fèi** to people setting up towels in the public bathroom. Better to know in advance of your trip how much (or how little) is expected of you so you don't embarrass yourself (and by extension, your countryfolk).

Here are some the general tipping conventions for various Chinese-speaking countries:

✔ In Taiwan, **xiǎo fèi** are generally included in restaurant bills. If not, 10 percent is standard. You can **gěi** 给 (給) (gay) (*give*) bellboys and porters a dollar (USD) per bag.

✔ In Hong Kong, most restaurants automatically include a 10-percent tip, but feel free to give an additional 5 percent if the **fúwù** 服务 (服務) (foo-woo) (*service*) is good. Small tips are also okay for taxi drivers, bellboys, and washroom attendants.

✔ Tipping in mainland China used to be rare, but the idea is finally catching on, especially now that service with a scowl rather than a smile is fast becoming a thing of the past. (For the longest time, workers simply had no incentive to work harder or with a more pleasant demeanor after the Cultural Revolution. Can you blame workers for having no reason to perform their duties with the idea of customer service in mind?) A 3-percent tip is standard in restaurants (still low compared to Taiwan and Hong Kong). Bellboys and room service attendants typically expect a dollar or two (USD). Tipping in U.S. currency is still very much appreciated, because it's worth about six times as much as the Chinese dollar.

If you get a bill and can't make heads or tails of it, you can always ask the following question to find out whether the tip is included:

Zhàngdān bāokuò fúwùfēi ma? 账单包括服务费吗? (賬單包括服務費嗎?) (jahng-dahn baow-kwaw foo-woo-fay mah?) (*Does the bill include a service charge/tip?*)

In English, when you say *15 percent,* you mean 15 percent out of a total of 100. The way to express **bǎifēnbǐ** 百分比 (bye-fun-bee) (*percentages*) in Chinese is to start with the larger denomination of **bǎi** 百 (bye) (*100*) first and then work your way backward with the percentage of that amount. Here are some examples:

> **bǎifēn zhī bǎi** 百分之百 (bye-fun jir bye) (*100 percent* [Literally: *100 out of 100 parts*])

> **bǎifēn zhī bāshíwǔ** 百分之八十五 (bye-fun jir bah-shir-woo) (*85 percent* [Literally: *85 out of 100 parts*])

> **bǎifēn zhī shíwǔ** 百分之十五 (bye-fun jir shir-woo) (*15 percent* [Literally: *15 out of 100 parts*])

> **bǎifēn zhī sān** 百分之三 (bye-fun jir sahn) (*3 percent* [Literally: *3 out of 100 parts*])

> **bǎifēn zhī líng diǎn sān** 百分之零点三 (百分只零點三) (bye-fun jir leeng dyan sahn) (*0.3 percent* [Literally: *0.3 out of 100 parts*])

For more information on numbers, head to Chapter 5.

Talkin' the Talk

Ben and Erin are in a restaurant. They get their bill and discuss how much of a tip to leave.

Erin:	**Wǒmen de zhàngdān yígòng sānshí kuài qián. Xiǎo fèi yīnggāi duōshǎo?**
	waw-men duh jahng-dahn ee-goong sahn-shir kwye chyan. shyaow fay eeng-guy dwaw-shaow?
	Our bill comes to $30 altogether. How much should the tip be?
Ben:	**Yīnwèi fúwù hěn hǎo, suǒyǐ xiǎo fèi kěyǐ bǎifēn zhī èr shí. Nǐ tóngyì ma?**
	een-way foo-woo hun how, swaw-yee shyaow fay kuh-yee bai-fun jir are shir. nee toong-ee mah?
	Because the service was really good, I think we can leave a 20-percent tip. Do you agree?
Erin:	**Tóngyì.**
	toong-ee.
	I agree.

Words to Know

zhàngdān 账单 (賬單)	jahng-dahn	the bill
yígòng 一共	ee-goong	altogether
yīnggāi 应该 (應該)	eeng-guy	should
yīnwèi ... suǒyǐ 因为 ... 所以 (因為 ... 所以)	een-way ... swaw-yee	because ... therefore
tóngyì 同意	toong ee	to agree

Fun & Games

Identify what the following illustrations depict in Chinese. See Appendix D for the correct answers.

A.

B.

C.

D.

E.

F.

A. _____

B. _____

C. _____

D. _____

E. _____

F. _____

Chapter 16

Getting Around

- -

In This Chapter

▶ Traveling by plane

▶ Breezing through customs

▶ Shuttling around town

- -

Traveling halfway around the world to **Zhōngguó** 中国 (中國) (joong-gwaw) (*China*) can be a long haul. Knowing the magic traveling words and phrases in Chinese can make your journey as efficient and comfortable as possible. This chapter helps you make your way around the airport and the airplane, survive the customs experience, and board different types of transportation after you reach your destination.

Flying Around the Airport

Consider yourself a veteran traveler just because you've been all through Europe and the Americas? Well, my friend, you're in for a rude awakening. When it comes to finding your way around China, English (or any other Western language) does you little good. You spend a lot of unproductive time trying to interpret the signs to get some sense of which line to stand in and where to go next at the **fēijīchǎng** 飞机场 (飛機場) (fay-jee-chahng) (*airport*). You need to at least know the **pīnyīn** 拼音 (pin-yin) (Literally: *spelled the way it sounds*) Romanization system, if not Chinese characters themselves. If you don't, you'll be up a creek without a paddle. You may end up following the guy next to you, even if it takes you to the bathroom rather than baggage claims. (See Chapter 1 for more about the **pīnyīn** system of spelling Chinese words.)

Good move to get a head start by reading *Chinese For Dummies* in advance of your trip. You can bone up on some essential words and phrases before the whole airport experience makes you want to get right back on the next plane bound for home.

Making it past the check-in counter

Ready to **bànlǐ dēngjī shǒuxù** 办理登记手续 (辦理登記手續) (bahn-lee duhng-jee show-shyew) (*check in*)? After lugging your bags up to this point, you finally get to **tuōyùn** 托运 (托運) (twaw-yewn) (*check*) your **xínglǐ** 行李 (sheeng-lee) (*luggage*). You receive a **dēngjīpái** 登机牌 (登機牌) (duhng-jee-pye) (*boarding pass*) at the check-in counter, at which point you're ready to make your way to the appropriate **chūkǒu** 出口 (choo-ko) (*gate*), taking only your **shǒutí xínglǐ** 手提行李 (show-tee sheeng-lee) (*carry-on luggage*).

All sorts of questions may be running through your mind about now. Here are some basic phrases that may come in handy during check-in:

- ✔ **Fēijī jǐ diǎn qǐfēi?** 飞机几点起飞? (飛機幾點起飛?) (fay-jee jee dyan chee-fay?) (*What time does it depart?*)

- ✔ **Wǒde hángbān hàomǎ shì duōshǎo?** 我的航班号码是多少? (我的航班號碼是多少?) (waw-duh hahng-bahn how-mah shir dwaw-shaow?) (*What's my flight number?*)

- ✔ **Wǒ xiǎng tuōyùn xíngli.** 我想托运行李. (我香托運行李.) (waw shyahng twaw-yewn sheeng-lee.) (*I'd like to check my luggage.*)

- ✔ **Wǒ xiǎng yào kào chuāng de wèizi.** 我想要靠窗的位子. (waw shyahng yaow cow chwahng duh way-dzuh.) (*I'd like a window seat.*)

- ✔ **Wǒ xiǎng yào kào guòdào de wèizi.** 我想要靠过道的位子. (我想要靠過道的位子.) (waw shyahng yaow cow gwaw-daow duh way-dzuh.) (*I'd like an aisle seat.*)

- ✔ **Zài jǐ hào mén hòujī?** 在几号门候机? (在幾號門候機?) (dzye jee how mun ho-jee?) (*Which gate do we leave from?*)

- ✔ **Zhè shì wǒde hùzhào.** 这是我的护照. (這是我的護照.) (jay shir waw-duh hoo-jaow.) (*Here's my passport.*)

After you check in, you may encounter all sorts of unpleasant surprises. Perhaps the plane can't **zhèngdiǎn qǐfēi** 正点起飞 (正點起飛) (juhng-dyan chee-fay) (*depart on time*) after all and the airline must **tuīchí** 推迟 (推遲) (tway-chir) (*postpone*) your departure or **qǔxiāo** 取消 (chyew-shyaow) (*cancel*) it altogether. Maybe the **tiānqì** 天气 (天氣) (tyan-chee) (*weather*) is causing the problems.

Talkin' the Talk

 Shí Píng is checking in at the airport in New York for a business trip to Beijing. She shows her ticket and passport to the **zhíyuán** (jir-ywan) (*agent*) and checks her luggage. (Track 22)

Zhíyuán: **Nín hǎo. Qǐng chūshì nínde jīpiào.**
neen how. cheeng choo-shir neen-duh jee-pyaow.
Hello. Your ticket, please.

Shí Píng: **Jiù zài zhèr.**
jyo dzye jar.
Here it is.

Zhíyuán: **Nín shì bú shì qù Běijīng? Néng kànkàn nínde hùzhào ma?**
neen shir boo shir chyew bay-jeeng? nuhng kahn-kahn neen-duh hoo-jaow mah?
Are you going to Beijing? May I see your passport?

Shí Píng: **Kěyǐ.**
kuh-yee.
Here you are.

Zhíyuán: **Yǒu jǐ jiàn xíngli?**
yo jee jyan sheeng-lee?
How many suitcases do you have?

Shí Píng: **Wǒ yǒu sānge xiāngzi.**
waw yo sahn-guh shyahng-dzuh.
I have three suitcases.

Zhíyuán: **Yǒu méiyǒu shǒutí xíngli?**
yo mayo show-tee sheeng-lee?
Do you have any carry-on luggage?

Shí Píng: **Wǒ zhǐ yǒu yíge gōngwénbāo.**
waw jir yo ee-guh goong-one-baow.
I have only one briefcase.

Zhíyuán: **Hǎo. Nín yào kào guòdào de wèizi háishì yào kào chuāng de wèizi?**
how. neen yow cow gwaw-daow duh way-dzuh hi-shir yaow cow chwahng duh way-dzuh?
All right. Would you like an aisle or a window seat?

Shí Píng: **Wǒ xiǎng yào kào guòdào de wèizi.**
waw shyahng yaow cow gwaw-daow duh way-dzuh.
I'd like an aisle seat.

Zhíyuán: **Hǎo. Zhèi shì nínde dēngjīpái. Qù Běijīng de 108 cì bānjī, 19 pái, B zuò.**
how. jay shir neen-duh duhng-jee-pye. chyew bay-jeeng duh ee-bye-leeng-bah tsuh bahn-jee, shir-jyo pye, B dzwaw.
Fine. Here's your boarding pass. Flight 108 to Beijing, Row 19, Seat B.

Shí Píng: **Xièxiè.**
shyeh-shyeh.
Thanks.

Zhíyuán: **Zhè shì nínde xínglǐ lǐngqǔdān. Dàole Běijīng yǐhòu kěyǐ lǐngqǔ nínde xínglǐ.**
jay shir neen-duh sheeng-lee leeng-chyew-dahn. dow-luh bay-jeeng ee-ho kuh-yee leeng-chyew neen-duh sheeng-lee.
Here are your luggage claim tags. After you arrive in Beijing, you can claim your luggage.

Shí Píng: **Xièxiè.**
shyeh-shyeh.
Thanks.

Zhíyuán: **Zhù nín yí lù píng ān.**
joo neen ee loo peeng ahn.
Have a nice trip.

Words to Know

jīpiào 机票	jee-pyaow	airplane ticket
hùzhào 护照 (護照)	hoo-jaow	passport
shǒutí xíngli 手提行李	show-tee sheeng-lee	carry-on luggage
gōngwénbāo 公文包	goong-one baow	briefcase
lǐngqǔdān 领取单 (領取單)	leeng-chyew-dahn	luggage claim tag
yí lù píng ān 一路平安	ee loo peeng ahn	have a nice trip

Boarding your flight

Okay! You're all set to board the **fēijī** 飞机 (飛機) (fay-jee) (*airplane*). Are you lucky enough to sit in the **tóudĕngcāng** 头等舱 (頭等艙) (toe-duhng-tsahng) (*first class*) section, or do you have to sit in **jīngjìcāng** 经济舱 (經濟艙) (jeeng-jee-tsahng) (*economy class*) the whole time? Either way, here are some people you see get on the plane (at least I hope you do):

- ✔ **chéngwùyuán** 乘务员 (乘務員) (chung-woo-ywan) (*flight attendants*)
- ✔ **jiàshǐyuán** 驾驶员 (駕駛員) (jyah-shih-ywan) (*pilot*)
- ✔ **jīzǔ** 机组 (機組) (jee-dzoo) (*crew*)

And if you're like me, you get worried about some things as the plane begins to taxi down the runway:

- ✔ **qǐfēi** 起飞 (起飛) (chee-fay) (*takeoff*)
- ✔ **qìliú** 气流 (氣流) (chee-lyo) (*turbulence*)
- ✔ **zhuólù** 着陆 (著陸) (jwaw-loo) (*landing*)

Aaah! I get nervous just thinking about them. It's okay, though. The **chéng-wùyuán** are on to people like you and me. That's why they make sure to tell you before takeoff where the **jiùshēngyī** 救生衣 (jyo-shung ee) (*life vests*) and **jǐnjí chūkǒu** 紧急出口 (緊急出口) (jin-jee-choo-ko) (*emergency exits*) are located. You may also hear them bark out the following instructions, if you haven't already managed to tune everything out:

✔ **Bǎ tuōpán cānzhuō shōu qǐlái.** 把托盘餐桌收起来. (把托盤餐桌收起來.) (bah twaw-pahn tsahn-jwaw show chee-lye.) (*Put your tray table back.*)

✔ **Bǎ nǐde zuòyǐ kàobèi fàngzhí.** 把你的座位靠背放直. (bah nee-duh dzwaw-ee cow-bay fahng-jir.) (*Put your seat back to the upright position.*)

✔ **Bù zhǔn chōuyān.** 不准抽烟. (不准抽煙.) (boo jwun cho-yan.) (*No smoking permitted.*)

✔ **Jìjǐn nǐde ānquándài.** 系紧你的安全带. (繫緊你的安全帶.) (jee-jin nee-duh ahn-chwan-dye.) (*Fasten your seat belt.*)

✔ **Rúguǒ kōngqì yālì yǒu biànhuà, yǎngqìzhào huì zìdòng luòxià.** 如果气压壓力有变化, 氧气罩会自动落下. (如果空氣壓力有變化, 氧氣罩會自動落下.) (roo-gwaw koong-chee yah-lee yo byan-hwah, yahng-chee-jaow hway dzuh-doong lwaw-shyah.) (*If there's any change in air pressure, the oxygen mask will automatically drop down.*)

You use the coverb **bǎ** 把 (bah) when you want to put the object right up front before you state the verb that tells what you did or will do with the object. (See Chapter 18 for more on this unique coverb.)

If you're not a nervous flyer, you'll probably spend all your time listening to music through the **ěrjī** 耳机 (耳機) (are-jee) (*headset*), flipping dials on the radio or channels on the television, or trying to sleep. Hopefully the flight is showing a good **diànyǐng** 电影 (電影) (dyan-yeeng) (*movie*) on such a long trip.

Going through customs

If you survive all the turbulence and the boring movie on your long flight without having a breakdown, good for you! The next test you have to get through is the **hǎiguān** 海关 (海關) (hi-gwahn) (*customs*) experience. After you get to customs, you see many **hǎiguān guānyuán** 海关关员 (海關關員) (hi-gwahn gwahn-ywan) (*customs officers*), none of whom may understand English. Table 16-1 lists the items you need to have ready at customs. The following phrases should come in handy, too:

✔ **Nǐ dǒng Yīngyǔ ma?** 你懂英语吗? (你懂英語嗎?) (nee doong eeng-yew mah?) (*Do you understand English?*)

✔ **Wǒ shì Jiānádà rén.** 我是加拿大人. (waw shir jyah-nah-dah run.) (*I'm Canadian.*)

✔ **Wǒ shì Měiguó rén.** 我是美国人. (我是美國人.) (waw shir may-gwaw run) (*I'm American.*)

✔ **Wǒ shì Yīngguó rén.** 我是英国人. (我是英國人.) (waw shir eeng-gwaw run.) (*I'm British.*)

✔ **Xǐshǒujiān zài nǎr?** 洗手间在哪儿? (洗手間在哪兒?) (she-show-jyan dzye nar?) (*Where are the restrooms?*)

Table 16-1	**Items to Have Ready at Customs**	
Chinese	*Pronunciation*	*English*
bāo 包	baow	*bag*
chūjìng dēngjì kǎ 出境登记卡 (出境登記卡)	choo-jeeng duhng-jee kah	*departure card*
jiànkāng zhèng 健康证 (健康證)	jyan-kahng jung	*health certificate*
jiǔ 酒	jyo	*alcohol* (to declare)
rùjìng dēngjì kǎ 入境登记卡 (入境登記卡)	roo-jeeng duhng-jee kah	*arrival card*
shēnbào de wùpǐn 申报的物品 (申報的物品)	shun-baow duh woo-peen	*articles to declare*
xingyān 香烟 (香煙)	shyahng-yan	*cigarettes* (to declare)
xiāngzi 箱子	shyahng-dzuh	*suitcase*
xínglǐ 行李	sheeng-lee	*luggage*

The **hǎiguān guānyuán** may ask you a couple of these important questions:

✔ **Nǐ dǎsuàn zài zhèr dāi duōjiǔ?** 你打算在这儿待多久? (你打算在這兒待多久?) (nee dah-swan dzye jar dye dwaw-jyo?) (*How long do you plan on staying?*)

✔ **Nǐ lái zhèr shì bàn gōngwù háishì lǚyóu?** 你来这儿是办公务还是旅游? (你來這兒是辦公務還是旅遊?) (nee lye jar shir bahn goong-woo hi-shir lyew-yo?) (*Are you here on business or as a tourist?*)

✔ **Nǐ yǒu méiyǒu yào shēnbào de wùpǐn?** 你有没有要申报的物品? (你有没有要申報的物品?) (nee yo mayo yaow shun-baow duh woo-peen?) (*Do you have anything you want to declare?*)

> ✔ **Qǐng gěi wǒ kànkàn nǐde hǎiguān shēnbàodān.** 请给我看看你的海关申报单. (請給我看看你的海關申報單.) (cheeng gay waw kahn-kahn nee-duh hi-gwan shun-baow-dahn.) (*Please show me your customs declaration form.*)

> ✔ **Qǐng gěi wǒ kànkàn nǐde hùzhào.** 请给我看看你的护照. (請給我看看你的護照.) (cheeng gay waw kahn-kahn nee-duh hoo-jaow.) (*Please show me your passport.*)

Customs agents aren't the only people with questions to ask. You may have some questions you want to try out yourself:

> ✔ **Wǒ yào fù shuì ma?** 我要付税吗? (我要付稅嗎?) (waw yaow foo shway mah?) (*Must I pay duty?*)

> ✔ **X guāng huì sǔnhuài wǒde jiāojuǎn ma?** X光会损坏我的胶卷 吗? (X光會損壞我的膠卷嗎?) (X gwahng hway swuhn-hwye waw-duh jyaow-jwan mah?) (*Will the X-ray damage my film?*)

> ✔ **Xínglǐ kéyǐ shōu qǐlái ma?** 行李可以收起来吗? (行李可以收起來嗎?) (sheeng-lee kuh-yee show chee-lye mah?) (*May I close my suitcases now?*)

> ✔ **Xínglǐ yào dǎkāi ma?** 行李要打开吗? (行李要打開嗎?) (sheeng-lee yaow dah-kye mah?) (*Should I open my luggage?*)

Talkin' the Talk

Georgia gets off her plane in Shanghai and begins the customs process by approaching an agent. (Track 23)

Agent:	**Qǐng gěi wǒ kànkàn nǐde hùzhào.**
	cheeng gay waw kahn-kahn nee-duh hoo-jaow.
	Please show me your passport.

Georgia shows him her passport, and the agent asks her some important questions.

Agent:	**Měiguórén. Nǐ yǒu méiyǒu yào shēnbào de wùpǐn?**
	may-gwaw-run. nee yo mayo yaow shun-baow duh woo-peen?
	American. Do you have anything you'd like to declare?

Georgia:	**Méiyǒu. Wǒ zhǐ yǒu yìtiáo xiāngyān.**
	mayo. waw jir yo ee-tyaow shyahng-yan.
	No. I have only a carton of cigarettes.

Agent:	**Nǐ lái zhèr shì bàn gōngwù háishì lǚyóu?**
	nee lye jar shir bahn goong-woo hi-shir lyew-yo?
	Are you here on business or as a tourist?
Georgia:	**Wǒ lái zuò shēngyì.**
	waw lye dzwaw shung-ee.
	I've come on business.
Agent:	**Nǐ kéyǐ zǒu le.**
	nee kuh-yee dzoe luh.
	You may go.

Words to Know

Qǐng gěi wǒ kànkàn nǐde hùzhào. 请给我看看你的护照. (請給我看看你的護照.)	cheeng gay waw kahn-kahn nee-duh hoo-jaow.	Please show me your passport.
yìtiáo xiāngyān 一条香烟 (一條香煙)	ee-tyaow shyahng-yan	a carton of cigarettes
gōngwù 公务 (公務)	goong-woo	to be on business
Nǐ kéyǐ zǒu le. 你可以走了.	nee kuh-yee dzoe luh.	You may go.

Navigating Around Town

It's Friday night, and you just had a pretty successful day doing business with your Chinese counterparts. You've finally mustered the courage to venture out of your hotel room for a night on the town. You decide to check out a popular dance hall, and you begin to determine what mode of transport can best get you there.

Renting a car is virtually impossible in China. Cars just aren't available. And even if you can find a rental, you may not want to get one, given the bureaucracy and driving conditions. Signs aren't printed in English, which is probably the main reason you shouldn't even attempt driving. Just think of the upside. You don't have to suddenly learn how to use a stick shift or purchase any extra car insurance. Let someone else worry about how to get you from point A to point B.

No matter what form of **jiāotōng** 交通 (jyaow-toong) (*transportation*) you end up taking, here are a few crucial words and phrases to know:

- **fāngxiàng** 方向 (fahng-shyahng) (*directions*)
- **dìtú** 地图 (地圖) (dee-too) (*map*)
- **Wǒ mílù le.** 我迷路了. (waw mee-loo luh.) (*I'm lost.*)

Hailing a cab

Although **zìxíngchē** 自行车 (自行車) (dzuh-sheeng-chuh) (*bicycles*), **mótuōchē** 摩托车 (摩托車) (maw-twaw-chuh) (*motorcycles*), **mǎchē** 马车 (馬車) (mah-chuh) (*horse-drawn carts*), and even **niú** 牛 (nyo) (*cows*) are still the main forms of transportation for the average individual in some parts of mainland China, most foreigners take taxis wherever they go. You can easily find taxis around hotels, and cabs are certainly more comfortable and convenient than having to deal with nonexistent rules of the road; breathing in air pollution while bicycling; finding your way through a maze of old alleyways; or, depending on the time of year, leaving yourself to the mercy of the natural elements.

Here's what you say to the hotel door attendant if you want help hailing a cab: **Wǒ yào jiào jìchéngchē.** 我要叫计程车. (我要叫計程車.) (waw yaow jyaow jee-chung-chuh.) (*I'd like a taxi.*)

After you're safely ensconced in the cab, you need to know how to say the following phrases:

- **Nǐ kéyǐ děng jǐ fēn zhōng ma?** 你可以等几分钟吗? (你可以等幾分鐘嗎?) (nee kuh-yee duhng jee fun joong mah?) (*Can you wait a few minutes?*)
- **Qǐng dǎ biǎo.** 请打表. (請打表.) (cheeng dah byaow.) (*Please turn on the meter.*)
- **Qǐng dài wǒ dào zhèige dìzhǐ.** 请带我到这个地址. (請帶我到這個地址.) (cheeng dye waw daow jay-guh dee-jir.) (*Please take me to this address.*)
- **Qǐng kāi kuài yìdiǎr.** 请开快一点儿. (請開快一點兒.) (cheeng kye kwye ee-dyar.) (*Please drive a little faster.*)
- **Qǐng kāi màn yìdiǎr.** 请开慢一点儿. (請開慢一點兒.) (cheeng kye mahn ee-dyar.) (*Please drive a little slower.*)
- **Qǐng zǒu fēngjǐng hǎo de lù.** 请走风景好的路. (請走風景好的路.) (cheeng dzoe fung-jeeng how duh loo.) (*Please take a scenic route.*)
- **Wǒ děi gǎn shíjiān.** 我得赶时间. (我得趕時間.) (waw day gahn shir-jyan.) (*I'm in a hurry.*)
- **Zài zhèr guǎi wār.** 在这儿拐弯儿. (在這兒拐彎兒.) (dzye jar gwye wahr.) (*Turn here.*)

Oh, and one more thing. As you set off with your taxi **sījī** 司机 (司機) (suh-jee) (*driver*), make sure you put on your **ānquándài** 安全带 (ahn-chwan-dye) (*seat belt*).

Finally, before you get out of the cab, these phrases may come in handy for price negotiations:

✔ **Bié qīpiàn wǒ.** 别欺骗我. (別欺騙我.) (byeh chee-pyan waw.) (*Don't cheat me.*)

✔ **Bú yòng zhǎo le.** 不用找了. (boo yoong jaow luh.) (*Keep the change.*)

✔ **Kāi wán xiào! Wǒ jùjué fù zhèmme duō qián.** 开玩笑! 我拒绝付这么多钱. (開玩笑! 我拒絕付這麼多錢.) (kye wahn shyaow! waw jyew-jweh foo juhmmuh dwaw chyan.) (*You've got to be kidding! I refuse to pay so much.*)

✔ **Qǐng gěi wǒ shōujù.** 请给我收据. (請給我收據.) (cheeng gay waw show-jyew.) (*Please give me a receipt.*)

✔ **Wǒ gāi gěi nǐ duōshǎo qián?** 我该给你多少钱? (我該給你多少錢?) (waw guy gay nee dwaw-shaow chyan?) (*How much do I owe you?*)

✔ **Wǒ huì àn biǎo fù kuǎn.** 我会按表付款. (我會按表付款.) (waw hway ahn byaow foo kwahn.) (*I'll pay what the meter says.*)

Because most people in China don't speak English, always remember to take a hotel card when you leave your hotel. Your card has the name and address in English and Chinese. You can always show the card to a taxi driver when you want to get back. If you're walking around town, you may want to take a map that shows local landmarks such as pagodas or train stations near your hotel.

Talkin' the Talk

Bill ventures out for a night on the town and needs a cab. He enlists the help of his hotel doorman.

Bill: **Wǒ yào jiào jìchéngchē.**
waw yaow jyaow jee-chung-chuh.
I'd like a taxi.

Doorman: **Hǎo.**
how.
Certainly.

Bill enters the cab and shows the driver a card with the name and address of a local nightclub.

Bill: **Qǐng dài wǒ dào zhèige yèzǒnghuì.**
cheeng dye waw daow jay-guh yeh-dzoong-hway.
Please take me to this nightclub.

Driver: **Méiyǒu wèntí.**
mayo one-tee.
No problem.

Bill: **Wǒ bùjí. Qǐng kāi màn yìdiǎr.**
waw boo-jee. cheeng kye mahn ee-dyar.
I'm not in a hurry. Please drive a little slower.

Bill finally reaches the nightclub after his scenic cab drive.

Bill: **Wǒ gāi gěi nǐ duōshǎo qián?**
waw guy gay nee dwaw-shaow chyan?
How much do I owe you?

Driver: **Shí kuài liǎng máo wǔ.**
shir kwye lyahng maow woo.
That will be $10.25.

Bill hands the driver $15.

Bill: **Qǐng gěi wǒ shōujù. Bú yòng zhǎo le.**
cheeng gay waw show-jyew. boo yoong jaow luh.
Please give me a receipt. Keep the change.

Driver: **Hǎo. Xièxiè.**
how. shyeh-shyeh.
Okay. Thanks.

Words to Know

yèzǒnghuì 夜总会 (夜總會)	yeh-dzoong-hway	nightclub
bùjí 不急	boo-jee	no rush/no hurry
shōujù 收据 (收據)	show-jyew	receipt
Bú yòng zhǎo le. 不用找了。	boo yoong jaow luh.	Keep the change.

Hopping on the bus

Gōnggòng qìchē 公共汽车 (公共汽車) (goong-goong chee-chuh) (*buses*) are almost as common as bicycles in China. They also cost much less than taxis. But here's the catch: Bus drivers usually don't speak a word of English, signs are only in Chinese, and the buses are always super crowded. Still, if you're game for a unique travel experience and you don't mind killing time waiting for the bus, put these phrases in your carry-on bag:

- ✔ **Chē piào duōshǎo qián?** 车票多少钱? (車票多少錢?) (chuh pyaow dwaw-shaow chyan?) (*How much is the fare?*)

- ✔ **Duōjiǔ lái yítàng?** 多久来一趟? (多久來一趟?) (dwaw-jyo lye ee-tahng?) (*How often does it come?*)

- ✔ **Gōnggòng qìchē zhàn zài nǎr?** 公共汽车站在哪儿? (公共汽車站在哪兒?) (goong-goong chee-chuh jahn dzye nar?) (*Where's the bus station?*)

- ✔ **Qǐng gàosù wǒ zài nǎr xià chē.** 请告诉我在哪儿下车. (請告訴我在哪兒下車.) (cheeng gaow-soo waw dzye nar shyah chuh.) (*Please let me know where to get off.*)

- ✔ **Yīnggāi zuò jǐ lù chē?** 应该坐几路车? (應該坐幾路車?) (eeng-guy dzwaw jee loo chuh?) (*Which [number] bus should I take?*)

Talkin' the Talk

Charlie is walking along the street, trying to find a bus that can take him to the famous Shilin night market in Taiwan. He sees his old friend Louise, and after saying hello, he asks her for help.

Charlie: **Qù Shílín yīnggāi zuò jǐ lù gōnggòng qìchē?**
chyew shir-leen eeng-guy dzwaw jee loo goong-goong chee-chuh?
Which bus should I take to go to Shilin?

Louise: **Yīnggāi zuò sān lù chē. Nèige gōnggòng qìchē zhàn jiù zài zhèr.**
eeng-guy dzwaw sahn loo chuh. nay-guh goong-goong chee-chuh jahn jyo dzye jar.
You should take the number 3 bus. That bus stop is right here.

Charlie: **Tài hǎo le. Duōjiǔ lái yítàng?**
tye how luh. dwaw-jyo lye ee-tahng?
That's great. How often does it come?

Louise: **Měi sānshí fēn zhōng. Hái hǎo.**
may sahn-shir fun joong. hi how.
Every 30 minutes. That's not too bad.

Charlie: **Xièxiè nǐ.**
shyeh-shyeh nee.
Thank you.

Words to Know

jǐ lù chē 几路车 (幾路車)	jee loo chuh	which number bus
gōnggòng qìchē 公共汽车 (公共汽車)	goong-goong chee-chuh	bus
gōnggòng qìchē zhàn 公共汽车站 (公共汽車站)	goong-goong chee-chuh jahn	bus stop
Hái hǎo. 还好 (還好).	hi how.	It's not too bad./ It's okay.

Riding the rails

If you want to get where you need to go really quickly, especially in Hong Kong or New York, the fastest way to get there may take you below the ground — to the **dìtiě** 地铁 (地鐵) (dee-tyeh) (*subway*). Most **dìtiě zhàn** 地铁站 (地鐵站) (dee-tyeh jahn) (*subway stations*) are pretty easy to navigate.

Unlike in Hong Kong, the subway system in mainland China is relatively new, and you find stations in less than a handful of cities. Above-ground **huǒchē** 火车 (火車) (hwaw-chuh) (*train*) travel, however, is tried and true — especially because China is such a huge place and distances between cities are so great. Unlike the number of subway stations, you can find plenty of **huǒchēzhàn** 火车站 (火車站) (hwaw-chuh-jahn) (*train stations*) in China. They even come equipped with waiting rooms.

If you plan to travel a long distance, be sure to book a soft sleeper — or at least ask for a soft seat — because they're the more comfortable accommodations and not as jam-packed as other parts of the train. Trust me. Soft sleepers are worth the extra cost. For more on the types of seats in trains, see Table 16-2.

Taking the subway around China

Hong Kong constantly upgrades and extends its subway system, making it quite reliable. Taipei also has an excellent and efficient subway system. In Shanghai, China's major commercial center of Pudong has a subway that connects the east and west sides of the Huangpu River.

And in Beijing, the 2008 Olympics prompted extensive subway expansion in preparation for the hordes that descended into its metro system. It now has 15 lines and close to 200 stations.

Table 16-2	Seating Accommodations on Trains	
Chinese	*Pronunciation*	*English*
ruǎnwò 软卧 (軟臥)	rwahn-waw	*soft sleeper*
ruǎnzuò 软座 (軟座)	rwan-dzwaw	*soft seat*
shàngpù 上铺 (上舖)	shahng-poo	*upper berth*
xiàpù 下铺 (下舖)	shyah-poo	*lower berth*
yìngwò 硬卧	eeng-waw	*hard sleeper*
yìngzuò 硬座	eeng-dzwaw	*hard seat*

February is a particularly risky month to attempt long-distance train travel, because the shortest month often features the Chinese New Year, and you're bound to meet what seems like the entire country traveling from one part of China to another. Make sure you consult a **shíkèbiǎo** 时刻表 (時刻表) (shir-kuh-byaow) (*time schedule*) in advance and note the correct **dàodá shíjiān** 到达时间 (到達時間) (daow-dah shir-jyan) (*arrival time*) and **kāichē shíjiān** 开车时间 (開車時間) (key-chuh shir-jyan) (*departure time*) of your train.

Before you **shàngchē** 上车 (上車) (shahng-chuh) (*board the train*) to enjoy your comfy, soft seat, you need to go to the **shòupiàochù** 售票处 (售票處) (show-pyaow-choo) (*ticket office*) to buy your ticket. You use the following words and phrases to get the job done:

- ✔ **dānchéngpiào** 单程票 (單程票) (dahn-chuhng-pyaow) (*one-way ticket*)
- ✔ **láihuípiào** 来回票 (來回票) (lye-hway-pyaow) (*round-trip ticket*)
- ✔ **mànchē** 慢车 (慢車) (mahn-chuh) (*local train*)
- ✔ **piào** 票 (pyaow) (*ticket*)

> ✔ **piàojià** 票价 (票價) (pyaow-jyah) (*fare*)
>
> ✔ **tèkuài** 特快 (tuh-kwye) (*express train*)

The following may come in handy at the train station:

> ✔ **Huŏchē cóng něige zhàntái kāi?** 火车从哪个站台开? (火車從哪個站台開?) (hwaw-chuh tsoong nay-guh jahn-tye kye?) (*Which gate does the train leave from?*)
>
> ✔ **Piàofáng zài năr?** 票房在哪儿? (票房在哪兒?) (pyaow-fahng dzye nar?) (*Where's the ticket office?*)
>
> Notice the different way of saying *ticket office* in this question. Options abound in the Chinese language.
>
> ✔ **Wŏ yào yìzhāng yìngwò piào.** 我要一张硬卧票. (我要一張硬臥票.) (waw yow ee-jahng eeng-waw pyaow.) (*I'd like a hard-sleeper ticket.*)

And when you finally hear the **lièchēyuán** 列车员 (列車員) (lyeh-chuh-ywan) (*conductor*) say **Shàng chē le!** 上车了! (上車了!) (shahng chuh luh!) (*All aboard!*), you can board and ask the following questions:

> ✔ **Cānchē zài năr?** 餐车在哪儿? (餐車在哪兒?) (tsahn-chuh dzye nar?) (*Where's the dining car?*)
>
> ✔ **Zhèige zuòwèi yŏu rén ma?** 这个座位有人吗? (這個座位有人嗎?) (jay-guh dzwaw-way yo run mah?) (*Is this seat taken?*)

Talkin' the Talk

Candice is at the Beijing train station to buy a round-trip ticket to Shanghai for tomorrow. She approaches a ticket agent to purchase her ticket.

Candice:	**Qĭngwèn, yŏu méiyŏu míngtiān qù Shànghăi de huŏchē piào?**
	cheeng-one, yo mayo meeng-tyan chyew shahng-hi duh hwaw-chuh pyaow?
	Excuse me, do you have any train tickets to Shanghai for tomorrow?

Ticket agent:	**Yŏu. Yào jĭ zhāng?**
	yo. yaow jee jahng?
	Yes. How many would you like?

Candice: **Zhǐ yì zhāng lái huí piào. Xiàge lǐbàiyī yào huí lái.**
jir ee jahng lye hway pyaow. shyah-guh lee-bye-ee yaow hway lye.
Just one round-trip ticket. I'd like to return next Monday.

Ticket agent: **Hǎo. Yào yìngwò, ruǎnwò, háishì ruǎnzuò?**
how. yaow eeng-waw, rwahn-waw, hi-shir rwahn-dzwaw?
Okay. Would you like a hard sleeper, a soft sleeper, or a soft seat?

Candice: **Wǒ yào yì zhāng ruǎnwò. Xièxiè.**
waw yaow ee jahng rwahn-waw. shyeh-shyeh.
I'd like a soft sleeper. Thanks.

Words to Know

míngtiān 明天	meeng-tyan	tomorrow
lái huí piào 来回票 (來回票)	lye hway pyaow	round-trip ticket
huí lái 回来 (回來)	hway lye	to return

Fun & Games

How do you say these types of transportation in Chinese? (Flip to Appendix D for the answers.)

A. _____

B. _____

C. _____

D. _____

E. _____

Chapter 17

Asking for Directions

· ·

In This Chapter

▶ Asking "where" questions

▶ Covering time and distances

▶ Picking out specific spots with ordinal numbers

▶ Pointing the way with directional coverbs

· ·

Everyone (yes, even you) has to ask for **fāngxiàng** 方向 (fahng-shyahng) (*directions*) at some time or another. Even if you just need to find the bathroom — when you've got to go, you'd better know.

You may find yourself baffled by the boulevards in Beihai or dumbfounded by directions in Dalian. This chapter helps you figure out exactly how to ask for directions before you ever **mílù** 迷路 (mee-loo) (*get lost*). Whether you lose your bearings in Beijing or wander off the path in Luoyang, this chapter gives you helpful tips that make it easier to find your way back home. Or at least back to your hotel.

You definitely need to know how to ask where certain places are in mainland China, where most people don't speak English. You have a greater likelihood of hailing an English-speaking cabbie in Taipei or Kowloon to take you where you need to go than you do in one of the cities or towns in mainland China, but you can't bank on that.

Avoiding 20 Questions: Just Ask "Where?"

Okay, so you're searching for the closest post office to mail a package home before your mother's birthday next week. A passerby tells you to go right down the street, but for the life of you, all you see are a couple of bookstores and an occasional subway station. Time to ask for directions. But how?

The easiest way to ask where something is in Chinese is to use the question word **nǎr** 哪儿 (哪兒) (nar) (*where*). But you can't just say **nǎr,** or folks still won't know what you're talking about. You have to use the coverb **zài** 在 (dzye), which can be translated as *in* or *at*, in front of **nǎr (zài nǎr).** (A *coverb* is officially a verb but functions as a preposition.) Just put the name of whatever you're looking for before the word **zài** to create a complete question:

> **Nǐ zài nǎr?** 你在哪儿? (你在哪兒?) (nee dzye nar?) (*Where are you?*)

> **Shūdiàn zài nǎr?** 书店在哪儿? (書店在哪兒?) (shoo-dyan dzye nar?) (*Where's the bookstore?*)

> **Yóujú zài nǎr?** 邮局在哪儿? (郵局在哪兒?) (yo-jyew dzye nar?) (*Where's the post office?*)

Here are some places you may be looking for when you lose your way:

- ✔ **cèsuǒ** 厕所 (廁所) (tsuh-swaw) (*bathroom*)
- ✔ **chūzū qìchēzhàn** 出租汽车站 (出租汽車站) (choo-dzoo chee-chuh-jahn) (*taxi stand*)
- ✔ **dìtiězhàn** 地铁站 (地鐵站) (dee-tyeh-jahn) (*subway station*)
- ✔ **fànguǎn** 饭馆 (飯館) (fahn-gwahn) (*restaurant*)
- ✔ **gōnggòng qìchē zhàn** 公共汽车站 (公共汽車站) (goong-goong chee-chuh jahn) (*bus stop*)
- ✔ **huǒchē zhàn** 火车站 (火車站) (hwaw-chuh-jahn) (*train station*)
- ✔ **jiēdào** 街道 (jyeh-daow) (*street*)
- ✔ **jízhěn shì** 急诊室 (急診室) (jee-juhn shir) (*emergency room*)
- ✔ **Měiguó dàshǐguǎn** 美国大使馆 (美國大使館) (may-gwaw dah-shir-gwahn) (*American embassy*)
- ✔ **piàofáng** 票房 (票房) (pyaow-fahng) (*ticket office*)
- ✔ **shūdiàn** 书店 (書店) (shoo-dyan) (*bookstore*)
- ✔ **xuéxiào** 学校 (學校) (shweh-shyaow) (*school*)
- ✔ **yínháng** 银行 (銀行) (een-hahng) (*bank*)
- ✔ **yóujú** 邮局 (郵局) (yo-jyew) (*post office*)

When you travel in unknown areas, you may need to determine whether you can walk or if you need to take a bus or taxi to reach your destination:

- ✔ **Hěn jìn ma?** 很近吗? (很進嗎?) (hun jeen mah?) (*Is it near?*)
- ✔ **Hěn yuǎn ma?** 很远吗? (很遠嗎?) (hun ywan mah?) (*Is it far?*)

Chapter 16 has the lowdown on all sorts of transportation.

Different strokes for different folks: Saying năr versus saying năli

Chinese people immediately know where you're from, where you've studied, or at least where your Chinese language teacher is from by the way you say the word *where.* If you say **năr** 哪儿 (哪兒) (nahr) with an *r* sound at the end of the word, you represent a northern Chinese accent commonly found in Beijing. If you say it with a *lee* sound at the end rather than an *r* sound, as in **năli** 哪里 (哪裡) (nah-lee), that indicates you've probably lived or studied in Taiwan.

The word **năr** spoken with a third (low falling and then rising) tone means *where,* but the same word said with a fourth (falling) tone, **nàr,** means *there,* so be particularly careful which tone you use when you ask for directions. The person you ask may think you're making a statement, not asking a question.

Talkin' the Talk

Wanda is about to leave her hotel in Beijing to head for the American embassy to renew her passport. She's not sure where to find it, so she asks a hotel attendant how to get there. (Track 24)

Wanda: **Qǐngwèn, Měiguó dàshǐguǎn zài năr?**
cheeng-one, may-gwaw dah-shir-gwahn dzye nar?
Excuse me, where's the American embassy?

Attendant: **Měiguó dàshǐguǎn zài Xiù Shuǐ Běi Jiē.**
may-gwaw dah-shir-gwahn dzye shyow shway bay jyeh.
The American embassy is on Xiu Shui Bei Street.

Wanda: **Hěn yuǎn ma?**
hun ywan mah?
Is it far?

Attendant: **Hěn yuǎn. Nǐ zuì hǎo zuò chūzū qìchē qù.**
hun ywan. nee dzway how zwaw choo-dzoo chee-chuh chyew.
Yes, it's quite far. You'd best take a taxi.

Wanda: **Xièxiè.**
shyeh-shyeh.
Thanks.

Words to Know

qǐng wèn 请问 (請問)	cheeng-one	excuse me
Hěn yuǎn. 很远. (很遠.)	hun ywan.	It's quite far.
zuò chūzū qìchē 坐出租汽车 (坐出租汽車)	dzwaw choo-dzoo chee-chuh	to take a taxi

Getting direction about directions

Knowing how to ask where you can find a particular place is the first step, but you also need to know how to get there. (Otherwise, why would you ask where it is in the first place, right?) Here's the simplest way to find out: **Qù _____ zěnme zǒu?** 去 _____ 怎么走? (去 _____ 怎麼走?) (chyew _____ dzummuh dzoe?) (*How do I get to_____?*)

Here are some examples of how to use this question pattern:

> **Qù fēijīchǎng zěnme zǒu?** 去飞机场怎么走? (去飛機場怎麼走?) (chyew fay-jee-chahng dzummuh dzoe?) (*How do I get to the airport?*)

> **Qù túshūguǎn zěnme zǒu?** 去图书馆怎么走? (去圖書館怎麼走?) (chyew too-shoo-gwahn dzummuh dzoe?) (*How do I get to the library?*)

> **Qù xuéxiào zěnme zǒu?** 去学校怎么走? (去學校怎麼走?) (chyew shweh-shyaow dzummuh dzoe?) (*How do I get to the school?*)

If you get lost in any city in mainland China, you can often get back on track by asking where **Zhōngshān Lù** 中山路 (joong-shahn loo) or **Jiěfàng Lù** 解放路 (jyeh-fahng loo) is. **Zhōngshān,** which literally means *the middle mountain,* refers to the birthplace of Dr. Sun Yat-sen, founder of the modern Chinese Republic (Taiwan) in 1911. **Jiěfàng,** on the other hand, means *liberation* and refers to the "liberation" of the mainland by the Communists in 1949. **Lù** just means *road.* Generally, these streets are located in the middle of town. They serve as the Chinese equivalent of Main Street in Anytown, USA. Always a safe bet.

Understanding the answers to "where" questions

Short of using international sign language with a pantomime act, you may want to get a handle on some basic terms that indicate direction and location. Read on for a quick list:

- ✔ **duìmiàn** 对面 (對面) (dway-myan) (*opposite*)
- ✔ **fùjìn** 附近 (foo-jeen) (*near*)
- ✔ **hòu** 后 (後) (ho) (*back*)
- ✔ **kàojìn** 靠近 (kaow-jeen) (*next to*)
- ✔ **lǐ** 里 (理) (lee) (*inside*)
- ✔ **qián** 前 (chyan) (*front*)
- ✔ **shàng** 上 (shahng) (*above*)
- ✔ **sìzhōu** 四周 (suh-joe) (*around*)
- ✔ **wài** 外 (why) (*outside*)
- ✔ **xià** 下 (shyah) (*below*)
- ✔ **yòu** 右 (yo) (*right*)
- ✔ **yòu zhuǎn** 右转 (右轉) (yo jwan) (*turn right*)
- ✔ **zhí zǒu** 直走 (jir dzoe) (*go straight ahead*)
- ✔ **zhuǎn wān** 转弯 (轉彎) (jwan wahn) (*turn around*)
- ✔ **zuǒ** 左 (dzwaw) (*left*)
- ✔ **zuǒ zhuǎn** 左转 (左轉) (dzwaw jwan) (*turn left*)

Three different, completely interchangeable word endings work with any of the location words:

- ✔ **biān** 边 (邊) (byan)
- ✔ **miàn** 面 (myan)
- ✔ **tóu** 头 (頭) (toe)

So, for example, to tell you that the bus stop is outside, someone may say any of the following sentences:

> **Chūzū qìchēzhàn zài wàibiān.** 出租汽车站在外边. (出租汽車站在外邊.) (choo-dzoo chee-chuh-jahn dzye why-byan.) (*The bus stop is outside.*)

> **Chūzū qìchēzhàn zài wàimiàn.** 出租汽车站在外面. (出租汽車站在外面). (choo-dzoo chee-chuh-jahn dzye why-myan.) (*The bus stop is outside.*)

> **Chūzū qìchēzhànzài wàitóu.** 出租汽车站在外头. (出租汽車站在外頭.) (choo-dzoo chee-chuh-jahn-dzye why-toe.) (*The bus stop is outside.*)

Sometimes the situation may require a more complex location expression, such as when your friendly direction-giver doesn't want to simply note where something is. Perhaps your helper wants to tell you where a certain action should take place. For example, if he or she wants to say *Please turn left in front of the school.,* here's what you'll hear:

> **Qǐng nǐ zài xuéxiào qiánbiān wǎng zuǒ zhuǎn.** 请你在学校前边往左转. (請你在學校前邊往左轉.) (cheeng nee dzye shweh-shyaow chyan-byan wahng dzwaw jwan.) (*Please turn left in front of the school.*)

> **Qǐng nǐ zài xuéxiào qiánmiàn wǎng zuǒ zhuǎn.** 请你在学校前面往左转. (請你在學校前面往左轉.) (cheeng nee dzye shweh-shyaow chyan-myan wahng dzwaw jwan.) (*Please turn left in front of the school.*)

> **Qǐng nǐ zài xuéxiào qiántóu wǎng zuǒ zhuǎn.** 请你在学校前头往左转. (請你在學校前頭往左轉.) (cheeng nee dzye shweh-shyaow chyan-toe wahng dzwaw jwan.) (*Please turn left in front of the school.*)

In such cases, the verb **děng** 等 (dung) (*to wait*) comes after the specified location (**xuéxiào qiánmiàn**). Here are some other examples:

> **Zài túshūguǎn qiántóu děng .** 在图书馆前头等. (在圖書館前頭等.) (dzye too-shoo-gwahn chyan-toe dung.) (*Wait in front of the library.*)

> **Zài wūzi lǐ wàibiān děng.** 在屋子里外边等. (在屋子理外邊等.) (dzye woo-dzuh lee why-byan dung.) (*Wait outside the room.*)

> **Zài xuéxiào hòumiàn děng.** 在学校后面等. (在學校後面等.) (dzye shweh-shyaow ho-myan dung.) (*Wait in back of the school.*)

Talkin' the Talk

Corey asks Casey for directions in Tainan. He wants to get to the post office. (Track 25)

Corey: **Qǐngwèn, Casey, yóujú zài nǎr?**
cheeng-one, Casey, yo-jyew dzye nar?
Excuse me, Casey, where's the post office?

Casey: **Yóujú jiù zài yínháng duìmiàn. Guò liǎng tiáo lù jiù shì.**
yo-jyew jyo dzye een-hahng dway-myan. gwaw lyahng tyaow loo jyo shir.
The post office is right opposite the bank. If you go two more blocks, it's right there.

Corey: **Xièxiè. Qù yóujú zěnme zǒu?**
shyeh-shyeh. chyew yo-jyew dzummuh dzoe?
Thank you. How should I walk to the post office?

Casey: **Wàng nán zǒu. Yìzhí zǒu jiù dào le.**
wahng nahn dzoe. ee-jir dzoe jyoe daow luh.
Walk south. Go straight, and you'll see it.

Words to Know

zài yínháng duìmiàn 在银行对面 (在銀行對面)	dzye een-hahng dway-myan	opposite the bank
zǒu (zǒu lù) 走路	dzoe (dzoe loo)	to walk
wàng 往	wahng	toward

Expressing Distances (Time and Space) with Lí

Even though you can use the **cóng . . . dào** pattern to literally say *from here to there* (**cóng zhèr dào nàr** 从这儿到那儿 [從這兒到那兒]) (tsoong jar daow nar) when you want to indicate the distance from one place to another, you need to use the "distance from" coverb **lí** 离 (離) (lee). The general sentence pattern looks something like this:

Place word + **lí** + place word + description of the distance

For example

> **Gōngyuán lí túshūguǎn hěn jìn.** 公园离图书馆很近. (公園離圖書館很近.) (goong-ywan lee too-shoo-gwan hun jeen.) (*The park is very close to the library.*)

> **Wǒ jiā lí nǐ jiā tǐng yuǎn.** 我家离你家挺远. (我家離你家挺遠.) (waw jyah lee nee jyah teeng ywan.) (*My home is really far from your home.*)

If you want to specify exactly how far one place is from another, you use the number of **lǐ** 里 (lee) (the Chinese equivalent of a kilometer) followed by the word **lǐ** and then the word **lù** 路 (loo) (Literally: *road*). Whether you say **sì lǐ lù** 四里路 (suh lee loo) (*4 kilometers*), **bā lǐ lù** 八里路 (bah lee loo) (*8 kilometers*), or **èrshísān lǐ lù** 二十三里路 (are-shir-sahn lee loo) (*23 kilometers*), people know the exact distance when you use this pattern. You also have to use the word **yǒu** 有 (yo) (*to have*) before the number of kilometers. If the answer includes an adjectival verb such as **yuǎn** 远 (遠) (ywan) (*far*) or **jìn** 近 (jin) (*close*) rather than a numerical distance, however, you don't need to specify the number of kilometers or use the word **yǒu.** (Count on Chapter 5 for information on Chinese numbers.)

Check out the following sample questions and answers that use these patterns:

> **Gōngyuán lí túshūguǎn duōme yuǎn?** 公园离图书馆多么远? (公園離圖書館多麼遠?) (goong-ywan lee too-shoo-gwahn dwaw-muh ywan?) (*How far is the park from the library?*)

> **Gōngyuán lí túshūguǎn yǒu bā lǐ lù.** 公园离图书馆有八里路. (公園離圖書館有八里路.) (goong-ywan lee too-shoo-gwahn yo bah lee loo.) (*The park is eight kilometers from the library.*)

> **Yínháng lí nǐ jiā duōme jìn?** 银行离你家多么近? (銀行離你家多麼進?) (eeng-hahng lee nee jyah dwaw-muh jin?) (*How close is the bank from your home?*)

> **Hěn jìn. Zhǐ yī lǐ lù.** 很近. 只一里路. (hun jin. jir ee lee loo.) (*Very close. Just one kilometer.*)

You may have some other questions when you inquire about locations and distances:

✔ **Yào duō cháng shíjiān?** 要多长时间? (要多長時間?) (yaow dwaw chahng shir-jyan?) (*How long will it take?*)

✔ **Zǒu de dào ma?** 走得到吗? (走得到嗎?) (dzoe duh daow mah?) (*Can I walk there?*)

✔ **Zǒu de dào, zǒu bú dào?** 走得到走不到? (dzoe duh daow, dzoe boo daow?) (*Can one walk there?*)

To indicate whether something is likely to happen or unlikely to be attained, the pattern you use includes *potential complements*. You use potential complements by putting the word **de** 得 (duh) or **bù** 不 (boo) between the verb and the complement to indicate whether a positive or negative potential is involved, respectively.

Consider the phrase **nǐ kànjiàn** 你看见 (你看見) (nee kahn-jyan) (*you see*). If you say **Nǐ kàn de jiàn ma?** 你看得见 吗? (你看得見嗎?) (nee kahn duh jyan ma?), you mean *Can you see?* If replace the positive **de** with the negative **bù** to ask **Nǐ kàn bú jiàn ma?** 你看不见 吗? (你看不見嗎?) (nee kahn boo jyan ma?), you mean *You can't see?* Finally, if you use both positive and negative potential forms in the same sentence by asking **Nǐ kàn de jiàn, kàn bú jiàn?** 你看得见, 看不见? (你看得見, 看不見?) (nee kahn duh jyan, kahn boo jyan?), you mean *Can you see [or not]?*

So in the earlier example **Zǒu de dào, zǒu bú dào?,** what you're really saying is *Can one can walk there [or not]?* Similarly, **Wǒmen lái de jí, lái bù jí?** 我们来得及, 来不及? (我們來得及來不及?) (waw-mun lye duh jee, lye boo jee?) means *Will we make it on time [or not]?*

Here are some other examples of this pattern:

xǐ gānjìng 洗干净 (洗乾淨) (she gahn-jeeng) (*to wash [and make clean]*)

xǐ de gānjìng 洗得干净 (洗得乾淨) (she duh gahn-jeeng) (*can be washed*)

xǐ bù gānjìng 洗不干净 (洗不乾淨) (she boo gahn-jeeng) (*can't be washed*)

Xǐ de gānjìng, xǐ bù gānjìng? 洗得干净, 洗不干净? (洗得不乾淨, 洗不乾淨?) (she duh gahn-jeeng, she boo gahn-jeeng?) (*Can you wash it?/Can it be washed?*)

zuò wán 做完 (dzwaw wahn) (*to finish [doing something]*)

zuò de wán 做得完 (dzwaw duh wahn) (*can finish*)

zuò bù wán 做不完 (dzwaw boo wahn) (*can't finish*)

Zuò de wán, zuò bù wán? 做得完, 做不完? (dzwaw duh wahn, dzwaw boo wahn?) (*Can you finish it?/Can it be finished?*)

Using Ordinal Numbers to Clarify Points of Reference

If someone has ever told you to make a right at the second **jiāotōng dēng** 交通灯 (交通燈) (jyaow-toong dung) (*traffic light*) or that her house is the third one on the left, she's used ordinal numbers. (You can find a list of ordinal numbers in Chapter 5; in this section, I just show you how they're used in giving Chinese directions.)

Simply using a numeral plus a classifier doesn't work in Chinese, such as when you say **sān ge** 三个 (三個) (sahn guh) (*three*) of something. If someone giving you directions says **sān ge jiāotōng dēng** 三个交通灯 (三個交通燈) (sahn guh jyaow-toong dung), you hear *three traffic lights.* To accurately express *the third traffic light,* your helper has to add the word **dì** 第 (dee) before the numeral to create **dì sān ge jiāotōng dēng** 第三个交通灯 (第三個交通燈) (dee sahn guh jyaow-toong dung).

As I note in Chapter 5, if you use an ordinal number followed by a noun, you must always have a classifier between them. You can't combine **dì sān** 第三 (dee sahn) (*the third*) with **qìchē** 汽车 (汽車) (chee-chuh) (*car*). You have to put the classifier **ge** between the number and the noun to say **dì sān ge qìchē** 第三个汽车 (第三個汽車) (dee sahn guh chee-chuh) (*the third car*).

Following are some examples of ways you may hear ordinal numbers in directions:

> **dì èr ge fángzi** 第二个房子 (第二個房子) (dee are guh fahng-dzuh) (*the second house*)

> **dì yī tiáo lù** 第一条路 (第一條路) (dee ee tyaow loo) (*the first street*)

> **zuǒ biān dì bā ge fángzi** 左边第八个房子 (左邊第八個房子) (dzwaw byan dee bah guh fahng-dzuh) (*the eighth house on the left*)

Specifying Cardinal Points

Your direction-givers can tell you to go right or left until they're blue in the face, but sometimes the best way to give you directions is to point you the right way with the cardinal points: north, south, east, or west.

In Chinese, however, you say them in this order:

- ✔ **dōng** 东 (東) (doong) (*east*)
- ✔ **nán** 南 (nahn) (*south*)
- ✔ **xī** 西 (she) (*west*)
- ✔ **běi** 北 (bay) (*north*)

Not precise enough? Try the following (also in the correct Chinese order):

- ✔ **dōng běi** 东北 (東北) (doong bay) (*northeast*)
- ✔ **xī běi** 西北 (she bay) (*northwest*)
- ✔ **dōng nán** 东南 (東南) (doong nahn) (*southeast*)
- ✔ **xī nán** 西南 (she nahn) (*southwest*)

When it comes to indicating north, south, east, and west (as well as left and right), you can use either **-biān** 边 (邊) (byan) or **-miàn** 面 (myan) as a word ending, but not **-tóu** 头 (頭) (to), which you can use with other position words such as front, back, inside, and outside. (I cover these position words earlier in the chapter.)

Giving directions often entails multiple instructions. "Make a right, and you're there." or "Go straight, and you'll see it right in front of you." doesn't always cut it. Luckily, a common Chinese pattern makes giving multiple directions easy:

> **xiān** 先 + Verb 1, **zài** 再 + Verb 2. (shyan + Verb 1, dzye + Verb 2.) (*First do Verb 1, and then do Verb 2.*)

Here are some examples:

> **Xiān wàng dōng zǒu, zài wàng yòu zhuǎn.** 先往东走, 再往右转. (先往 東走, 再往右轉.) (shyan wahng doong dzoe, dzye wahng yo jwan.) (*First walk east, and then turn right.*)

> **Xiān zhí zǒu, zài wàng xī zǒu.** 先直走, 再往西走. (shyan jir dzoe, dzye wahng she dzoe.) (*First go straight, and then turn west.*)

Talkin' the Talk

Linda is walking around Shanghai looking for the Shanghai Museum. She begins to wonder if she's going in the right direction, so she decides to ask a stranger how to get there.

Linda: **Qǐngwèn, Shànghǎi bówùguǎn lí zhèr hěn yuǎn ma?**
cheeng-one, shahng-hi baw-woo-gwahn lee jar hun ywan mah?
Excuse me, is the Shanghai Museum very far from here?

Stranger: **Bù yuǎn. Shànghǎi bówùguǎn jiù zài rénmín dà dào.**
boo ywan. shahng-hi baw-woo-gwahn jyo dzye run-meen dah daow.
It's not far at all. The Shanghai Museum is on the Avenue of the People.

Linda: **Rénmín dà dào lí zhèr duōme yuǎn?**
run-meen dah daow lee jar dwaw-muh ywan?
How far is the Avenue of the People from here?

Stranger: **Rénmín dà dào lí zhèr zhǐ yǒu yì lǐ lù zuǒyòu.**
run-meen dah daow lee jar jir yo ee lee loo dzwaw-yo.
The Avenue of the People is only about one kilometer from here.

Linda: **Cóng zhèr zǒu de dào, zǒu bú dào?**
tsoong jar dzoe duh daow, dzoe boo daow?
Can I walk there from here?

Stranger: **Kěndìng zǒu de dào. Nǐ xiān wàng nán zǒu, zài dì èr tiáo lù wàng xī zhuǎn. Dì yī ge lóu jiù shì.**
kun-deeng dzoe duh daow. nee shyan wahng nahn dzoe, dzye dee are tyaow loo wahng she jwan. dee ee guh low jyoe shir.
It's certainly walkable. First walk north, and then turn west at the second street. It'll be the first building you see.

Linda: **Fēicháng gǎnxiè nǐ.**
fay-chahng gahn-shyeh nee.
I'm extremely grateful [for your help].

Stranger: **Méi shì.**
may shir.
It's nothing.

Words to Know

bówùguǎn 博物馆 (博物館)	baw-woo-gwahn	museum
zuǒyòu 左右	dzwaw-yo	approximately
kěndìng 肯定	kun-deeng	definitely
xiān...zài... 先...再	shyan...dzye...	first...then...
fēicháng gǎnxiè 非常感谢 (非常感謝)	fay-chahng gahn-shyeh	many thanks
Méi shì. 没事.	may shir.	It's nothing.

Fun & Games

Use Chinese cardinal directions to indicate whether each building in the illustration is to the north, south, east, or west. (Check out Appendix D for the answers.)

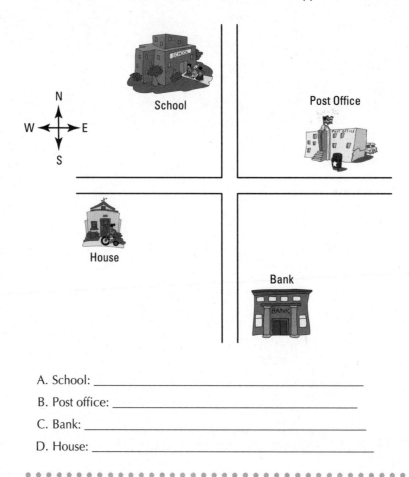

A. School: _____

B. Post office: _____

C. Bank: _____

D. House: _____

Chapter 18

Finding a Place to Stay

In This Chapter

▶ Booking your room reservation

▶ Checking in upon arrival

▶ Requesting hotel service

▶ Paying your bill

T he right hotel can make or break a vacation. Whether you stay in a capital city or a little backwater town with only one hotel to its name, you still need to know how to check in, check out, and ask for anything you need in between (including the bill). This chapter runs you through the gamut of booking your hotel, checking in at the front desk, checking out at the designated time, and dealing with all sorts of issues that may come up in between.

First, however, I have an astounding fact for you: You have not one, not two, but as many as five ways to say the word *hotel* in Chinese:

✔ **bīnguǎn** 宾馆 (賓館) (been-gwahn) (Literally: *a place for guests*)

✔ **fàndiàn** 饭店 (飯店) (fahn-dyan) (Literally: *a place for meals*)

✔ **jiǔdiàn** 酒店 (jyo-dyan) (Literally: *a place for wine*)

✔ **lǚguǎn** 旅馆 (旅館) (lyew-gwahn) (*hotel*)

✔ **zhāodàisuǒ** 招待所 (jaow-dye-swaw) (Literally: *a place to receive people*)

Making a Room Reservation

Thinking of **yùdìng** 预定 (預定) (yew-deeng) (*reserving*) a hotel **fángjiān** 房间 (房間) (fahng-jyan) (*room*)? What kind do you want? A single room all for yourself? A double room for you and your special someone? Or perhaps a suite for a special occasion like your 50th wedding anniversary?

You have many kinds of rooms to choose from, depending on your budget and your unique needs:

- ✔ **dānrén fángjiān** 单人房间 (單人房間) (dahn-run fahng-jyan) (*single room*)

- ✔ **shuāngrén fángjiān** 双人房间 (雙人房間) (shwahng-run fahng-jyan) (*double room*)

- ✔ **tàojiān** 套间 (套間) (taow-jyan) (*a suite*)

- ✔ **yíge ānjìng de fángjiān** 一个安静的房间 (一個安靜的房間) (ee-guh ahn-jeeng duh fahng-jyan) (*a quiet room*)

- ✔ **yíge bù xīyān de fángjiān** 一个不吸烟的房间 (一個不吸煙的房間) (ee-guh boo she-yan duh fahng-jyan) (*a nonsmoking room*)

- ✔ **yíge cháo yuànzi de fángjiān** 一个朝院子的房间 (一個朝院子的房間) (ee-guh chaow ywan-dzuh duh fahng-jyan) (*a room facing the courtyard*)

- ✔ **yíge dài yángtái de fángjiān** 一个带阳台的房间 (一個帶陽臺的房間) (ee-guh dye yahng-tye duh fahng-jyan) (*a room with a balcony*)

- ✔ **yíge fāngbiàn cánjí rén de fángjiān** 一个方便残疾人的房间 (一個方便殘疾人的房間) (ee-guh fahng-byan tsahn-jee run duh fahng-jyan) (*a room equipped for handicapped people*)

- ✔ **yíge guāngxiàn hǎo de fángjiān** 一个光线好的房间 (一個光線好的房間) (ee-guh gwahng-shyan how duh fahng-jyan) (*a bright room*)

- ✔ **yíge hǎi jīng de fángjiān** 一个海景的房间 (一個海景的房間) (ee-guh hi jeeng duh fahng-jyan) (*a room with an ocean view*)

- ✔ **yíge yǒu kōngtiáo de fángjiān** 一个有空调的房间 (一個有空調的房間) (ee-guh yo koong-tyaow duh fahng-jyan) (*a room with air conditioning*)

Whatever the occasion and whatever kind of room you want, you need to know how to make a reservation. Just make sure you know your budget in advance (and stick to it). You're sure to find a decent hotel no matter the price range if you spend some time checking out the competition.

Here are some things you may want to ask or specify over the phone as you begin the search for your ideal hotel:

- ✔ **Nǐmen de fángjiān yǒu méiyǒu wǎngluò liánjié?** 你们的房间有没有网络连接? (你們的房間有沒有網絡連接?) (nee-men duh fahng-jyan yo mayo wahng-lwaw lyan-jyeh?) (*Do your rooms have Internet access?*)

- ✔ **Nǐmen hái yǒu fángjiān ma?** 你们还有房间吗? (你們還有房間嗎?) (nee-mun hi yo fahng-jyan mah?) (*Do you have any rooms available?*)

- ✔ **Nǐmen fángjiān de jiàgé shì duōshǎo?** 你们房间的价格是多少? (你們房間的價格是多少?) (nee-mun fahng-jyan duh jyah-guh shir dwaw-shaow?) (*How much are your rooms?*)

✔ **Nǐmen shōu bù shōu xìnyòng kǎ?** 你们收不收信用卡? (你們收不收信用卡?) (nee-men show boo show sheen-yoong kah?) (*Do you accept credit cards?*)

✔ **Wǒ yào yíge fángjiān zhù liǎng ge wǎnshàng.** 我要一个房间住两个晚上. (我要一個房間住兩個晚上.) (waw yaow ee-guh fahng-jyan joo lyahng guh wahn-shahng.) (*I'd like a room for two nights.*)

✔ **Yǒu méiyǒu shāngwù zhōngxīn?** 有没有商务中心? (有沒有商務中心?) (yo mayo shahng-woo joong-sheen?) (*Is there a business center?*)

When you do finally pick up your phone to reserve a room, make sure you have your credit card in front of you (refer to Chapter 15 for more money talk).

Talkin' the Talk

Eli calls a well-known hotel chain in Hong Kong to make a three-day reservation for his whole family. The hotel clerk quickly answers his call. (Track 26)

Eli:	**Qǐngwèn, nǐmen fángjiān de jiàgé shì duōshǎo?** cheeng-one, nee-men fahng-jyan duh jyah-guh shir dwaw-shaow? *May I ask, how much are your rooms?*
Hotel clerk:	**Wǒmen de fángjiān yì tiān wǎnshàng yì bǎi wǔ shí kuài měi yuán.** waw-men duh fahng-jyan ee tyan wahn-shahng ee bye woo shir kwye may ywan. *Our rooms are USD $150 per night.*
Eli:	**Nà shì dānrén fángjiān hái shì shuāngrén fángjiān de jiàgé?** nah shir dahn-run fahng-jyan hi shir shwahng-run fahng-jyan duh jyah-guh? *Is that the price of a single room or a double?*
Hotel clerk:	**Dānrén fángjiān hé shuāngrén fángjiān de jiàgé dōu yíyàng.** dahn-run fahng-jyan huh shwahng-run fahng-jyan duh jyah-guh doe ee-yahng. *The prices of our single and double rooms are the same.*

Eli: **Hǎo jíle. Wǒ yào liǎngge dānrén fángjiān yíge shuāngrén fángjiān.**
how jee-luh. waw yaow lyahng-guh dahn-run fahng-jyan ee-guh shwahng-run fahng-jyan.
Great. I'd like two single rooms and one double.

Hotel clerk: **Méiyǒu wèntí. Nǐmen yào dāi jǐ ge wǎnshàng?**
mayo one-tee. nee-men yaow dye jee guh wahn-shahng?
No problem. How many nights will you be staying?

Eli: **Yígòng sān ge wǎnshàng.**
ee-goong sahn guh wahn-shahng.
Altogether, three nights.

Hotel clerk: **Hǎo. Nà yígòng yìqiān sānbǎi wǔ shí kuài.**
how. nah ee-goong jyo bye kwye.
Very well. That will be $1,350 altogether.

Words to Know

jiàgé 价格 (價格)	jyah-guh	price
hé 和	huh	and
dōu yíyàng 都一样 (都一樣)	doe ee-yahng	they're both the same
dāi 待	dye	to stay
yígòng 一共	ee-goong	altogether

The coverb **hé** 和 (huh) (*and*), along with the noun that always follows it, precedes the main verb or adjective of a sentence. (What's a *coverb?* Basically, it's a word that's technically a verb but typically acts as a preposition.) Some synonyms of **hé** are **gēn** 跟 (gun), **yǔ** 与 (與) (yew), and **tóng** 同 (toong), although **tóng** translates more closely as *with*.

CULTURAL WISDOM

Hotel or apartment?

China's booming economy has become a magnet for foreign businesses, and scores of foreign business people have begun taking up residence there. Because living in mainland China can be quite expensive and nice apartments that don't come with long waiting lists are hard to come by, many foreigners opt to stay in a permanent hotel room or a serviced apartment connected to a foreign-run hotel. A friend of mine in Shanghai rents out his nice-sized apartment for around USD $2,000 per month, comparable to the rent of major U.S. cities like New York or Chicago. And you can expect the hotels to run at least $150 per night, just like in metropolitan U.S. cities.

Checking In Before You Hit the Pool

Before you can take advantage of any conveniences your hotel offers (flip to the following section), you have to officially **bànlǐ rùzhù shǒuxù** 办理入住手续 (辦理入住手續) (bahn-lee roo-joo show-shyew) (*check in*). You don't want to be caught red handed running in the gym or relaxing in the hot tub unless you're a bona fide guest, right? (Don't answer that.)

When you walk up to the **fàndiàn qiántái** 饭店前台 (飯店前台) (fahn-dyan chyan-tye) (*reception desk*), you invariably find yourself needing to say one of the following sentences:

✔ **Nǐmen hái yǒu fángjiān ma?** 你们还有房间吗? (你們還有房間嗎?) (nee-men hi yo fahng-jyan mah?) (*Do you have any rooms available?*)

✔ **Wǒ méiyǒu yùdìng fángjiān.** 我没有预定房间. (我沒有預定房間.) (waw mayo yew-deeng fahng-jyan.) (*I don't have a reservation.*)

✔ **Wǒ yǐjīng yùdìng le fángjiān.** 我已经预定了房间. (我已經預定了房間.) (waw ee-jeeng yew-deeng luh fahng-jyan.) (*I already made a reservation.*)

If you're in luck, the hotel has at least one **kōng** 空 (koong) (*empty/vacant*) room. If the hotel has no available space, you'll hear **Duìbùqǐ, wǒmen kèmǎn le.** 对不起, 我们客满了. (對不起, 我們客滿了.) (dway-boo-chee, waw-men kuh-mahn luh.) (*Sorry, there are no vacancies./We're full.*)

The **qiántái fúwùyuán** 前台服务员 (前台服務員) (chyan-tye foo-woo-ywan) (*front desk clerk*) asks you to **tián** 填 (tyan) (*fill out*) a couple of **biǎo** 表 (byaow) (*forms*) to book your room, so have a pen and some form of **zhèngjiàn** 证件 (證件) (juhng-jyan) (*ID*) ready — especially your **hùzhào** 护照 (護照) (hoo-jaow) (*passport*). Voilà! You're officially a hotel **kèrén** 客人 (kuh-run) (*guest*).

After you successfully manage to check in, a **xíngliyuán** 行李员 (行李員) (sheeng-lee-ywan) (*porter/bellboy*) immediately appears to help take your **xíngli** 行李 (sheeng-lee) (*luggage*) to your room. After he lets you in, he gives you the **yàoshi** 钥匙 (鑰匙) (yaow-shir) (*key*) if you didn't get it from the **qiántái fúwùyuán** downstairs.

Talkin' the Talk

Adele arrives in Taiwan and wants to check into a hotel in downtown Taipei, but the clerk informs her that the hotel has no vacancy. (Track 27)

Adele:	**Nǐ hǎo. Qǐngwèn, nǐmen hái yǒu fángjiān ma?** nee how. cheeng-one, nee-men hi yo fahng-jyan mah? *Hello. May I ask, do you have any rooms available?*
Clerk:	**Duìbùqǐ, wǒmen jīntiān kèmǎn le. Méiyǒu kōng fángjiān le.** dway-boo-chee, waw-men jin-tyan kuh-mahn luh. mayo koong fahng-jyan luh. *I'm sorry, but we're full today. There aren't any vacant rooms.*
Adele:	**Zāogāo! Nǐ néng bù néng tuījiàn biéde lǚguǎn?** dzaow-gaow! nee nung boo nung tway-jyan byeh-duh lyew-gwahn? *Rats! Could you perhaps recommend another hotel, then?*
Clerk:	**Kéyǐ. Gébì de lǚguǎn yǒu kōng fángjiān. Nǐ zuì hǎo zǒu guò qù shì shì kàn.** kuh-yee. guh-bee duh lyew-gwahn yo koong fahng-jyan. nee dzway how dzoe gwaw chyew shir shir kahn. *Yes. The hotel next door has vacancies. You may as well walk over there and have a look.*
Adele:	**Xièxiè.** shyeh-shyeh. *Thank you.*

Words to Know

duìbùqǐ 对不起 (對不起)	dway-boo-chee	I'm sorry
zāogāo 糟糕	dzaow-gaow	rats/what a shame
tuījiàn 推荐 (推薦)	tway-jyan	recommend
biéde 别的	byeh-duh	other
lǚguǎn 旅馆 (旅館)	lyew-gwahn	hotel
gébì 隔壁	guh-bee	next door

Taking Advantage of Hotel Service

After you check into your hotel (refer to the preceding section), you may find yourself mysteriously lingering a bit in the **dàtīng** 大厅 (大廳) (dah-teeng) (*lobby*), visually casing the joint long enough to take in all sorts of amenities. The following sections introduce you to both the comfort services and customer services hotels have to offer.

REMEMBER

Depending on your service needs, you interact with many different employees on any given hotel stay:

- ✔ **fúwùtái jīnglǐ** 服务台经理 (服務台經理) (foo-woo-tye jeeng-lee) (*concierge*)
- ✔ **fúwùyuán** 服务员 (服務員) (foo-woo-ywan) (*attendant*)
- ✔ **fúwùyuán lǐngbān** 服务员领班 (服務員領班) (foo-woo-ywan leeng-bahn) (*bell captain*)
- ✔ **zhùlǐ jīnglǐ** 助理经理 (助理經理) (joo-lee jeeng-lee) (*assistant manager*)
- ✔ **zǒngjīnglǐ** 总经理 (總經理) (dzoong-jeeng-lee) (*general manager*)

Counting on convenience

Most hotels let you put in for a wake-up call so that you don't have to worry about setting an alarm. All you have to say is **Qǐng nǐ jiào wǒ qǐchuáng.** 请你叫我起床. (請你叫我起床.) (cheeng nee jyaow waw chee-chwahng.) (Literally: *Please call me to get out of bed.*)

After you're awake, the luxuries at your disposal may include the following:

- **ànmō yùgāng** 按摩浴缸 (ahn-maw yew-gahng) (*hot tub*)
- **diànshì** 电视 (電視) (dyan-shir) (*television*)
- **gānxǐ fúwù** 干洗服务 (乾洗服務) (gahn-she foo-woo) (*dry cleaning service*)
- **lǚguǎn fàndiàn** 旅馆饭店 (旅館飯店) (lyew-gwahn fahn-dyan) (*hotel restaurant*)
- **shāngwù zhōngxīn** 商务中心 (商務中心) (shahng-woo joong-sheen) (*business center*)
- **tǐyùguǎn** 体育馆 (體育館) (tee-yew-gwahn) (*gym*)
- **xǐyī fúwù** 洗衣服务 (洗衣服務) (she-ee foo-woo) (*laundry service*)
- **yóuyǒngchí** 游泳池 (yo-yoong-chir) (*swimming pool*)

Getting problems fixed

Uh oh . . . you're finally ensconced in your big, beautiful hotel room when you discover that the **mén suǒ bú shàng** 门锁不上 (門鎖不上) (mun swaw boo shahng) (*door doesn't lock*) and the **kōngtiáo huài le** 空调坏了 (空調壞了) (koong-tyaow hwye luh) (*air conditioning doesn't work*). To make matters worse, your **chuānghu dǎ bù kāi** 窗户打不开 (窗戶打不開) (chwahng-hoo dah boo kye) (*window won't open*). Heat wave! It may be hard to believe, but in addition to all that, your **mǎtǒng dǔzhùle** 马桶堵住了 (馬桶堵住了) (mah-toong doo-joo-luh) (*toilet is clogged*). Time to call the nearest **kèfáng fúwùyuán** 客房服务员 (客房服務員) (kuh-fahng foo-woo-ywan) (*hotel housekeeper*) for help.

Call quick if the following pieces of equipment are **huàile** 坏了 (壞了) (hwye-luh) (*broken*) and need immediate fixing:

- **chāzuò** 插座 (chah-dzwaw) (*electric outlet*)
- **kāiguān** 开关 (開關) (kye-gwahn) (*light switch*)
- **kōngtiáo** 空调 (空調) (koong-tyaow) (*air conditioner*)
- **mǎtǒng** 马桶 (馬桶) (mah-toong) (*toilet*)

- **nuǎnqì** 暖气 (暖氣) (nwan-chee) (*heater*)
- **yáokòng qì** 遥控器 (遙控器) (yaow-koong chee) (*remote control*)

Even if you aren't having an equipment emergency, you may want housekeeping to send the following items right over:

- **chuīfēngjī** 吹风机 (吹風機) (chway-fung-jee) (*hair dryer*)
- **máojīn** 毛巾 (maow-jeen) (*towel*)
- **máotǎn** 毛毯 (maow-tahn) (*blanket*)
- **wèishēngzhǐ** 卫生纸 (衛生紙) (way-shung-jir) (*toilet paper*)
- **zhěntóu** 枕头 (枕頭) (jun-toe) (*pillow*)

Maybe you just need someone to **dǎsǎo fángjiān** 打扫房间 (打掃房間) (dah-saow fahng-jyan) (*clean the room*). Oh well. Even the best hotels need some tweaking every now and then.

Hey! I almost forgot one of the best kinds of service you can take advantage of on occasion: room service! Before you decide to order room service for food, however, just remember that it's often twice as expensive as dining in the hotel restaurant, because the service is more convenient.

To make a comparison by saying that something is a number of times more expensive than something else, you first use the word **guì** 贵 (貴) (gway) (*expensive*), followed by the number of times you think it's more expensive and the word **bèi** 倍 (bay) (roughly translated as *times*). You can compare the relative cost of two products or services by using the word **bǐ** 比 (bee) (*compared to*) in the following pattern:

> X **bǐ** Y **guì** # **bèi** X 比 Y 贵 (貴) # 倍

Here are some examples:

> **Zhège fángjiān bǐ nèige guì shí bèi.** 这个房间比那个贵十倍. (這個房間比那個貴十倍.) (jay-guh fahng-jyan bee nay-guh gway shir bay.) (*This room is ten times more expensive than that one.*)

> **Zuò chūzūchē bǐ zuò gōnggòng qìchē guì wǔ bèi.** 坐出租车比坐公共汽车贵五倍. (坐出租車比坐公共汽車貴五倍.) (zwaw choo-dzoo-chuh bee dzwaw goong-goong chee-chuh gway woo bay.) (*Taking a cab is five times more expensive than taking the bus.*)

Never drink directly from the tap in your Chinese hotel; the water isn't safe. Every hotel room in China has a large flask of boiling water that you can use to make tea or for drinking water. You can brush your teeth with tap water because you just spit it out. Local Chinese don't dare drink the tap water either, so you're in good company.

Talkin' the Talk

Carl enters his hotel room after he checks in, only to discover the bathroom faucet is broken. He calls for housekeeping and a few minutes later hears a knock on his door.

Housekeeper: **Kèfáng fúwùyuán!**
kuh-fahng foo-woo-ywan!
Housekeeping!

Carl: **Qǐng jìn!**
cheeng jin!
Come on in!

Housekeeper: **Yǒu shénme wèntí?**
yo shummuh one-tee?
What seems to be the trouble?

Carl: **Zhèige shuǐlóngtóu huàile. Yě méiyǒu rèshuǐ.**
jay-guh shway-loong-toe hwye-luh. yeah mayo ruh-shway.
This faucet is broken. There's also no hot water.

Housekeeper: **Hěn duìbùqǐ. Mǎshàng sòng shuǐnuǎngōng guòlái kànkàn.**
hun dway-boo-chee. mah-shahng soong shway-nwan-goong gwaw-lye kahn-kahn.
I'm so sorry. We'll send a plumber right away to have a look.

Carl: **Xièxiè.**
shyeh-shyeh.
Thank you.

As the housekeeper starts to leave, Carl suddenly remembers some other things that the housekeeper may be able to take care of as long as she's there.

Carl: **Xiǎojiě, nǐmen yǒu méiyǒu xǐyī fúwù?**
shyaow-jyeh, nee-men yo mayo she-ee foo-woo?
Miss, do you have any laundry service?

Housekeeper: **Yǒu.**
yo.
Yes, we do.

Carl: **Hǎo jíle. Jīntiān kěyǐ bǎ zhè xiē yīfú xǐ hǎo ma?**
how jee-luh. jin-tyan kuh-yee bah jay shyeh ee-foo she how mah?
Great. Can I have these clothes cleaned today?

Housekeeper: **Kěyǐ.**
kuh-yee.
Yes.

Carl: **Yóuqíshì zhèige wūdiǎn. Néng bùnéng qùdiào?**
yo-chee-shir jay-guh woo-dyan. nung boo-nung chyew-dyaow?
Especially this stain. Can it be removed?

Housekeeper: **Méiyǒu wèntí.**
mayo one-tee.
No problem.

Carl: **Hǎo. Xièxiè.**
how. shyeh-shyeh.
Great. Thanks.

Words to Know

Qǐng jìn! 请进! (請進!)	cheeng jin!	Come on in!
mǎshàng 马上 (馬上)	mah-shahng	immediately
shuǐnuǎngōng 水暖工	shway-nwan-goong	plumber
yóuqíshì 尤其是	yo-chee-shir	especially
wūdiǎn 污点 (污點)	woo-dyan	stain
qùdiào 去掉	chyew-dyaow	erase/remove

GRAMMATICALLY SPEAKING

As you can see in the previous Talkin' the Talk dialogue, the coverb **bǎ** 把 (bah) often appears right after the subject of the sentence, separating it from the direct object, which is always something concrete rather than an abstract idea. It separates the indirect and direct objects.

You don't have the following sentence pattern:

Subject + Verb + Complement (+ Indirect Object) + Object

Instead, you have this one:

Subject + **bă** + Object + Verb + Complement (+ Indirect Object)

Here are some examples:

Qǐng nǐ bă nǐde hùzhào ná gěi qiántái fúwùyuán. 请你把你的护照拿给前台服务员. (請你把你的護照拿給前台服務員.) (cheeng nee bah nee-duh hoo-jaow nah gay chyan-tye foo-woo-ywan.) (*Please give your passport to the front desk clerk.*)

Wǒ bă shū jiè gěi nǐ. 我把书接给你. (我把書借給你.) (waw bah shoo jyeh gay nee.) (*I'll loan you the book.*)

Checking Out Before Heading Out

That oh-so-depressing time has come again. Time to say goodbye. Time to **téngchū** 腾出 (騰出) (tuhng-choo) (*vacate*) your hotel room and **tuìfáng** 退房 (tway-fahng) (*check out*).

You may need to say some of the following as you begin the end of your stay:

✔ **Jiézhàng yǐhòu wǒ néng bùnéng bă bāoguǒ liú zài qiántái?** 结帐以后我能不能把包裹留在前台? (結帳以後我能不能把包裹留在前台?) (jyeh-jahng ee-ho waw nung boo-nung bah baow-gwaw lyo dzye chyan-tye?) (*After checking out, may I leave my bags at the front desk?*)

✔ **Nǐmen jiēshòu shénme xìnyòng kǎ?** 你们接收什么信用卡? (你們接收甚麼信用卡?) (nee-men jyeh-show shummuh sheen-yoong kah?) (*Which credit cards do you accept?*)

✔ **Wǒ bù yīnggāi fù zhè xiàng.** 我不应该付这项. (我不應該付這項.) (waw boo eeng-gye foo jay shyahng.) (*I shouldn't be charged for this.*)

✔ **Wǒ yào fù zhàng.** 我要付账. (我要付賬.) (waw yaow foo jahng.) (*I'd like to pay the bill.*)

✔ **Yǒu méiyǒu qù fēijīchǎng de bānchē?** 有没有去飞机场的班车? (有沒有去飛機場的班車?) (yo mayo chyew fay-jee-chahng duh ban-chuh?) (*Is there a shuttle to the airport?*)

✔ **Zhè búshì wǒde zhāngdàn.** 这不是我的账单. (這不是我的賬單.) (jay boo-shir waw-duh jahng-dahn.) (*This isn't my bill.*)

Talkin' the Talk

Nancy is ready to check out after her three-day stay at a five-star hotel in Shanghai. She approaches the reception clerk to check out.

Nancy: **Nǐ hǎo. Wǒ jīntiān yào tuìfáng, suǒyǐ yào fù zhàng.**
nee how. waw jin-tyan yaow tway-fahng, swaw-yee yaow foo jahng.
Hello. I'd like to check out today, so I'd like to pay the bill.

Clerk: **Qǐngwèn, nín de fángjiān hàomǎ shì duōshǎo?**
cheeng-one, neen duh fahng-jyan how-mah shir dwaw-shaow?
May I ask, what's your room number?

Nancy: **Wǔlíngliù hào fángjiān.**
woo-leeng-lyo how fahng-jyan.
Room 506.

Clerk: **Hǎo. Zhè shì nínde zhàngdān. Yígòng yìqiān wǔbǎi kuài.**
how. jay shir neen-duh jahng-dahn. ee-goong ee-chyan woo-bye kwye.
Okay. This is your bill. It's $1,500 altogether.

Nancy pays the bill with her credit card.

Nancy: **Zhè shì wǒmen fángjiān de yàoshi.**
jay shir waw-mun fahng-jyan duh yaow-shir.
This is my room key.

Clerk: **Xièxiè.**
shyeh-shyeh.
Thank you.

Nancy: **Jiézhàng yǐhòu wǒ néng bùnéng bǎ bāoguǒ liú zài qiántái?**
jyeh-jahng ee-ho waw nung boo-nung bah baow-gwaw lyo dzye chyan-tye?
After checking out, may I leave my bags at the front desk?

Clerk: **Kěyǐ. Méiyǒu wèntí.**
kuh-yee. mayo one-tee.
Yes. No problem.

Words to Know

tuìfáng 退房	tway-fahng	check out
suǒyǐ 所以	swaw-yee	so; therefore
Nín de fángjiān hàomǎ shì duōshǎo? 您的房间号码是多少? (您的房間號碼是多少?)	neen duh fahng-jyan how-mah shir dwaw-shaow?	What's your room number?
zhàngdān 账单 (賬單)	jahng-dahn	bill
yàoshi 钥匙 (鑰匙)	yaow-shir	key

Fun & Games

Fill in the blanks, using the following words: **tuìfáng** 退房, **zhàngdān** 账单 (賬單), **fángjiān** 房间 (房間), **kèmǎn** 客满 (客滿), and **qǐchuáng** 起床. You can find the answer key in Appendix D.

1. **Nǐmen de** _____ **yǒu méiyǒu wǎngluò liánjié?** 你们的 _____有没有网络连接? (你們的 _____有沒有網絡連接?)

   Do your rooms have Internet access?

2. **Duìbùqǐ, wǒmen** _____ **le.** 对不起, 我们 _____了. (對不起, 我們 _____了.)

   I'm sorry, we have no vacancies.

3. **Qǐng nǐ jiào wǒ** _____. 请你叫我 _____. (請你叫我 _____.)

   Please give me a wake-up call.

4. **Zhè búshì wǒde** _____. 这不是我的 _____. (這不是我的 _____.)

   This isn't my bill.

5. **Wǒ jīntiān yào** _____. 我今天要 _____.

   I'd like to check out today.

Chapter 19

Handling Emergencies

In This Chapter

▶ Yelling for help

▶ Visiting your doctor

▶ Going to the authorities

▶ Looking for legal advice

*Y*ou can easily plan the fun and exciting things you want to experience while you travel or go out with friends, but you can't predict needing to call the police to report a theft or rushing to an emergency room with **lánmò yán** 阑尾炎 (闌尾炎) (lahn-maw yeahn) (*appendicitis*) on your trip to the Great Wall. Such things can and do happen, and this chapter gives you the language tools you need to communicate your problems during your times of need.

Calling for Help in Times of Need

When you're faced with an emergency, the last way you want to spend your time is searching for an oversized Chinese-English dictionary to figure out how to quickly call for help. Try memorizing these phrases before a situation arises:

✔ **Jiào jǐngchá!** 叫警察 (jyaow jeeng-chah!) (*Call the police!*)

✔ **Jiào jiùhùchē!** 叫救护车! (叫救護車! (jyaow jyo-hoo-chuh!) (*Call an ambulance!*)

✔ **Jiù mìng!** 救命! (jyo meeng!) (*Help!/Save me!*)

✔ **Zháohuǒ lā!** 着火啦! (jaow-hwaw lah!) (*Fire!*)

✔ **Zhuā zéi!** 抓贼 (抓贼!) (jwah dzay!) (*Stop, thief!*)

Be careful when you say the words **jiào** 叫 (jyaow) (*to call*) and **jiù** 救 (jyo) (*to save*) in the preceding phrases. You don't want to mistakenly ask someone to save the police when you want him to call the police.

Sometimes you have to ask for someone who speaks English. Here are some phrases you can quickly blurt out during emergencies:

✔ **Nǐ shuō Yīngwén ma?** 你说英文吗? (你說英文嗎?) (nee shwaw eeng-one mah?) (*Do you speak English?*)

✔ **Wǒ xūyào yíge jiǎng Yīngwén de lǜshī.** 我需要一个讲英文的律师. (我需要一個講英文的律師.) (waw shyew-yaow ee-guh jyahng eeng-one duh lyew-shir.) (*I need a lawyer who speaks English.*)

✔ **Yǒu méiyǒu jiǎng Yīngwén de dàifu?** 有没有讲英文的大夫? (有沒有講英文的大夫?) (yo mayo jyahng eeng-one duh dye-foo?) (*Are there any English-speaking doctors?*)

When you finally get someone on the line who can help you, you need to know what to say to get immediate help:

✔ **Wǒ bèi rén qiǎng le.** 我被人抢了. (我被人搶了.) (waw bay run chyahng luh.) (*I've been robbed.*)

✔ **Wǒ yào huì bào yíge chē huò.** 我要汇报一个车祸. (我要匯報一個車禍.) (waw yaow hway baow yee-guh chuh hwaw.) (*I'd like to report a car accident.*)

✔ **Yǒu rén shòu shāng le.** 有人受伤了. (有人受傷了.) (yo run show shahng luh.) (*People are injured.*)

Receiving Medical Care

It's everyone's greatest nightmare — getting sick and not knowing why or how to make it better. If you suddenly find yourself in the **yīyuàn** 医院 (醫院) (ee-ywan) (*hospital*) or otherwise visiting an **yīshēng** 医生 (醫生) (ee-shung) (*doctor*), you need to explain what ails you — often in a hurry. Doing so may be easier said than done, especially if you have to explain yourself in Chinese (or help a Chinese-speaking victim who's having trouble communicating), but don't worry. In the following sections, I walk you through your doctor's visit step by step.

When you travel, don't forget to bring your prescription medicines. Carry them in a separate carry-on bag or in your purse. You don't want to pack them in a piece of check-in luggage, never to be seen again if the luggage gets lost.

Here are a couple of additional medical-emergency tips for traveling in China:

- Unless you're in a big city like Beijing or Shanghai, if you get seriously ill while staying in mainland China, your best bet is to fly to Hong Kong or back home for medical care. Don't forget to check into evacuation insurance before you go.

- **Warning:** Chinese people don't have O-negative blood, so Chinese hospitals don't store it. If you have a medical emergency in China that requires O-negative blood, you should check directly with your country's nearest embassy or consulate for help. You may need to be airlifted out to get the appropriate care. You may also want to take your own hypodermic needles in case you need an injection because you can't guarantee that the needles you may come across are sterilized. Better safe than sorry away from home.

Deciding whether to see a doctor

If your luck is good, you'll never need to use any of the phrases I present in this chapter. If you end up running out of luck, however, keep reading. Even if you've never smoked a day in your life, you can still develop a cough or even bronchitis. Time to see a **yīshēng**.

Talkin' the Talk

Dàlín and his wife, Miǎn, are on their first trip back to China in 20 years. Miǎn becomes concerned about a sudden onset of dizziness. The two discuss her symptoms.

Dàlín: **Nǐ zěnme bùshūfu?**
nee dzummuh boo-shoo-foo?
What's wrong?

Miǎn: **Wǒ gǎnjué bùshūfu kěshì bù zhīdào wǒ déle shénme bìng.**
waw gahn-jweh boo-shoo-foo kuh-shir boo jir-daow waw duh-luh shummuh beeng.
I don't feel well, but I don't know what I have.

Dàlín: **Nǐ fā shāo ma?**
nee fah shaow mah?
Are you running a fever?

Miǎn: **Méiyǒu, dànshì wǒ tóuyūn. Yěxǔ wǒ xūyào kàn nèikē yīshēng.**

mayo, dahn-shir waw toe-yewn. yeh-shyew waw shyew-yaow kahn nay-kuh ee-shung.

No, but I feel dizzy. Perhaps I need to see an internist.

Dàlín calls the nearest medical clinic to make an appointment and then returns to Miǎn.

Dàlín: **Wǒ jīntiān xiàwǔ sān diǎn zhōng yuē le yíge shíjiān. Nǐ zuì hǎo zànshí zuò xiàlái.**

waw jin-tyan shyah-woo sahn dyan joong yweh luh ee-guh shir-jyan. nee dzway how dzahn-shir dzwaw shyah-lye.

I've made an appointment for 3:00 this afternoon. In the meantime, you'd better sit down for a while.

Words to Know

Nǐ zěnme bùshūfu? 你怎么不舒服? (你怎麼不舒服?)	nee dzummuh boo-shoo-foo?	What's wrong?
Nǐ fā shāo ma? 你发烧吗? (你發燒嗎?)	nee fah shaow mah?	Are you running a fever?
zànshí 暂时 (暫時)	dzahn-shir	in the meantime
Wǒ tóuyūn. 我头晕. (我頭暈.)	waw toe yewn.	I feel dizzy.

Although verbs don't express tense in Chinese, you often connect them to things called *aspect markers,* which come directly after the verb and indicate the degree of completion of an action. The aspect markers **xiàlái** 下来 (下來) (shyah-lye) and **xiàqù** 下去 (shyah-chyew) are two such examples. **Xiàlái** refers to an action that slowly turns into a non-action or a calmer state, such as **zuò xiàlái** 坐下来 (dzwaw shyah-lye) (*to sit down and rest*) in the previous Talkin' the Talk section. **Xiàqù** refers to continuing action.

Describing what ails you

First things first: You can't tell the doctor where it hurts if you don't know the word for what hurts. (Sure, you can point, I guess, but that only goes so far; when was the last time you tried pointing to internal organs?) Table 19-1 spells out the general body parts.

Table 19-1	Basic Body Words	
Chinese	*Pronunciation*	*English*
tóu 头 (頭)	toe	*head*
ěrduō 耳朵	are-dwaw	*ear*
liǎn 脸 (臉)	lyan	*face*
yǎnjīng 眼睛	yan-jeeng	*eye*
bízi 鼻子	bee-dzuh	*nose*
bózi 脖子	baw-dzuh	*neck*
hóulóng 喉咙 (喉嚨)	ho-loong	*throat*
jiānbǎng 肩膀	jyan-bahng	*shoulder*
gēbo 胳膊	guh-baw	*arm*
shǒu 手	show	*hand*
shǒuzhǐ 手指	show-jir	*finger*
xiōng 胸	shyoong	*chest*
fèi 肺	fay	*lungs*
xīn 心	shin	*heart*
dùzi 肚子	doo-dzuh	*stomach*
gān 肝	gahn	*liver*
shèn 肾	shun	*kidney*
bèi 背	bay	*back*
tuǐ 腿	tway	*leg*
jiǎo 脚 (腳)	jyaow	*foot*
jiǎozhǐ 脚趾 (腳趾)	jyaow-jir	*toe*
shēntǐ 身体 (身體)	shun-tee	*body*
gǔtóu 骨头 (骨頭)	goo-toe	*bone*
jīròu 肌肉	jee-row	*muscles*
shénjīng 神经 (神經)	shun-jeeng	*nerves*

Maybe you're just now checking your old **wēndùjì** 温度计 (溫度計) (one-doo-jee) (*thermometer*) and finding out **Wǒ fā shāo le!** 我发烧了! (我發燒了!) (waw fah shaow luh) (*I have a fever!*) Time to figure out what the problem is. Whether you make a sudden trip to the **jízhěnshì** 急诊室 (急診室) (jee-jun-shir) (*emergency room*) or take a normal visit to a private doctor's office, you'll probably field the same basic questions about your symptoms. Table 19-2 lists some symptoms you may have.

Table 19-2	Common Medical Symptoms	
Chinese	*Pronunciation*	*English*
bèi tòng 背痛	bay toong	*backache*
biànmì 便秘	byan-mee	*constipation*
ěr tòng 耳痛	are toong	*earache*
ěxīn 恶心 (噁心)	uh-sheen	*nauseous*
fāshāo 发烧 (發燒)	fah-shaow	*to have a fever*
hóulóng téng 喉咙痛 (喉嚨痛)	ho-loong tung	*sore throat*
lādùzi 拉肚子	lah-doo-dzuh	*diarrhea*
pàngle 胖了	pahng-luh	*to put on weight*
shòule 瘦了	show-luh	*to lose weight*
tóuténg 头疼 (頭疼)	toe-tung	*headache*
wèi tòng 胃痛	way toong	*stomachache*
xiàntǐ zhǒngle 腺体肿了 (腺體腫了)	shyan-tee joong-luh	*swollen glands*
yá tòng 牙痛	yah toong	*toothache*

In an emergency, you may not have the energy to remember both the pronunciation *and* the proper tone for the word you mean to use. You may want to say you're feeling kind of **tóuyūn** 头晕 (頭暈) (toe-yewn) (*dizzy*), but if it comes out sounding like **tuōyùn** 托运 (托運) (twaw-yewn) instead, you alert your caregiver that you're sending your luggage on ahead of you.

Talkin' the Talk

Kristen shows up for her appointment to see **Huò Dàifu** (Dr. Huo). Because this is Kristen's first visit to Dr. Huo, the **jiēdàiyuán** (jyeh-dye-ywan) (*receptionist*) needs her to fill out some forms before she sees the doctor to discuss her symptoms. (Track 28)

Jiēdàiyuán: **Nǐ shì lái kànbìng de ma?**
nee shir lye kahn-beeng duh mah?
Have you come to see a doctor?

Kristen: **Shì de.**
shir duh.
Yes.

Jiēdàiyuán: **Yǒu méiyǒu yīliáo bǎoxiǎn?**
yo mayo ee-lyaow baow-shyan?
Do you have any medical insurance?

Kristen: **Yǒu.**
yo.
Yes, I do.

Jiēdàiyuán: **Hǎo. Qǐng qiān yíxià zhèi zhāng biǎo.**
how. cheeng chyan ee-shyah jay jahng byaow.
All right. Please fill out this form.

A short while later, the receptionist introduces Kristen to a **hùshì** (hoo-shir) (*nurse*), who plans to take her blood pressure.

Jiēdàiyuán: **Hùshì huì xiān liáng yíxià xuèyā.**
hoo-shir hway shyan lyahng ee-shyah shweh-yah.
The nurse will first take your blood pressure.

Hùshì: **Qǐng juǎnqǐ nǐde xiùzi.**
cheeng jwan-chee nee-duh shyo-dzuh.
Please roll up your sleeve.

Hùshì: **Hǎo. Huò Dàifu xiànzài gěi nǐ kànbìng.**
how. hwaw dye-foo shyan-dzye gay nee kahn-beeng.
All right. Dr. Huo will see you now.

Kristen enters Dr. Huo's office, and after a few basic introductory questions, Dr. Huo asks her what brings her to his office.

Huò Dàifu: **Yǒu shénme zhèngzhuàng?**
yo shummuh juhng-jwahng?
What sorts of symptoms do you have?

Kristen: **Wǒde hóulóng cóng zuótiān jiù tòngle.**
waw-duh ho-loong tsoong dzwaw-tyan jyo toong-luh.
I've had this pain in my throat since yesterday.

Huò Dàifu: **Hǎo. Wǒ xiān yòng tīngzhěnqì tīng yíxià nǐde xīnzàng.**
how. waw shyan yoong teeng-jun-chee teeng ee-shyah nee-duh shin-dzahng.
All right. I'm first going to use a stethoscope to listen to your heart.

Dr. Huo puts the stethoscope to Kristen's chest.

Huò Dàifu: **Shēn hūxī.**
shun hoo-she.
Take a deep breath.

Dr. Huo finishes listening with the stethoscope and takes out a tongue depressor.

Huò Dàifu: **Qǐng bǎ zuǐ zhāngkāi, bǎ shétóu shēn chūlái . . . duì le. Nǐde hóulóng hǎoxiàng yǒu yìdiǎn fāyán.**
cheeng bah dzway jahng-kye, bah shuh-to shun choo-lye . . . dway luh. nee-duh ho-loong how-shyahng yo ee-dyan fah-yan.
Please open your mouth and stick out your tongue . . . yes. Your throat seems to be inflamed.

Words to Know

Yǒu méiyǒu yīliáo bǎoxiǎn? 有没有医疗保险? (有没有醫療保險?)	yo mayo ee-lyaow baow-shyan?	Do you have any medical insurance?
hǎo 好	how	all right
Qǐng qiān yíxià zhèi zhāng biǎo. 请签一下这张表. (請簽一下這張表.)	cheeng chyan ee-shyah jay jahng byaow.	Please fill out this form.
fāyán le 发炎了 (發炎了)	fah-yan luh	it's inflamed

Discussing your medical history

When you see a doctor for the first time, he or she will want to find out about your **bìng lì** 病历 (病歷) (beeng lee) (*medical history*). You'll hear the following query: **Nǐ jiā yǒu méiyǒu _____ de bìnglì?** 你家有没有 _____ 的病历? (你家有沒有 _____ 的病歷?) (nee jyah yo mayo _____ duh beeng-lee?) (*Does your family have any history of _____?*)

Table 19-3 lists some of the more serious illnesses that hopefully neither you nor your family members have ever had.

Table 19-3	Serious Illnesses	
Chinese	*Pronunciation*	*English*
áizhèng 癌症	eye-juhng	*cancer*
àizǐbìng 艾滋病	eye-dzuh-beeng	*AIDS*
bǐngxíng gānyán 丙型肝炎	beeng-sheeng gahn-yan	*hepatitis C*
fèi'ái 肺癌	fay-eye	*lung cancer*
fèi jiéhé 肺结核 (肺結核)	fay jyeh-huh	*tuberculosis*
huòluàn 霍乱 (霍亂)	hwaw-lwan	*cholera*
jiǎxíng gānyán 甲型肝炎	jya-sheeng gahn-yan	*hepatitis A*
lìjí 痢疾	lee-jee	*dysentery*
qìchuǎnbìng 气喘病 (氣喘病)	chee-chwan-beeng	*asthma*
shuǐ dòu 水痘	shway-doe	*chicken pox*
tángniàobìng 糖尿病	tahng-nyaow-beeng	*diabetes*
xīnzàng yǒu máobìng 心脏有毛病 (心臟有毛病)	shin-dzahng yo maow-beeng	*heart trouble*
yǐxíng gānyán 已型肝炎	ee-sheeng gahn-yan	*hepatitis B*

Making a diagnosis

Did your doctor say those magic words: **Méi shénme** 没什么 (沒甚麼) (may shummuh) (*It's nothing*)? Yeah, neither did mine. Too bad. I bet you've heard stories about how doctors who use traditional medical techniques from ancient cultures can just take one look at a person and immediately know what ails them. The truth is, aside from simple colds and the flu, most doctors still need to take all kinds of tests to give a proper diagnosis. They may even need to perform the following tasks:

- **huà yàn** 化验 (化驗) (hwah yan) (*lab tests*)

- **xīndiàntú** 心电图 (心電圖) (shin-dyan-too) (*electrocardiogram*)

- **huàyàn yíxià xiǎobiàn** 化验一下小便 (化驗一下小便) (hwah-yan ee-shyah shyaow-byan) (*have your urine tested*)

When the doctor is ready to give you the verdict, here are some of the conditions you may hear (the minor ones, at least; check out Table 19-3 for more serious diagnoses):

- **bìngdú** 病毒 (beeng-doo) (*virus*)

- **gǎnmào** 感冒 (gahn-maow) (*a cold*)

- **gǎnrǎn** 感染 (gahn-rahn) (*infection*)

- **guòmín** 过敏 (過敏) (gwaw-meen) (*allergies*)

- **liúgǎn** 流感 (lyo-gahn) (*flu*)

- **qìguǎnyán** 气管炎 (氣管炎) (chee-gwahn-yan) (*bronchitis*)

Talkin' the Talk

Pete takes his daughter, Lauren, to the **yīshēng** (*doctor*) after he notices her bad cough. The doctor takes her temperature and discusses what she may have with the family.

Yīshēng: **Lauren, hǎo xiāoxi! Nǐde tǐwēn zhèngcháng.**
Lauren, how shyaow-she! nee-duh tee-one juhng-chahng.
Lauren, good news! Your temperature is normal.

Lauren: **Hǎo jí le.**
how jee luh.
Great.

Yīshēng: **Kěnéng zhǐ shì gǎnmào.**
kuh-nung jir shir gahn-maow.
Perhaps it's just a little cold.

Pete: **Hái chuánrǎn ma?**
hi chwahn-rahn mah?
Is it still contagious?

Yīshēng: **Bú huì.**
             boo hway.
             No.

Lauren: **Yánzhòng ma?**
             yan-joong mah?
             Is it serious?

Yīshēng: **Bù yánzhòng. Nǐ zuì hǎo xiūxi jǐ tiān hē hěn duō shuǐ, jiù hǎo le.**
             boo yan-joong. nee dzway how shyow-she jee tyan huh hun dwaw shwun, jyo how luh.
             No. You should rest for a few days and drink lots of liquids, and it should get better.

Pete: **Tā děi zài chuángshàng tăng duōjiǔ?**
             tah day dzye chwahng-shahng tahng dwaw-jyo?
             How long must she rest in bed?

Yīshēng: **Zuì hǎo liǎng sān tiān.**
             dzway how lyahng sahn tyan.
             Ideally for two or three days.

Words to Know

Hǎo xiāoxi! 好消息!	how shyaow-she!	*Good news!*
Yánzhòng ma? 严重吗? (嚴重嗎?)	yan-joong mah?	Is it serious?
Hē hěn duō shuǐ. 喝很多水.	huh hun dwaw shway.	*Drink lots of liquids.*

In Chinese, you generally put a negative prefix, such as **bù** 不 (boo), in front of the verb you're negating. It sounds redundant in English to literally translate a response as *not serious* when someone asks about the seriousness of a situation. It's more colloquial and appropriate to translate it as *no,* as you see in the previous Talkin' the Talk section when Lauren asks the doctor if her ailment is serious.

Treating yourself to better health

Not everything can be cured with a bowl of **jī tāng** 鸡汤 (雞湯) (jee tahng) (*chicken soup*), despite what my grandmother told me. If your grandmother cooks as well as mine did, however, the soup couldn't hurt . . .

Your doctor may prescribe some **yào** 药 (藥) (yaow) (*medicine*) to make you feel better. After you **tián** 填 (填) (tyan) (*fill*) your **yīliào chǔ fāng** 医疗处方 (醫療處方) (ee-lyaow choo fahng) (*prescription*), you may find the following instructions on the bottle:

- ✔ **Fàn hòu chī.** 饭后吃. (飯後吃.) (fahn ho chir.) (*Take after eating.*)
- ✔ **Měi sìge xiǎoshí chī yícì.** 每四个小时吃一次. (每四個小時吃一次.) (may suh-guh shyaow-shir chir ee-tsuh.) (*Take one tablet every four hours.*)
- ✔ **Měi tiān chī liǎng cì, měi cì sān piàn.** 每天吃两次, 每次三片. (每天吃兩次, 每次三片.) (may tyan chir lyahng tsuh, may tsuh sahn pyan.) (*Take three tablets twice a day.*)

Calling the Police

Ever have your pocketbook **tōu le** (toe luh) (*stolen*)? Being a victim is an awful feeling, as I can tell you from experience. You feel angry at such a scary experience, especially if it happens in another country and the **zéi** 贼 (賊) (dzay) (*thief*) **táopǎo** 逃跑 (taow-paow) (*escapes*) quickly.

I hope you're never the victim of a crime like theft (or something worse). Still, you should always be prepared with some key words you can use when the **jǐngchá** 警察 (jeeng-chah) (*police*) finally pull up in the **jǐngchē** 警车 (警車) (jeeng-chuh) (*police car*) and take you back to the **jǐngchájú** 警察局 (jeeng-chah-jyew) (*police station*) to identify a potential **zéi**. Hopefully the culprit will be **zhuā le** 抓了 (jwah luh) (*arrested*).

You may also find yourself in an emergency that doesn't involve you. If you ever witness an accident, here are some phrases you can relay to the police, emergency workers, or victims:

- ✔ **Bié kū. Jǐngchá hé jiùhùchē láile.** 别哭. 警察和救护车来了. (別哭. 警察和救護車來了.) (byeh koo. jeeng-chah huh jyo-hoo-chuh lye-luh.) (*Don't cry. The police and the ambulance have arrived.*)
- ✔ **Tā bèi qìchē yàzháo le.** 他被车压着了. (他被車压着了.) (tah bay chee-chuh yah-jaow luh.) (*He was run over by a car.*)
- ✔ **Tā zài liúxiě.** 他在流血. (tah dzye lyo-shyeh.) (*He's bleeding.*)

Acquiring Legal Help

Nine out of ten foreigners never need to look for a lawyer during a stay in China, which isn't as litigious a society as the United States, to be sure. If you do need a **lǜshī** 律师 (律師) (lyew-shir) (*lawyer*), however, your best bet is to check with your country's **dàshǐguǎn** 大使馆 (大使館) (dah-shir-gwahn) (*embassy*) or **língshìguǎn** 领事馆 (領事館) (leeng-shir-gwahn) (*consulate*) for advice.

It can be very annoying and stressful to have to deal with **lǜshī,** no matter what country you're in, but you have to admit — they do know the **fǎlǜ** 法律 (fah-lyew) (*law*). And if you have to go to **fǎyuàn** 法院 (fah-ywan) (*court*) for any serious incident, you want the judge to **pànjué** 判决 (判決) (pahn-jweh) (*make a decision*) in your favor. Moral of the story: Good **lǜshī** are worth their weight in gold, even if you still consider them sharks in the end.

Identify the following body parts in Chinese. Check Appendix D for the answers.

1. Arm: _____

2. Shoulder: _____

3. Finger: _____

4. Leg: _____

5. Neck: _____

6. Chest: _____

7. Eye: _____

8. Ear: _____

9. Nose: _____

Part IV
The Part of Tens

The 5th Wave

By Rich Tennant

"We're still learning the language, and Martin tends to act out things he doesn't know the word for. He tried buying a toilet seat the other day, and they almost threw him out of the store."

In this part . . .

This part is short and sweet. I give you practical tips to keep in mind when learning Chinese. Equally important, I give you ten things to avoid doing when you're in China or with Chinese acquaintances.

Chapter 20

Ten Ways to Learn Chinese Quickly

*T*his chapter contains ten good activities that can help speed up your Chinese learning curve. Having useful, easy-to-access, and easy-to-follow learning tools makes a big difference in your progress. And besides, you can have fun with them, too.

Listen to Chinese-Language Tapes, CDs, and CD-ROMs

Just imagine trying to figure out what Chinese tones sound like without actually hearing them spoken out loud; it's kind of like imagining what Beethoven's Fifth sounds like based on a written description. Even if you read this book cover to cover, you'll be hard pressed to figure out just what the first, second, third, and fourth tones actually sound like unless you listen to the accompanying audio tracks. Be creative with your discovery of the language (and your language listening) by picking up all the language tapes, CDs, and CD-ROMs you can find out there. Keep mimicking what you hear over and over again so that your pronunciation and intonation become better with each go-round. Pretty soon, you'll be able to tell a native Mandarin speaker from a native Cantonese speaker.

Check Out a Peking Opera Performance

Okay, I admit that the first time I attended a performance of Peking Opera, I wished I had brought a pair of ear plugs. The opera is an acquired taste, to be sure. Kind of like caviar. But I recommend spending time cultivating an appreciation for it. Peking Opera originated in the late 1700s, when opera troupes originally staged performances for the royal family. Only later did it become such a public art, and now it's all the rage for any person who claims to appreciate Chinese culture. The makeup, costumes, cacophonous music, and stylized movements are predictable and much treasured by the Chinese people. Listening to Peking Opera not only helps you develop an appreciation for a great Chinese art form but also fine-tunes your recognition of the pronunciation of standard Mandarin. You can even learn a few tunes at the same time. A win-win situation all around.

Cook with a Wok

You may be surprised what cooking with a wok can do for your Chinese. Not only do you start eating healthier, but you also soak in Chinese words by osmosis because you're forced to visit some Asian food markets to gather the ingredients you need to cook with. Ever hear of **dòufu** 豆腐 (doe-foo) (*soybean curd*)? How about bok choi? Okay, so that's Cantonese, but the Mandarin is **bái cài** 白菜 (bye tsye) (*Chinese cabbage*). The best traditional Chinese cooking, all done with a wok, puts you in the proper frame of mind to want to absorb some more Chinese language. Try following some recipes from a Chinese cookbook and repeat the names of the ingredients over and over. And if you're not a great cook, get into the habit of eating at Chinese restaurants and mastering the names of at least ten dishes before the end of the meal.

Shop for Food in Chinatown

Mingle with the Mandarin-speaking masses while you attune your ear to the sounds and tones of Chinese. Buying food is only one of the fun things to do in Chinatown, of course, but it's one worth doing often. Not only do you cultivate a good ear for Chinese, but you also become privy to the gestures that often go along with the sounds.

Surf the Net

Tons of information on Chinese language and culture is only a mouse click away. Now that you're in the information age, take advantage of it. Everything from writing Chinese characters to discovering Peking Opera is out there. (Head to the earlier section "Check Out a Peking Opera Performance" for more on that particular option.) Whatever motivated you to start speaking Chinese in the first place, the World Wide Web keeps you involved. Just do a quick search for places such as Shanghai, Beijing, or Taipei or for cultural keywords such as *wok* or *pagoda*. You'll be amazed at what you can come up with.

Watch Kung-Fu Flicks

Bruce Lee is only the tip of the iceberg. Go to your local public library and ask to see the list of kung-fu movies. Everything from Hong Kong action films to mainland martial arts flicks — you should find them all there. Pick whatever interests you. Directors like Zhang Yimou and Chen Kaige have become famous around the world. (Okay, so they didn't direct kung-fu movies . . . but they're still worth checking out.)

The best way to grasp Chinese is to watch the films over and over to see how many words and phrases you can pick up in one sitting. You soon become adept at anticipating which gestures go with which words, and you develop a great ear for all those tones.

Exchange Language Lessons

Finding a language partner has to be one of the best ways to pick up Chinese. You get to learn the language, but you also develop a friendship along the way. Tons of students come to the United States every year from China. Whether you're in school at the moment or just live near one, you should have no problem putting up a sign offering a language exchange. And don't forget to ask your language partner to compare notes about Chinese and American culture. That's when the real fun begins.

Make Chinese Friends

Possibilities for meeting Chinese-speaking people are endless. Check out the cubicle next to you at your office or the desk ahead of you in class. Or how about the mother of the kid who's in your child's karate class? Wherever you go, you have a chance to make a new friend who not only knows Chinese but can also teach you a little about the culture. You may even find a new friend to see that kung-fu movie with or to help you navigate grocery shopping in Chinatown (not to mention how to use a wok after you buy all your food).

Study Chinese Calligraphy

Chinese calligraphy is one of the most beautiful art forms in the world. Why not pick up a brush and create those beautiful strokes yourself on rice paper? The whole ritual of preparing the ink and paper is an exercise in patience and meditation, and you get to appreciate the difficulty Chinese schoolchildren have in learning to write Chinese. You can discover how to write your name in Chinese (have your English name transliterated, because there's no alphabet in Chinese) and then practice writing those characters over and over until you can sign your name to a Chinese New Year's card and mail it to a friend.

Be Curious and Creative

If you look for opportunities to practice Chinese, I guarantee you can find them. Be imaginative. And stop worrying about failing. In fact, make as many mistakes as it takes so that you can make a mental note of what you should do or say differently the next time around. Give yourself a pat on the back every time you discover something new in Chinese or figure out a novel way to find out more about the Chinese language and people. Keep yakking away with the new words and phrases you find in this book and enjoy watching the reactions on people's faces when you open your mouth.

Chapter 21

Ten Things Never to Do in China

In This Chapter

▶ Understanding Chinese etiquette

▶ Being gracious and humble in social situations

This chapter may save you from certain embarrassment and possibly even outright humiliation one day. It gives you ten important tips on what not to do if you really want to win friends and make a good impression with your Chinese acquaintances. Take my tips to heart.

Never Accept a Compliment Graciously

You may find yourself at a loss for words when you compliment a Chinese host on a wonderful meal and you get in response, "No, no, the food was really horrible." You hear the same thing when you tell a Chinese parent how smart or handsome his son is; he meets the compliment with a rebuff of "No, he's really stupid." or "He's not good looking at all." These people aren't being nasty — just humble and polite. Moral of the story here: Feign humility, even if it kills you! A little less boasting and fewer self-congratulatory remarks go a long way toward scoring cultural sensitivity points with the Chinese.

To deflect a compliment, you can say something like **Nálǐ, nálǐ.** 哪里哪里. (哪裡哪裡.) (nah-lee nah-lee.) if you're speaking with someone from Taiwan or **Nǎr de huà.** 哪儿的话. (哪兒的話.) (nar duh hwah.) if you're speaking with someone from mainland China. They both mean *No, no, I don't deserve any praise.* (Chapter 4 shows you some other ways to reject compliments.)

Never Make Someone Lose Face

The worst thing you can possibly do to Chinese acquaintances is publicly humiliate or otherwise embarrass them. Doing so makes them lose face. Don't point out a mistake in front of others or yell at someone.

The good news is that you can actually help someone gain face by complimenting them and giving credit where credit is due. Do so whenever the opportunity arises. Your graciousness is much appreciated.

Never Get Angry in Public

Public displays of anger are frowned upon by the Chinese and are most uncomfortable for them to deal with — especially if the people getting angry are foreign tourists, for example. This concept goes right along with the faux pas of making someone (usually the Chinese host) lose face, which I cover in the preceding section. The Chinese place a premium on group harmony, so foreigners should try to swallow hard, be polite, and cope privately.

Never Address People by Their First Names First

Chinese people have first and last names like everyone else. However, in China, the last name always comes first. The family (and the collective in general) always takes precedence over the individual. Joe Smith in Minnesota is known as Smith Joe (or the equivalent) in Shanghai. If a man is introduced to you as Lǐ Míng, you can safely refer to him as Mr. Lǐ (not Mr. Míng).

Unlike people in the West, the Chinese don't feel very comfortable calling each other by their first names. Only family members and a few close friends ever refer to Lǐ Míng, for example, as simply Míng. They may, however, add the prefix **lǎo** 老 (laow) (*old*) or **xiǎo** 小 (shyaow) (*young*) before the family name to show familiarity and closeness. **Lǎo Lǐ** 老李 (laow lee) (*Old Lǐ*) may refer to his younger friend as **Xiǎo Chén** 小陈 (小陳) (shyaow chun) (*Young Chén*).

Never Take Food with the Wrong End of Your Chopsticks

The next time you gather around a dinner table with a Chinese host, you may discover that serving spoons for the many communal dishes are nonexistent. Rather, everyone serves themselves (or others) by turning their chopsticks upside down to take food from the main dishes before putting the food on the individual plates. Why upside down? Because you don't want to put the part of the chopsticks that goes in your mouth in the communal food bowls everyone eats from.

Never Drink Alcohol Without First Offering a Toast

Chinese banquets include eight to ten courses of food and plenty of alcohol. Sometimes you drink rice wine, and sometimes you drink industrial-strength **Máo Tái** 茅台 (maow tye), known to put a foreigner or two under the table in no time. One way to slow the drinking is to observe Chinese etiquette by always offering a toast to the host or someone else at the table before taking a sip yourself (yes, before every sip). Toasting not only prevents you from drinking too much too quickly but also shows your gratitude toward the host and your regard for the other guests.

All you need to do is raise your glass with your right hand, holding the bottom of the glass from underneath with your left hand, say the name of the person who you want to toast, look directly at them with a smile, give a nod as a form of respect, and then take a little sip.

If someone toasts you with a **gān bēi** 干杯 (gahn bay), however, watch out. **Gān bēi** means *bottoms up,* and you may be expected to drink the whole drink rather quickly. Don't worry. You can always say **suí yì** 随意 (sway ee) (*as you wish*) in return and take just a little sip instead.

Never Let Someone Else Pay the Bill Without Fighting for It

Most Westerners are stunned the first time they witness the many noisy, fairly chaotic scenes at the end of Chinese restaurant meals. The time to pay the bill has come, and everyone is simply doing what they're expected to do — fight to be the one to pay it. The Chinese feel that vociferously and strenuously attempting to wrest the bill out of the very hands of whoever happens to have it is simply good manners. This struggle may go back and forth for a good few minutes until someone "wins" and pays the bill. The gesture of being eager and willing to pay is always appreciated.

Never Show Up Empty-Handed

Gifts are exchanged frequently between the Chinese, and not just on special occasions. If you have dinner in someone's house to meet a prospective business partner or for any other pre-arranged meeting, both parties commonly exchange gifts as small tokens of friendship and good will. Westerners are often surprised at the number of gifts the Chinese hosts give. The general rule of thumb is to bring many little (gender non-specific) gifts when you travel to China. You never know when you'll meet someone who wants to present you with a special memento, so you should arrive with your own as well.

Never Accept Food, Drinks, or Gifts Without First Refusing a Few Times

No self-respecting guests immediately accept whatever food, drink, or gift may be offered to them in someone's home no matter how eager they may be to receive it. Proper Chinese etiquette prevents you from doing anything that makes you appear greedy or eager to receive any offerings, so be sure to politely refuse a couple of times. For example, if someone tries to serve you food, immediately say **Zìjǐ lái.** 自己来。(自己來。) (dzuh-jee lye.) (*I'll take it myself.*). You should do this several times and then let the person serve you anyway. At least he'll know you didn't want him to go to all the trouble.

Never Take the First "No, Thank You" Literally

Chinese people automatically decline food or drinks several times — even if they really feel hungry or thirsty. They might say something like **bú yòng, bú yòng** 不用，不用 (boo yoong, boo yoong) (*no need, no need*). Never take the first refusal literally. Even if they say it once or twice, offer it again. A good guest is supposed to refuse at least once, but a good host is also supposed to make the offer at least twice.

Part V
Appendixes

The 5th Wave   By Rich Tennant

"Is there an easy phrase in Chinese for removing a squid from a cowboy hat that won't make me look like a tourist?"

In this part . . .

The appendixes in this part give you easy-to-access Chinese reference sources. I provide a mini-dictionary with some of the words you use most often. Next, I include a simple list of verbs in Chinese, because Chinese has no equivalent of English verb conjugation. Then I list the audio tracks included with this book so you can read along as you listen and then practice speaking Chinese with the correct tones. Finally, you get the answers to the Fun & Games exercises that appear at the end of the chapters.

Chinese-English Mini-Dictionary

A

ǎi (eye): short

àirén (eye-run): spouse (used only in the PRC)

āiyá (eye-yah): oh my goodness!

ānjìng (ahn-jeeng): quiet

ānpái (ahn-pye): to arrange

ānquán dài (ahn-chwan dye): seat belt

B

bàba (bah-bah): father

bǎifēn bǐ (bye-fun bee): percentage

bàn (bahn): half

bāngmáng (bahng-mahng): to help

bàngōngshì (bahn-goong-shir): office

bàngōngzhuō (bahn-goong-jwaw): desk

bànyè (bahn-yeh): midnight

bàoqiàn (baow-chyan): I'm sorry

bàozhǐ (baow-jir): newspaper

biéde (byeh-duh): other

bìng (beeng): to be sick

bīnguǎn (been-gwahn): hotel

bō (baw): to dial

bówùguǎn (baw-woo-gwahn): museum

bù (boo): not; no

búkèqì (boo-kuh-chee): you're welcome

bǔchōng (boo-choong): to add

búcuò (boo-tswaw): not bad; really good

bùzhǎng (boo-jahng): department head; minister

C

cá (tsah): to sweep

cài (tsye): food

càidān (tsye-dahn): menu

cānguǎn (tsahn-gwahn): restaurant

cānjīnzhǐ (tsahn-jeen-jir): napkin

cèsuǒ (tsuh-swaw): toilet

chá (chah): tea; to look something up

chángcháng (chahng-chahng): often

chángtú diànhuà (chahng-too dyan-hwah): long-distance phone call

chāojí shìchǎng (chaow-jee shir-chahng): supermarket

chātóu (chah-toe): adaptor

chāzi (chah-dzuh): fork

chéngshì (chung-shir): city

chī yào (chir yaow): to take medicine

chīfàn (chir-fahn): to eat

chuān (chwahn): to wear

chuáng (chwahng): bed

chuánzhēn jī (chwan-juhn-jee): fax machine

chūfā (choo-fah): to leave the house; to set off

chūzū (choo-dzoo): to rent

chūzū chē (choo-dzoo chuh): taxi

cóng (tsoong): from

cōngmíng (tsoong-meeng): intelligent

cuò (tswaw): incorrect; mistake

D

dà (dah): big

dǎ (dah): to do, play, or hit

dàlù (dah-loo): mainland (China)

dānchéng piào (dahn-chuhng pyaow): one-way ticket

dāngrán (dahng-rahn): of course

dànshì (dahn-shir): but; however

dàshǐguǎn (dah-shir-gwahn): embassy

dàtīng (dah-teeng): lobby

děng (duhng): to wait

dēng jīpái (duhng jee-pye): boarding pass

diǎn (dyan): to order (food)

diànhuà (dyan-hwah): telephone

diànhuà hàomǎ (dyan-hwah how-mah): telephone number

diànhuà hàomǎbù (dyan-hwah how-mah-boo): telephone book

diànnǎo (dyan-now): computer

diànshì (dyan-shir): television

diàntī (dyan-tee): elevator

diànyǐng (dyan-yeeng): movie

diànzǐ yóujiàn (dyan-dzuh yo-jyan): e-mail

diànzǐ yóuxiāng dìzhǐ (dyan-dzuh yo-shyahng dee-jir): e-mail address

dìfāng (dee-fahng): place

dìng wèi (deeng way): to make a reservation

dìqū (dee-chyew): area; location

dìtiě (dee-tyeh): subway

dìtú (dee-too): map

dìzhǐ (dee-jir): address

dōngxī (doong-she): thing

dōu (doe): both; all

duìbùqǐ (dway-boo-chee): excuse me; I'm sorry

duìfāng fùfèi diànhuà (dway-fahng foo-fay dyan-hwah): collect call

duìhuàn lǜ (dway-hwahn lyew): exchange rate

duìhuànchù (dway-hwahn-choo): exchange bureaus

duìmiàn (dway-myan): opposite

dùjià (doo-jyah): on vacation

duō (dwaw): many

duō jiǔ (dwaw-jyoe): how long

duōshǎo (dwaw-shaow): how much

E

è (uh): hungry

érzi (are-dzuh): son

F

fǎlǜ (fah-lyew): law

fàn (fahn): food

fàndiàn (fahn-dyan): restaurant

fàndiàn qiántái (fahn-dyan chyan-tye): reception desk

fáng jià (fahng-jyah): to take a vacation

fángjiān (fahng-jyan): room

fànguǎn (fahn-gwahn): hotel

fángzi (fahng-dzuh): house

fàntīng (fahn-teeng): dining room

fēijī (fay-jee): airplane

fēijīchǎng (fay-jee-chahng): airport

féizào (fay-dzaow): soap

fēn (fun): minute; one cent

fùjìn (foo-jeen): area; vicinity

fùmǔ (foo-moo): parents

fù qián (foo chyan): to pay

fùqīn (foo-cheen): father

fúwùqì (foo-woo-chee): server

fúwùtái jīnglǐ (foo-woo-tye jeeng-lee): concierge

fúwùyuán (foo-woo-ywan): attendant

G

gǎibiàn (guy-byan): to change (attitude/behavior)

Gǎngbì (gahng-bee): Hong Kong dollar

gāngbǐ (gahng-bee): pen

gānjìng (gahn-jeeng): clean

gǎnxiè (gahn-shyeh): many thanks

gāofēngqī (gaow-fung-chee): rush hour

gàosù (gaow-soo): to tell

gāosù gōnglù (gaow-soo goong-loo): freeway

gāoxìng (gaow-sheeng): happy

gěi (gay): to give

gèng (guhng): more

gèrén diànnǎo (guh-run dyan-now): PC (personal computer)

gōnggòng qìchē (goong-goong chee-chuh): public bus

gōnggòng qìchē zhàn (goong-goong chee-chuh jahn): bus stop

gōnglù (goong-loo): highway

gōngsī (goong-suh): company

gōngwénbāo (goong-one-baow): briefcase

gōngxǐ (goong-she): congratulations

gōngyòng diànhuà (goong-yoong dyan-hwah): public telephone

gōngzuò (goong-dzwaw): to work; job

guà (gwah): to hang up

guǎn (gwan): to care about

guāngguāng tuán (gwahn-gwahng twahn): tour group

guāngpán (gwahng-pahn): music CD

gǔdài (goo-dye): ancient; antique

guì (gway): expensive

guójì diànhuà (gwaw-jee dyan-hwah): international phone call

guójì wǎngluò (gwaw-jee wahng-lwaw): the Internet

guójiā (gwaw-jyah): country

guóyǔ (gwaw-yew): Mandarin (term used in Taiwan)

H

hǎiguān (hi-gwahn): customs

háizi (hi-dzuh): child

Hànyǔ (hahn-yew): Chinese language

hǎo (how): good

hǎokàn (how-kahn): pretty

hàomǎ (how-mah): number

hē (huh): to drink

hétóng (huh-toong): contract

huài (hwye): broken; bad

huàn (hwahn): to change (trains, money, and so on)

huángdēngjī (hwahn-duhng-jee): slide projector

huángdēngpiàn (hwahn-duhng-pyan): slides

huānyíng (hwahn-yeeng): welcome

huí (hway): to answer; to return

huì (hway): to know how to do something

huí lái (hway lye): to return (come back)

huìyì (hway-ee): meeting

huò zhe (hwaw juh): or

huòbì (hwaw-bee): currency

huǒchē zhàn (hwaw-chuh jahn): train station

hùshī (hoo-shir): nurse

hùtóu (hoo-toe): bank account

hùzhào (hoo-jaow): passport

J

jǐ (jee): several; how many

jiā (jyah): family; home

jiàgé (jyah-guh): price

jiàn (jyan): to see; also used as a classifier

jiǎnchá (jyan-chah): to examine

jiǎng (jyahng): to talk

jiànshēn yùndòng (jyan-shun yewn-doong): to work out

jiǎnsuǒ (jyan-swaw): to search

jiànyì (jyan-ee): to suggest; suggestion

jiào (jyaow): to be called

jiāo (jyaow): to teach

jiàoshòu (jyaow-show): professor

jiāotōng (jyaow-toong): transportation

jiàrì (jyah-ir): vacation day

jí (jee): hurry

jiè (jyeh): to borrow; to loan

jiē (jyeh): to answer the phone; street

jiéhūn (jyeh-hwun): to marry

jiějué (jyeh-jweh): to resolve; to solve

jiérì (jyeh-ir): holiday

jièshào (jyeh-shaow): to introduce

jiéyú (jyeh-yew): account balance

jìn (jin): close

jǐngchá (jeeng-chah): police

jǐngchájú (jeeng-chah-jyew): police station

jīngjìcāng (jeeng-jee-tsahng): economy class

jīngjìrén (jeeng-jee-run): broker

jīnglǐ (jeeng-lee): manager

jǐnjí chūkǒu (jin-jee choo-koe): emergency exits

jīntiān (jin-tyan): today

jiǔ (jyoe): wine; alcohol

jiùhùchē (jyoe-hoo-chuh): ambulance

jiùshēng yī (jyoe-shung ee): life vests

jízhěnshì (jee-juhn-shir): emergency room

K

kāfēi (kah-fay): coffee 咖啡

kāfēitīng (kah-fay-teeng): café 咖啡厅

kāi (kye): to open 開

kāi chē (kye chuh): to drive 開車

kāihuì (kye-hway): to have a meeting 開會

kāimén (kye-mun): to open the door 開門

kāishǐ (kye-shir): to start 開始

kàn (kahn): to read; to see 看

kànbìng (kahn-beeng): to see a doctor

kàojìn (cow-jeen): next to

kè (kuh): class (academic)

kě (kuh): thirsty

kè hù (kuh hoo): client

kěndìng (kuhn-deeng): definitely

kěnéng (kuh-nung): perhaps

kěpà (kuh-pah): scary

kèrén (kuh-run): guest

kěxí (kuh-she): too bad; unfortunately

kěyǐ (kuh-yee): can; to be able to

kōngtiáo (koong-tyaow): air conditioning

kòngwèi (koong-way): vacant

kuài (kwye): fast; dollar

kuàijì (kwye-jee): accounting

kuàizi (kwye-dzuh): chopsticks

L

lái (lye): to come

láihuí piào (lye-hway pyaow): round-trip ticket

lǎo (laow): old; overdone

lǎobǎn (laow-bahn): a boss

lǎoshī (laow-shir): teacher

lèi (lay): tired

léishè guāngdié (lay-shuh gwahng-dyeh): CD-ROM

lěng (luhng): cold

lǐ (lee): inside; Chinese equivalent of a kilometer

liáotiān (lyaow-tyan): to chat

lǐbài (lee-bye): to pray; week

líkāi (lee-kye): to leave

lǐngqǔdān (leeng-chyew-dahn): luggage claim tag

línshìguǎn (leeng-shir-gwahn): consulate

lǐtáng (lee-tahng): auditorium

liúhuà (lyoe-hwah): to leave a message

liúlǎn (lyoe-lahn): to browse

liúxíng (lyoe-sheeng): popular

lǐwù (lee-woo): gifts

lóushàng (low-shahng): upstairs

lóuxià (low-shyah): downstairs

lù (loo): road

lǚguǎn (lyew-gwahn): hotel

lǜshī (lyew-shir): lawyer

lùxiàngjī (loo-shyahng-jee): video recorder

lǚxíng (lyew-sheeng): to travel

lǚxíng dàilǐrén (lyew-sheeng dye-lee-run): travel agent

lǚxíng zhīpiào (lyew-sheeng jir-pyaow): traveler's checks

lǚxíngshè (lyew-sheeng-shuh): travel agency

lùyīn diànhuà (loo-een dyan-hwah): answering machine

lǚyóu (lyew-yoe): tour

lǚyóu shǒucè (lyew-yoe show-tsuh): guidebook

M

máfan (mah-fahn): annoying

mài (my): to sell

mǎi (my): to buy

māma (mah-mah): mother

màn (mahn): slow

mànchē (mahn-chuh): local train

máng (mahng): busy

máojīn (maow-jeen): towel

máotǎn (maow-tahn): blanket

màoyì zhǎnxiāohuì (maow-ee jahn-shyaow-hway): trade show

měige (may-guh): each

Měiguó (may-gwaw): America

Měiguóren (may-gwaw-run): American

méiyǒu (mayo): don't have

Měiyuán (may-ywan): U.S. dollar

mén (mun): door

ménkǒu (mun-ko): entrance

miàn (myan): face

miǎnfèi (myan-fay): free

miàntiáo (myan-tyaow): noodles

mǐfàn (mee-fahn): rice

mílù (mee-loo): to get lost

mìmǎ (mee-mah): personal identification number (PIN); password

míngnián (meeng-nyan): next year

míngpiàn (meeng-pyan): business card

míngtiān (meeng-tyan): tomorrow

mìshū (mee-shoo): secretary

mǔqīn (moo-cheen): mother

N

ná (nah): to pick up

nà (nah): that

nǎ (nah): which

nán péngyǒu (nahn pung-yo): boyfriend

nào zhōng (now-joong): alarm clock

nǎr (nar): where

nàr (nar): there

nǐ (nee): you

niánjì (nyan-jee): age

niánqīng (nyan-cheeng): young

nǐmen (nee-mun): you (plural)

nín (neen): you (polite)

nuǎnhuó (nwan-hwaw): warm

nǚpéngyǒu (nyew-puhng-yo): girlfriend

O

Ōu yuán (oh ywan): Euro

Ōuzhōu (oh-joe): Europe

P

pànjué (pahn-jweh): to make a decision legal

pēngtiáo yìshù (puhng-tyaow ee-shoo): culinary arts

péngyǒu (puhng-yo): friend

piányì (pyan-yee): cheap

piānzi (pyan-dzuh): movie

piào (pyaow): ticket

piàoliàng (pyaow-lyahng): pretty

píngcháng (peeng-chahng): usually; often

pǐntuō (peen-twaw): pint

pīnyīn (peen-yeen): Chinese Romanization system

Pǔtōnghuà (poo-toong-hwah): Mandarin (term used in mainland China)

Q

qián (chyan): front; money

qiān chū (chyan choo): to log off

qiánbāo (chyan-baow): wallet

qiānbǐ (chyan-bee): pencil

qiántái fúwùyuán (chyan-tye foo-woo-ywan): receptionist

qiānzhèng (chyan-juhng): visa

qiáo (chyaow): bridge

qìchē (chee-chuh): car

qǐfēi (chee-fay): to take off (airplane)

qíguài (chee-gwye): strange

qiān rù (chyan roo): to log on

qíng (cheeng): affection

qìng (cheeng): to celebrate

qǐng (cheeng): please

qīng (cheeng): clear

qīngzǎo (cheeng-dzaow): time (midnight to 6:00 am)

qítā (chee-tah): other; anything else

qīzi (chee-dzuh): wife

qù (chyew): to go

qǔ qián (chyew chyan): to withdraw money

quánbù (chwan-boo): entire; the whole thing

qùdiào (chyew-dyaow): erase; remove

qùnián (chyew-nyan): last year

qúnzi (chwun-dzuh): skirt

qǔxiāo (chyew-shyaow): to cancel

R

ràng (rahng): to let; to allow

rè (ruh): hot

rén (run): person

rénmínbì (run-meen-bee): PRC dollar

rènshi (run-shir): to know someone

Rì yuán (ir ywan): Japanese dollar

Rìběn (ir-bun): Japan

rìlì (ir-lee): calendar

rìqī (ir-chee): date

róngxìng (roong-sheeng): to be honored

róngyì (roong-ee): easy

ròu (row): meat

ruǎnjiàn (rwahn-jyan): software

S

shàng (shahng): above; on top; to go up; to get on

shāngdiàn (shahng-dyan): store

shàngge xīngqī (shahng-guh sheeng-chee): last week

shàngge yuè (shahng-guh yweh): last month

shàngwǎng (shahng-wahng): to go online

shāngwù zhōngxīn (shahng-woo joong-sheen): business center

shāngyè (shahng-yeh): business

shéi (shay): who; whom

shēn (shun): dark; deep

shēngqì (shung-chee): angry

shēngrì (shung-ir): birthday

shēngyì huǒbàn (shuhng yee hwaw bahn): business partner

shēngyīn (shung-een): voice

shénme (shummuh): what

shēntǐ (shun-tee): body

shì (shir): yes; is

shīfu (shir-foo): master; cook

shíhòu (shir-ho): time

shíjiānbiǎo (shir-jyan-byaow): schedule

shìpǐn záhuò (shir-peen dzah-hwaw): groceries

shuzāi (shway-dzye): flood

shōudào (show-daow): to receive

shǒujī (show-jee): cellphone

shǒujī hàomǎ (show-jee how-mah): cellphone number

shōujù (show-jyew): receipt

shòushāng (show-shahng): to be injured

shǒutí xínglǐ (show-tee sheeng-lee): carry-on luggage

shǒutíshì (show-tee-shir): laptop

shū (shoo): to lose; book

shuāng (shwahng): a pair

shuāngrén fángjiān (shwahng-run fahng-jyan): double room

shūfu (shoo-foo): comfortable

shuǐguǒ (shway-gwaw): fruit

shuìjiào (shway-jyaow): sleep

shuō (shwaw): to speak

sījī (suh-jee): driver

sìzhōu (suh-joe): around

sòng (soong): to send

sōng (soong): loose

sùcài (soo-tsye): vegetarian dishes

suì (sway): age

suǒ (swaw): to lock

sùshè (soo-shuh): dormitory

T

tā (tah): he; him

tāde (tah-duh): his

tài (tye): too much

táishì (tye-shir): desktop

tàitài (tye-tye): wife (term used mostly in Taiwan)

Táiwān (tye-wahn): Taiwan

tàiyáng yǎnjìng (tye-yahng yan-jeeng): sunglasses

tāmen (tah-mun): they; them

tāng (tahng): soup

tánpàn (tah-pahn): negotiate

tǎnzi (tahn-dzuh): blanket

tàojiān (taow-jyan): suite

tǎolùn (taow-loon): to discuss

tèsè (tuh-suh): special

tián (tyan): to fill out a form

tiānqì (tyan-chee): weather

tiàowǔ (tiaow-woo): to dance

tīng (teeng): to listen to

tóngshì (toong-shir): colleague

tóngwū (toong-woo): roommate

tóngyì (toong-ee): to agree

tóuděng cāng (toe-dung-tsahng): first class

tóuténg (toe-tung): headache

tuīchí (tway-chir): postponed

tuìfáng (tway-fahng): to check out of a room

tuìhuí (tway-hway): to return merchandise

tuìkuǎn (tway-kwahn): refund

tuōyùn (twaw-yewn): to check in luggage

W

wài (wye): outside

wàibì (wye-bee): foreign currency

wàijiāoguān (wye-jyaow-gwahn): diplomat

wǎnfàn (wahn-fahn): dinner

wǎngluò liánjié (wahng-lwaw lyan-jyeh): Internet access

wǎngshàng fúwù tígōng shāng (wahng-shahng foo-woo tee-goong shahng): Internet service provider

wǎngzhàn (wahng-jahn): website

wǎnhuì (wahn-hway): party

wǎnshàng (wahn-shahng): evening (6:00 p.m. to midnight)

wéi (way): hello (on phone only)

wèishēng zhǐ (way-shung jir): toilet paper

wèishénme (way-shummuh): why

wénjiàn (one-jyan): a file

wènlù (one-loo): to ask for directions

wèntí (one-tee): problem

wǒ (waw): I; me

wǒde (waw-duh): mine

wǒmen (waw-mun): we; us

wòshì (waw-shir): bedroom

wǔfàn (woo-fahn): lunch

wǔyuè (woo-yweh): May

X

xǐ (she): to wash

xià (shyah): below; next; to go down; to get off

xiàge (shyah-guh): next

xiàge xīngqī (shyah-guh sheeng-chee): next week

xiàge yuè (shyah-guh yweh): next month

xiǎng (shyahng): to think

Xiānggǎng (shyahng-gahng): Hong Kong

xiàngmù (shyahng-moo): item

xiāngzi (shyahng-dzuh): suitcase

xiànjīn (shyan-jeen): cash

xiánliáo (shyan-lyaow): small talk

xiántán (shyan-tahn): to chat

xiànzài (shyan-dzye): now

xiǎo (shyaow): small

xiǎofèi (shyaow-fay): tip

xiǎo géjiān (shyaow guh-jyan): cubicle

xiǎo xīn (shyaow sheen): be careful

xiàwǔ (shyah-woo): afternoon (noon to 6:00 p.m.)

xiàzài (shyah-dzye): to download

xīcān (she-tsahn): Western food

xièxiè (shyeh-shyeh): thanks

xiézi (shyeh-dzuh): shoes

xǐhuān (she-hwahn): to like

xīn (shin): new

Xīn bì (shin bee): Singapore dollar

xínglǐ (sheeng-lee): luggage

xīngqī'èr (sheeng-chee-are): Tuesday

xīngqīliù (sheeng-chee-lyo): Saturday

xīngqīsān (sheeng-chee-sahn):
Wednesday

xīngqīsì (sheeng-chee-suh): Thursday

xīngqītiān (sheeng-chee-tyan): Sunday

xīngqīwǔ (sheeng-chee-woo): Friday

xīngqīyī (sheeng-chee-ee): Monday

xīn Táibì (shin tye-bee): New Taiwan
dollars

xìnxī (sheen-she): message

xìnyòng kǎ (sheen-yoong kah): credit
card

xǐshǒu jiān (she-show-jyan): bathroom

xiūxi (shyo-she): to rest

xǐyī fúwù (she-ee foo-woo): laundry
service

xuǎnzé (shwan-dzuh): to choose

xuéshēng (shweh-shung): student

xuéxí (shweh-she): to study

xuéxiào (shweh-shyaow): school

xūyào (shyew-yaow): to need

Y

yǎnjìng (yan-jeeng): glasses

yǎnjīng (yan-jeeng): eye

yǎnshì (yan-shir): a presentation

yào (yaow): to want; medicine

yàofáng (yaow-fahng): pharmacy

yáokòng qì (yaow-koong chee): remote
control

yàoshi (yaow-shir): key

yàowán (yaow-wahn): pill

yáshuā (yah-shwah): toothbrush

yáyī (yah-ee): dentist

Yàzhōu (yah-joe): Asia

yě (yeah): also

yī (ee): one

yìchéng (ee-chung): agenda

yīfu (ee-foo): clothing

yǐhòu (ee-ho): after

yìhuǎr jiàn (ee-hwar jyan): see you later

yìhuǎr (ee-hwar): in a little while

yìjiàn (ee-jyan): opinion

yíng (eeng): to win

yìngbì (eeng-bee): coins

yīnggāi (eeng-guy): should

yínháng (een-hahng): bank

Yīngwén (eeng-one): English language

Yīngyǔ (eeng-yew): English language

yǐnliào (een-lyaow): drinks

yīnwèi (een-way): because

yīnyuè (een-yweh): music

yìqǐ (ee-chee): together

yīshēng (ee-shung): doctor

yǐwéi (ee-way): to consider

yìxiē (ee-shyeh): a few

yíyàng (ee-yahng): the same

yīyuàn (ee-ywan): hospital

yǐzi (ee-dzuh): chair

yòng (yoong): to use

yònghù xìngmíng (yoong-hoo sheeng-
meeng): user name

yòu (yo): right

yǒu (yo): to have

yǒu shēng yóujiàn (yo shung yo-jyan):
voicemail

yóujú (yo-jyew): post office

yóulǎn (yo-lahn): to sightsee

yǔ (yew): rain

yuán (ywan): Chinese dollar

yuǎn (ywan): far

yùdìng (yew-deeng): to make a reservation

Yuènán (yweh-nahn): Vietnam

yùndòng (yewn-doong): exercise

yùnqì (yewn-chee): luck

yǔsǎn (yew-sahn): umbrella

yùsuàn (yew-swan): budget

yǔyī (yew-ee): raincoat

Z

zàijiàn (dzye-jyan): goodbye

zánmen (dzahn-mun): we; us (informal)

zǎofàn (dzaow-fahn): breakfast

zāogāo (dzaow-gaow): Rats!; what a shame

zǎoshàng (dzaow-shahng): morning (6:00 a.m. to noon)

zázhì (dzah-jir): magazine

zéi (dzay): thief

zěnme (dzummah): how

zhàngdān (jahng-dahn): bill

zhàngfu (jahng-foo): husband

zhàntái (jahn-tye): platform

zhǎo (jaow): to look for

zhāohu (jaow-hoo): greeting

zhàopiàn (jaow-pyan): photo

zhàoxiàng (jaow-shyahng): to take pictures

zhàoxiàng jī (jaow-shyahng jee): camera

zhēn (juhn): really; truly

zhèngdiǎn (juhng-dyan): on time

zhèngjiàn (juhng-jyan): ID

zhí (jir): straight

zhǐ (jir): only

zhīdào (jir-daow): to know information

zhìliàng (jir-lyahng): quality

zhīpiào (jir-pyaow): check (money)

zhīpiào bù (jir-pyaow boo): checkbook

zhōng (joong): time; size medium

Zhōngguó (joong-gwaw): China

Zhōngguó rén (joong-gwaw run): Chinese person

Zhōngwén (joong-one): Chinese language

zhōngwǔ (joong-woo): noon

zhōngyú (joong-yew): finally

zhōumò (joe-maw): weekend

zhù (joo): to reside

zhuǎn (jwan): to transfer; to turn

zhūbǎo (joo-baow): jewelry

zhǔguǎn (joo-gwan): CEO

zhuólù (jwaw-loo): landing

zhuōzi (jwaw-dzuh): table

zìdòng lóutī (dzuh-doong low-tee): escalator

zìdòng tíkuǎn kǎ (dzuh-doong tee-kwan kah): ATM card

zìdòng tíkuǎnjī (dzuh-doong tee-kwan-jee): ATM

zìjǐ (dzuh-jee): self

zǒngcái (dzoong-tsye): president of a company

zǒngshì (dzoong-shir): always

zǒngsuàn (dzoong-swahn): finally

zǒu (dzoe): to walk

zūfèi (dzoo-fay): rent

zǔfù (dzoo-foo): grandfather

zuì (dzway): the most

zuǒ (dzwaw): left

zuótiān (dzwaw-tyan): yesterday

English-Chinese Mini-Dictionary

A

above: **shàng** (shahng)

account balance: **jiéyú** (jyeh-yew)

accounting: **kuàijì** (kwye-jee)

adaptor: **chātóu** (chah-toe)

add: **bǔchōng** (boo-choong)

address: **dìzhǐ** (dee-jir)

affection: **qíng** (cheeng)

after: **yǐhòu** (ee-ho)

afternoon (noon to 6:00 p.m.): **xiàwǔ** (shyah-woo)

age: **niánjì; suì** (nyan-jee; sway)

agenda: **yìchéng** (ee-chung)

agree: **tóngyì** (toong-ee)

air conditioning: **kōngtiáo** (koong-tyaow)

airplane: **fēijī** (fay-jee)

airport: **fēijīchǎng** (fay-jee-chahng)

alarm clock: **nào zhōng** (naow-joong)

alcohol: **jiǔ** (jyoe)

all: **dōu** (doe)

allow: **ràng** (rahng)

also: **yě** (yeh)

always: **zǒngshì** (dzoong-shir)

ambulance: **jiùhùchē** (jyoe-hoo-chuh)

America: **Měiguó** (may-gwaw)

American: **Měiguórén** (may-gwaw-run)

ancient: **gǔdài** (goo-dye)

angry: **shēngqì** (shung-chee)

annoying: **máfan** (mah-fahn)

answer the phone: **jiē** (jyeh)

answer: **huí** (hway)

answering machine: **lùyīn diànhuà** (loo-een dyan-hwah)

antique: **gǔdài** (goo-dye)

anything else: **qítā** (chee-tah)

area (location): **dìqū** (dee-chyew)

area (vicinity): **fùjìn** (foo-jeen)

around: **sìzhōu** (suh-joe)

arrange: **ānpái** (ahn-pye)

Asia: **Yàzhōu** (yah-joe)

ask for directions: **wènlù** (one-loo)

ATM card: **zìdòng tíkuǎn kǎ** (dzuh-doong tee-kwan kah)

ATM: **zìdòng tíkuǎnjī** (dzuh-doong tee-kwan-jee)

attendant: **fúwùyuán** (foo-woo-ywan)

auditorium: **lǐtáng** (lee-tahng)

B

bad: **huài** (hwye)

bank: **yínháng** (een-hahng)

bank account: **hùtóu** (hoo-toe)

bathroom: **xǐshǒu jiān** (she-show jyan)

be able to: **kěyǐ** (kuh-yee)

be called: **jiào** (jyaow)

be careful: **xiǎo xīn** (shyaow sheen)

be honored: **róngxìng** (roong-sheeng)

be injured: **shòushāng** (show-shahng)

be sick: **bìng** (beeng)

because: **yīnwèi** (een-way)

bed: **chuáng** (chwahng)

bedroom: **wòshì** (waw-shir)

below: **xià** (shyah)

big: **dà** (dah)

bill: **zhàngdān** (jahng-dahn)

birthday: **shēngrì** (shung-ir)

blanket: **máotǎn; tǎnzi** (maow-tahn; tahn-dzuh)

boarding pass: **dēngjī pái** (dung-jee pye)

body: **shēntǐ** (shun-tee)

book: **shū** (shoo)

borrow: **jiè** (jyeh)

boss: **lǎobǎn** (laow-bahn)

both: **dōu** (doe)

boyfriend: **nán péngyǒu** (nahn pung-yo)

breakfast: **zǎofàn** (dzaow-fahn)

bridge: **qiáo** (chyaow)

briefcase: **gōngwénbāo** (goong-one-baow)

broken: **huài** (hwye)

broker: **jīngjìrén** (jeeng-jee-run)

browse: **liúlǎn** (lyo-lahn)

budget: **yùsuàn** (yew-swan)

bus stop: **gōnggòng qìchē zhàn** (goong-goong chee-chuh jahn)

business: **shēngyì** (shung-yee)

business card: **míngpiàn** (meeng-pyan)

business center: **shāngwù zhōngxīn** (shahng-woo joong-sheen)

business partner: **shēngyì huǒbàn** (shung-yee hwaw-bahn)

busy: **máng** (mahng)

but: **dànshì** (dahn-shir)

buy: **mǎi** (my)

C

café: **kāfēitīng** (kah-fay-teeng)

calendar: **rìlì** (ir-lee)

camera: **zhàoxiàng jī** (jaow-shyahng-jee)

can: **kěyǐ** (kuh-yee)

cancel: **qǔxiāo** (chyew-shyaow)

car: **qìchē** (chee-chuh)

care about: **guǎn** (gwan)

carry-on luggage: **shǒutí xínglǐ** (show-tee sheeng-lee)

cash: **xiànjīn** (shyan-jeen)

CD (music): **guāngpán** (gwahng-pahn)

CD-ROM: **léishè guāngdié** (lay-shuh gwahng-dyeh)

celebrate: **qìng** (cheeng)

cellphone: **shǒujī** (show-jee)

cellphone number: **shǒujī hàomǎ** (show-jee how-mah)

CEO: **zhǔguǎn** (joo-gwan)

chair: **yǐzi** (ee-dzuh)

change (attitude/behavior): **gǎibiàn** (guy-byan)

change (trains, money, and so on): **huàn** (hwahn-chuh)

chat: **liáotiān; xiántán** (lyaow-tyan; shyan-tahn)

cheap: **piányì** (pyan-yee)

check (money): **zhīpiào** (jir-pyaow)

check in luggage: **tuōyùn** (twaw-yewn)

check out of a room: **tuìfáng** (tway-fahng)

checkbook: **zhīpiào bù** (jir-pyaow boo)

child: **háizi** (hi-dzuh)

China: **Zhōngguó** (joong-gwaw)

Chinese (language): **Hànyǔ; Zhōngwén** (hahn-yew; joong-one)

Chinese dollar: **yuán** (ywan)

Chinese person: **Zhōngguó rén** (joong-gwaw-run)

Chinese Romanization system: **pīnyīn** (peen-yeen)

choose: **xuǎnzé** (shwan-dzuh)

chopsticks: **kuàizi** (kwye-dzuh)

city: **chéngshì** (chung-shir)

class (academic): **kè** (kuh)

clean: **gānjìng** (gahn-jeeng)

clear: **qīng** (cheeng)

client: **kè hù** (kuh hoo)

close: **jìn** (jeen)

clothing: **yīfu** (ee-foo)

coffee: **kāfēi** (kah-fay)

coins: **yìngbì** (eeng-bee)

cold: **lěng** (luhng)

colleague: **tóngshì** (toong-shir)

collect call: **duìfāng fùfèi diànhuà** (dway-fahng foo-fay dyan-hwah)

come: **lái** (lye)

comfortable: **shūfu** (shoo-foo)

company: **gōngsī** (goong-suh)

computer: **diànnǎo** (dyan-now)

concierge: **fúwùtái jīnglǐ** (foo-woo-tye jeeng-lee)

congratulations: **gōngxǐ** (goong-she)

consider: **yǐwéi** (ee-way)

consulate: **lǐnshìguǎn** (leeng-shir-gwahn)

contract: **hétóng** (huh-toong)

cook: **shīfu** (shir-foo)

country: **guójiā** (gwaw-jyah)

credit card: **xìnyòng kǎ** (sheen-yoong-kah)

cubicle: **xiǎo géjiān** (shyaow guh-jyan)

culinary arts: **pēngtiáo yìshù** (puhng-tyaow ee-shoo)

currency: **huòbì** (hwaw-bee)

customs: **hǎiguān** (hi-gwahn)

D

dance: **tiàowǔ** (tiaow-woo)

dark: **shēn** (shun)

date: **rìqī** (ir-chee)

deep: **shēn** (shun)

definitely: **kěndìng** (kuhn-deeng)

dentist: **yáyī** (yah-ee)

department head: **bùzhǎng** (boo-jahng)

desk: **bàngōng zhuō** (bahn-goong jwaw)

desktop: **táishì** (tye-shir)

dial: **bō** (baw)

dining room: **fàntīng** (fahn-teeng)

dinner: **wǎnfàn** (wahn-fahn)

diplomat: **wàijiāoguān** (wye-jyaow-gwahn)

discuss: **tǎolùn** (taow-loon)

do: **dǎ** (dah)

doctor: **yīshēng** (ee-shung)

dollar: **kuài** (kwye)

don't have: **méiyǒu** (mayo)

door: **mén** (mun)

dormitory: **sùshè** (soo-shuh)

double room: **shuāngrén fángjiān** (shwahng-run fahng-jyan)

download: **xiàzài** (shyah-dzye)

downstairs: **lóuxià** (low-shyah)

drink: **hē** (huh)

drinks: **yǐnliào** (een-lyaow)

drive: **kāi chē** (kye-chuh)

driver: **sījī** (suh-jee)

E

each: **měige** (may-guh)

easy: **róngyì** (roong-ee)

eat: **chīfàn** (chir-fahn)

economy class: **jīngjìcāng**
(jeeng-jee-tsahng)

elevator: **diàntī** (dyan-tee)

e-mail: **diànzǐ yóujiàn** (dyan-dzuh yo-jyan)

e-mail address: **diànzǐ yóuxiāng dìzhǐ**
(dyan-dzuh yo-shyahng dee-jir)

embassy: **dàshǐguǎn** (dah-shir-gwahn)

emergency exits: **jǐnjí chūkǒu** (jeen-jee
choo-ko)

emergency room: **jízhěnshì** (jee-jun-shir)

English (language): **Yīngwén; Yīngyǔ**
(eeng-one; eeng-yew)

entire: **quánbù** (chwan-boo)

entrance: **ménkǒu** (mun-ko)

erase: **qùdiào** (chyew-dyaow)

escalator: **zìdòng lóutī** (dzuh-doong
low-tee)

Euro: **Ōu yuán** (oh-ywan)

Europe: **Ōuzhōu** (oh-joe)

evening (6:00 p.m. to midnight):
wǎnshàng (wahn-shahng)

examine: **jiǎnchá** (jyan-chah)

exchange bureaus: **duìhuànchù**
(dway-hwahn-choo)

exchange rate: **duìhuàn lǜ** (dway-hwahn
lyew)

excuse me: **duìbùqǐ** (dway-boo-chee)

exercise: **yùndòng** (yewn-doong)

expensive: **guì** (gway)

eye: **yǎnjīng** (yan-jeeng)

F

face: **miàn** (myan)

family: **jiā** (jyah)

far: **yuǎn** (ywan)

fast: **kuài** (kwye)

father: **bàba; fùqīn** (bah-bah; foo-cheen)

fax machine: **chuánzhēn jī**
(chwahn-juhn jee)

few: **yìxiē** (ee-shyeh)

file: **wénjiàn** (one-jyan)

fill out (a form): **tián** (tyan)

finally: **zhōngyú** (joong-yew)

first class: **tóuděngcāng**
(toe-dung-tsahng)

flood: **shuǐzāi** (shway-dzye)

food: **cài; fàn** (tsye; fahn)

foreign currency: **wàibì** (wye-bee)

fork: **chāzi** (chah-dzuh)

free: **miǎnfèi** (myan-fay)

freeway: **gāosù gōnglù** (gaow-soo
goong-loo)

Friday: **xīngqīwǔ** (sheeng-chee-woo)

friend: **péngyǒu** (puhng-yo)

from: **cóng** (tsoong)

front: **qián** (chyan)

fruit: **shuǐguǒ** (shway-gwaw)

G

get lost: **mílù** (mee-loo)

get off: **xià** (shyah)

get on: **shàng** (shahng)

gifts: **lǐwù** (lee-woo)

girlfriend: **nǚpéngyǒu** (nyew-puhng-yoe)

give: **gěi** (gay)

glasses: **yǎnjìng** (yan-jeeng)

go: **qù** (chyew)

go down: **xià** (shyah)

go online: **shàngwǎng** (shahng-wahng)

go up: **shàng** (shahng)

good: **hǎo** (how)

goodbye: **zàijiàn** (dzye-jyan)

grandfather: **zǔfù** (dzoo-foo)

greeting: **zhāohu** (jaow-hoo)

groceries: **shípǐn záhuò** (shir-peen dzah-hwaw)

guest: **kèrén** (kuh-run)

guidebook: **lǚyóu shǒucè** (lyew-yo show-tsuh)

H

half: **bàn** (bahn)

hang up: **guà** (guah)

happy: **gāoxìng** (gaow-sheeng)

have: **yǒu** (yo)

have a meeting: **kāihuì** (kye-hway)

he: **tā** (tah)

headache: **tóuténg** (toe-tuhng)

hello (on phone only): **wéi** (way)

help: **bāngmáng** (bahng-mahng)

highway: **gōnglù** (goong-loo)

him: **tā** (tah)

his: **tāde** (tah-duh)

hit: **dǎ** (dah)

holiday: **jiérì** (jyeh-ir)

home: **jiā** (jyah)

Hong Kong: **Xiānggǎng** (shyahng-gahng)

Hong Kong dollar: **Gǎngbì** (gahng-bee)

hospital: **yīyuàn** (ee-ywan)

hot: **rè** (ruh)

hotel: **bīnguǎn; fànguǎn; lǚguǎn** (been-gwahn; fahn-gwahn; lyew-gwahn)

house: **fángzi** (fahng-dzuh)

how: **zěnme** (dzummuh)

however: **dànshì** (dahn-shir)

how long: **duō jiǔ** (dwaw jyoe)

how many: **jǐ** (jee)

how much: **duōshǎo** (dwaw-shaow)

hungry: **è** (uh)

hurry: **jí** (jee)

husband: **zhàngfu** (jahng-foo)

I

I: **wǒ** (waw)

ID: **zhèngjiàn** (juhng-jyan)

I'm sorry: **bàoqiàn; duìbùqǐ** (baow-chyan; dway-boo-chee)

in a little while: **yīhuǐr** (ee-hwar)

incorrect: **cuò** (tswaw)

inside: **lǐ** (lee)

intelligent: **cōngmíng** (tsoong-meeng)

international phone call: **guójì diànhuà** (gwaw-jee dyan-hwah)

Internet: **guójì wǎngluò** (gwaw-jee wahng-lwaw)

Internet access: **wǎngluò liánjié** (wahng-lwaw lyan-jyeh)

Internet service provider: **wǎngshàng fúwù tígōng shāng** (wahng-shahng foo-woo tee-goong shahng)

introduce: **jièshào** (jyeh-shaow)

is: **shì** (shir)

item: **xiàngmù** (shyahng-moo)

J

Japan: **Rìběn** (ir-bun)

Japanese dollar: **Rì yuán** (ir ywan)

jewelry: **zhūbǎo** (joo-baow)

job: **gōngzuò** (goong-dzwaw)

K

key: **yàoshi** (yaow-shir)

kilometer (Chinese equivalent): **lǐ** (lee)

know (how to do something): **huì** (hway)

know (information): **zhīdào** (jir-daow)

know (someone): **rènshi** (run-shir)

L

landing: **zhuólù** (jwaw-loo)

laptop: **shǒutíshì** (show-tee-shir)

last month: **shàngge yuè** (shahng-guh yweh)

last week: **shàngge xīngqī** (shahng-guh sheeng-chee)

last year: **qùnián** (chyew-nyan)

laundry service: **xǐyī fúwù** (she-ee foo-woo)

law: **fǎlǜ** (fah-lyew)

lawyer: **lǜshī** (lyew-shir)

leave: **líkāi** (lee-kye)

leave a message: **liúhuà** (lyoe-hwah)

leave the house: **chūfā** (choo-fah)

left: **zuǒ** (dzwaw)

let: **ràng** (rahng)

life vests: **jiùshēng yī** (jyoe-shung ee)

like: **xǐhuān** (she-hwahn)

listen to: **tīng** (teeng)

loan: **jiè** (jyeh)

lobby: **dàtīng** (dah-teeng)

local train: **mànchē** (mahn-chuh)

location: **dìqū** (dee-chyew)

lock: **suǒ** (swaw)

log off: **qiān chū** (chyan choo)

log on: **qiān rù** (chyan roo)

long-distance phone call: **chángtú diàn-huà** (chahng-too dyan-hwah)

look for: **zhǎo** (jaow)

look something up: **chá** (chah)

loose: **sōng** (soong)

lose: **shū** (shoo)

luck: **yùnqì** (yewn-chee)

luggage: **xínglǐ** (sheeng-lee)

luggage claim tag: **lǐngqǔdān** (leeng-chyew-dahn)

lunch: **wǔfàn** (woo-fahn)

M

magazine: **zázhì** (dzah-jir)

mainland (China): **dàlù** (dah-loo)

make a legal decision: **pànjué** (pahn-jweh)

make a reservation (seats): **dìng wèi** (deeng-way)

make a reservation (room, tickets, and so on): **yùdìng** (yew-deeng)

manager: **jīnglǐ** (jeeng-lee)

Mandarin: **guóyǔ; pǔtōnghuà; Hànyǔ** (gwaw-yew [term used in Taiwan]; poo-toong-hwah [term used in mainland China]; hahn-yew [politically neutral term used in both Taiwan and mainland China])

many: **duō** (dwaw)

many thanks: **gǎnxiè** (gahn-shyeh)

map: **dìtú** (dee-too)

marry: **jiéhūn** (jyeh-hwun)

master: **shīfu** (shir-foo)

May: **wǔyuè** (woo-yweh)

me: **wǒ** (waw)

meat: **ròu** (row)

medicine: **yào** (yaow)

meeting: **huìyì** (hway-ee)

menu: **càidān** (tsye-dahn)

message: **xìnxī** (sheen-she)

midnight: **bànyè** (bahn-yeh)

mine: **wǒde** (waw-duh)

minister (official): **bùzhǎng** (boo-jahng)

minute: **fēn** (fun)

mistake: **cuò** (tswaw)

Monday: **xīngqīyī** (sheeng-chee-ee)

money: **qián** (chyan)

more: **gèng** (guhng)

morning (6:00 a.m. to noon): **zǎoshàng** (dzaow-shahng)

most: **zuì** (dzway)

mother: **māma; mǔqīn** (mah-mah; moo-cheen)

movie: **diànyǐng; piānzi** (dyan-yeeng; pyan-dzuh)

museum: **bówùguǎn** (baw-woo-gwahn)

music: **yīnyuè** (een-yweh)

my: **wǒde** (waw-duh)

N

napkin: **cānjīnzhǐ** (tsahn-jeen-jir)

need: **xūyào** (shyew-yaow)

negotiate: **tánpàn** (tahn-pahn)

neighborhood: **fùjìn** (foo-jeen)

new: **xīn** (shin)

newspaper: **bàozhǐ** (baow-jir)

next: **xià; xiàge** (shyah; shyah-guh)

next month: **xiàge yuè** (shyah-guh yweh)

next to: **kàojìn** (cow-jeen)

next week: **xiàge xīngqī** (shyah-guh sheeng-chee)

next year: **míngnián** (meeng-nyan)

no: **bù** (boo)

noodles: **miàntiáo** (myan-tyaow)

noon: **zhōngwǔ** (joong-woo)

not bad: **búcuò** (boo-tswaw)

not: **bù** (boo)

now: **xiànzài** (shyan-dzye)

number: **hàomǎ** (how-mah)

nurse: **hùshì** (hoo-shir)

O

of course: **dāngrán** (dahng-rahn)

office: **bàngōngshì** (bahn-goong-shir)

often: **chángcháng; píngcháng** (chahng-chahng; peeng-chahng)

Oh my goodness!: **āiyà** (eye-yah)

old: **lǎo** (laow)

on time: **zhèngdiǎn** (juhng-dyan)

on top: **shàng** (shahng)

on vacation: **dùjià** (doo-jyah)

one: **yī** (ee)

one cent: **fēn** (fun)

one-way ticket: **dānchéng piào** (dahn-chuhng pyaow)

only: **zhǐ** (jir)

open: **kāi** (kye)

open the door: **kāimén** (kye-mun)

opinion: **yìjiàn** (ee-jyan)

opposite: **duìmiàn** (dway-myan)

or: **huòzhe** (hwaw-juh)

order (food): **diǎn** (dyan)

other: **biéde** (byeh-duh)

other: **qítā** (chee-tah)

overdone: **lǎo** (laow)

outside: **wài** (wye)

P

pair: **shuāng** (shwahng)

parents: **fùmǔ** (foo-moo)

party: **wǎnhuì** (wahn-hway)

passport: **hùzhào** (hoo-jaow)

password: **mìmǎ** (mee-mah)

pay: **fù qián** (foo chyan)

PC (personal computer): **gèrén diànnǎo** (guh-run dyan-now)

pen: **gāngbǐ** (gahng-bee)

pencil: **qiānbǐ** (chyan-bee)

percentage: **bǎifēn bǐ** (bye-fun bee)

perhaps: **kěnéng** (kuh-nuhng)

person: **rén** (run)

pharmacy: **yàofáng** (yaow-fahng)

phone book: **diànhuà hàomǎbù** (dyan-hwah how-mah-boo)

photo: **zhàopiàn** (jaow-pyan)

pick up: **ná** (nah)

pill: **yàowán** (yaow-wahn)

PIN: **mìmǎ** (mee-mah)

pint: **pǐntuō** (peen-twaw)

place: **dìfāng** (dee-fahng)

platform: **zhàntái** (jahn-tye)

play: **dǎ** (dah [used with a follow-up word referring to a particular sport])

play: **wán** (wahn [general usage])

please: **qǐng** (cheeng)

police: **jǐngchá** (jeeng-chah)

police station: **jǐngchájú** (jeeng-chah-jyew)

popular: **liúxíng** (lyo-sheeng)

post office: **yóujú** (yo-jyew)

postponed: **tuīchí** (tway-chir)

pray: **lǐbài** (lee-bye)

PRC dollar: **rénmínbì** (run-meen-bee)

presentation: **yǎnshì** (yan-shir)

president (of company): **zǒngcái** (dzoong-tsye)

pretty: **hǎokàn** (how-kahn)

pretty: **piàoliàng** (pyaow-lyahng)

price: **jiàgé** (jyah-guh)

problem: **wèntí** (one-tee)

professor: **jiàoshòu** (jyaow-show)

public bus: **gōnggòng qìchē** (goong-goong chee-chuh)

public telephone: **gōngyòng diànhuà** (goong-yoong dyan-hwah)

Q

quality: **zhìliàng** (jir-lyahng)

quiet: **ānjìng** (ahn-jeeng)

R

rain: **yǔ** (yew)

raincoat: **yǔyī** (yew-ee)

Rats!: **zāogāo** (dzaow-gaow)

read: **kàn** (kahn)

really: **zhēn** (juhn)

really good: **búcuò** (boo-tswaw)

receipt: **shōujù** (show-jyew)

receive: **shōudào** (show-daow)

reception desk: **fàndiàn qiántái** (fahn-dyan chyan-tye)

receptionist: **qiántái fúwùyuán** (chyan-tye foo-woo-ywan)

refund: **tuìkuǎn** (tway-kwahn)

remote control: **yáokòng qì** (yaow-koong chee)

remove: **qùdiào** (chyew-dyaow)

rent (noun): **zūfèi** (dzoo-fay)

rent (verb): **chūzū** (choo-dzoo)

reside: **zhù** (joo)

resolve: **jiějué** (jyeh-jweh)

rest: **xiūxi** (shyo-she)

restaurant: **cānguǎn; fàndiàn** (tsahn-gwahn; fahn-dyan)

return: **huí** (hway)

return (come back): **huílái** (hway-lye)

return (merchandise): **tuìhuí** (tway-hway)

rice: **mǐfàn** (mee-fahn)

right: **yòu** (yo)

road: **lù** (loo)

room: **fángjiān** (fahng-jyan)

roommate: **tóngwū** (toong-woo)

round-trip ticket: **láihuí piào** (lye-hway pyaow)

rush hour: **gāofēngqī** (gaow-fuhng-chee)

S

same: **yíyàng** (ee-yahng)

Saturday: **xīngqīliù** (sheeng-chee-lyo)

scary: **kěpà** (kuh-pah)

schedule: **shíjiānbiǎo** (shir-jyan-byaow)

school: **xuéxiào** (shweh-shyaow)

search: **jiǎnsuǒ** (jyan-swaw)

seat belt: **ānquán dài** (ahn-chwan dye)

secretary: **mìshū** (mee-shoo)

see: **kàn** (kahn)

see a doctor: **kànbìng** (kahn-beeng)

see you later: **yīhuǐr jiàn** (ee-hwar jyan)

see: **jiàn** (jyan [also used as a classifier])

self: **zìjǐ** (dzuh-jee)

sell: **mài** (my)

send: **sòng** (soong)

server: **fúwùqì** (foo-woo-chee)

set off (leave): **chūfā** (choo-fah)

several: **jǐ** (jee)

shoes: **xiézi** (shyeh-dzuh)

short: **ǎi** (eye)

should: **yīnggāi** (eeng-guy)

sightsee: **yóulǎn** (yo-lahn)

Singapore dollar: **Xīn bì** (shin bee)

skirt: **qúnzi** (chwun-dzuh)

sleep: **shuìjiào** (shway-jyaow)

slide projector: **huàndēngjī** (hwahn-duhng-jee)

slow: **màn** (mahn)

small: **xiǎo** (shyaow)

small talk: **xiánliáo** (shyan-lyaow)

soap: **féizào** (fay dzaow)

software: **ruǎnjiàn** (rwahn-jyan)

solve: **jiějué** (jyeh-jweh)

son: **érzi** (are-dzuh)

soup: **tāng** (tahng)

speak: **shuō** (shwaw)

special: **tèsè** (tuh-suh)

spouse: **àirén** (eye-run [used only in the PRC])

start: **kāishǐ** (kye-shir)

store: **shāngdiàn** (shahng-dyan)

straight: **zhí** (jir)

strange: **qíguài** (chee-gwye)

street: **jiē** (jyeh)

student: **xuéshēng** (shweh-shung)

study: **xuéxí** (shweh-she)

subway: **dìtiě** (dee-tyeh)

suggest: **jiànyì** (jyan-ee)

suggestion: **jiànyì** (jyan-ee)

suitcase: **xiāngzi** (shyahng-dzuh)

suite: **tàojiān** (taow-jyan)

Sunday: **xīngqītiān** (sheeng-chee-tyan)

sunglasses: **tàiyáng yǎnjìng** (tye-yahng yan-jeeng)

supermarket: **chāojí shìchǎng** (chaow-jee shir-chahng)

sweep: **cá** (tsah)

T

table: **zhuōzi** (jwaw-dzuh)

Taiwan: **Táiwān** (tye-wahn)

take a vacation: **fàng jià** (fahng-jyah)

take medicine: **chī yào** (chir-yaow)

take off (airplane): **qǐfēi** (chee-fay)

take pictures: **zhàoxiàng** (jaow-shyahng)

talk: **jiǎng** (jyahng)

taxi: **chūzū chē** (choo-dzoo-chuh)

tea: **chá** (chah)

teach: **jiāo** (jyaow)

teacher: **lǎoshī** (laow-shir)

telephone: **diànhuà** (dyan-hwah)

telephone book: **diànhuà hàomǎbù** (dyan-hwah how-mah-boo)

telephone number: **diànhuà hàomǎ** (dyan-hwah how-mah)

tell: **gàosù** (gaow-soo)

thanks: **xièxiè** (shyeh-shyeh)

that: **nà** (nah)

That's awful!: **zāogāo** (dzaow-gaow)

them: **tāmen** (tah-mun)

there: **nàr** (nahr)

they: **tāmen** (tah-mun)

thief: **zéi** (dzay)

thing: **dōngxi** (doong-she)

think: **xiǎng** (shyahng)

thirsty: **kě** (kuh)

Thursday: **xīngqīsì** (sheeng-chee-suh)

ticket: **piào** (pyaow)

time: **shíhòu** (shir-ho)

time (midnight to 6:00 a.m.): **qīngzǎo** (cheeng-dzaow)

time: **zhōng** (joong)

tip: **xiǎofèi** (shyaow-fay)

tired: **lèi** (lay)

today: **jīntiān** (jin-tyan)

together: **yìqǐ** (ee-chee)

toilet: **cèsuǒ** (tsuh-swaw)

toilet paper: **wèishēng zhǐ** (way-shung jir)

tomorrow: **míngtiān** (meeng-tyan)

too bad: **kěxī** (kuh-she)

too much: **tài** (tye)

toothbrush: **yáshuā** (yah-shwah)

tour: **lǚyóu** (lyew-yo)

tour group: **guānguāng tuán** (gwahng-gwahng twahn)

towel: **máojīn** (maow-jeen)

trade show: **màoyì zhǎnxiāohuì** (maow-ee jahn-shyaow-hway)

train station: **huǒchē zhàn** (hwaw-chuh jahn)

transfer: **zhuǎn** (jwan)

transparency: **tóuyǐngpiàn** (toe-eeng-pyan)

transportation: **jiāotōng** (jyaow-toong)

travel: **lǚxíng** (lyew-sheeng)

travel agency: **lǚxíngshè** (lyew-sheeng-shuh)

travel agent: **lǚxíng dàilǐrén** (lyew-sheeng-dye-lee-run)

traveler's checks: **lǚxíng zhīpiào** (lyew-sheeng jir-pyaow)

truly: **zhēn** (juhn)

Tuesday: **xīngqī'èr** (sheeng-chee-are)

turn: **zhuǎn** (jwan)

TV: **diànshì** (dyan-shir)

U

U.S. dollar: **Měiyuán** (may-ywan)

umbrella: **yǔsǎn** (yew-sahn)

unfortunately: **kěxī** (kuh-she)

upstairs: **lóushàng** (low-shahng)

us: **wǒmen** (waw-mun)

us (informal): **zánmen** (dzahn-mun)

use: **yòng** (yoong)

user name: **yònghù xìngmíng** (yoong-hoo sheeng-meeng)

usually: **píngcháng** (peeng-chahng)

V

vacant: **kòngwèi** (koong-way)

vacation day: **jiàrì** (jyah-ir)

vegetarian dishes: **sùcài** (soo-tsye)

vicinity: **fùjìn** (foo-jeen)

video recorder: **lùxiàngjī** (loo-shyahng-jee)

Vietnam: **Yuènán** (yweh-nahn)

visa: **qiānzhèng** (chyan-juhng)

voice: **shēngyīn** (shung-een)

voicemail: **yǒu shēng yóujiàn** (yo shung yo-jyan)

W

wait: **děng** (duhng)

walk: **zǒu** (dzoe)

wallet: **qiánbāo** (chyan-baow)

want: **yào** (yaow)

warm: **nuǎnhuó** (nwan-hwaw)

wash: **xǐ** (she)

we: **wǒmen** (waw-mun)

we (informal): **zánmen** (dzahn-mun)

wear: **chuān** (chwahn)

weather: **tiānqì** (tyan-chee)

website: **wǎngzhàn** (wahng-jahn)

Wednesday: **xīngqīsān** (sheeng-chee-sahn)

week: **lǐbài** (lee-bye)

weekend: **zhōumò** (joe-maw)

welcome: **huānyíng** (hwahn-yeeng)

Western food: **xīcān** (she-tsahn)

what: **shénme** (shummuh)

what a shame: **zāogāo** (dzaow-gaow)

where: **nǎr** (nar)

which: **nǎ** (nah)

who: **shéi** (shay)

whom: **shéi** (shay)

whole thing: **quánbù** (chwan-boo)

why: **wèishénme** (way-shummuh)

wife: **qīzi** (chee-dzuh)

wife: **tàitài** (tye-tye [used mostly in Taiwan])

win: **yíng** (eeng)

wine: **jiǔ** (jyoe)

withdraw money: **qǔ qián** (chyew chyan)

work: **gōngzuò** (goong-dzwaw)

work out: **jiànshēn yùndòng** (jyan-shun yewn-doong)

Y

yes: **shì** (shir)

yesterday: **zuótiān** (dzwaw-tyan)

you: **nǐ** (nee)

you (plural): **nǐmen** (nee-mun)

you (polite): **nín** (neen)

you're welcome: **búkèqì** (boo-kuh-chee)

young: **niánqīng** (nyan-cheeng)

Appendix B

Chinese Verbs

*H*ere's a handy list of useful Chinese verbs. For a general description of how verbs work in Chinese, see Chapter 3.

àn (ahn): to press

ānpái (ahn-pye): to arrange; to schedule

ānzhuāng (ahn-jwahng): to install

bāngmáng (bahng-mahng): to help

bō (baw): to dial

cānjiā (tsahn-jyah): to participate

chàng (chahng): to sing

chī (chir): to eat

chídào (chir-daow): to be late

chóngxīn kāijī (choong-sheen kye-jee): to reboot

chuān (chwan): to wear

chuī (chway): to blow

cún qián (tswun chyan): to deposit money

dǎ (dah): to hit; to strike; to play

dài (dye): to bring; to carry; to wear (accessories)

děng (duhng): to wait

diǎn (dyan): to order (food)

dǒng (doong): to understand

è (uh): to be hungry

fēi (fay): to fly

fù zhàng (foo jahng): to pay a bill

gǎibiàn (gye-byan): to change

gǎnjué (gahn-jweh): to feel

gǎnxiè (gahn-shyeh): to thank

gàosù (gaow-soo): to tell

gāoxìng (gaow-sheeng): to be happy

gěi (gay): to give

gōngzuò (goong-dzwaw): to work

guà (gwah): to hang up

guān (gwan): to close

gūjì (goo-jee): to estimate

guò (gwaw): to pass

hē (huh): to drink

hézuò (huh-dzwaw): to cooperate

huà (hwah): to paint

huàn (hwahn): to exchange

huānyíng (hwahn-eeng): to welcome

huí (hway): to return

huì (hway): to know how to do something

hūxī (hoo-she): to breathe

jiàn (jyan): to see

jiǎng (jyahng): to speak

jiànlì (jyan-lee): to set up

jiànyì (jyan-ee): to suggest

jiào (jyaow): to call

jiē (jyeh): to answer (a phone call)

jiè (jyeh): to loan; to borrow

jiěfàng (jyeh-fahng): to liberate

jiéhūn (jyeh-hwun): to marry

jiějué (jyeh-jweh): to solve

jièshào (jyeh-shaow): to introduce

jiézhàng (jyeh-jahng): to pay the bill

jiù (jyoe): to save (a life)

juédìng (jyweh-deeng): to decide

kāi (kye): to open

kāi chē (kye chuh): to drive

kāihuì (kye-hway): to have or be in a meeting

kàn (kahn): to read; to look; to see

kě (kuh): to be thirsty

lái (lye): to come

liànxí (lyan-she): to practice

líkāi (lee-kye): to leave

liú (lyoe): to leave (an object; a message)

mà (mah): to scold

mǎi (my): to buy

mài (my): to sell

máng (mahng): to be busy

mílù (mee-loo): to get lost

ná (nah): to pick up; to take

néng (nuhng): to be able to

pànjué (pahn-jweh): to make a legal decision

qiān rù (chyan roo): to log on

qiān chū (chyan choo): to log off

qǐng (cheeng): to invite

qù (chyew): to go

qǔ qián (chyew chyan): to withdraw money

qǔxiāo (chyew-shyaow): to cancel

ràng (rahng): to permit

rènshi (run-shir): to know (a person); to recognize

shàng (shahng): to get on

shàngwǎng (shahng-wahng): to go online

shì (shir): to be

shōu (show): to receive

shòu (show): to accept (money, tickets, and so on)

shū (shoo): to lose

shuō (shwaw): to speak

sòng (soong): to send

tánpàn (tahn-pahn): to negotiate

tǎolùn (taow-lwun): to discuss

tián (tyan): to fill out (a form)

tīng (teeng): to hear; to listen to

tóngyì (toong-ee): to agree

tuìfáng (tway-fahng): to check out (of hotel room)

tuìhuí (tway-hway): to return (merchandise)

tuōyùn (twaw-yewn): to check in luggage

wǎn (wahn): to play

wàng (wahng): to forget

wèn (one): to ask

xǐ (she): to wash

xià (shyah): to get off

xiǎng (shyahng): to think; to miss

xiàzài (shyah-dzye): to download

xǐhuān (she-hwan): to like; to enjoy

xīn (sheen): to believe

xuǎnzé (shwan-dzuh): to choose

xuéxí (shweh-she): to study

yǎnshì (yan shir): to give a presentation

yào (yaow): to want

yíng (eeng): to win

yòng (yoong): to use

yǒu (yo): to have; there are

yóulǎn (yo-lahn): to sightsee

yóuyǒng (yo-yoong): to swim

yuànyì (ywan-yee): to be willing to

yùsuàn (yew-swan): to budget

zhǎo (jaow): to look for

zhàoxiàng (jaow-shyahng): to take pictures

zhīdào (jir-daow): to know (a fact)

zhù (joo): to reside; to extend wishes

zhuā (jwah): to catch

zhuǎn (jwan): to transfer; to turn

zhuāngrù (jwahng-roo): to pack

zhuǎnzū (jwan-dzoo): to sublet

zhǔchí (joo-chir): to lead

zǒu (lù) (dzoe [loo]): to walk

zū (dzoo): to rent

zuò (dzwaw): to do; to make; to sit

zuò fàn (dzwaw fahn): to cook

Appendix C
On the CD

Note: If you are using a digital or enhanced digital version of this book, this appendix does not apply.

Track Listing

The following is a list of the tracks that appear on this book's audio CD. Note that this is an audio-only CD, so it'll play in any standard CD player or in your computer's CD-ROM drive.

Track 1: Introduction

Track 2: Consonant sounds

Track 3: Tones

Track 4: Going out to dinner

Track 5: Introductions

Track 6: Going to see a movie

Track 7: Calling a realtor

Track 8: Asking for the time

Track 9: Discussing professions

Track 10: Going to a restaurant

Track 11: Shopping at the food market

Track 12: Shopping for clothes

Track 13: Going to the museum

Track 14: Making a phone call

Track 15: Starting a meeting

Track 16: Going to a seaside resort

Track 17: Going to a basketball game

Track 18: Discussing vacation plans

Track 19: Making plans with a travel agent

Track 20: Exchanging money

Track 21: Opening an account at the bank

Track 22: Checking in at the airport

Track 23: Going through customs

Track 24: Getting directions to the embassy

Track 25: Asking for directions to the post office

Track 26: Making a hotel reservation

Track 27: Inquiring about hotel vacancies

Track 28: Arriving at the doctor's office

Customer Care

If you have trouble with the CD, please call the Wiley Product Technical Support phone number at 800-762-2974. Outside the United States, call 1-317-572-3994. You can also contact Wiley Product Technical Support at http://support.wiley.com. Wiley will provide technical support only for installation and other general quality control items.

To place additional orders or to request information about other Wiley products, please call 877-762-2974.

Appendix D
Answer Key

The following are all of the answers to the Fun & Games exercises.

Chapter 2

c, a, d, c, c

Chapter 3

b, e, a, d, c

Chapter 4

Activity 1: **hǎo, míngzi, Déguórén, bàofēngxuě, jiàn**

Activity 2:

1. (C) **Hǎo jiǔ méi jiàn.**
2. (D) **Wǎn ān.**
3. (E) **Zǎo.**
4. (F) **Nǎr de huà.**
5. (A) **Hěn gāoxìng jiàndào nǐ.**
6. (B) **Yílù pīng'ān.**

Chapter 5

wǔ, qī, shí, sānshí, liùshí, jiǔshí

Chapter 6

> **yùshì:** *bathroom*
>
> **wòshì:** *bedroom*
>
> **fàntīng:** *dining room*
>
> **tǎnzi:** *blanket*
>
> **yángtái:** *balcony*

   zhěntóu: *pillow*

   bèizi: *quilt*

   shūzhuō: *desk*

   shāfā: *sofa*

Chapter 7

   yīshēng: *doctor*

   lǎoshī: *teacher*

   fēixíngyuán: *pilot*

   kuàijì: *accountant*

Chapter 8

   A. **píngguǒ** (*apple*)

   B. **júzi** (*orange*)

   C. **shēngcài** (*lettuce*)

   D. **fānqié** (*tomato*)

   E. **hú luóbō** (*carrot*)

   F. **yángcōng** (*onion*)

   G. **xīlánhuā** (*broccoli*)

Chapter 9

   A. **zhūbǎo diàn** (*jewelry store*)

   B. **cài shìchǎng:** (*food market*)

   B. **huādiàn:** (*flower shop*)

   D. **yàofáng:** (*drugstore*)

   E. **wánjù diàn:** (*toy store*)

Chapter 10

   1. f

   2. e

   3. d

   4. c

   5. a

   6. b

Chapter 11

Just a moment.: **Shǎoděng**

Is she at home?: **Tā zài ma?**

Hello?: **Wéi?**

Sorry, you dialed the wrong number.: **Duìbùqǐ, nǐ bōcuòle hàomǎ.**

Please leave a message.: **Qǐng nǐ liú yíge huà.**

Chapter 12

1. c
2. e
3. b
4. d
5. a

Chapter 13

A. **dǎ pīngpōngqiú**

B. **tán gāngqín**

C. **dǎ gōngfu**

D. **chuī chángdí**

E. **pá shān**

Chapter 14

1. **Àiěrlán**
2. **liù yuè bā hào**
3. **fó miào**
4. **yáshuā**
5. **Kāi wǎn xiào**

Chapter 15

A. **zìdòng tīkuǎnjī** (*ATM*)

B. **chūnàyuán** (*bank teller*)

C. **yínháng** (*bank*)

D. **hùzhào** (*passport*)

E. **xìnyòng kǎ** (*credit card*)

F. **qiánbāo** (*wallet*)

Chapter 16

A. **fēijī**

B. **huǒchē**

C. **dìtiě**

D. **gōnggòng qìchē**

E. **chūzū chē**

Chapter 17

A. **Xuéxiào zài běibiān/běimiàn.** (*The school is to the north.*)

B. **Yóujú zài dōngbiān/dōngmiàn.** (*The post office is to the east.*)

C. **Yínháng zài nánbiān/nánmiàn.** (*The bank is to the south.*)

D. **Fángzi zài xībiān/xīmiàn.** (*The house is to the west.*)

Chapter 18

1. **fángjiān**

2. **kèmǎn**

3. **qǐchuáng**

4. **zhàngdān**

5. **tuìfáng**

Chapter 19

1. **gēbō:** *arm*

2. **jiānbǎng:** *shoulder*

3. **shǒuzhǐ:** *finger*

4. **tuǐ:** *leg*

5. **bózi:** *neck*

6. **xiōngqiāng:** *chest*

7. **yǎnjīng:** *eye*

8. **ěrduō:** *ear*

9. **bízi:** *nose*

John Wiley & Sons, Inc.
End-User License Agreement

READ THIS. You should carefully read these terms and conditions before opening the software packet(s) included with this book "Book". This is a license agreement "Agreement" between you and John Wiley & Sons, Inc. "WILEY". By opening the accompanying software packet(s), you acknowledge that you have read and accept the following terms and conditions. If you do not agree and do not want to be bound by such terms and conditions, promptly return the Book and the unopened software packet(s) to the place you obtained them for a full refund.

1. **License Grant.** WILEY grants to you (either an individual or entity) a nonexclusive license to use one copy of the enclosed software program(s) (collectively, the "Software") solely for your own personal or business purposes on a single computer (whether a standard computer or a workstation component of a multi-user network). The Software is in use on a computer when it is loaded into temporary memory (RAM) or installed into permanent memory (hard disk, CD-ROM, or other storage device). WILEY reserves all rights not expressly granted herein.

2. **Ownership.** WILEY is the owner of all right, title, and interest, including copyright, in and to the compilation of the Software recorded on the physical packet included with this Book "Software Media". Copyright to the individual programs recorded on the Software Media is owned by the author or other authorized copyright owner of each program. Ownership of the Software and all proprietary rights relating thereto remain with WILEY and its licensers.

3. **Restrictions on Use and Transfer.**

    (a) You may only (i) make one copy of the Software for backup or archival purposes, or (ii) transfer the Software to a single hard disk, provided that you keep the original for backup or archival purposes. You may not (i) rent or lease the Software, (ii) copy or reproduce the Software through a LAN or other network system or through any computer subscriber system or bulletin-board system, or (iii) modify, adapt, or create derivative works based on the Software.

    (b) You may not reverse engineer, decompile, or disassemble the Software. You may transfer the Software and user documentation on a permanent basis, provided that the transferee agrees to accept the terms and conditions of this Agreement and you retain no copies. If the Software is an update or has been updated, any transfer must include the most recent update and all prior versions.

4. **Restrictions on Use of Individual Programs.** You must follow the individual requirements and restrictions detailed for each individual program in the "About the CD" appendix of this Book or on the Software Media. These limitations are also contained in the individual license agreements recorded on the Software Media. These limitations may include a requirement that after using the program for a specified period of time, the user must pay a registration fee or discontinue use. By opening the Software packet(s), you agree to abide by the licenses and restrictions for these individual programs that are detailed in the "About the CD" appendix and/or on the Software Media. None of the material on this Software Media or listed in this Book may ever be redistributed, in original or modified form, for commercial purposes.

5. **Limited Warranty.**

   (a) WILEY warrants that the Software and Software Media are free from defects in materials and workmanship under normal use for a period of sixty (60) days from the date of purchase of this Book. If WILEY receives notification within the warranty period of defects in materials or workmanship, WILEY will replace the defective Software Media.

   (b) WILEY AND THE AUTHOR(S) OF THE BOOK DISCLAIM ALL OTHER WARRANTIES, EXPRESS OR IMPLIED, INCLUDING WITHOUT LIMITATION IMPLIED WARRANTIES OF MERCHANTABILITY AND FITNESS FOR A PARTICULAR PURPOSE, WITH RESPECT TO THE SOFTWARE, THE PROGRAMS, THE SOURCE CODE CONTAINED THEREIN, AND/OR THE TECHNIQUES DESCRIBED IN THIS BOOK. WILEY DOES NOT WARRANT THAT THE FUNCTIONS CONTAINED IN THE SOFTWARE WILL MEET YOUR REQUIREMENTS OR THAT THE OPERATION OF THE SOFTWARE WILL BE ERROR FREE.

   (c) This limited warranty gives you specific legal rights, and you may have other rights that vary from jurisdiction to jurisdiction.

6. **Remedies.**

   (a) WILEY's entire liability and your exclusive remedy for defects in materials and workmanship shall be limited to replacement of the Software Media, which may be returned to WILEY with a copy of your receipt at the following address: Software Media Fulfillment Department, Attn.: *Chinese For Dummies,* 2nd Edition, John Wiley & Sons, Inc., 10475 Crosspoint Blvd., Indianapolis, IN 46256, or by calling 1-800-762-2974. Please allow four to six weeks for delivery. This Limited Warranty is void if failure of the Software Media has resulted from accident, abuse, or misapplication. Any replacement Software Media will be warranted for the remainder of the original warranty period or thirty (30) days, whichever is longer.

   (b) In no event shall WILEY or the author be liable for any damages whatsoever (including without limitation damages for loss of business profits, business interruption, loss of business information, or any other pecuniary loss) arising from the use of or inability to use the Book or the Software, even if WILEY has been advised of the possibility of such damages.

   (c) Because some jurisdictions do not allow the exclusion or limitation of liability for consequential or incidental damages, the above limitation or exclusion may not apply to you.

7. **U.S. Government Restricted Rights.** Use, duplication, or disclosure of the Software for or on behalf of the United States of America, its agencies and/or instrumentalities "U.S. Government" is subject to restrictions as stated in paragraph (c)(1)(ii) of the Rights in Technical Data and Computer Software clause of DFARS 252.227-7013, or subparagraphs (c)(1) and (2) of the Commercial Computer Software - Restricted Rights clause at FAR 52.227-19, and in similar clauses in the NASA FAR supplement, as applicable.

8. **General.** This Agreement constitutes the entire understanding of the parties and revokes and supersedes all prior agreements, oral or written, between them and may not be modified or amended except in a writing signed by both parties hereto that specifically refers to this Agreement. This Agreement shall take precedence over any other documents that may be in conflict herewith. If any one or more provisions contained in this Agreement are held by any court or tribunal to be invalid, illegal, or otherwise unenforceable, each and every other provision shall remain in full force and effect.

Index

• *U* •

• *V* •

• *W* •

• *Ƴ* •